ETHNOPOLITICAL
WARFARE

ETHNOPOLITICAL WARFARE

Causes, Consequences, and Possible Solutions

Edited by
Daniel Chirot and
Martin E. P. Seligman

AMERICAN PSYCHOLOGICAL ASSOCIATION
Washington, DC

D443
E77
2001

Published by
American Psychological Association
750 First Street, NE
Washington, DC 20002

Copies may be ordered from
APA Order Department
P.O. Box 92984
Washington, DC 20090-2984

In the U.K., Europe, Africa, and the
   Middle East, copies may be ordered from
American Psychological Association
3 Henrietta Street
Covent Garden, London
WC2E 8LU England

Typeset in Goudy by World Composition Services, Inc., Sterling, VA

Printer: Edwards Brothers, Inc., Ann Arbor, MI
Cover Designer: Kathleen Sims Graphic Design, Washington, DC
Technical/Production Editor: Jennifer Powers

The opinions and statements published are the responsibility of the authors, and such
opinions and statements do not necessarily represent the policies of the APA.

Library of Congress Cataloging-in-Publication Data

Ethnopolitical warfare : causes, consequences, and possible solutions / edited by Daniel
Chirot and Martin Seligman.
    p. cm.
  Includes bibliographical references and index.
  ISBN 1-55798-737-8 (alk. paper)
    1. World politics—20th century. 2. Ethnic relations. 3. Minorities.
4. Genocide—History—20th century. 5. Nationalism. 6. Ethnic groups—Political
activity. I. Chirot, Daniel. II. Seligman, Martin E. P.
D443.E77 2000
305.8—dc21   00-059351

British Library Cataloguing-in-Publication Data
A CIP record is available from the British Library.

Printed in the United States of America
First Edition

First, we dedicate this book to our many friends and relatives who, in the past century, have suffered so unjustly from ethnopolitical warfare.

The editors of this book are long-time friends who graduated together in 1960 from the Albany Academy. So, our second dedication is to two of our masters from the academy: To Frank Nash, who taught us to love the written word, and to David Midgley, who gave us our first glimpse of the study of politics.

CONTENTS

CONTRIBUTORS

Fikret Adanir, Fakultät für Geschichtswissenschaft, Ruhr-Universität Bochum, Germany

Inger Agger, Center for Development Research, Copenhagen, Denmark

Ed Cairns, Centre for the Study of Conflict, University of Ulster, Coleraine, Northern Ireland

Miguel Angel Centeno, Wilson College, Princeton University

Daniel Chirot, Henry M. Jackson School of International Studies, University of Washington, Seattle

Tony Gallagher, Graduate School of Education, Queen's University Belfast, Northern Ireland

Misha Glenny, Author and Journalist, London

Brandon Hamber, Centre for the Study of Violence and Reconciliation, Johannesburg, South Africa

Patrick Heuveline, Population Research Center, National Opinion Research Center, and the University of Chicago

Miles Hewstone, School of Psychology, Cardiff University, Wales, U.K.

Ken Jowitt, Department of Political Science, University of California, Berkeley and Hoover Institution, Stanford University

Reşat Kasaba, Henry M. Jackson School of International Studies, University of Washington, Seattle

Ben Kiernan, Genocide Studies Program, Yale University

Ian S. Lustick, Department of Political Science, University of Pennsylvania, Philadelphia

Clark McCauley, Department of Psychology, Bryn Mawr College, PA

Anthony Oberschall, Department of Sociology, University of North Carolina at Chapel Hill

Brendan O'Leary, Department of Government, London School of Political Science and Economics, London

Gérard Prunier, Centre National de la Recherche Scientifique, Paris
Martin E. P. Seligman, Department of Psychology, University of
Pennsylvania, Philadelphia
John Shelton Reed, Howard W. Odum Institute for Research in Social
Science, University of North Carolina at Chapel Hill
Ervin Staub, Department of Psychology, University of Massachusetts,
Amherst
Peter Suedfeld, Department of Psychology, University of British
Columbia, Vancouver, Canada
Aili Mari Tripp, Department of Political Science, College of Letters and
Science, University of Wisconsin, Madison
Crawford Young, Department of Political Science, College of Letters
and Science, University of Wisconsin, Madison

PREFACE

MARTIN E. P. SELIGMAN

I want to introduce this volume by telling you its history and the charge I delivered to its authors. The history began in August 1996 at the Toronto meeting of the American Psychological Association (APA), when I was approached by the president of CPA—not the Canadian Psychological Association and not the California Psychological Association—the Croatian Psychological Association.

He said "help," and I said "sure." Then I began to ask around within organized American psychology about where this help might be. I found that we didn't have much help to offer. APA, like the United States in general, tends to be isolationist; problems in the United States come first, and there is not much attention left over for the world's problems.

The next scene in this story takes place in Vancouver. My family and I were vacationing near the United States–Canadian border when I received a telephone call telling me that I had been elected APA president. We drove up to Vancouver, and Peter Suedfeld, who had been nominated as president of the Canadian Psychological Association, was the first person that I called there. Over sushi I asked Peter if there was a joint project that the two associations might do together. We began to talk about ethnopolitical warfare. We agreed that with the death of fascism and the dying of communism, the wars that our children and grandchildren were most likely to face would be racial and ethnic. Was there anything organized psychology in Canada and the United States could do about that?

We decided that if he was elected, we would form a joint task force of the CPA and the APA. Peter was elected, and we then asked Mike Wessells, a well-known peace psychologist from Randolph-Macon College, and Dan Chirot, a brilliant sociologist and political scientist from the University of Washington, to cochair a task force. They gathered together 12 experts on ethnopolitical warfare in March 1997 in Philadelphia to set an agenda for the two associations.

I had the privilege of opening the meeting and said, "We could have a special issue of the *American Psychologist*, or we could put out a series of volumes, but I would like us to do something more than that. I'd like us to think ambitiously." Barbara Smith, the vice president of International Rescue, was sitting on my right. She then gave the most stirring speech I heard during my presidency.

She said, "You want something ambitious, Marty. I'll tell you what I want: I want a new profession. I go to Bosnia, I go to Rwanda. I look around and say "Where is everybody? I am one of the only psychologists there. I want a new profession."

Mike Wessells then chimed in, "You know, Marty, all you have to do is look down the main street of Luanda and you will see more child amputees in one glance than you will in a lifetime in North America. I also want a new profession."

Barbara continued, "Marty, you're the head of the largest labor union of mental health workers in the world, and your people are constantly complaining about the nature of their jobs. There may not be enough jobs, but there is plenty of work. If we do the work, the jobs will follow. I want a new profession."

We rose in a body and decided that was just what we would try to do.

Now the history branches into two different streams, both focused on the creation of a new profession, a profession in which some psychologists could devote their lives to the prediction, prevention, understanding, and healing of ethnopolitical warfare.

The first stream was to sponsor scholarship and conferences that would become the database for the new profession, and the second stream was to create postdoctoral training. This volume and the conference on which this volume is based (Conference on Ethnopolitical Warfare: Causes and Solutions, University of Belfast, Londonderry, Northern Ireland, June 27–July 3, 1998) is the first step in the stream of scholarship. It came about through the good offices of Mari Fitzduff, our host in Londonderry, and Judy Rodin, president of the University of Pennsylvania and head of the Penn National Commission on Society, Culture and Community. Mari, Judy, and I, as members of this commission, began to talk about broadening the mission of the commission beyond the United States and its internal problems of loss of civility. Genocide seemed to us to be located at the extreme end of a continuum that has mere incivility at the gentle end. We then met with a group of generous donors, who prefer anonymity, and they wrote an enormously generous check, saying "just do it." So we called together the leading experts on the genocides of the 20th century for a meeting in Londonderry in the summer of 1998.

The intellectual background for this meeting emerged wholly from the brow of one person, Dan Chirot. Dan suggested that the genocides of the

20th century could be divided into six stages, where Stage 6 was Rwanda and Nazi Germany—out-and-out racial murder—and Stage 1 was South Africa, where reconciliation and forgiveness now seem possible, when only a decade ago, a bloodbath seemed the likely outcome. Dan asked, "When does a society move up the scale of violence to Stage 6 or down toward reconciliation and Stage 1?" Dan's question is the inspiration of the meeting and of this volume.

The other stream of creating a new profession has also begun: the Solomon Asch Institute of the University of Pennsylvania, under the direction of Paul Rozin and Rick McCauley. It offered its first postdoctoral training in the psychology of ethnopolitical warfare in the summer of 1999. Penn will collaborate with the University of Ulster and the University of Capetown, South Africa, to create the cadres of the new profession. Working in psychology's venerable scientist–practitioner model, postdoctoral students will do scholarship on ethnopolitical warfare and then be placed for a year in the field. The Mellon Foundation and the National Institute of Mental Health are supporting this endeavor.

Now for the charge I delivered to the scholars whose work makes up this volume. First some excuses. I am an interloper in the field of ethnopolitical warfare. I have spent my life working on helplessness, depression, optimism, and pessimism, and I am an "individual" psychologist. I have never worked on group processes. So I have doubts that there is anything of intellectual substance that I might have to say to introduce a volume to people who have or intend to devote their careers to work on genocide. But I believe that I have one thing of use to say.

Psychologists are fond of the distinction between the "idiographic" and the "nomothetic." The *idiographic* is the story of one life. But in this context, it is also the story of one holocaust. The other side of the psychology is the *nomothetic*, the search for the regularities and the laws—the science of psychology. Regularities can be extracted only from a number of instances, which are then compared to control groups. It can be argued that in the 20th century there have been 15 genocides or ethnopolitical wars so severe that they approached genocidal proportions, as in Bosnia, and there have been at least 15 instances in which genocide might have happened, but didn't. For a nomothetic psychologist, this allows the movement from the idiographic to the nomothetic. This allows the beginning of a science of genocide. The only silver lining I can see in the horrors of the 20th century is that the N is now large enough to ask scientific questions, questions of prediction and prevention and about movement from one stage to another.

For example, Kathleen Jamieson, arguably the world's expert on political rhetoric, said, "With N's of 15 genocides or near genocides and 15 escapes from genocide, you can look at rhetoric, asking rigorously what rhetoric leads down towards Rwanda, Bosnia, and Nazi Germany, and what rhetoric leads up toward South Africa."

Which leads me to the charge.

My friend and collaborator, Lester Luborsky, told me recently of his father's happiest childhood memory. Lester's father, Meyer, and his grandfather, Jehuda Leb, lived in a small twin-village in Southern Russia, Utik-Mulif. On New Year's day of the 20th century, a century ago, the villagers walked back and forth across the bridge over the Dniester, shaking hands and rejoicing. "This is the dawn of a peaceful era; at last this terrible century has come to an end."

So it is given to you to create a science of ethnopolitical warfare by isolating the causal variables that move societies toward genocide or toward reconciliation. It is given to you to use this science to prevent what happened in the 20th century from happening once again in the 21st century.

ACKNOWLEDGMENTS

We would like to thank Mari Fitzduff, who is a professor at the University of Ulster and the director of Initiative on Conflict Resolution and Ethnicity (INCORE) in Derry, Northern Ireland. Without her, the conference that led to this book would have been impossible. Professor Fitzduff, her assistant Catherine Sharkey, and the rest of her exceptionally able staff made all the arrangements so that all the attendees had a stimulating, interesting, and very pleasant time in Northern Ireland. She also made sure that we got a complete picture of just how complex the ethnopolitical conflict there really is and why it is so hard to solve it. At the same time, we were able to learn why INCORE's work in finding solutions has been so effective.

We are grateful to the Canadian Psychological Association and its president at that time, Peter Suedfeld, who contributed to the planning of the conference and helped to make it intellectually coherent. The conference resulted from a joint presidential initiative of Peter Suedfeld and Martin Seligman, 1998 president of the American Psychological Association (APA). The APA provided important support for the conference and the subsequent production of this book, and we are particularly indebted to Ray Fowler, APA's chief executive officer.

At APA Books, we have benefited from the sound advice and help of Gary R. VandenBos, the publisher, and from the work of Margaret Schlegel, development editor, and Jennifer Powers, technical/production editor, who guided the manuscript through publication.

The Solomon Asch Center for the Study of Ethnopolitical Conflict at the University of Pennsylvania helped fund the conference and the subsequent work on these collected papers. The center was aided by, among others, the Mellon Foundation, whose support we gratefully acknowledge.

Finally, we must thank Janet Wilt, our excellent editorial assistant at the University of Washington.

I

THEORIES OF NATIONALISM
AND ETHNIC CONFLICT

1

INTRODUCTION

DANIEL CHIROT

How far along are we in the quest for an explanation of ethnic conflict and, more specifically, how well do we understand why such conflicts sometimes escalate to become genocidal, while at other times they moderate and move toward resolution? The chapters in this volume suggest that we know a lot about specific cases, that they can be explained in ad hoc ways, but that we lack strong general theories able to explain why such different outcomes occur. Nevertheless, we do have some theoretical insights, and the work in this volume points to the progress we have made.

To take two dramatic and geographically adjoining cases discussed in this volume, Tanzania and Rwanda, it is perfectly obvious after reading the chapters by Aili Mari Tripp and Crawford Young (chapter 16) and by Gérard Prunier (chapter 8) that specialists can explain why the former is a rare model of ethnic peace in Africa and the latter is the worst case of ethnic war on that continent. A social psychologist might point to the dyadic polarization in Rwanda, and to the zero-sum political game that made conflict almost inevitable in a resource-poor environment, while contrasting this to multiple and cross-cutting ethnic allegiances in Tanzania that made politics a non-ethnic game. The role of Julius Nyerere as a relatively benign, honest, and determinedly non-ethnic political leader helped greatly. But Nyerere would have been less successful if the existing situation had made a few groups think they could gain power by appealing to ethnic identities.

Rwanda provides us with a social psychological experiment that no psychologist could ever carry out in a laboratory, where life-and-death zero-sum games are frowned upon by human subjects review boards. Create two groups with strongly antagonistic, hereditarily determined identities, and set them loose in an impoverished environment to compete over increasingly scarce resources. Then see what happens. The outcome was perfectly consistent with what we know about group conflict. As the much milder experiments discussed in the chapters by Clark McCauley (21) and by Miles

Hewstone and Ed Cairns (20) suggest, it takes far less to create severe tension. Yet, it is precisely because we can never experimentally manipulate real-life situations and whole societies that we obviously need to go further in order to establish stronger theories able to explain why some situations turn into genocides, but others, which certainly seemed to have the potential for genocide, such as South Africa, have not evolved in that direction.

Ken Jowitt (chapter 2) suggests a theoretically elegant distinction between different types of identities. Ethnic identity is not automatically violent because identities that allow both entry and exit are much less likely to lead to political violence. There are hundreds, even thousands, of historical cases of ethnicities that allowed relatively easy entry and exit. That is why, despite countless legends to the contrary, there are no genetically unmixed people, and no national entities that have always consisted of just one homogeneous group. To take the example of Rwanda, Tutsi and Hutu identities were historically not barricaded but were relatively open and mixed, so that by the late 19th century the two groups were thoroughly intertwined and shared the same language, culture, and institutions. They were no longer, in that sense, ethnic groups at all, even if they had originated as different peoples. Only under Belgian colonialism were rules established that gradually closed off entry and exit to create what Jowitt calls "barricaded ethnic identities." These deny individuals the right to decide their degree of participation, deny entry to outsiders, and consider any exit to be high treason. Barricaded identities are more prone to violence. When barricaded groups come into conflict with other ethnic groups, their fundamental existence is brought into question, and issues of group honor become matters of life and death. (This conclusion applies as well to religious conflict, which is theoretically very similar to, and in cases such as Northern Ireland and the former Yugoslavia, virtually identical to, ethnic conflict in the modern world.)

The lack of resources and demographic overcrowding in Rwanda made political conflict more desperate because control of the government was the only major source of wealth, but it was the prior history of increasingly barricaded ethnic identities under Belgian colonial rule and in the postcolonial era that turned this conflict into the awful ethnic war that still continues in both Rwanda and its socially similar neighbor Burundi. Eventually, what had once been a fluid and tolerant situation came to deny individuals the right to choose their ethnopolitical identities, and when the genocide began in 1994, Hutus who were not allies of the ruling group were labeled traitors and slaughtered, too.

Jowitt's model also accounts for the savage "auto-genocide" that took place under Khmer Rouge rule in Cambodia. There, the Vietnamese were identified as the main enemy, and the fiercely barricaded Khmer Rouge leadership lived in deadly fear of being exterminated by the Vietnamese.

Whether this perception was correct or not is another matter, and in his many writings, Ben Kiernan (chapter 6) has shown that it was the result of a misreading of history born in the colonial era when France ruled Indochina. But whether realistic or not, the perception was there, and it accounts for much of the viciousness of the regime. When Khmer Rouge spokesman Khieu Samphan claimed that very few Cambodians had been killed, but mostly Vietnamese and "Cambodians with Vietnamese minds," he was not necessarily being disingenuous. He was being as honest as Adolf Hitler was in his claims that Jews threatened the life of the German people. In both cases, barricaded identities had led to what psychologists might wish to call "self-induced paranoia." Of course, in the eyes of the ideologues leading the Khmer Rouge and the Nazis, their fear of threatening alien ethnic groups who were thought to control both vast internal and international resources seemed utterly realistic.

Western social scientists are extremely suspicious of both nationalism and ethnic consciousness, and psychologists interested in promoting ethnic peace are no exception. Brendan O'Leary's (chapter 3) demonstration that such sentiments will remain strong is therefore of crucial theoretical importance. In the modern world, the village, the family, and the clan are no longer the primary focus of allegiance. Rather, the state is the focus of political identity, and if particular religious or ethnic groups feel that the state in which they live discriminates against them, and that redress is impossible, they will eventually attempt to seize that state, or secede to form their own state. (Any group that claims its own state is, de facto, claiming to be a nation.) This is why any form of nationalism based on an exclusionary, barricaded identity is so dangerous; it refuses to treat different ethnicities or religions as equal nationals, and this eventually leads to conflict.

This is a lesson well worth learning, and that needs to be pointed out to those who believe that somehow ethnopolitical conflict can be avoided by getting people to interact and know each other better. Very obviously it is psychologically easier to hate and kill a stranger who has no identity other than that imposed by group stereotypes, but several of the chapters in this volume show that it is also quite possible to hate and kill neighbors one knows very well. The critical distinction between peaceful and conflictual relations may have little to do with personal contact and understanding, but rather, as O'Leary and Jowitt suggest, they may be a function of the different ideologies promoted by various nationalist and ethnic groups. That does not answer the question of why, in some cases, more closed identities prevail, but it does warn us that once these are strongly present we face a high potential for deadly conflict in times of crisis.

Despite the widespread notion that ethnic conflict, especially in its most violent forms, is an "irrational" and "mass" response to tension, the fact is that in the 20th century, states have killed many more people than have less organized groups acting against states. In the very worst cases, deliberate and rationally planned, ideologically motivated state actions, not spontaneous and irrational crowd hysteria, have done the killing. Dominant state elites trying to maintain their nation's purity and their own monopoly on power have been responsible for the worst ethnopolitically motivated outrages. That was certainly the case in all of the extreme cases discussed in this volume: the slaughter of the Armenians by the Ottoman state in 1915, the Nazi Holocaust, the Khmer Rouge "auto-genocide," the killings and ethnic cleansings in former Yugoslavia, and the Rwandan genocide. Thus, the issue of how to create open, inclusive, and genuinely democratic forms of nationalism is a key to understanding how to diminish violence generated by ethnic and religious conflicts.

This is where political science and psychology have much to learn from each other, as neither is able to handle the difficult subject of how to do this. Barricaded, fearful nationalisms have been so common in the 20th century that it seems foolhardy to attack them as if believers merely were in need of psychological counseling. Yet, the mechanisms through which such beliefs become entrenched and dangerous are not well understood by experts in politics. Indeed, very often, we are left with inaccurate and overly general allusions to "national cultures" or, at the other end, explanations that blame individual leaders or outside forces in ways that make most participants in such conflicts helpless pawns.

LEVELS OF ETHNOPOLITICAL CONFLICT

One of the important conclusions of the Conference on Ethnopolitical Warfare, where this volume's papers were first presented, was that it is possible to establish a scale of intensity for ethnopolitical conflicts and that individual cases may move up or down on that scale to become more or less severe. Table 1.1 sets out different levels of conflict. Some cases not discussed in this volume are included simply to make the picture more complete. Comparing the cases in these different levels can tell us something about why conflicts escalate or de-escalate.

Genocides

The genocidal conflicts discussed in the volume, although covering four different parts of the world, show that some strong general conclusions can be made. One important consideration must be taken into account. All such events have generated an immense amount of controversy. Almost every aspect of the history leading up to these events is contested, and the

TABLE 1.1
Levels of Ethnic Conflict: Examples and Cases Discussed in This Volume

Levels of Ethnic Conflict	Cases	Remarks
Genocides	Armenians, 1915 Jews, 1939–1945 Cambodia, 1975–1979 Rwanda, 1994	Outright genocides have been rare, but viewed as a part of a continuum of conflict they should be interpreted as being part of a larger phenomenon.
War short of genocide	Kurds in Turkey, present Yugoslav wars, 1990s *Guatemala, 1970s–1980s* *Sri Lanka, present*	This is a much more common type of case than outright genocide which can, however, produce many massacres. In Guatemala, the war was largely (but not entirely) fought along ethnic lines.
Conflict, low-level war	Israel-occupied West Bank/Gaza, 1967–present Northern Ireland, 1969–present South Africa before 1991 Many cases in Latin America	Even more common, these types of semi-wars have occurred in dozens of cases. They heat up and cool down but can remain unresolved for decades. These are the kinds of ethnic wars that can most likely be stopped with proper mediation but that can escalate if mishandled. See below for examples of reconciliation.
Conflict, no war, occasional violence	Israel-Israeli Arabs, 1948–present U.S. South before 1970s *Many cases in India* *Southern Mexico, present*	Very common, such cases may be held in check by effective repression and co-optation, as in Israel and Mexico. In India, they occasionally flare into much more severe warfare, as in Kashmir.
No serious conflict despite high level of awareness about and important political role of ethnic, religious, and regional differences	Tanzania—many groups *Switzerland—regions* *Germany—regions* *China—Han regions* *Finland—Swedes*	There are many examples. These illustrations show that potential ethnic conflicts need not be actualized, much less turn into wars. China has problems with its non-Han minorities but has few other ethnic conflicts despite many linguistic and regional differences.
Past conflict followed by reconciliation	South Africa Northern Ireland U.S. South *Muslims in Thailand* *Malaysia—Chinese* *Spain—Basques*	In all these cases, tensions in the recent past produced either wars or high levels of confrontation that seemed to be headed toward civil war but all have produced substantial reconciliation in the 1980s and 1990s.

Note. Cases in italics are mentioned for purposes of illustration and were not presented during the conference.

events themselves are the subject of bitter controversies. Merely untangling competing claims and counterclaims can be unnerving, even with the best of good will. For example, many Armenian nationalists now claim that Turks had long-standing genocidal intentions against Armenians and still do, while Turkish nationalists claim that the killings were part of a brutal but two-sided war for control over eastern Anatolia. Many who have commented on the killings in Cambodia deny that there was any ethnic element involved and claim that to say there was in some sense lessens the responsibility of communism. Many Rwandan intellectuals, particularly among the Tutsi, assert that ethnicity had little to do with the genocide. As for the Nazi Holocaust, even though few of the actual facts are disputed by serious historians, the motives and causes of this catastrophe (Jewish historians use the Hebrew word *Shoah*, which means catastrophe) are harshly contested.

In all these cases political leaders in charge of states and all its means of violence initiated mass murder in order to hold on to power and to further nationalist visions of what kinds of states they wished to rule. In all these cases, those targeted for death or expulsion were felt to be hereditarily antagonistic to the projects of the rulers and a mortal danger to the rulers' ambitions. Thus, not just individuals but whole categories of people were exterminated. In Cambodia, of course, the reality was that most of the killing was of Khmers by Khmers, and there, notions of ethnicity mixed with those of hereditarily determined class. In that respect, the Cambodian case bears some resemblance to the worst non-ethnic massacres conducted in the 20th century by other Communist regimes. When Joseph Stalin caused between 25 and 30 million deaths in the Soviet Union, this was on grounds that targeted groups were class enemies. In principle, that might mean that they could be redeemed, but in fact whole families were condemned, especially during the collectivization campaigns against supposedly prosperous peasants. Similarly, in China and North Korea, whole groups were persecuted and millions killed as class enemies, and those of their descendants who survived were labeled hereditary class enemies. In all these cases, political leaders convinced their followers that the danger applied to their entire group, so that mass murder was the best, most viable solution (Chirot, 1996).

If we compare the two most clear-cut cases of planned genocide in the 20th century, in Rwanda in 1994 and in Hitler's Germany, when there was no doubt that whole categories were sentenced to death—every man, woman, and child—by the ruling states, we are faced with a tremendous paradox. However cruel and unjustified the Rwandan slaughter may have been, it is fairly clear from Prunier's account (chapter 8 & Prunier, 1997) that the ruling Hutu elite's power was genuinely threatened by the invasion of a Tutsi-led army. That is not to say that far better solutions could not have been found to create a more equitable, democratic system of sharing power. After all, Communist elites all over Eastern Europe gave up power without fighting to the death in 1989, and in South Africa, the White power structure compromised with the African National Congress to effect a peaceful power sharing arrangement. But at least, any objective observer would have agreed that the Hutu elite had reasons for being fearful, and this gave the extremists among them grounds for planning an extreme solution. But what objective outsider would have considered Jews in Germany in 1932 to be the main cause of Germany's many misfortunes?

This is the problem Peter Suedfeld (chapter 4) tries to resolve, a problem that has become the source of so much controversy. Although he is an eminent psychologist, Suedfeld's answer is more based on the history of ideas than on either social structural or purely psychological factors. There is much to be said for his argument that German intellectuals' unsuccessful attempts to reconcile themselves to modernity lies at the heart of the Holocaust and that the various structural (World War I, the inflation of 1923, the Depression of 1929) or psychological (Hitler's paranoia, the disorienting effects of catastrophic social and political conditions, German authoritarianism) explanations fall short of being satisfactory. If Suedfeld is right, the many continuing attempts by intellectuals to reject modernity, even in such bastions of prosperity and democracy as the United States and Western Europe, augur poorly for the future. Who knows what strange new theories these intellectuals will propose and when these may feed ethnonationalist fears in the future? What innocent groups will suffer?

Questions of intentions arise, also, in the Armenian and Cambodian cases. Fikret Adanir's (chapter 5) nuanced explanation of the 1915 Armenian genocide suggests that it was more similar to the Rwandan case than to what the Nazis did. There was a realistic fear on the part of the Ottoman authorities that Armenian nationalists might create an Armenian Republic in eastern Anatolia, allied to the Russians, and that this would bring down the Ottoman Empire. Again, this hardly justifies the Ottoman government's response, but it does make it clear that this was not so much part of a long-term genocidal plan as a reaction to an immediate political problem that had its origins decades, not centuries, earlier. In fact, the Armenian nationalists' view, that the Turks were trying to exterminate Armenians long before 1915, is as much based on a false reconstruction of history as the Turkish nationalist claim that what happened in 1915 was only part of a normal war between roughly equal sides. As long as both extreme interpretations persist, of course, historical reconciliation between Armenians and Turks remains impossible. Here, without really going into details, Adanir implicitly shows us that the task of the objective historian is as difficult and often as vital for reconciliation as that of the psychological therapist trying to overcome the trauma produced by ethnopolitical conflict. But it is a difficult task fraught with professional, and sometimes personal, danger.

In Cambodia, the Khmer Rouge's seemingly successful attempt to kill every Vietnamese under their control was a pure ethnic genocide. But the Vietnamese made up only a small proportion of those killed in Cambodia. As Patrick Heuveline (chapter 7) shows, recent demographic analysis suggests that prior estimates of over one million deaths were, if anything, low estimates. Two million deaths is not an unreasonable number. Surely, this is not really genocide in the ethnic sense because, whatever Khmer Rouge leaders may have said about "Vietnamese minds," they were killing their own people. Here again, ideology was paramount. Kiernan's writings (Kiernan, 1998) have shown that it was the leadership's vision of an idyllic, powerful, ancient agrarian Khmer empire, combined with a utopian, socialist egalitarianism that lay behind its plan for Cambodia. Added to this was a racially tinged fear of being overwhelmed by Cambodia's Vietnamese neighbors and the years of accumulated hatred generated by the Khmer Rouge's war against the right-wing government and its American backer. The American bombing of Cambodia, the way in which Cambodian Communists were used and sacrificed by the Vietnamese Communists in their own war effort, and the poverty and isolation of Cambodia after 1975 all played a part. But without their utopian ideology combined with neo-Darwinian racism, without a serious misreading of their ancient history, and without Marxist–Maoist fantasies about the power of peasant communal solidarity to overcome all obstacles, the Cambodian tragedy would never have reached such extreme proportions. The psychology of fear and resentment that motivated much of the killing was not unique, but when combined with a peculiarly barricaded and delusional ideology, it produced an almost unparalleled horror.

Aside from state action and murderous ideologies, the common element uniting all these cases is that those in charge were overwhelmed by a mortal fear that if they did not destroy their real or imagined enemies first, they would themselves be annihilated. Unfortunately, the psychology of extreme fear is not well understood. Individual panic is one thing, but the collective panic that lasts a long time and produces well thought out ideological visions is a different kind of phenomenon. Nor is political science, especially in its most up-to-date form, rational choice theory, well equipped to explain ideologies that can be so destructive. In fact, when leaders see that their ideologies are not working, but are leading to catastrophe, they become all the more intransigent. Hitler, the Khmer Rouge, the Rwandan elite, or for that matter Stalin, Kim Il Sung, and Mao Tse-tung did not abandon their ideological dreams when they saw that they were producing immense suffering, millions of deaths, and national tragedies. On the contrary, they redoubled their efforts to impose their visions. If the plan had not worked so far, that meant that there were still dangerous enemies around who had to be eliminated, traitors to the cause who had to be found and purged.

It is clear that the psychological mechanisms that transform ordinary people into vicious killers are not well understood. Conformity and fear of being left out of the group play a role, of course, but the ideologies that drive the leaders responsible for initiating these atrocities have not been explored particularly well. On close inspection, it turns out that the leaders were not "mad" or "irrational" but that they were driven by an ideological view of the world that left them few other options.

In commenting on these issues, McCauley (chapter 21) points out that psychologists have much more work to do to understand both how people identify with their ethnic group or nation and how they become killers in order to defend such identities. Research on group psychology suggests that it is a mistake to treat such extreme behavior as "sick," and to look to abnormal psychology for answers. In fact, it is possible to mobilize completely normal people for genocidal killing.

Major Ethnopolitical Warfare That Stopped Short of Genocide

Among the whole range of potential ethnic conflicts that have occurred in the 20th century, few have resulted in genocides. Many more have produced wars that, however serious, remained less than genocidal, although in some cases, what has come to be called "ethnic cleansing" was so widely practiced as to amount to a kind of quasi-genocide.

Certainly, that is what happened during the several Yugoslav wars in the 1990s. Serbs and Croats massively expelled each other, and both Serbs and Croats expelled Muslims from areas they controlled in Bosnia. Serbs tried to expel Albanians from Kosovo, and many Serbs have been, in turn, expelled from Kosovo by the Albanians who triumphed after NATO's war against Serbia. In all these cases, there were bitter fighting, torture, rape, massacres, looting, and a whole range of the usual brutal tactics. The Serbian and Croat states, or their co-ethnic puppets in Bosnia, committed most of the atrocities; some were committed by Muslims in Bosnia. The outrages against Serbs committed by Albanians after the 1999 NATO war seem to have been more spontaneous than centrally planned and executed by any recognized political authority. Yet even in Yugoslavia, it would be difficult to claim that actual genocides were planned. Why did such horrors occur, and why were they not even worse?

Neither of these two questions are easily answered. Serbs, Croats, and Albanians were in conflict well before the collapse of Yugoslavia, and both Serbian and Croatian nationalist politicians were able to use prior conflicts, especially the memories of the massacres during World War II, as well as carefully nurtured stories that presented their people as eternal historical victims, to promote hatred, fear, and a desire for revenge. As Anthony

Oberschall (chapter 9) carefully shows, once the process has begun, and one population is convinced that its survival depends on destroying the others before it is itself victimized, it becomes relatively easy to turn prior neighbors and co-workers against each other. It takes only a few activists who commit outrages to persuade everyone that vengeful wars of extermination have begun. Then, whoever does not agree to turn against the other ethnic group can be labeled a traitor. Identities are barricaded against other ethnic groups. Individuals disappear and are replaced by collectivities who treat each other as groups of uniformly guilty, hostile enemies. But what starts the whole cycle?

Misha Glenny (chapter 10), who has recently published a large book on Balkan history (Glenny, 2000), suggests that the great European powers bear much of the blame for having turned various Balkan ethnicities into mutually hostile nations. He agrees with the overwhelming majority of serious scholars of this area when he points out that these are not ancient hatreds but are the products of late 19th- and early 20th-century nationalist conflicts promoted by outsiders. The very definition of ethnic nations entitled to rule ethnically pure states was once quite alien to the Balkans, as it was to most of the world. But the concept developed in the advanced parts of Europe and spread from there, thus creating the terrible 20th-century tragedies in Central and Eastern Europe that we know all too well. (In chapter 5, Adanir argues that it was this same impulse, imported from the West, that created the pressures for pure ethnic nations within the Ottoman Empire, and led to the genocide against the Armenians.) From the time of the Balkan Wars before World War I to the culminating ethnic massacres of Serbs, Jews, and Gypsies perpetrated by Croatian allies of the Germans and Italians during World War II, a pattern of historical mistrust and fear was set. It was these historical memories, still very much alive in the 1980s, only 40 years after the end of World War II, that resurfaced during the economic and political crisis accompanying the collapse of communism. The spark needed to set off a new blaze was the presence of ambitious politicians able to capitalize on the rampant insecurities of the peoples of Yugoslavia.

There is more to the story, of course, including the damages left by four decades of Communist rule, which defined ethnicity and region as the main bargaining chips in the competition for the allocation of centrally distributed resources. There was the ultimate economic failure of communism, without which people would not have become so desperate or insecure. In the end, however, economic and political failure only produce the likelihood of crisis, they do not determine whether that will take the form of ethnopolitical warfare. That was largely determined by the fact that ethnicity continued under communism to be the chief way in which people could identify themselves as political beings except if they chose to be loyal

Communists. With the fall of communism, there were few if any alternative ways for people to find support groups or identities except through their ethnic memberships.

That the outcome was not even bloodier only points to the fact that outright genocides are not easily conducted. The presence of international observers hardly stopped the war, but it made the participants a bit more cautious, because of the danger that NATO would intervene, as it finally did in both Bosnia and Kosovo against the Serbs who were the worst offenders. Although this is mere speculation, it is quite plausible that without this admittedly small restraint, the wars conducted by the Serbs would have been even bloodier. As for the Croats, they were brutal, too, as Misha Glenny has shown in his many writings, but they were always more aware of the importance of maintaining the sympathy of some of the Western powers. Thus, even though international intervention came too late to stop terrible outrages, the Yugoslav case shows that in some circumstances only the realistic threat of outside intervention can stop a genocide. In this respect, it is probably instructive to compare what happened in Yugoslavia in the 1990s to what happened to the Armenians in 1915. The Ottoman authorities' primary goal was to empty eastern Anatolia of Armenians rather than exterminating all Armenians from the face of the earth. In the main cities of western Anatolia and in Istanbul, where large Armenian populations resided, most were left alone. But the brutality of the forced exodus and the conditions under which it was conducted led to so many deaths that, as Adanir points out, the term *genocide* is appropriate. In Yugoslavia, it stopped just short of that.

We should not forget that there have been many ethnic wars that never threatened to degenerate into genocide or massive ethnic cleansing at all. In what ways are they different? Cases such as the Kurdish War and the many ethnic internal wars in Latin America point to a possible answer.

Reşat Kasaba (chapter 11) emphasizes the complex nature of the war between Kurds and the Turkish state, a war that still continues, despite some recent signs of a possible resolution. Turkey's regard for European opinion has placed some limits on its own use of force. Then, too, millions of Kurds are integrated into Turkish society at many levels, including the elite, and there is no deep-seated ethnic or religious prejudice against Kurds among Turks, or vice versa. Conversely, since the time of Ataturk, the Turkish state has denied Kurds any cultural (that is, primarily linguistic) recognition, and this has provided grounds for grievance among some Kurdish intellectuals. At the same time, the southeastern part of Turkey, where Kurds are in the majority, is also the poorest and least developed part of the country. So, when some Marxist Kurdish intellectuals began a liberation movement, they found some popular support. Then, the brutal clumsiness of the Turkish army did the rest, fanning what might have remained a fairly small conflict into a large one with tens of thousands of people killed in the past couple of decades. This war, in turn, has certainly contributed to the development of Kurdish nationalism, even though Kurds remain very split over the issue. The majority would probably prefer integration with Turkey along with some cultural autonomy. Even though the Turkish army resists this, there has never been, and is certainly not now any intention of conducting, either a genocide or massive ethnic cleansing. What the Turkish military wants is to absorb Kurds into a Turkish national identity, something quite different from what has happened in Yugoslavia between Serbs, Croats, Bosnian Muslims, and Albanians. Thus, whereas by 1995 it seemed utterly quixotic to believe that some sort of reconciliation was possible in Yugoslavia (despite American policy statements to the contrary), in Turkey a more reasonable and conciliatory approach to the Kurdish problem by the Turkish government still has a substantial chance of succeeding. In Yugoslavia, partition is the only solution by now. In Turkey, better options remain, although with time, if the war continues, and if the Turkish military ever begin to massacre large numbers of Kurds, the situation could easily become irreconcilable.

Had we included a chapter on Sri Lanka, we might well have concluded that there, also, the situation has gradually moved beyond any realistic possibility of reconciliation between Tamils and Singhalese. Conversely, had we included a chapter on Guatemala, we might have found that there, despite many tens of thousands of deaths in a brutal civil war with strong ethnic elements between Mayan and European or mixed segments of the population, reconciliation is possible, as a modicum of cultural autonomy and respect for the original Mayan cultures would go a long way toward resolving the problem. In Guatemala, as in the case of the Kurds, the Mayan population consists of many different linguistic groups who do not really form a national entity, and much mixing has occurred, so that coexistence within the same state, and even full reconciliation is a realistic option.

For our purposes, these cases show how important it is to distinguish between cases and to know why some are more amenable to resolution than others. It is not helpful to lump them all together, as do some human rights activists. The Turkish state and government should not be placed in the same boat as the Serbian state run by Slobodan Milosevic, and if there is to be international intervention, it should be of a very different sort in Turkey than it was in Yugoslavia.

Miguel Centeno's chapter (12) stands out as a very suggestive but different kind of essay. He explains that Latin American nationalisms have seldom directed their hostility toward outsiders. One reason for this has been that they shared so much in common with their neighbors. Yet, internal wars of repression, particularly against Indians or against ideological and class enemies, have been more common and, on the whole, far bloodier than international wars. Latin American elites have tended to share cultural outlooks across borders more than they have with many of their own people. In view of the continent's domination by military governments for so long, international war has been surprisingly rare, especially in the 20th century. Nationalism has not been as deep or as institutionalized as in some other parts of the world, particularly Europe.

This raises a very disturbing issue. We know that there have been many potential ethnic conflicts that have simply fizzled out, for example, the one between Catholic Bavarians and Protestant north Germans. After all, there the religious and linguistic differences were as great as, say, between Croats and Serbs. Also, there had been a tradition of war on religious grounds in the 17th century. Among scholars of German history, there is some agreement that the wars fought by Germany under Bismarck, who united Germany, and then World Wars I and II ended all possibility of internal German disunity by creating such a strong sense of shared destiny. Unpleasant as the conclusion may be, it may be that one of the best ways of reducing internal ethnic conflict is to find an outside enemy and fight a war.

Strong nationalism reduces internal ethnic differences. On the contrary, where nationalism is weak and the state does not take strong measures to foster it, all kinds of internal cultural differences, ranging from linguistic to religious to merely regional can become a primary focus of identity and lead to internal ethnopolitical warfare. Thus, the attempts of some nation-states to force cultural homogeneity on their people, so decried as forced assimilation, has, in many cases, worked and produced internally more peaceful nations. Waging war against a common outside enemy is often the best way to accelerate this process, although of course, in Western Europe, that has had its own extremely bloody consequences.

Low-Level Ethnopolitical War

Not all ethnic conflicts that turn into war wind up with mass killing or expulsions. A good example is the Northern Irish conflict explained by Tony Gallagher (chapter 13). Whatever one may think of the British, in the 20th century, and certainly after 1969, they were not going to allow either side in Northern Ireland or their own troops to engage in genocidal massacres. Thus, even though the conflict has killed over 3,600, the casualties could not reach the same proportions that occurred where state-controlled forces led the killings. Great Britain is a democracy, and British public opinion would never have tolerated state-led genocidal behavior or massive ethnic cleansing. Furthermore, the British themselves never felt fundamentally threatened by events in Northern Ireland. Some extremist Protestants and Catholics did think they were mortally endangered, but they were not in command of the armed forces or police. However painful the Northern

Irish situation may have been, for the governing authority, it was never a matter of life and death or even the top political issue. Thus, terrorism's destructive powers could be limited by British military power while the occupying British authorities kept the two sides sufficiently apart to prevent an all-out civil war. In these circumstances, neither the level of killing nor the British government's position ever precluded reconciliation.

This applies as well to South Africa, although there the stakes for the governing Whites were far higher than they were for the British rulers of Northern Ireland. In the case of South Africa, both international pressure and the fact that the Whites depended on non-White labor made a genocidal solution unlikely. The fact that the Whites had a functioning democracy among themselves also made it possible for dissident White opinion to make itself heard, and it afforded some partial source of help for non-Whites. However much repression and censorship there was, many details about the abuses of power carried out by the Apartheid government got out. Furthermore, Whites were not a single ethnic group, anymore than were non-Whites, but were themselves divided. As Brandon Hamber (chapter 15) points out, South Africa is an extremely complex ethnic mosaic. This is not to say that it was a pluralistic society in the American sense, because the majority under White rule was heavily discriminated against, repressed, and disenfranchised. But extreme ethnic complexity made genocide less of an option than if there had been only two or three clearly defined ethnic groups in South Africa. Thus, South Africa averted a genocidal internal war, although it came a lot closer to this than Northern Ireland.

Finally, although it is not the main point of his chapter, Ian Lustick (chapter 14) raises the question of relations between the Israeli government and the Palestinians in the occupied territories of the West Bank and Gaza. There has been warfare between them, although it was severely constrained by overwhelming and effective Israeli military power. In this case, very few observers ever thought any kind of integration between the two populations would ever be possible, no matter how long Israel occupied these territories or how many Palestinians got jobs in the Israeli economy. Extremists on both sides demanded that the war be taken to extremes. Because the Israelis were so much stronger, why was genocide or massive ethnic cleansing never envisioned? (In fact, recent Israeli scholarship suggests that during the 1947–1948 Israeli–Arab war, there was considerable, deliberate ethnic cleansing by the Jews of Arabs, but such a policy was never massively applied after the 1967 war.) One important reason, perhaps the single most important, was that no Israeli government could countenance the enormous negative publicity this would have generated in Western Europe and especially the United States, without whose support Israel's very survival would have been in doubt. Then, too, as a full democracy for its Jews, Israel had dissenters who wanted a milder policy toward Arabs and who would have protested and publicized outrages against Arabs.

Thus, in all three of these otherwise very different cases, international opinion and observation made a difference and reduced the brutality of the powerful governments who could have done far worse than they actually did. In all three cases, democracy, however imperfect, played a role, too, in limiting violence. In that sense, Ervin Staub's (chapter 18) comment that observers, both internal and external, may be vital to reduce conflict, is an apt one.

All of the cases of outright genocide in our century, or even of massive ethnic cleansing, were either in states that were extremely isolated or that thought that their closest big-power allies would agree with their actions. Nazi Germany itself waited until 1941, when it finally attacked the Soviet Union, to begin the whole-scale extermination of Jews, even though the intention had been there from the start of Nazi rule. Before 1939, Hitler did not want to precipitate a war before he felt ready, and between 1939 and 1941, he wanted to stay in the good graces of the Soviets whom he thought (quite wrongly) to be controlled by Jews. Cambodia was almost totally isolated when it conducted its mass killings. The Ottoman Empire felt (correctly) that its only big-power ally, Germany, would say nothing. Rwanda, in what was one of the most shameful episodes of recent history, felt that its big power ally, France, would keep international pressure at bay during the genocide because, as Prunier (chapter 8) writes, the French had not complained about prior, lesser episodes of killing. And, indeed, Rwanda turned out to be right: The French and the Americans, joined by the United Nations, at first denied that what was going on was genocidal.

External pressure can have considerable effect. In Yugoslavia, when the Americans finally got up the nerve to use military force, the Serbian war against Bosnian Muslims stopped. Had the United States or Western Europe acted earlier, there almost certainly would have been far fewer deaths in Bosnia. Relatively fast action in Kosovo prevented a larger tragedy, and the death rate was less than in Bosnia.

Therefore, one of the conclusion we can draw is that international action, even at the level of simply providing observers, can have some effect. But the threat of serious diplomatic, economic, or even military action can do much more.

Ethnopolitical Conflicts Without Wars

This book is more concerned with the very violent episodes of ethnopolitical warfare in the 20th century than with the far more common cases of conflict with relatively few deaths or the extremely common potential cases that produce practically no violence. At the extremes, there are potential cases that produce no real conflict at all. We discussed only one such case, the one in Tanzania, which is particularly interesting because it is in a part of the world rife with ethnopolitical conflicts of the worst sort. But an imaginative historian could point to hundreds of cases, ranging from Germany's regions whose religious and linguistic differences might have produced conflict; to Paraguay, which has done the best job in Latin America of incorporating some elements of Native American linguistic culture into the dominant Spanish-speaking culture; to China, where the many different regional languages do not seem to pose a separatist problem or much conflict except among the minorities that are explicitly defined as non-Chinese, chiefly Tibetans and Muslim Turkic speakers such as Uighurs.

There is no need to point to potential conflicts that are long dead or never developed, such as between Burgundians and the French, or Frisians and Dutch, or Thais and Laotians or, to take a more contentious and surprising one, between Tatars and Russians in the 1990s. This last case is interesting because some Tatar ethnic entrepreneurs did try to make an issue of the differences between Muslim Tatars and Russians, but unlike in Chechnya, this never turned into violence or anything close to a serious secessionist movement. Who remembers that at one time there was the potential for conflict between minority but economically dominant Swedes and majority but poorer Finns? And why do the Swiss, divided by language, religion, and high mountains, stick together with very little conflict? When the French speakers in the canton of Berne demanded autonomy a few years ago, they got their own canton, Jura, and everyone promptly forgot about the matter.

Why so many potential conflicts do not exist or remain at very low levels of violence is a question we did not take up in this book except for Tanzania, so we cannot draw any conclusions from the fact that such cases are widespread. Nevertheless, that fact must be kept in mind, lest we think that such conflicts are universal wherever any linguistic, religious, regional, or other cultural differences based on skin color or economic class happen to exist. As Jowitt (chapter 2) says about ethnicity, it need not always produce barricaded identities or conflict.

More relevant for our purposes are the cases where conflict has existed, but remained contained or moved toward resolution. Just as some conflicts, such as that between Serbs and Croats, may remain quiescent for decades and then suddenly become much more intense, so there are reverse cases where the situation becomes calmer. If every situation in which there are visible cultural differences and any past history of conflict in which some groups have felt victimized by others has the potential to become more severe, it is equally true that most conflictual situations may be improved or may remain nonviolent. Among the many interesting examples of such nonviolent ethnopolitical conflicts there are the Canadian–French Québec-ois conflict, the Flemish–Walloon one in Belgium, and some of the ethnic–regional conflicts in India. (Of course, some Indian conflicts, such as that in Kashmir, turn into violent wars, and we can imagine circumstances in which Canada's troubles could become more violent.) The situation in southern Mexico between Native cultures and the dominant Hispanic Mexicans has remained relatively, although not absolutely, peaceful. There have been deaths, but when compared to our extreme cases, or even Northern Ireland, the recent situation in Mexico has been fairly restrained.

What keeps some existing ethnopolitical conflicts relatively calm? A look at the essays on Jewish–Arab relations within the borders of 1948 Israel and of race relations in the American South yield some partial answers, even though, again, the two cases are very different from each other.

The case of Israel presents us with one of the world's most effective examples of semi-benign repression that has not and is not leading toward real reconciliation. Since independence, those Palestinians who remained within the 1948 borders of Israel have been granted an unequal form of citizenship. In matters of housing, economic opportunity, public facilities, and access to good jobs, they have been heavily discriminated against. But they have been allowed free expression and have benefited from some government programs. There has been almost no violence. How have the Israelis managed this?

Lustick (chapter 14) explains that enough Arabs have benefited, and their society has been sufficiently penetrated by Israeli intelligence to keep the situation under very firm control. Repression has not been so extreme as to drive the local population to desperation, but it has been great enough to prevent effective mobilization against Israel. It becomes obvious from this story that many official Israelis once believed that they could work out the same kind of compromise with Arabs in the territories occupied after 1967, but this failed. Whereas Israeli Arabs compose less than 15% of Israel's population, the population in the occupied territories is overwhelmingly Arab and was harder to penetrate or seduce. The effort to do so eventually broke down. Eventually, a Palestinian revolt changed the minds of some Israeli leaders and led to effort to find a compromise that would create a separate Palestinian state in the occupied territories.

The danger in Israel is that an independent Palestinian state may inspire enough dissatisfied Arab Israelis to become political activists so that the half-century of benign repression will finally fall apart. Then, Israel will face the same problem that other ethnically polarized modern nation-states face: repress harder or work toward some form of conciliatory integration. But until now, neither option has been necessary.

The American South after the Civil War is another example of discriminatory repression that worked for a long time, although with substantial localized violence. As in South Africa, genocide and ethnic cleansing were never considered because, while Whites dominated the situation completely, the Southern African American population was required for its labor. Yet, in the long run, the Southern situation proved to be impossibly volatile for three reasons. First, the situation so blatantly contradicted the stated ideals of the United States about equality and fairness that a large part of the country, if not the South, felt uneasy about this discrimination. Second, it was only a matter of time until the African American population organized itself sufficiently to mount effective protests. Finally, as the Southern economy became less rural, the whole social and economic basis of Jim Crow laws weakened. Eventually, few Southern Whites had much of an economic stake in maintaining the situation, even if that did not, of itself, change attitudes.

The most interesting question to ask is why, when the civil rights struggle of the 1950s to 1970s erupted, this did not lead to more violence and an attempt to forcefully repress African American demands. There were some extremist Whites who wanted to do just that, but they met with no success. Why not? That is the question John Reed (chapter 17) answers. As one of the successful cases of movement toward peaceful resolution, the American South can be compared to South Africa and Northern Ireland.

MOVING TOWARD RESOLUTION AND BREAKING THE CYCLE OF REVENGE

In South Africa, as in Northern Ireland and in the American South during the struggle for civil rights from the 1950s to the 1970s, there came a point when it became clear that the struggle to suppress non-Whites, Catholics, and African Americans was no longer worth it for most of the dominant group. The costs were high and rising, and outside pressure was mounting. Final success against those out of power, barring genocide or ethnic cleansing, was impossible, and extreme solutions were impossible because of structural constraints. South Africa would have lost too much of its labor force and was already suffering from the partial but growing economic embargo imposed on it.

In South Africa, the fall of communism and the fact that South Africa no longer could claim a strategic role in the East–West struggle meant that external pressure would only grow. At the same time, the African National Congress's abandonment of extreme socialist measures made it somewhat less threatening. In Northern Ireland, the growing wealth of the Catholic Republic of Ireland, its integration in the European Union, and the political moderation of the Republic may have made the Republic seem less threatening to the Protestants. Even more important was the growing European and

British pressure on the Protestants to compromise and grant the Catholics civil rights. In the American South, the fact that state power (that is, the federal government) was increasingly involved against segregation vastly increased the cost of White Southern resistance. Any violence is too much, but as John Reed writes, there were, during this period (1960s and 1970s), fewer than about 50 civil-rights-related murders. This is a tiny number compared to other cases of violent ethnic conflict over any comparable period of time.

Ultimately, the case of the American South presents one of the world's outstanding success stories. No American could be fooled into thinking there is racial harmony, but a considerable amount of reconciliation has taken place, there are thousands of African American political officials in the South, the level of interracial violence is low, and the civil rights struggle has been won. Aside from the fact that this was helped by the federal government's intervention, it was also helped by the fact that most civil rights leaders appealed to values shared, at least in principle, by most White Southerners. The movement was led by Protestant clergy who were of the same religion as the Whites; both sides claimed to be inspired by America's democratic ideals; and the movement's leadership threatened neither confiscation of White property nor massive retribution. Therefore, the costs of giving in were relatively low compared to the costs of trying to maintain segregation.

The Southern case cannot be easily replicated elsewhere, but it does show that fostering reconciliation requires the aggrieved party to abandon some, perhaps most, claims to retribution. It requires the costs of continued struggle to be higher than the costs of settlement. It requires both sides to find some common values. It requires some outside force, either international or domestic, to impose a prohibition against extreme measures such as genocide or ethnic cleansing. When terrible acts of murder occur, there has to be a credible military or police force than can promise that the killings will neither spread nor be tolerated, so that panic is avoided and extremist political forces find no purchase. Finally, the solution requires at least some politicians to emerge who have a broad enough vision to give up the extreme claims of their side. A democratic system, even if it limits the political freedom to the controlling side, is essential for this because it prepares the way for open debate.

The White South African and the Northern Irish electorates, when faced by the realities of their situation, voted against the extremists. Politicians with some vision always exist, but they have to have the opportunity to gain power. Nelson Mandela is an extraordinarily forgiving man, considering what was done to him and his people. But he had to be given a chance to exercise power. Martin Luther King, Jr., who inspired Mandela, was also an exceptional conciliator and unifier of the races. But both these men had to be given a chance. Potential Mandelas or Kings in Yugoslavia or Rwanda were murdered, exiled, or jailed and never had a chance.

True conciliators are those who can provide reassurance that there will be no widespread reprisals for past abuses. Property will not be confiscated, and whatever wrongs have been committed in the past will lead to legal action only in a very few and extreme cases. In other words, the larger social group responsible for discrimination—the Southern American Whites, the South African Whites, and the Protestants in Northern Ireland—had to be assured that they would not be treated as a single guilty body, but rather as individuals who would be exonerated from communal guilt. That may be the single key element in the reconciliations that tie these otherwise quite different cases together.

The issues of justice and revenge looms large. As Hamber (chapter 15) emphasizes, many of the former victims or relatives of victims of apartheid in South Africa believe that the Reconciliation Commission set up to expose and forgive past abuses is letting off criminal officials in return for insincere, shallow "confessions." If we consider the meaning of the word *justice* in criminal proceedings, it is quite obvious that in many cases, despite frequent assertions to the contrary, victims and their relatives mean *revenge*. This is a sensitive subject because the legal systems developed in Western Europe have gradually moved toward notions of prevention and rehabilitation rather than punishment for the sake of revenge. Nor do modern legal systems permit individuals to take revenge in their own hands.

Ethnic warfare is a form of violence that invites collective revenge, and if there is no outside authority to impose justice, ethnic communities may feel entirely justified in seeking to take matters into their own hands. South Africa has taken steps to prevent just that by, first of all, individualizing responsibility and, second, emphasizing the possibility of forgiveness. To identify particular persons as responsible rather than "Whites" or "Afrikaners" is meant to defuse intercommunal hostility. Whether this is "just" or not, it is the only path to eventual reconciliation, because when one community visits retribution on another, this only leads to continuing or renewed warfare. Satisfying abstract notions of justice, even by demanding that a particularly responsible community pay significant reparations, invites the very opposite of reconciliation. We can all agree that for victims of past abuse, this may seem unfair and psychologically unsatisfying. But it is necessary.

Even if past abuses are individualized, how severely should they be punished, and how many should be punished? All systems of ethnic oppression involved the collaboration of large portions of the population. In the case of South Africa, as in the American South, not only were most Whites complicit, but so were many non-Whites. In cases of genocide, for example, in the case of the Nazis, of Rwanda, and of the Ottoman genocide of Armenians, hundreds of thousands of individuals, ranging from the top officials through ordinary soldiers and cooperating civilians, were responsible for mass murder. The same has been true in the Yugoslav wars of the 1990s. Who, then, should be brought to trial? It is relatively painless but psychologically frustrating to bring a few individuals, even a few dozen, to trial and to sentence them. No victim of the Nazi Holocaust was fooled into thinking that an appropriate number of Germans had been punished for their crimes, however much satisfaction they may have felt at hearing about Hermann Göring's suicide and Joachim von Ribbentrop's hanging. Surely, victims of the Yugoslav wars must feel that bringing a handful of killers and torturers to trial before an international tribunal is, at best, a tiny gesture. But if there is to be reconciliation, how much farther should justice be pushed before it begins to appear like collective revenge? Once that threshold is passed, the community being punished may feel that there is no point in trying to achieve reconciliation and that either renewed war or flight are better options than waiting for massive retribution.

That is precisely what the government of South Africa wishes to avoid. Whether or not South Africa will succeed remains to be seen. Could the current crime wave, calls for greater retribution from some circles, and the continuing but unpublicized flight of Whites and East Indians erode the process of reconciliation? Perhaps, but we can still agree that the course being followed by South Africa, to try to overcome past abuses with a minimum of punishment and through strict attempts to blame individuals rather than whole communities, is the only possible road to reconciliation. This, obviously, was the path followed in the American South as well. Only a few individuals responsible for the most flagrant criminal acts have been punished for what was a much larger pattern of past abuse.

Prunier (chapter 8) presents us with the contrasting case of Rwanda, where attempts at reconciliation have failed and where civil war continues. Ultimately, he predicted, there will be further rounds of bloody massacres, and another genocide cannot be excluded. Moderate Tutsis and Hutus are being killed by their own extremists. If the international tribunal set up to deal with Rwanda has moved slowly, retributions and counter-retributions between the two communities have killed thousands more since 1994. In this case, it is hard to see what steps could possibly bring about meaningful reconciliation.

In every case of ethnic conflict, it is when whole communities are blamed, rather than individuals, that escalation or continuation of the conflict becomes almost inevitable. It is when individuals are blamed and distinctions made within ethnic communities that reconciliation becomes possible.

This leaves open a fascinating question. Under what circumstances can wronged individuals learn to forgive and to abandon a quest for revenge? It is because Nelson Mandela has done this that he is recognized as a great man. Forgiveness, especially by those who have been so victimized, is rare, and it should be the task of future psychological research to identify what motivates such exceptional cases. Much more common, both among leaders and ordinary people, are those who harbor deep grudges for past wrongs and even extend them historically to include whole communities for many generations.

WHAT CAN PSYCHOLOGY CONTRIBUTE?

It would be naïve to believe that human beings are inherently peaceful and that conflict is unnatural. On the other hand, conflict and war can be controlled. Once we recognize that there are structural conditions that bring about conflict, we might be able to set up a "world watch" to warn us of situations that are degenerating into serious conflicts. Then, outside pressure might be brought to bear before it is too late.

This is one of the suggestions made in Staub's chapter (18). Chaotic political and economic conditions, the nurturing of past grievances and increasing calls for barricading ethnic identities against hostile others, and calls for revenge are clear signs of coming trouble. Even if scholars rarely have the capacity to influence government policies very much, they can point to warning signs that would at least alert policy makers and publics in advanced, powerful democracies to tell them where ethnopolitical warfare is likely to break out. But that seems more the province of political science than of psychology.

Inger Agger's chapter (19) is an excellent discussion of what psychologists can do in order to alleviate individual trauma. Her work in Bosnia has led her to conclude that we should beware of facile and politically appealing generalizations. For example, she notes that despite all the attention given to rape during the war, few women clients thought this was the major issue. The war itself, the loss of home and disappearance of family members, the loss of livelihood and all sense of stability—these were the major reasons for trauma. From her chapter it becomes clear that psychologists are well equipped to offer counseling and individual healing to victims of such conflicts, and this kind of work can make an important contribution even if we do not yet have good theoretical ways of explaining, much less halting, ethnopolitical warfare.

The chapters by Hewstone and Cairns (20) and by McCauley (21) review in some detail most of the psychological theories worked out about the causes of group conflict, and they apply these to ethnopolitical hostilities. It would not be particularly useful to summarize these two elegant essays, as they are themselves excellent summaries of very large bodies of literature.

They both show that until now psychology's contribution to our understanding of this phenomenon has been modest but should grow significantly.

The structural conditions that lead to ethnic conflict and warfare, and even the structural conditions that can contribute to solutions, are fairly well understood. What we do not know is what goes on inside the minds of those directly involved. Why do some politicians, like Yitzhak Rabin, Nelson Mandela, or Frederik de Klerck, come to adopt a broader vision, while others, like Benjamin Netanyahu or Slobodan Milosevic, do not? What are the psychodynamics that produce extremists? After all, most Palestinians; most Israeli Jews; most Irish Protestants and Catholics; most Black and White Southerners; and most Croats, Serbs, and Bosnians are not extremists. Under what circumstances does fear so pervade the mentality of whole people that they listen to, and even sometimes elect, extremists? What kinds of community will satisfy modern individuals without forcing them to give up their individuality? How can individualism be fostered, in order to make "barricaded" identities less likely, but without producing the decay of social solidarity? What breaks the cycle of revenge seeking?

What the chapters by McCauley (21) and Hewstone and Cairns (20) also make clear, as do the theoretical political science chapters by O'Leary (3) and Jowitt (2), is that we do not understand the process of identity formation very well. Ethnic identities may not always be primary and, in fact, rarely are. Nor are national identities. And no serious scholar today believes that ethnic or national identities are primordial, in the sense of being eternal and carried through generations without change. Nevertheless, McCauley insists that some sort of identity larger than the individual and longer lasting than single lives may be necessary for almost all of us. At times some groups have made their ethnic or national identities their most important ones. In modern times that has been particularly true in times of great stress, as Staub emphasizes. After all, however historically constructed the "ethnic" identities of Hutus and Tutsis may have been, or Croats and Serbs, or Jews and Aryan Germans, when the moments of crisis came, that was all that counted. In times of ethnopolitical warfare, and in the conditions leading up to them, the leaders and main followers of ethnic entrepreneurs who lead ethnopolitical movements behave as if such identities were indeed primordial. So, despite our well-placed scholarly skepticism about the scientific accuracy of such claims, we cannot simply dismiss them. Rather, we should know more about the psychological processes that cause large numbers of people to adopt attitudes which strike us as "unreasonable," "false," and even "irrational." Obviously in some cases we are dealing with cynical manipulation of public opinion, or cowardly acceptance of social and political pressures that override commons sense and human decency. But why does this happen sometimes, and not at other times? Who is psychologically prepared to resist such pressures, and who is not? Finally, we cannot overlook the fact that many extreme ethnopolitical warriors do, after all, believe in their cause, however wrong we may think they are. What deep psychological urges within some of us make us so want to identify with larger ethnic groups that we are driven to such extremes?

It would be nice to say that we have solved these problems. Instead we conclude by saying that we have inventoried much that is known about ethnopolitical warfare and also much that we do not know. It is particularly at the intersection of social psychology and the other social sciences that much fundamental research remains to be done. Eventually, we will be able to talk about the possibility of taking long-range preventive action on the basis of a more solid scientific foundation.

REFERENCES

Chirot, D. (1996). *Modern tyrants: The power and prevalence of evil in our age.* Princeton, NJ: Princeton University Press.

Glenny, M. (2000). *The Balkans: Nationalism, war, and the great powers 1809–1999.* New York: Viking Penguin.

Kiernan, B. (1998). *The Pol Pot regime: Race, power, and genocide in Cambodia, 1975–1979.* New Haven, CT: Yale University Press.

Prunier, G. (1997). *The Rwanda crisis: History of a genocide.* New York: Columbia University Press.

2

ETHNICITY: NICE, NASTY, AND NIHILISTIC

KEN JOWITT

Ethnicity is a remarkable and recent form of attempted group security, dignified identity, and material advantage peculiar to egalitarian settings. No one captures this hybrid of equality and solidarity more evocatively than Shaw (1951) in *Saint Joan* when he has Joan deny the status or corporate superiority of the nobility by addressing a member of the nobility familiarly (equally) as Polly and justifies it by saying "we are both French."

Weber (1968) specified the novelty of ethnicity with the observation that "ethnic honor is a *specific honor of the masses* . . . accessible to *anybody* who belongs to the subjectively believed community of descent." He also argued that "ethnic membership does not constitute a group; it only facilitates group formation of any kind, particularly in the political sphere" (pp. 385–398). Implicit in this statement is the existence of actors who can choose among second-order identities with relative ease, regularity, and success, of a society with a high degree of "combinatorial freedom" (Deutsch, 1963), that is, the ability in ordinary, not only emergency, circumstances to standardize intrinsically diverse social identities (e.g., as citizens) and combine them in novel ways.

As a historically recent form of identification, ethnicity combines and rejects features from both traditional corporate and modern individual identity. Ethnicity emphasizes group solidarity but is not stratified internally and invidiously like traditional corporate groups; it allows for individual choice while emphasizing group origin and loyalty. Framed in behavioral terms, ethnic identification allows for exit from a group without excommunication—and for reentry without official certification. Conceptually, this means ethnicity is a mode of identification, not a categorical identity.

The significance of this is twofold: Not every ethnic conflict is "platonically" set for all time, and all too many—quite often radically different—types of conflict and violence are conflated and confused under the heading of "ethnic" violence. Which means one should distinguish the types of conflict and violence that are frequently said to be ethnic. (For a quite different, but in key respects complementary, construct of ethnic political consciousness, see Price, 1997). I will distinguish three ideal typically distinct forms of ethnic conflict and connect them to three distinct settings, a *setting* being a particular combination of identity and entity.

ETHNIC CONFLICT IN THE CORPORATE SETTING

In the first setting, traditional corporate identities prevail. Identities of the pre-ethnic order are, to use Coser's (1974) term, *greedy*. One might think of them as Jehovah identities. Ideal typically, corporate identities are given and fixed (not chosen or exchangeable), nonbiodegradable wholes (not limited roles). They claim all of one's self.

A striking example is the Medieval Roman Catholic Church. The expressive phrase "no salvation outside the Church" captures perfectly the corporate quality of the Church. *The* Church was an absolute, categorical, superior whole outside of which no "real" identity was available. Like, and long before *the* Bolshevik Party, *the* Church authoritatively monopolized and absolutized the terms of its members' identity and fate. In a similar non-ethnic vein, the Church was (and remains) internally and invidiously stratified into superior and inferior components: priests and laity.

Corporate identities manifest themselves as barricaded (social) entities whose primary imperative is "absolute" separation from what are seen as contaminating others (Douglas, 1966). This imperative sets the terms for identity (not identification), organization, and action. Social, religious, ideological, cultural, and political connections among members who share a barricaded identity are dogmatically and hysterically defined and defended, as are disconnections from nonmembers.

Contamination is the great fear within a barricaded entity. This fear produces urgent attempts to impose and maintain an absolutely overriding solidary identity for all members (regardless of their particular functions) in order to prevent infiltration by enemies. In this vein, a premium is placed on concretizing signs of identity and membership, creating identity "moats and drawbridges" between the barricaded identity/ entity and "others"—both externally and internally. In fact, the presence of internal barricades may be the best indicator of a pre- and anti-ethnic barricaded identity. Examples include the status of Levites in the Old Testament; the SS in the Nazi regime; and in a less ideologically consistent sense, the place of male middle-class Protestants in 19th-century Western liberal capitalist nations.

Violence between barricaded entities tends to be recurrent. The threshold for violence is very low. Where individualism is absent, violence is more likely to be present. It is easier to gas "the Jew," lynch "the Black," starve "the Catholic," or shoot "the Protestant" than to murder an individual with a recognized name and ethical worth. Also, as Chirot (1995) has noted, a society of barricaded identities means that the scope of violence is greater because it is legitimate to do violence to any member of the group in retaliation for violence done to anyone in your group. Finally, where corporate entities and barricaded identities prevail, there is a genealogy of violence. Violence between groups does not end with the death of particular individuals. It ends only with the death of the entire intergenerational family. In *The Godfather* (Puzo, 1969), Don Cicci attempts to kill the young boy Vito Andolini precisely because Don Cicci knows that when Vito grows up he will attempt to kill him—and does.

ETHNIC CONFLICT IN THE INDIVIDUAL SETTING

In the second type of setting, individual identity is primary (not exclusive). In an ideal typical sense, individual identities are the polar opposite of corporate identities. An individual identity is made up of partial roles not nonbiodegradable wholes. To be an individual is to be "Lutheran" not "Roman Catholic." The difference should be clear if you ask yourself the simple question, Does anyone ever refer to a lapsed Lutheran, an ex-Lutheran, or ask whether someone is a practicing Lutheran?

Individual identities are typical of bounded social, cultural, religions, and political entities where resemblance, not difference, and relative, not absolute, claims of state, civic, and ethnic membership set the terms for identification (not identity), organization, and action. In bounded settings, that is, societies where state and social identities are relativized—not absolutized as in barricaded settings or weakly connected as in frontier settings— conflict is tempered by the individual's ability to more readily and regularly alternate emphases on complementary (what Mao Tse-tung [1966, 1967] called non-antagonistic) identities: state, civic, and ethnic.[1] In settings of this order, ethnic conflict is rarely violent, due to the elastic quality of ethnic identification, which in contrast to the sticky quality of ethnic identity and molasses quality of a barricaded identity offers a possible, not imperative, form of identity.

---

[1] In fact, one might understand non-antagonistic contradictions as cross-cutting cleavages and antagonistic contradictions as superimposed cleavages—in the first case between actors with "generous" identities and in the second between actors with "greedy" ones.

But then how does one explain the phenomenon of ethnic barricading in countries and societies that are presumably based on individual identity? How does one explain the movement from ethnic identification to ethnic identity and differentiate the latter from what I have referred to as pre-ethnic, corporate identity? To do so one must conceptually distinguish between situational and integral barricading.

When, in response to physical danger, status deprivation, and/or economic discrimination, individuals with "generous" ethnic identifications adopt "stingy" ethnic identities, one can speak of situational not integral barricading. In contrast to integrally barricaded identities in corporate societies, ethnically barricaded identities have a rationale and source of discipline that are more chosen and less derived, more instrumental and strategic, and less metaphysical. The practical significance of this is that while violence in both settings can be horrific, situationally shaped ethnic barricades should be more easy to dismantle than either pre-ethnic, socially barricaded identities á la caste, or supra-ethnic ideologically barricaded identities á la Leninism and Nazism. The reason? In societies where individualism is a moral imperative (not a suspect form of selfishness), there exists a defining principle and (latent/manifest) agent of opposition to categorical identities. In traditional corporate (i.e., pre-ethnic) and ideological (i.e., supra-ethnic) revolutionary regimes, individual liberty and equality lack a philosophical and ideologically principled, not only a practical, base.

ETHNIC CONFLICT IN THE EGO SETTING

In the third type of setting, ego identities prevail—identities that differ from both corporate and individual identities insofar as egoism recognizes no authoritative or imperative "ought." It recognizes no discipline—religious, legal, ethical, political, or ideological—and no authoritative and consistent limitation of ego other than external obstacle (power) or internal disability (weakness).

Ego identities prevail in frontier conditions characterized by weak social connections, blurred institutional distinctions, and violent weakness—nasty, even murderous conditions that are more visceral than ideological, with a frame of reference and effective political circumference that is more local than national, more national than regional, and more regional than global. Murderous and immoral as behavior in these settings may be and is, the violence is "ghetto violence," typical of weak states and societies like Russia, Chechnya, Bosnia, Albania, Somalia, Afghanistan, and the Congo (former Zaire). Violent weakness tends to be sporadic, dispersed, and difficult to eradicate, precisely because of its low level of organizational and ideological discipline.

EXAMPLES OF ETHNIC CONDITIONS

What conclusions can one reach on the basis of these conceptual and typological constructs? First, they should not be reified. We must always recognize that empirically real identities and entities practically relate what ideal types conceptually separate. The point is not to have untidy realities conform to tidy ideal types but to use tidy types to make sense of intrinsically untidy realities. Given our concerns, that means identifying and characterizing the locus, weight, and role that ethnic identification, and/or ethnic identity, and/or pre-ethnic corporate identity, and/or supra-ethnic ideological identities play within a given unit at a particular time and over time. Some cases will be "obedient." They will closely approximate one or the other of the types I have introduced. Other cases will be quite "disobedient" mixes of conflicting and, to varying degrees blurred, identities requiring nuanced analytic specification of their composition and development. Whether obedient or disobedient, the ideal types I have introduced can play a strategic role in framing any such analysis.

I will examine three cases in an effort to practice what I have just preached. I will start with a conceptually obedient case. Congo has all the defining features of a frontier: an extraordinarily weak state, the absence of any disciplining ideology, and widespread violent weakness. Congo is also a clear example of a futile frontier insofar as one cannot locate any endogenous type (bounded or barricaded) or site of leadership, ideological articulation, or institutional innovation. Consequently, in the absence of disciplining external actions, the frontier condition of violent weakness in the Congo will have a long half-life.

Northern Ireland is a predictably disobedient case. Can one characterize Northern Ireland's development after 1968 parsimoniously and accurately in terms of frontier, barricaded, and bounded identities? After all, for some 30 years Northern Ireland has been divided into and by highly barricaded entities and greedy identities that seem to make any conceptual distinction between situationally generated ethnic barricades and integral corporate identities hard to sustain. What, if anything, does this distinction tell us when applied to the case of Northern Ireland?

To begin with, integrally barricaded corporate identities and entities actively attempt to internally eliminate opposing modes of identity. But the democratic Western world has been a main, persistent, and accepted point of political reference and preference inside each of the situationally barricaded communities in Northern Ireland, that is, a reference and preference that contradicts and critiques barricaded identities. To that symbolic reference one must add the growing potential for and reality of individual identities in an increasingly middle-class, educated, urban society (Protestant and Catholic), with a corresponding secular culture that favors ethnic identification as a competing alternative to ethnic/corporate identity. To conclude this somewhat arithmetical exercise, if we now add the dramatic changes in the international situation after the Cold War and the consequent changes in the calculations of British and Irish elites, one can explain the rapid—and I think decisive—move from violent confrontation between categorically hostile barricaded identities to a more tolerant civic–ethnic confrontation within a bounded parliamentary setting. A tense but tolerant confrontation that will be predictably and sporadically challenged by violently weak frontier remnants who, seeing their barricades fall, resist the conclusion that the new political "boundaries [in Northern Ireland] are falling in pleasant places," to quote Psalm 16.

And what of Russia? Can we interpret this very untidy reality with the types I have introduced? Russia is a striking example of a frontier setting, filled with weakly connected political "companions," "khoroshie rebiate" (good old boys), "Mafia," what Verdery has called "unruly coalitions," egos undisciplined by anything but expediency or weakness; blurred institutional distinctions between commercial, crony, and criminal capitalism; weak institutional connections between Moscow and the regions, between parties and their constituencies, between monetary and barter economies; and multiple, persistent acts of violent weakness. It is a frontier setting masked by an anemically bounded façade of electoral democracy that since the fall of 1998 has been subjected to its greatest test. The issue facing Russia is whether it will (a) persist in its largely frontier condition; (b) find the leverage to replace the current democratic malarkey with a bounded civic polyarchy; or (c), in response to its futile, frustrating, humiliating frontier realities, generate a novel and powerful set of as yet unnamed barricaded identities— ideological, political, and organizational—and once again confront the world with a potentially unbounded challenge and threat (Jowitt, 1998b).

Whether ethnic violence is on the rise, or, as Yahya Sadowski (1999) has argued, we are simply more aware of it now that the Cold War threat of nuclear war has receded and, embarrassed by the fact that it has broken out in a part of Europe, we should recognize the kind of ethnic violence we face in the world today. For the most part, it is the violent weakness typical of frontier settings: visceral, pre-ideological, parochial, and more or less disorganized. Congo, Somalia, Cambodia, and Afghanistan approximate the type quite well. Rwanda is more complicated.

The Rwandan case is not simply on the organized scale of a disorganized (frontier) category. The killing of Tutsis was highly organized—by Colonel Theonesta Bagosora, Director of Services in the Rwanda Ministry of Defense, who effectively mobilized the Presidential Guard along with local Gendarmeries and French-trained militia units, the Interahamwe—for the purpose of eliminating an entire ethnic group. What one saw in Rwanda was the transformation of a frontier-like setting of violent weakness into one of pre-ideological barricaded entities combining corporate and ethnic features, who viewed each other as immediate and absolute threats to each other's existence. The current efforts in Rwanda to create a genuine national identity that will relativize and replace these absolutely barricaded identities with ethnic identification benefits, if such a term can be used in this context, from the very success each group had in destroying the other's solidary organization and identity and from the widespread social and psychological exhaustion.

Rwanda is not typical. Murderous though it is, most ethnic violence today is parochial and relatively disorganized and is due in good measure to the weakness of the state in frontier settings and the absence, at least for the historical moment, of a global anti-Western ideology (à la Nazism and Leninism) with the ability to co-opt a particular ethnicity as its primary social base, but not its primary ideological rationale. As a rule, frontier settings of violent weakness are more futile than fertile in their ability to generate a new way of life. The prevalence of weak social connections, blurred institutional distinctions, and violent weakness favor acts of prevention over acts of institutional innovation and foundation.[2] Consequently, in the absence of powerful exogenous interventions, frontier settings of violent weakness are likely to have a very long half-life. There is no necessity that they evolve into either bounded or barricaded entities.

However, for all of this, it is necessary to recognize that frontier settings of ethnoviolence may act as fertile laboratories where novel ideological idioms, political organization, and charismatic leaders originate. Which means we must develop the ability to specify and understand the conditions that favor (a) the persistence of violently weak nasty frontier settings; (b) the emergence and predominance within them of nice ethnic–national identifications bounded (relativized) by civic and state identification; (c) the emergence and predominance of barricaded ethnic identities that subordinate civic and state identifications in pursuit of nasty ethnically chauvinistic programs; and (d) the emergence in and transformation of frontier settings by supra-ethnic ideologically barricaded revolutionary movements like the Nazis, the Khmer Rouge, Mao's Great Proletarian Cultural Revolution, and Stalin's regime that subordinated ethnic, civic, and state identities in pursuit of nihilistic programs.

The distinguishing feature of ideologically barricaded revolutionary movements and regimes like the Nazi and Stalin's Soviet Union is their ambivalent identification with a particular ethnic host, an ambivalence that manifests itself on the one hand as a tendency to confuse—particularly in

---

[2] I am currently writing a book-length manuscript in which I deal more fully with this phenomenon and more generally with the social conditions and identities I call *frontier*, *barricade*, and *boundary*.

certain developmental points—the ethnic host with the ideological mission (e.g., "socialism in one country" or conflating ethnic Germans with the "Aryan race"), and on the other as strenuous and periodic political and ideological efforts to resist and characterize that very development as a parochial ethnic corruption of the universal revolutionary mission. These latter efforts find their most striking expression in the regime's strident assertion and defense of the categorically invidious status distinction between the superior Communist Party cadre and SS and inferior subjects, by ethnicity and/or class.

If the nicest form of ethnic-based conflict occurs in bounded settings where the prevailing identity is individual, then the best way to prevent the emergence of barricaded identities and movements capable of generating murderously novel forms of membership, power, and global purpose is to create a culture of individualism. But cultural revolutions are the rarest type of revolution and by no means typically benign in their outcome, as the Great Proletarian Cultural Revolution demonstrated.

Does that leave us helpless? Not entirely. A satisfying, or second-best, solution would be to favor the emergence and success of a particular type of authoritarian rule, one in which the dominant political (or military) elite is not the captive of any particular social (e.g., ethnic, religious, class, or regional) group, defines its interest in local, not universal terms, and emphasizes the state more than the ethnic dimension of the nation.

Elite autonomy from its primary social base provides rulers with maneuverability between and among differing ethnic, social, religions, and regional groups, the opportunity to avoid rigid patterns of domination/subordination—to create more boundaries than barricades. In a related vein, elites with local political interests and identities are much less likely to create ideological and coercive barricades between their host populations and themselves. By choice and necessity, elites with local rather than universal orientations and self-identification must be more responsive to and respectful of their immediate social bases of support. And, under many but not all circumstances, concern for the territorial sovereignty of the state will inhibit irredentist tendencies.

How then does one explain Slobodan Milosevic's rule, his indirect/covert support of ethnic cleansing in Bosnia, and his overt, brutal direction of ethnic cleansing in Kosovo? To begin with, Milosevic's emergence as the major political figure in Serbia is intimately connected to his privileging the ethnic component of Serbian national identity over the state dimension and privileging both at the expense of the civic. Second, the threatened dismemberment of the Serbian territorial nation–state by Kosovo Liberation Army (KLA) secession efforts followed in 1999 by NATO's increasing support for both the KLA and a NATO protectorate in Kosovo explained and provided the pretext for the expanded scope and intensity of Serbian violence in Kosovo. As for Milosevic's policy toward Bosnia, the disintegration of Yugoslavia created a frontier-like situation in which the boundaries of new successor states were unclear. Where an existing polity (imperial or national) disintegrates, an ethnic state leadership, like the Serbian and Croatian (the Turkish after World War I, and the Israeli in 1948) will try to politically and physically include as many conationals as possible in the new successor states, and exclude (politically and physically) as many non-ethnic nationals as possible.

Ethnic conflict of a nonviolent order is most likely in a liberal democratic capitalist regime, a setting in which conflict is diluted by the prevalence of relative boundaries and multiple identities centered in the individual with the related possibility of movement between identifications without excommunication.[3] The most extensive and persistent violence with ethnic dimensions is likely to occur within the radius of a barricaded ideological (supra-ethnic) polity that combines an internally invidious hierarchical form of domination and fear of contamination with a modern technological reach and capacity. Regimes of this order are a global and powerful threat.

In between these polarities one can specify three other forms of rule with lesser and greater potential for ethnoconflict and violence. An authoritarian polity that has an autonomous elite, a local definition, and high state (vs. ethnic) emphasis, is likely to be less unstable and experience less violence than a frontier polity in which wildcat violence is likely to be the rule. And each of these polities is likely to be less violent than a barricaded ethnic polity in which the dominant political, military, and/or religious elite is both recruited from and exclusively loyal to a particular ethnic base à la Serbia.

Most discussions of ethnicity recognize and emphasize the intensely emotional quality of its identity claims. This is correctly seen as a signature feature of ethnic identity or identification. And, it is precisely this feature that is regularly and stereotypically cast as irrational and dangerous. But in our Enlightenment rush to entirely rid ourselves of the irrational, we should not lose sight of the fact that the sense of collective distinction and affective recognition ethnic identification provides is not automatically irrational or dangerous.

A strong state and prosperous economy are not the only or most robust bases for a tolerant democratic nation. Our practical efforts to lessen the likelihood of civic boundaries becoming corporate barricades must include the recognition that "man" does not live by bread and power alone, that mutual ethnic recognition of a certain order, that is, "ethnic lite," if you will, contributes rather than subtracts from social coherence. In liberal

---

[3]Which is not to say that movement of this order does not bring about censure from and displeasure on the part of those for whom any given (religious, political, social, or cultural) identification is an identity. It is to say that this censure and displeasure have limited punitive correlates.

capitalist countries where the primary and dominant identity (philosophical, ideological, political, economic, and psychological) is the individual, ethnicity, far from being simply a dangerous atavism, is a positive—yes, positive—element.

The Enlightenment dream of a universal civic/civil society is not only a utopia; it is a negative one. We must recognize ethnic identification as a flying buttress that in its ambivalent, hybrid manner, actually contributes to our individualism by adding an invaluable dimension to it—a dimension that is not simply socially effective, but socially affective. Without ethnicity's social affect, the effect of a one-dimensional Lockeian individualism may create (some say it already has) a "stirner egoism"—Max Stirner's (1971) egoism: a society populated by narcissistic selves.

Our goal should be to construct societies where the option of ethnic identification prevails over the imperative of ethnic identity (Jowitt, 1998a), not to eliminate ethnicity per se. We should oppose social definitions and organizations that diminish the individual's ability to relativize his and her ethnic identification. We should favor social definitions and organizations where ethnic identification makes partial, contingent, and relative claims that shrink those of a potentially greedy state, and stretch those of a potentially stingy individualism.

REFERENCES

Chirot, D. (1995, Fall). Modernism without liberalism. *Contentions, 13,* 141–166.

Coser, L. A. (1974). *Greedy institutions: Patterns of undivided commitment.* New York: Free Press.

Deutsch, K. (1963). *Nerves of government.* New York: Free Press.

Douglas, M. (1966). *Purity and danger: An analysis of concepts of pollution and taboo.* London: Routledge & Kegan Paul.

Jowitt, K. (1998a). In praise of the ordinary. In A. Michnik (Ed.), *Letters from freedom* (pp. xiii–xxxiii). Berkeley: University of California Press.

Jowitt, K. (1998b). Russia disconnected. *Irish Slavonic Studies, 19,* 1–9.

Mao Tse-tung. (1966). *On the correct handling of contradictions among the people.* Beijing, China: Foreign Languages Press.

Mao Tse-tung. (1967). *On contradictions.* Beijing, China: Foreign Languages Press.

Price, R. (1997, June). Race and reconciliation in the New South Africa. *Politics and Society, 25*(2), 152.

Puzo, M. (1969). *The godfather.* New York: Putnam.

Sadowski, Y. (1999). *Is chaos a strategic myth? Bosnia and myths and ethnic conflict.* Unpublished manuscript.

Shaw, G. B. (1951). *Saint Joan.* Baltimore: Penguin Books.

Stirner, M. (1971). *The ego and his own.* London: Cape.

Weber, M. (1968). *Economy and society.* New York: Bedminster Press.

3

NATIONALISM AND ETHNICITY: RESEARCH AGENDAS ON THEORIES OF THEIR SOURCES AND THEIR REGULATION

BRENDAN O'LEARY

As a political scientist writing for psychologists I have decided not to summarize what political scientists and political sociologists claim to know about nationalism and ethnicity. Instead, I will rapidly, and with maximum feasible insensitivity, address two topics: (a) how political sociologists and political scientists explain nationalism or, alternatively, what they consider worthy of explanatory attention and (b) how political sociologists, political scientists, and political philosophers explain (and justify) the regulation of national and ethnic differences.

EXPLAINING NATIONALISM IN POLITICAL SCIENCE AND POLITICAL SOCIOLOGY

Debate among political scientists and sociologists about how best to understand nationalism can be classified in four ways. The first two ways can be presented in a cross-tabulation on the basis of the answers given to two questions, presented in Table 3.1. They are answers to the two following issues.

I would like to thank participants at the Understanding Nationalism Conference at the Institute for Advanced Study at Princeton University, December 1997, for comments on a previous version of this presentation, especially Ian Lustick, Daniel Chirot, and Alex Motyl. I would also like to thank John McGarry.

TABLE 3.1
The Place of Nationalism in World-Time

Base of nationalism's appeal	Modernity (industria)	Posttribal (industria and agraria	Primordial (industria, agraria, and foragia)
Ideas	Kedourie	Hastings, 1997	Popper, 1945
Interests	V, RC (e.g., Banton, Goodin, Hechter); V, M (e.g., Hobsbawm, Mandel)		van den Berghe, 1990
Identities	Walzer	Armstrong	Isaacs, 1975
Ideas and interests			
Interests and identities	Gellner, Non-V, RC (Laitin); Non-V, M (Anderson, 1983, 1991)	Rousseau	
Ideas and identities	Greenfield, 1992	Smith (A. D.) 1986, 1994	Herder
Ideas, interests, and identities	Connor, 1994	Horowitz, 1985, 1989a & b	

Note. V = vulgar; RC = rational choice; Non-V = non-vulgar; M = Marxism.

1. The Place of Nationalism in World-Time

This issue differentiates among the following.

- *Modernists*, who maintain that nationalism is a distinctively modern (industrial, capitalist, post-Reformation) phenomenon, perhaps anticipated in a few pre-modern (agrarian, pre-capitalist, pre-Reformation) polities but never fully realized therein.
- *Ethnocontinuists*, who maintain that nations (or most nations) are built on ethnic cores, or *ethnie*, and insist that such ethnie were widespread and persistent in pre-modern polities and social systems, although not all of them. Although they may accept that it may not be true that for every nation, n_i, in modernity, there corresponds an historically previous ethnie, e_i, in pre-modernity, they nevertheless think that an authentic ethnic past mightily assists nation-building, and that the absence of an authentic ethnic past significantly assists nation-building failures.
- *Primordialists*, who maintain that nations and nationalism are expressions of persistent and permanent (genetic or natural)

features of humans as collectivities. Nations are, so to speak, expressions of ethnic nepotism, or large-scale contemporary expressions of the urge to live with one's kin. Hard-line primordialism emphasizes the genetic roots of ethnonational sentiment; soft-line primordialism emphasizes the durability of collective ethnic identities acquired in childhood.

2. The Basis of the Appeal of Nationalism

This issue differentiates among the following.

- *Idealists*, who explain the salience and impact of ideas by their persuasive, discursive, cognitive, and emotional traits (I include postmodernists within this category, their philosophical ignorance notwithstanding).
- *Instrumentalists*, who explain the appeal of ideas by the interests that they serve.
- *Identificationists*, who explain the appeal of ideas by their roles in identity formation, affirmation, and expression.

This differentiation of the sources of the appeal of nationalism is not mutually exclusive. It is possible to believe in the importance of both ideas and interests; to believe in the importance of both interests and identities; to believe in the importance of ideas and identities; and last, to accommodate all three explanatory sources of the appeal of nationalism (ideas, interests, and identities). The answers given to the questions of the placement of nationalism in world-time and the bases of its appeal can be summarized in the cells of Table 3.1, which indicate the approaches of some of the major thinkers on the subjects.

Debates over the placement of nationalism in world-time are partly structured by disagreement over terms (e.g., over the meaning of nations, ethnic groups, etc.) and partly by normative fears and beliefs. For example, (a) the fear of tribalism makes many treat nationalism as a permanent threat to liberalism (Popper, 1945), and (b) the desire to transcend nationalism makes many emphasize the contingency of nationalism (Hobsbawm, 1990). Some of this debate, however, is open, in principle, to historical and empirical research, for example, the dependence or otherwise of actually existing nations on previously existing ethnie, the subject that Ernest Gellner (1964) marvelously captured in his question, "Do nations have navels"?

Debates over the bases of the appeal of nationalism are partly methodological; for example, rational choice theorists maintain that we should test the limits of rational and narrowly instrumentalist explanations. They are also partly normative. For example, *nationophiles* prefer to emphasize the salience of identity, whereas *nationophobes* prefer to emphasize the role of interests; nationophobes also tend to emphasize what they see as the cognitively challenged nature of nationalists.

This brutal summary, and its tabular representation, surveys the standard range of variation in explanatory accounts of nationalism in political science, political sociology and, I would add, in history—or at least those sections of that profession that do not think truth lies somewhere in an as yet undiscovered archive. Two other and related big questions structure debate among political scientists and sociologists.

3. Is the Salience of Nationalism Variable Across Elites and Masses?

This question is perhaps the tacit theme in analysis of the political history of nationalism. There are at least three stylized answers in the literature and a related difference on the sources of nationalist extremism.

- The first answer, perhaps best represented by Paul Brass's (1990) work on India, suggests that elites use and abuse the identities and ideas of the masses because of the interests of elites. Brass's work is sophisticated but, his critics maintain, fails satisfactorily to explain why elites choose ethnic identities for mobilization rather than other identities.
- The second answer suggests that elites both construct and then use and abuse the national identities and ideas of the masses— whose identities and ideas are therefore plainly inauthentic. (Although the expression "false consciousness" is rarely heard these days, it is plainly signaled.) This pattern of thought is the one that liberal and leftist teachers manage to impart to their weaker students, even if that is not their intention. It is difficult to convict real academics of this pattern of thought but, if pressed, I would maintain that this perspective is the burden of John Breuilly's (1982) *Nationalism and the State* and of Eric Hobsbawm's (1990) recent work—although the latter, through dependence on Ernest Gellner (1983), does seek to explain why ethnonational identities might have appeals rooted in the experiences of what he scornfully called the "lesser examination passing" classes.
- The third answer, and the one I am most comfortable with, sees elites, as much as the masses, as constrained by their ethnonational identities, although these identities themselves may be capable of slow and occasionally sudden shifts. In different ways and with different methodologies, this perspective is held by Walker Connor (1994), the most brilliant essayist on ethnonationalism; by Donald Horowitz (1985), the most comprehen-

sive and lucid comparative analyst of ethnic conflict; and by David Laitin, whose insightful "soft rational choice" perspective on the choices of language repertoires in Africa manages to respect the interests and intelligence of elites and masses.

- The fourth answer is more nuanced. It focuses on the sources of nationalist extremism—assuming that all are vulnerable, in principle, to the alleged "bacillus." Here there is an interesting disjunction. Conservatives, such as Elie Kedourie (1960, 1971), and Marxists such as Ernest Mandel, maintain that ethnonational extremism, especially its dehumanizing varieties, is the special vice of modern intellectuals, perhaps especially of certain kinds of petty bourgeois with status anxieties. By contrast, liberals and libertarians tend to see the masses, unschooled in a free society, sunk in closed tribalism, in pre-enlightenment, as the potential fonts of genocide, ethnic expulsion, and worse. In this perspective, the treason of intellectuals is to play on these mass susceptibilities—although plainly they are not held to have created them.

4. Is (or When Is) Nationalism Strong, Moderate, or Weak?

The last big question concerns the strength of nationalism. It sets an important research agenda, vital to our times and our century. Questions addressed here include the following:

- Is nationalism strong in the sense that, in crisis conditions, it will trump all other ideas, or isms (e.g., liberalism, socialism, conservatism), especially if these are non-national? Intelligent people, who minimize their wishful thinking, know the answer to this question. Of course!
- Is nationalism strong intellectually or ideologically, in the sense of providing a repertoire of answers for the design of political institutions and the shaping of public policy, or is it, alternatively, always enmeshed with other intellectual and ideological traditions because it lacks a sufficient prescriptive core to survive on its own?
- Is nationalism strong in the sense that, in crisis conditions, its power is such that it trumps all other identities—conferring belief systems, such as religious, civic, administrative, and personal identities and all other interest-conferring roles?
- Is nationalism strong when nationalities are threatened or made insecure but are otherwise moderate or weak? Alternatively, is it the product of "the sleep of reason"—a monster that is either

dormant or in control but incapable of being emasculated or eliminated?

- Is nationalism strong only in the transition to modernity but weaker thereafter?
- Is nationalism strong only when democratic (or demotic) but otherwise fragile?
- Is nationalism war-provoking, and is it more war-provoking than other idea isms or identity-affirming beliefs? Likewise, does nationalism provoke genocide and ethnic expulsions and other horrific phenomena?

This chapter cannot address all the subthemes and sub-subthemes raised in the four big questions. But I would claim, provisionally, that these four questions compromise the bulk of the explaining of nationalism that takes place in political science and political sociology. We should, perhaps, ask ourselves whether these are the only or the right questions that our disciplines should address.

My brutal review suggests the following. Our disciplines do correctly address the issue best formulated by Gellner (1964). And that is this simple query: Why is there nationalism in our times, and why was there no (or in the weaker thesis, very little) nationalism in pre-modern times? If the question is correctly formulated the answer must be sought both in the constants of human nature—best addressed by anthropologists and psychologists—and in the transformation of our economic and political systems by the bundle of elements we correctly call modernity. It is, of course, open to people to deny that the question is correctly formulated: to maintain that *nationalism* is merely the word we give to a range of phenomena that have always been with us. I think they are wrong, but I am open to persuasion. If the question is correctly formulated, then the question becomes, does Gellner or anyone else have a convincing answer? My answer, crudely, is not yet. I am convinced, however, that the answer lies in accounting for the nationalization of states, a phenomenon that is related to the democratization, industrialization, and militarization of the world in the past two centuries.

THE REGULATION OF ETHNONATIONAL DIFFERENCES

There is, or so I would claim, an emergent field of inquiry within political science and political philosophy devoted to the regulation of ethnic and national differences; for the want of a better term let us call its domain *national and ethnic conflict regulation*. From political science some of the major contributions to its development have come from Ted Gurr (1993), Milton Esman (1973, 1987, 1994), Donald Horowitz (1989a), David Laitin, Arend Lijphart (1977a, 1977b), Ian Lustick (1979, 1993), and Erik Nordlinger

(1972), and from political philosophy some of the major contributions have come from Charles Taylor, Will Kymlicka, and Michael Walzer. Most of my own recent work with John McGarry (McGarry & O'Leary, 1995) is within this field.

How does this second field of work relate to the first field of work, the one asking the big questions about the nature of nationalism? The answer is not as direct as one might think. Explanations of nationalism in general do not necessarily determine analyses of its regulation, nor prescriptions for its regulation. That is not to say that there are no relationships. Modernists tend to have greater optimism about the management and transcendence of national and ethnic conflict than do ethnocontinuists and primordialists. Those who emphasize the salience of ideas in explaining nationalism tend to emphasize the possibilities for conflict resolution created through alternative ideological mobilization or educational transcendence. Those who emphasize the salience of interests tend to explain ethnic relations through a realist focus on the balance of power between groups. Those who emphasize identities focus on the recognition and the misrecognition of collective identities.

Domestic Differences

McGarry and I maintain that there is a finite set of macro-domestic strategies (combinations of goals and instruments) available to states for the regulation of ethnonational differences, summarized in our END/MEND taxonomy (in Table 3.2). They are structured by a grand strategic question, whether to eliminate differences or to manage them. The eight strategies are not mutually exclusive; different strategies can be applied to different groups and, indeed, different strategies can be applied to different people within the same groups. The strategies are available to modern states but may be applied to pre-modern peoples within their jurisdictions. The research agenda that flows from this taxonomy has three components:

- *Empirical and explanatory*—to seek to specify when and why states adopt each strategy and the limits to the realization of each strategy, for example, an argument which purports to demonstrate that stable majoritarian federations require a *Staats Volk*, a dominant people.
- *Empirical and ethical*—to seek to specify the ethical and political arguments used to justify each strategy (which may, one day, help in early warning monitoring).
- *Normative and practical*—to specify which strategies are compatible with reasonable liberal democratic norms and the circumstances in which they are likely to be successful (which may, one day, assist feasible constitutional engineering).

TABLE 3.2
Domestic Strategies for the Regulation of Ethnonational Differences

End—eliminate ethnonational differences	Mend—manage ethnonational differences
1. Genocide Eliminate people *Goal:* ethnic purity	1. Control Manage people *Goal:* ethnic hierarchy; organize the dominant, disorganize the dominated
2. Integration ↔ Assimilation Eliminate relevance of ethnic differences *Goal:* eliminate differences from public life ↔ national homogenization	2. Consociation Manage people while preserving differences *Goal:* ethnic equality and pluralism for the consociated (future integration not excluded)
3. Ethnic expulsion Eliminate people from territories *Goal:* ethnic purity	3. Arbitration Manage people impartially *Goal:* manage differences to promote accommodation or later integration
4. Territorial elimination Eliminate people and territory through downsizing or resizing *Goal:* greater ethnonational homogenization	4. Territorial management Manage people and territories *Goal:* ethnic federalism or autonomy, equality and diversity for stake-holders

External Differences

In contrast to eight domestic strategies (some of which admittedly have major external ramifications), I have identified a set of five external orientations for rulers confronted by ethnic and national conflicts which have inter-state, or inter-imperial, or inter-imperial and inter-state implications (see Table 3.3).

The research agenda implicit in this taxonomy is similar to the one suggested by Table 3.2:

- *Empirical and explanatory*—to specify the development of each of these orientations, to account for their rise, and in some cases, fall, and to specify their limitations.
- *Empirical and ethical*—to specify what rulers, agents, and intellectuals advocate each orientation and why.
- *Normative and practical*—to specify which orientations are compatible with reasonable liberal democratic norms and the circumstances in which they are likely to be successful (which may, one day, assist feasible constitutional engineering).

Political scientists share with politicians the capacity to reduce the amount of reliable knowledge in the world. So, we are obliged to be humble.

TABLE 3.3
External Strategies for the regulation of Ethnonational Differences

Strategic approach to external ethno-national questions	Norms	Goals
Imperialism	No recognition of equals; instrumental external orientations (balance of power)	World empire
Westphalian Statism	States are equals; no interference in others' domestic ethnonational affairs	Interstate world; confederalist world
Westphalian Liberal Individualist Statism	States are equals; no interference in others' domestic ethnonational affairs except to protect fundamental individualist human rights	Confederalist liberal individualism
Westphalian Communitarian Statism	States are equals; no interference in others' domestic ethnonational affairs except to protect pluralism and legitimate group rights	Confederalist communitarianism
Cosmopolitanism	States and nations are undesirable; external interference in states is justified in defense of correct cosmopolitan values (be they liberal, socialist, or theological)	Correct cosmopolis

Note. Bold rows are compatible with nationalism; imperialism is unstably compatible with national chauvinism in the metropolis.

Brutally simple as they may be, however, these tables do offer everyone interested in these matters a way of ordering their thoughts, even if they provide no answers.

REFERENCES

Alter, P. (1985). *Nationalism.* London: Edward Arnold.

Anderson, B. (1983). *Imagined communities: Reflections on the origins and spread of nationalism.* London: Verso.

Anderson, B. (1991). *Imagined communities: Reflections on the origins and spread of nationalism* (2nd ed.). London: Verso.

Avineri, S. (1962). Hegel and nationalism. *Review of Politics, 24,* 461–484.

Banton, M. (1980). Ethnic groups and the theories of rational choice. In UNESCO (Ed.), *Sociological theories: Race and colonialism* (pp. 275–299). Paris: UNESCO.

Banton, M. (1983). *Racial and ethnic competition*. Cambridge, England: Cambridge University Press.

Banton, M. (1994). Modelling ethnic and national relations. *Ethnic and Racial Studies, 17*(1), 1–19.

Barnard, F. M. (1965). *Herder's social and political thought: From enlightenment to nationalism*. Oxford, England: Clarendon Press.

Barnard, F. M. (1988). *Self-direction and political legitimacy: Rousseau and Herder*. Oxford, England: Clarendon Press.

Barry, B. (1983). Self-government revisited. In D. Miller & L. Siedentop (Eds.), *The nature of political theory* (pp. 121–154). Oxford, England: Clarendon Press.

Barry, B. (1987). Nationalism. In D. Miller, J. Coleman, W. Connolly, & A. Ryan (Eds.), *The Basil Blackwell encyclopaedia of political thought* (pp. 352–354). Oxford, England: Basil Blackwell.

Benner, E. (1995). *Really existing nationalisms: A post-communist view from Marx and Engels*. Oxford, England: Clarendon Press.

Berlin, I. (1976). *Vico and Herder*. London: Hogarth Press.

Berlin, I. (1992). The bent twig: On the rise of nationalism. In H. Hardy (Ed.), *The crooked timber of humanity* (pp. 238–262). New York: Random House.

Brass, P. (1990). *The politics of India since independence*. New York: Cambridge University Press.

Brass, P. (1991). *Ethnicity and nationalism: Theory and comparison*. New Delhi, India: Sage.

Brass, P. R. (1996). Introduction: Discourses of ethnicity, communalism, and violence. In P. R. Brass (Ed.), *Riots and pogroms* (pp. 1–55). Basingstoke, England: Macmillan.

Breton, A. (1964). An economic theory of nationalism. *Journal of Political Economy, 72*, 376–386.

Breuilly, J. (1982). *Nationalism and the state*. Manchester, England: University of Manchester Press.

Brubaker, R. (1996). *Nationalism reframed: Nationhood and the national question in the new Europe*. Cambridge, England: Cambridge University Press.

Canovan, M. (1996). *Nationhood and political theory*. Cheltenham, England: Edward Elger.

Connor, W. (1994). *Ethnonationalism: The quest for understanding*. Princeton, NJ: Princeton University Press.

Emerson, R. (1960). *From empire to nation: The rise to self-assertion of Asian and African peoples*. Boston: Beacon Press.

Esman, M. (1973). The management of communal conflict. *Public Policy, 21*(1), 49–78.

Esman, M. (1987). Ethnic politics and economic power. *Comparative Politics, 19*, 395–418.

Esman, M. (1994). *Ethnic politics*. Ithaca, NY: Cornell University Press.

Gellner, E. (1964). *Thought and change*. London: Weidenfeld & Nicolson.

Gellner, E. (1983). *Nations and nationalism*. Oxford, England: Basil Blackwell.

Greenfeld, L. (1992). *Nationalism: Five roads to modernity*. Cambridge, MA: Harvard University Press.

Gurr, T. R. (1993). *Minorities at risk: A global view of ethnopolitical conflicts*. Washington, DC: United States Institute of Peace Press.

Halperin, M., Scheffer, D., & Small, P. (1992). *Self-determination in the new world order*. Washington, DC: Carnegie Endowment for International Peace.

Hastings, A. (1997). *The construction of nationhood: Ethnicity, religion and nationalism*. Cambridge, England: Cambridge University Press.

Hechter, M. (1983). A theory of group solidarity. In M. Hechter (Ed.), *The microfoundations of macrosociology* (pp. 16–57). Philadelphia: Temple University Press.

Hechter, M. (1985). Internal colonialism revisited. In E. Tiryakian & R. Rogowski (Eds.), *New nationalisms of the developed West*. London: Allen & Unwin.

Hechter, M. (1986a). Rational choice theory and the study of race and ethnic relations. In J. Rex & D. Mason (Eds.), *Theories of race and ethnic relations* (pp. 264–279). Cambridge, England: Cambridge University Press.

Hechter, M. (1986b). Theories of ethnic relations. In J. Stack (Ed.), *The primordial challenge: Ethnicity in the contemporary world*. New York: Greenwood Press.

Hobsbawm, E. (1990). *Nations and nationalism since 1870*. Cambridge, England: Cambridge University Press.

Hobsbawm, E., & Ranger, T. (Eds.). (1983). *The invention of tradition*. Cambridge, England: Cambridge University Press.

Horowitz, D. (1985). *Ethnic groups in conflict*. Berkeley: University of California Press.

Horowitz, D. (1989a). Ethnic conflict management for policymakers. In J. P. Montville (Ed.), *Conflict and peacemaking in multiethnic societies* (pp. 115–130). Lexington, MA: Heath.

Horowitz, D. (1989b). Making moderation pay: The comparative politics of ethnic conflict management. In J. P. Montville (Ed.), *Conflict and peacemaking in multiethnic societies* (pp. 471–475). Lexington, MA: Heath.

Hutchinson, J. (1994). Modern nationalism. In J. White (Ed.), *Fontana movements and ideas*. London: Fontana.

Isaacs, H. (1975). *Idols of the tribe: Group identity and political change*. New York: Harper & Row.

Kedourie, E. (1960). *Nationalism*. London: Hutchinson.

Kedourie, E. (Ed.). (1971). *Nationalism in Asia and Africa*. London: Wiedenfeld & Nicholson.

Lijphart, A. (1977a). *Democracy in plural societies: A comparative exploration*. New Haven, CT: Yale University Press.

Lijphart, A. (1977b). Political theories and the explanation of ethnic conflict in the Western world: Falsified predictions and plausible postdictions. In M.

Esman (Ed.), *Ethnic conflict in the Western world* (pp. 46–64). Ithaca, NY: Cornell University Press.

Lustick, I. (1979). Stability in deeply divided societies: Consociationalism versus control. *World Politics, 31*, 325–344.

Lustick, I. (1993). *Unsettled states, disputed lands: Britain and Ireland, France and Algeria, Israel and the West Bank-Gaza.* Ithaca, NY: Cornell University Press.

McGarry, J., & O'Leary, B. (Eds.). (1993). *The politics of ethnic conflict regulation: Case studies of protracted ethnic conflicts.* New York: Routledge.

McGarry, J., & O'Leary, B. (1994). The political regulation of national and ethnic conflict. *Parliamentary Affairs, 46*(1), 94–117.

McGarry, J., & O'Leary, B. (1995). *Explaining Northern Ireland: Broken images.* Oxford, England: Basil Blackwell.

McNeill, W. (1986). *Polyethnicity and world history: National unity in world history.* Toronto, Ontario, Canada: Toronto University Press.

Miller, D. (1995). *On nationality.* Oxford, England: Oxford University Press.

Nordlinger, E. (1972). Conflict regulation in divided societies. *Occasional Papers in International Affairs, 29.* Cambridge, MA: Harvard University, Center for International Affairs.

O'Leary, B. (1997). On the nature of nationalism: A critical appraisal of Ernest Gellner's writings on nationalism. *British Journal of Political Science, 27*, 191–222.

O'Leary, B. (1998). What is living and what is dead in Ernest Gellner's philosophy of nationalism? In J. Hall (Ed.), *The state of the nation: Ernest Gellner's theory of nationalism* (pp. 40–90). Cambridge, England: Cambridge University Press.

O'Leary, B., Lyne, T., Marshall, J., & Rowthorn, B. (1993). *Northern Ireland: Sharing authority.* London: Institute for Public Policy Research.

O'Leary, B., & McGarry, J. (1996). *The politics of antagonism: Understanding Northern Ireland* (2nd ed.). London: Athlone.

O'Leary, B., & Schöpflin, E. (Eds.). (in press). *Understanding nationalism.* Cheltenham, England: Edward Elgar.

Popper, K. (1945). *The open society and its enemies* (Two volumes). London: Routledge.

Smith, A. (1996). Memory and modernity: Reflections on Ernest Gellner's theory of nationalism. *Nations and Nationalism, 2*(3), 371–388.

Smith, A., & Gellner, E. (1996). The Warwick debate. *Nations and Nationalism, 2*(3), 357–365.

Smith, A. D. (1986). *The ethnic origins of nations.* Oxford, England: Basil Blackwell.

Smith, A. D. (1994). The question of national identity: Ancient, medieval or modern? *Ethnic and Racial Studies, 17*(3), 375–399.

van den Berghe, P. (Ed.). (1990). *State, violence and ethnicity.* Boulder: University Press of Colorado.

II

GENOCIDES

4

THEORIES OF THE HOLOCAUST: TRYING TO EXPLAIN THE UNIMAGINABLE

PETER SUEDFELD

In trying to understand ethnopolitical violence, one of the darkest and most discomforting areas of human behavior, it may be useful to make a distinction between ethnic war and ethnic persecution. *Ethnic war* describes a situation in which opposing protagonists can deploy troops armed and organized for military action—or conventional armed forces on one side and substantial guerrilla or terrorist groups on the other—with each force strong enough and motivated enough to inflict painful damage. Such conflicts are not completely unlike interstate wars, and the conduct of the participants is probably affected by such matters as fear of the enemy's resistance, retaliation, and vengeance. Recent events in Chechnya, Bosnia, and Sri Lanka fit this category.

Ethnic persecution, whose dynamics may be quite different, occurs when only one side possesses armed and organized military forces, which it puts into action not against opponents, but against victims. Here, we can speak of genocides and massacres, as in Nazi-ruled Europe between 1933 and 1945 and in Cambodia between 1975 and 1979.

There certainly have been mixed cases, but in many historical episodes the categorization can be quite clear-cut. The precipitating causes and predictive signals of the two types of violence may differ markedly. For example, physical fear of the other group as an impetus for preemptive or preventive violence is less probable in the one-sided case, because a weak and unarmed group is not a threat. The same is true of the role of past

I am grateful to Dr. Phyllis J. Johnson and Dr. R. Ned Lebow for their insightful comments on earlier versions of this chapter.

humiliation (cf. Lindner, 1998): Unless there had been a reversal of relative power, a defenseless target community is unlikely to have humiliated a stronger group. Conversely, the perpetrators' feeling of superiority and impunity is perhaps more likely to characterize instances of persecution. Thus, the war–persecution distinction may be important clues in searching for the governing conditions involved in the causation, nature, and possible termination of ethnopolitical conflicts.

Of course, war can turn into persecution, and vice versa. An attempted or feared genocide can be prevented, repelled, or avenged by forces siding with the original target group. This was cited as the motivation for the Turkish invasion of Cyprus in 1974, Turkey claiming that sporadic violence by Greek Cypriots against Turks was the forerunner of planned genocide. It is also possible for victory over an armed foe to turn into a massacre of its noncombatant kinfolk, as happened in the German army's response to early defeats at the hands of Herero warriors in Southwest Africa in 1904. After the course of the war was reversed and German supremacy was assured, the victors went on killing until approximately three-quarters of the entire Herero population were dead. Still other cases are even more complex—and confused—with guerrilla or terrorist actions, large-scale military combat, and genocidal massacres following each other in rapid succession or occurring simultaneously.

CASE STUDIES VERSUS COMPARATIVE STUDIES

The epistemology of research in this field is split between particularism and universalism, as is illustrated both by the chapters in this volume and by a section in the July 1998 issue of *American Psychologist* entitled "Ethnic Conflict: Global Challenges and Psychological Perspectives" (Mays, Bullock, Rosenzweig, & Wessells, 1998).

The journal contains five articles, with one each analyzing ethnic violence in Rwanda, Northern Ireland, Israel, and Sri Lanka and one covering three Latin American nations. Like the chapters of this book, the articles demonstrate that social scientists have considerable knowledge about the country or area in which they specialize, and they can trace the background and track the events of outbreaks of mass violence there. One may agree or disagree with the authors' interpretations and conclusions, but each article reveals a rich and articulated knowledge of the societal and historical roots of the problem. As qualitative case studies, these articles are impressive. They may also be useful in pointing to ways of helping the people involved in the particular conflict being studied.

Other scholars are using the tools of the social and behavioral sciences to identify common factors that affect the occurrence or nonoccurrence of violent conflicts across different times and places, the characteristics of such conflicts, ways in which they might be de-escalated and ended, and methods for helping their victims (e.g., Kressel, 1996; Staub, 1989). Idiographic case studies can help in this effort, but the main thrust has to be nomothetic and comparative. Much of the research on causation has focused on historical antecedents and political structures (e.g., Horowitz, 1985); psychological factors, although salient in the study of violence and aggression generally, have only recently attracted much attention in the context of ethnic conflict. The relative importance of local knowledge and trans-situational principles, and the roles of psychological and politico-economic factors, still remain to be elucidated.

The effects of ethnic conflict may be more universal than its causes. Until evidence shows otherwise, it would probably be logical to assume that the psychological impact of traumatic events related to such conflicts is similar to that of other traumatic events with the same characteristics (life-threatening violence, deprivation, separation from family, dislocation, etc.). Scientists taking a comparative, psychological approach to causes or consequences may seem, and be, ignorant of the specifics of particular instances of violence—they may not know much about the colonial period of Rwanda or the historic suppression of Mayans in Guatemala—but they may recognize the basic aspects of human psychology that would make timely and effective intervention possible anywhere.

There have been scientific efforts to find objective predictors of genocide without detailed study of its deep origins—for example, through the content analysis of political communications (Winter & Molano, 1998)—but it seems important to conduct thorough case studies as well as comparative ones. We need to find out whether each occurrence of mass murder is sui generis, with no common thread: Perhaps there is no cause in common between the Holocaust and the "classicide" committed by the Khmer Rouge, or the wars between Serbs and Croats, Hutus and Tutsis, and so on. If this proves to be true, experts on a particular country may be valuable in that specific context, but their knowledge will be irrelevant to other areas of the world. Alternatively, persecutions could perhaps be classified into a finite number of categories by shared causal factors, such as the acting out of festering resentments upon the removal of a suppressing force, as in the inheritor states of Yugoslavia and the Soviet Union, alerting observers to potential trouble spots. Or, perhaps, all such events have some characteristics in common, as theorists like Kelman (1973) and Staub (1989) have suggested (discussed later), making it possible to apply universal criteria for prediction and intervention.

THE EXAMPLE OF THE HOLOCAUST

The event that has sparked the greatest number of attempted explanations has generally become the modern—and therefore the best known—exemplar of one-sided genocidal persecution: the organized effort of the Third Reich and its collaborators to make Germany, Europe, and possibly the world, *Judenrein*—cleansed of Jews. It is historically unusual for any nation to attempt to extirpate an internal ethnic group whose members are by any objective measure loyal, patriotic, productive, and thoroughly assimilated into the polity; it was unprecedented that a nation seriously aspired to wipe an entire widespread ethnoreligious community off the face of the earth. The Holocaust was singular: In the words of a man who survived its worst horrors, it was "unilateral, systematic, mechanized, willed, at a governmental level, perpetrated upon innocent and defenseless populations and legitimized by the doctrine of contempt" (Levi, 1988, p. 86). The additional fact that the nation involved was at the time generally considered a highly developed and civilized one put its actions beyond the realms even of imagination. In fact, many European Jews continued to believe to the end that such a mass slaughter just could not happen, that there was no way that Germany could commit it, that the cattle cars full of "deportees" were just taking them to resettlement somewhere.

Because of the historical uniqueness and magnitude of the Holocaust, many scholars have advanced explanations of why it happened and of how it both resembled and differed from other ethnic persecutions. Here, if anywhere, we should be able to expect some illumination of the dark corners of the genocidal impulse and perhaps a test of Kurt Lewin's famous dictum that there is nothing as practical as a good theory. A "practical" theory in the current context would be one that enables us not merely to formulate post hoc explanations for lethal conflicts, but to predict them and thus perhaps to head them off through political, psychological, or military means. Prediction and prevention are not the only realistic goals: Understanding the causes of persecution can also help in facilitating reconciliation between members of the opposing groups and in the reconstruction not only of a damaged physical environment but also of damaged psyches and social relations. Not least may be the effect on survivors, for many of whom the sheer randomness and incomprehensibility of the event can be among its most painful consequences. Understanding the causes of the persecution may restore meaning to their lives, reduce self-blame, and reestablish order in their psychological universe (Frankl, 1963; McCann & Pearlman, 1990).

This chapter provides a summary of attempts to explain why an event such as the Holocaust could take place when and where it did. Although it is not a bibliography, much less a detailed review, of all such writings—either would be a book in itself—it will consider the major causes that scholars consider to have played a part. It will also offer some suggestions as to where each of the theories falls short of a convincing explanation, usually because it does not account for the special horrors of the Holocaust or for why Germany, and Germany alone, embarked on this course.

The theories reflect the background of their authors: Some emphasize historical factors, others economic, sociological, or psychological ones. Some try to explain the ideologies, decisions, and behavior of Nazi leaders, others, the acts of "ordinary Germans." Because of the salience of the Holocaust, together they form the most comprehensive body of theoretical explanations in the literature of ethnopolitical warfare and genocide. Two fairly recent propositions, those of Goldhagen (1996) and Kaplan (1994), are treated in somewhat more detail than older ones. Goldhagen's argument deserves special treatment because it has attracted so much attention and has become the best-known example of theories ascribing the Holocaust to something unique about Germans (and, by implication, an event that was bound to happen sooner or later). Perhaps paradoxically, Kaplan's ideas need to be presented in some detail because, in spite of being intriguing, they are not well-known, and partly because his writing links the Holocaust to developments in the present. Both Goldhagen's and Kaplan's explanations are ingeniously and persuasively argued, and both invoke psychological issues of ideology and values.

DEMONIC THEORIES

Some of the best-known accounts of the idea of the universal destruction of the Jews blame it on one man: Adolf Hitler. According to this view, Hitler's anti-Semitism was not only *a*, but *the*, moving force of the Holocaust.

This perspective underlies the many attempts to psychoanalyze Hitler, the speculations about his genital malformation, sexual repression or perversion, inferiority complex, frustration over failed artistic ambitions, fear of having "Jewish blood" himself, resentment because a Jewish doctor was unable to cure his mother's cancer, and so forth (e.g., Bullock, 1964; Langer, 1972; Waite, 1976; and, for an excellent overview, see Rosenbaum, 1998). It has the appeal, to some people, of letting tens of millions of Nazis, sympathizers, and collaborators—in fact, everyone but Hitler himself—off the moral hook. But although there is no reason to doubt that Hitler fully intended the elimination of the Jews and took the needed steps to realize his intention, it is equally clear that he did not force this program on an unwilling populace (Barkai, 1994). It also appears impossible, so far at least, to pinpoint anything so unique in Hitler's family background or personal history that it would explain his unparalleled ability to bring about the Holocaust by his own sole efforts.

Somewhat broader versions of this approach blame the Holocaust on the small group of leaders surrounding Hitler, or on a larger Nazi coterie that includes the SS, the special police units engaged in hunting down Jews in occupied territories, and the like (summarized in Kressel, 1996). As in Hitler-centered theories, the attempts to understand the personality characteristics of Nazi leaders or of SS troopers are interesting and illuminating. However, they fail to explain why many people with similar backgrounds and personalities did not move into the same positions; nor do they address the question of why so many people who did not belong in any of these categories or to any of these organizations collaborated in mass murder.

Actually, some quirky theories do propose that Hitler and/or the central figures of the German government did not really mean the genocide to happen and did not know it was happening (Irving, 1977). In this so-called functionalist view, the "Final Solution" was implemented as the result of dispersed centers of power competing for more influence and resources by sequentially escalating their anti-Jewish activities and added to the disorganization of the Nazi governmental apparatus and the increasing stresses of a costly war effort. In contrast, intentionalists argue that this progression was in fact planned by the central leaders, especially Hitler, and point to *Mein Kampf* and other early statements that give an accurate forecast of how events unfolded (Mason, 1981). Records of the Wannsee Conference and many other documents support this interpretation (Bauer, 1982; Browning, 1992b, especially chapter 5; Hiden & Farquharson, 1989). The weight of the evidence is on the intentionalist side but, once again, this is minimally helpful in understanding the roots of the Holocaust beyond the implication that we should not ignore the long-held political philosophy of leaders who come to power in potentially explosive situations.

SOCIAL, POLITICAL, AND ECONOMIC CHAOS

Another suggestion is that it was the pre-Nazi life conditions of the German people that led to the Holocaust. Historians, political scientists, and economists have attributed the growth of Nazism to the nation's experiences between 1918 and 1933: a war characterized by massive human and material sacrifice, prolonged stalemate, and eventual defeat; a demeaning peace treaty that exacerbated both economic and psychological losses; waves of economic chaos (hyperinflation, depression, and unemployment) leading workers, peasants, and middle-class Germans to fear for their security; and a perceived level of cultural and moral anarchy that violated the traditional beliefs of the mass public (e.g., Lasswell as cited in Nolte, 1967/1984; Lederer, 1979). The weak Weimar Republic was unable to restore the economy, to control political violence, or to rally the people behind its rather laissez-faire form of democracy, while an active communist movement was perceived as being likely to impose Bolshevism on the hapless German people. This combination of severe stressors understandably led to a societal desire to find someone to blame and someone to lead the way back to respect, prosperity, and security; Jews and Hitler, respectively, fulfilled those needs.

Some of these factors may in fact have been important in explaining the Nazi accession to power, but we do not know which were important for what segments or individuals in the population. We do know that major support for the Nazis and/or for the Holocaust came from many rich industrialists, as well as from economically threatened members of the lower middle class and from workers and peasants, all of whom may have seen the Nazis as a shield against chaos and/or Bolshevism (Mayer, 1989).

Intellectuals and professionals were also enthusiastic subscribers to the anti-Semitic agenda. Professors, judges, lawyers, and physicians took prominent part in persecuting Jewish colleagues and justifying the elimination of Jews from national life (just as they were to participate in the actual killing; Müller-Hill, 1994). As early as 1920, long before any serious economic problems, schools and universities led by people from the educated upper and upper-middle class were promulgating anti-Semitic rules and teachings, barring Jewish students from organizations and even preventing them from enrolling. This pattern, cutting across class lines, is difficult to explain fully as a reaction to societal upheaval (Goldhagen, 1996).

Socioeconomic analyses may in fact provide valid, if partial, explanations for the widespread support of the Nazis and perhaps even for the citizenry's approval of anti-Semitic measures. But as an understanding of the leap from discrimination against a minority group—not, after all, unusual in any country or historical period—to a concerted effort to annihilate it seems to be outside their scope.

Another problem with this explanation is how to draw useful inferences from it. The exact conditions of Germany between the wars will probably never be duplicated in any other country or time; what were the critical factors that could have predicted the outcome? Costly, lost wars followed by economic disaster and political upheaval are not uncommon. Yet, there were no widespread organized massacres of minority groups in France after the Franco-Prussian War or in the American South after the Civil War.

PRAGMATISM: ACTUAL GAINS AND POTENTIAL LOSSES

Another type of explanation invokes both economics and individual psychology, material gain, and potential loss in terms of quasi-behavioristic reinforcement theory. Participating in the persecution led to positive reinforcement (loot, promotion, power, and respect). There is no doubt that the Holocaust provided economic benefits to the Nazi state and to many individuals. The extent of this enrichment is still emerging from the files of Swiss banks and stolen art collections. The elimination of Jews from economic competition and the confiscation of their possessions provided advantages to Gentiles across many strata of society, and the availability of slave laborers was certainly a boost to German industry (Mayer, 1989). However, it has also been argued that the cost of carrying out the Holocaust—in time, administrative complications, and diversion of resources that could have been used for the war effort—was greater than the profits (Hilberg, 1980). The secondary importance of cheap labor is proven by the fact that these workers were starved, tortured, and murdered even though such treatment reduced the productivity of the labor force (Speer, 1970). Whether the economic advantages to individuals were of a level that would enable an otherwise benign or neutral person to accept the Holocaust is still another question. It also seems unlikely that people who are not inclined to commit atrocities could be brought to do so by the prospect of a promotion in their organization; besides, many perpetrators were "unofficial" volunteers who had no such prospects.

The aversive reinforcement component of behavioristic theory as applied to the Holocaust is even more questionable. This is the frequently raised excuse of the killers that their refusal to participate would have led to their own death or imprisonment. Historical accounts agree that Germans, including police, soldiers, and SS men, were not severely punished if they chose to stay aloof from active persecution. In general, they were given another opportunity, after which they might be transferred to other duties. In some cases, such personnel were actually transferred from units in the East back to Germany, which one would expect to be more of a reward than a punishment (e.g., Browning, 1992a; Goldhagen, 1996).

SOCIO–PSYCHOLOGICAL THEORIES

A more convincing psychologically based approach to the problem is to try to explain something that both the Hitler-centered and the socioeconomic arguments leave out. It also moves away from a concentration on the Nazi elite and its "true believers" to the question that to many seems the most baffling. Why did the German nation—a leader in science, scholarship, and the arts—succumb to either one leader or to adversity in such a barbaric way, engaging with very little hesitation in the mass murder of its own citizens and neighbors? What conditions led people to turn lethal force against fellow Germans who had lived, worked, and played with them; went to war on the same side; spoke the same language; and frequently intermarried?

Social psychologists argue that human beings in general are creatures of obedience to authority and conformity to their peers and that traditional German family structure and child-rearing practices, reinforced by and reinforcing social and political hierarchies, led to exaggerated levels of both obedience and conformity. Thus, the Germans were merely exhibiting, in perhaps an exaggerated form, universal tendencies. Psychological research including the work of Milgram, Asch, Janis, Adorno, et al., Altemeyer, and others, has been cited to support these hypotheses (see Suedfeld, 2000). Psychohistorians have hypothesized that violence turned outward was the result of mass repression and projection, among other defense mechanisms, operating in the German unconscious, again, much as they do universally, but, perhaps because of the particularly strict, hierarchical family structure of Germany, in a more virulent form. Incidentally, both traditionally authoritarian child-rearing and the breakdown of traditional family structures have recently been mentioned as factors in the Rwandan violence (Smith, 1998).

The "authoritarian German family" explanation is balanced by an argument that the youth who followed Hitler suffered from deficiencies of conscience because, during their formative years—the years of World War I—their parents had been absent fighting or working in war industries, returning (if at all) with the mark of defeat and poverty. Because of this, the parents could not satisfy the child's need for an authoritative and admirable role model, and Hitler and the Nazis stepped in to fill that need (Loewenberg, 1983). If this reasoning is correct, it may have been the partition and occupation of Germany, the economic boom in the West and Soviet domination in the East, that prevented the same pattern from recurring after the World War II.

A more sophisticated and less essentialist version of these arguments is the attempt to identify sociopsychological factors that can increase the likelihood that any nation or group will turn to ethnic persecution (e.g., Kelman, 1973). Perhaps the best developed of these descriptions is Ervin Staub's (1989), which ranges from instigating factors such as difficult life conditions and conflict over desired goods to ideological, cultural, and historical influences; the use of euphemistic language; and the incremental escalation of devaluation, discrimination, and eventually, violence.

Does the Holocaust fit into this system? Probably like most mass persecutions, it meets some criteria better than others. Of the three instigating conditions for genocide listed by Staub (1998), one—difficult life conditions—was clearly present in Weimar Germany. The other two—intense conflicts and self-interest—were by objective measures marginal as far as Gentile–Jewish relations were concerned, although some Germans may have perceived them as important, and Nazi propaganda certainly magnified their severity. Again, though, even if a non-Jewish German felt that there was a struggle over desirable goods, it is still difficult to understand the leap from feeling stress and insecurity, from blaming the Jews to murdering one's Jewish neighbors and their children.

The effects of difficult life conditions seem unpredictable. Other things being equal, one might expect the populace to rally around a slogan of "Let us all pull together as good Germans" just as willingly as around *"Die Juden sind unser Unglück"* ("The Jews are our misfortune," a commonly seen slogan at Nazi rallies). And the question remains: In the midst of a worldwide depression with its accompanying anxieties and uncertainties, why—of all the nations with vulnerable minorities in their midst—did Germany embark on its program of annihilation?

Staub (1989) has pointed out that genocidal ideologies must—like all other ideologies—be compatible with the preexisting values and culture of the society if they are to become widely accepted. Thus, the theory connects in a more complex way with those based on German traditions and social and familial structures. This interaction may explain why Nazism triumphed in Germany over communism, which was a strong contender for power and shared some of the characteristics of the Nazi program.

One major strength of Staub's viewpoint (as of the other social psychological theories, such as those of Kelman [1973], Kressel [1996], and Winter & Molano [1998]) is its universality: The same antecedent conditions will increase or decrease the probability of genocide regardless of where, when, or what nation may be involved. It is not necessary to assume or argue that Germans are somehow unique in their propensity for authoritarianism, ethnocentrism, or mass murder.

A UNIQUE FORM OF ANTI-SEMITISM

In the theories just discussed, one intuitively obvious aspect of the German persecution is missing: ideology, specifically hatred for Jews. In fact, at least one prominent theorist has explicitly denied a central role for anti-Semitism as the root of the Holocaust (Bauman, 1991). A contrary view, promulgated in a best-selling and highly controversial book by Daniel Goldhagen (1996), is that Germany and its people are unique, precisely in the nature of their anti-Semitism, which led directly to genocide against the Jews (Fischer, 1998). According to Goldhagen, most explanations—such as those summarized in this chapter—assume the origins of the Holocaust to lie in pressures that overcame the reluctance of ordinary Germans to participate in, or at least assent to, mass murder.

This, says Goldhagen, is a mistaken assumption. Most Germans were in fact quite favorable to the idea of annihilating the Jews, and their actions were motivated by this attitude rather than by obedience, fear, greed, or other secondary factors. The Nazis, in Goldhagen's view, merely liberated the German populace to act out the lethal anti-Semitism that under previous regimes could be expressed only symbolically and partially.

Besides analyzing German history, Goldhagen supported his thesis by looking at the behavior of Germans toward their Jewish victims. The Holocaust saw uncountable examples of voluntary and unnecessary cruelty: many episodes of German civilians spontaneously attacking Jews and organizing riots, and gratuitous brutality, degradation, and torture that preceded or accompanied massacres in the streets, ghettoes, fields, and camps. Logically, one would not expect a people unwillingly acting as executioners to spontaneously torment and mock those about to die, to send photographs of their deeds home to their family, or to continue the killing even after they had received orders to stop.

Goldhagen posited that theories attributing the acceptance of the Holocaust to a small minority, to fear, or to pragmatism are all disconfirmed by the historical record. The genocidal acts were perpetrated by "ordinary" Germans, not just Nazi thugs or SS troopers (Browning, 1992a). Those who refused to participate were not subject to severe punishment, and they themselves considered their reluctance a sign of weakness rather than of moral strength. Any explanation based on a rational actor or unemotional bureaucrat model is contradicted by the diversion of men, supplies, and transport from military needs to continuing the killing. Adolf Eichmann, supposedly the very model of a bureaucrat unmotivated by personal hatred and wanting only to do his job (Arendt, 1977), was among those who disobeyed orders and refused to redirect these resources against the Russian advance.

According to Goldhagen, Germany had long nurtured a special "eliminationist" form of anti-Semitism, calling for the elimination of Jews and of Jewish influence from German society. This began with the view, shared across early Christianity and throughout medieval Europe, that the existence of Jews violated the moral order and imperiled the faith of Christians because Jews—the original people of the Bible—had rejected and killed God (that is, Jesus). This made Jews the personification of evil (Bauer, 1997; Katz, 1994).

In the 19th century, the emphasis changed from theological to secular concepts: Jews were not of the *Volk;* did not share the mystical blood tie that bonded all *real* Germans; and were asocial, immoral, and ambitious to control Germany (Elias, 1996). Even liberal Germans argued that the Jews would have to reform to "earn" civil rights, reform essentially being the abandonment of their Jewishness. When this failed to happen, the perceived recalcitrance of Jews as evil doers was reinforced.

Then popular scientific theories concerning inherited differences among ethnic groups led to the wide acceptance of the idea that the antisocial characteristics ascribed to Jews were racial rather than solely religious, resided "in the blood." In consequence, conversion to Christianity no longer exempted Jews (or even their Christian-born offspring) from their inherent stigma. Jewry held a central place in German thinking as the source of all that had gone wrong, and eliminationist anti-Semitism pervaded the ideology of Nazis, anti-Nazis, and passive bystanders alike. "When the Nazis did assume power, they found themselves the masters of a society already imbued with notions about Jews that were ready to be mobilized for the most extreme form of 'elimination' imaginable" (Goldhagen, 1996, p. 23).

Goldhagen's book has aroused considerable controversy, not least because of his harsh criticism of other Holocaust scholars and supposed misrepresentation of some of their thinking. Aside from those issues, the theory is not convincing in explaining either the causes or the nature of a unique German anti-Semitism. The same philosophical and racial ideas permeated other European nations from the Middle Ages through the 19th century (cf. Girard, 1980). Germany's history—a divided and weak nation, a lost war followed by economic and social disorder—is not unique. Nor is it clear that either the history or the prejudice inescapably leads to murderous persecution. And if one does accept the basic premise, it is difficult to explain why many Germans refused to participate. Even some of the killers showed considerable anguish over the tasks that they carried out, at least before they became hardened (Browning, 1992a). A more difficult problem for the theory is the willingness, and often the eagerness, of the citizenry of so many Nazi-occupied or influenced territories outside Germany (especially Latvia, Lithuania, Croatia, and the Ukraine, but to some extent most of the others as well) to participate in the persecution. The projected annihilation of the Gypsies and of at least a large proportion of Slavic communities to the East (Hilberg, 1980) also remains outside Goldhagen's explanatory schema.

Last, the special roles of Nazi leaders, ideology, and organization are slighted. Had Hitler been killed during World War I, or had the Weimar Republic been succeeded by a communist (or even a conservative *Junker*) government, would Germany still have attempted to annihilate the Jewish people? Goldhagen's analysis seems to imply that it would have, but the conclusion is not very persuasive.

THE WILL TO POWER, SCIENTISM,
AND POSTMODERN PHILOSOPHY

A last theoretical approach also ascribes special qualities to Germany, but these qualities link the Holocaust to salient aspects of modern and postmodern philosophies: scientism and the cult of power. Here the question of how such an "advanced" country could perpetrate such atrocities is answered in an unexpected way: The atrocities were possible exactly because

Germany was so advanced in science, technology, and philosophy. These theories are less well-known than the ones discussed earlier, and they propose intriguing interpretations of Nazi ideology. One might argue that the core concept is the depersonalization of human beings, as faceless parts of a mass whose only role is to play a part in the designs of the powerful.

One such argument goes as follows,

> In my mind it is no accident that the great evils of the period 1933–1945 were perpetrated in a country that was the world leader in theoretical science and mathematics. It was not necessary for the policy makers to have understood mathematics; it sufficed that a certain spirit—part of which was mathematical—was in the air . . . . (Davis & Hersh, 1986, pp. 290–291)

The passage goes on to cite George Steiner, who had theorized that the Holocaust was a reaction against the impossible, perfectionistic goals set for humankind by Jewish monotheism, Christian piety, and Marxist messianism.[1] It concludes,

> I will add one more vision of perfection to Steiner's list: the Greek idea of a perfect truth attainable through mathematical abstraction. I should like to suggest that advanced mathematization, through abstraction and subsequent loss of meaning, played a role. (Davis & Hirsh, 1986, pp. 290–291)

Gasman noted that in his Table Talks, Hitler frequently used the word *Wissenschaft* (science):

> From the content of Hitler's conversations it is patently clear that he thought of himself as rooted in the rational and scientific tradition of modern European civilisation and that he was certain that there was a basis in science for all the beliefs and policies which he espoused. (Gasman, as cited in Webster, 1995, p. 500)

Rassenwissenschaft or *Rassenkunde* (race science, race studies) was invoked and seriously pursued as the basis for classifying ethnic groups and arranging them hierarchically. Professors, researchers, and institutes devoted themselves to this painstaking task, using elaborate equipment and methodology. The end product was a taxonomy of races arranged by levels of deservingness—deservingness of life. This abstract classification, ignoring the reality of individual human beings, made it possible to view actions against them also in the abstract.

---

[1] One might also refer to the idealized concept of the all-conquering Aryan super-race. This mythologized history ranged from Armenius, the annihilator of Roman legions, to the Teutonic Knights and the Ring Cycle. German victory in the Franco-Prussian War had reinforced this proud self-perception, but the defeat of 1918 and its aftermath were failures to reach perfection, which may be added to the ones identified by Steiner.

Given the psychological disappearance of actual human suffering, it followed that when one knew one's goal, the will to power justified whatever deeds were necessary to reach it. Here, again, the laws of nature and of science were invoked: "the law of nature which demands that all living things mutually devour each other" (Hitler, quoted by Cameron & Stevens, as cited in Kaplan, 1994, p. 69). This pseudoscientific, or scientistic, formula was grafted onto the old romantic and mystical belief in the *Volksgemeinschaft*, a transcendental essence that engulfed its individual members, a mythical, self-perpetuating organism that united all of its living members with their Teutonic ancestors, the unity and destiny of the Germanic people, and their land—"blood and soil" (Barkai, 1994). In Kaplan's words, Nazism was "romanticized scientism" (p. 69), a combination of natural and supernatural forces, of religion and science in the service of "metapolitics."

Nazi writings emphasized that the purification of the race was a natural imperative that could be understood through the concepts of science. Jews were the anti-type of the Aryan, everything bad as a counterfoil to the all-good true Nordic European—a view adopted from the writings of earlier race theorists such as Chamberlain and Gobineau (Yahil, 1990). The Nazis' similes were biomedical: Jews were like tuberculosis bacilli, or like rats that spread plague. The state, and the *Volk*, were like a living organism that had to defend itself and to expand, to destroy its enemies, to control its destiny. "The law of existence prescribes uninterrupted killing, so that the better may live" (Hitler, as cited in Kaplan, 1994, p. 65). People were killed for the sake of the health of the group, as organs may be excised in therapeutic surgery: Nazism, according to Rudolf Hess, was "nothing but applied biology."

Nazism was in fact social Darwinism carried to its logical limits and combined with Nietzschean concepts of the superior man, the importance of the will, and the primacy of action over thought (Mosse & Lampert, 1980). The power to survive, grow, and thrive was the core imperative. "Limitless ambition for one's group . . . led simply and directly to the goal of limitless power. In exchange, the will to power became perfectly arbitrary and opportunistic in its manipulation of ideals and ideas" (Kaplan, 1994, p. 104). The concepts of individual conscience, or of morality above power, were considered to be mere myths; in the service of the Will to Power, it was perfectly reasonable to kill not only actual enemies, but even those who inhabited living space that the German people could use (*Lebensraum*, the ostensible reason for eastward expansion and the subjugation of the Slavic nations).

Kaplan asked how the Holocaust could have happened in a nation that gave the world much of its art, science, and even moral philosophy. The answer lies in the Nazi view that the war for survival, between transcendental forces in an epic and everlasting battle, outweighs all other considerations. Nazi ideology reversed the customary relationship between power and values.

Whereas most philosophies and political theories hold that power is exerted to advance a set of important values or goals, for the Nazis exerting power was the central value and goal, and other components of ideology were recruited to explain and clarify it.

This is where Kaplan drew the parallel with postmodern thinking,[2] with philosophers like Martin Heidegger, foreshadowed by Nietzsche and Hegel, among others, who exalt power and the "will to be," the submerging of individual life in the destiny of the group. Heidegger, the eminent philosopher, university rector (president), and Nazi, is obviously the prototype, as in the following passage: "The Führer himself is the only present embodiment of German nation and its law . . . . To oppose him would be treason against Being" (as cited in Kaplan, 1994, p. 60). The postmodernists' obsession with power and their scorn for the Enlightenment—with its emphasis on the individual and its ideas of discoverable truths, unalienable human rights and freedoms, abstract rules of justice, and procedural safeguards—find a congenial forerunner here.

The Nazis were inconsistent in their reliance on what they thought of as science. On the one hand, they believed it to be the foundation stone of their racial theories; on the other hand, they also believed that those who held power could mold the truth to their own desires. Kaplan (1994) again quoted Hitler: "There is no such thing as truth . . . either in the moral or in the scientific sense" (p. 49).

There is an interesting conjunction here with some postmodern thinkers, who also exalt power and also deny the basic precepts of science—above all the idea that there is such a thing as objective truth, potentially attainable through disinterested (not uninterested) research. On the contrary, they reinterpret the scientific search for truth as just another arena in the struggle for power. All supposed truths are social constructions, imposed by dominant groups on subordinate ones in order to repress the latter's alternative truths (Gross, Levitt, & Lewis, 1996). "Modern humanism is . . . mistaken in drawing [a] line between knowledge and power," wrote Foucault (1980, p. 53).

For Kaplan, as well as for other critics, this position epitomizes the subordination of truth and of humane values to force. If we reject the idea that there are universal truths, which can be recognized or discovered through the systematic appraisal of hypotheses and facts, we are left with "a jumble of superstitions and untestable propositions, all of which are as good as any other" (Chirot, 1995, p. 160).

It would be far-fetched to indict this philosophy—the will to power, the viewing of people merely as members of an abstract category, and the

---

[2] Interestingly, Bauman (1991) proposed that the Holocaust was quintessentially *modern*: organized, orderly, dispassionate, rationalized, scientific, and technological.

belief in communal rather than universal truths—as an accessory to the crimes of the Nazis. However, in one version or another it provided intellectual impetus and justification for the massacres not only of the Nazis but of Joseph Stalin, Mao Tse-tung, Pol Pot, and the proliferating ideological murderers of the late 20th century.

Large-scale ethnopolitical[3] violence is one of the most horrifying and awesome of human activities. Some commentators feel that analyzing such events should be avoided, particularly in the case of the Holocaust. According to some, trying to understand the crimes of the Nazis trivializes or distorts the magnitude of the acts and of the suffering (e.g., Bauer, 1978; Friedländer, 1992). Others (e.g., Lanzmann, 1991) fear that if people think they can understand why the Holocaust happened, they will be inclined to excuse the perpetrators—"*Tout comprendre c'est tout pardonner.*" But the horrific nature of events or of deeds should make us try even harder to comprehend them. There seems to be no logical reason why learning the factors that influenced someone to commit an atrocity should incline us to forgiveness, although it is possible that explanations will be used as excuses. The connection between understanding and pardoning is a question that requires research, which at the moment is nonexistent.[4] Thus, the argument for not studying the Holocaust is not grounded in evidence.

I find the argument for studying it more persuasive. The evil that people can do is part of human nature. It must therefore be within the realm of scholarship and research if we hope to understand human beings, and even more so if we hope someday to be able to prevent some of the tragedies that might otherwise occur because of our ignorance.

This is the reason for undertaking the preceding rapid voyage through some of the prominent theories of why the Holocaust happened. The theories can be divided along a number of dimensions. Some of these—by no means an exhaustive taxonomy—include the following:

1. Specificity to the Nazi Holocaust versus generalizability, with Goldhagen's eliminationism at one pole and Staub's psychosocial formulation at the other.[5]
2. Historical continuity, tracing the origins of the Holocaust back to early Christianity, to the Middle Ages, to the 19th century, or only to the post–World War I period.

---

[3] "Ethnopolitical" is a simplification; in different instances, there may be religious or economic as well as ethnic and political bases for conflict, or several of these in combination.
[4] The equating of the two concepts may be due to a semantic ambiguity—for example, when we call someone "an understanding person," forgiveness is implied.
[5] As this chapter was completed, a newly published article argued that the Holocaust was related to an evolutionary tendency toward xenophobia (Brannigan, 1998). I have not yet had a chance to read this article, but it may represent the extreme of the "universalist" position.

3. External versus internal causes, for example, socioeconomic upheaval or the workings of the individual unconscious.
4. The degree of mutability, ranging from almost none to very high. The former is illustrated by Goldhagen's thesis: in the face of rooted and pervasive eliminationist anti-Semitism, an eventual attempt to annihilate all Jews—a Holocaust, if not the Holocaust—seems unavoidable. High mutability is implied in the Hitler-centered analyses: If Hitler was the sole prime mover, then a single event, trivial from a contemporary perspective, would have prevented the *Shoah*. Hitler might easily have been killed at the front in World War I or have had a successful artistic career turning him away from politics, and so on. Bernstein's caveat must be borne in mind here: "not to regard the future from which the writers speak as the inevitable outcome of the past" (1994, p. 69).
5. The scope of responsibility, focusing on a single person, on a small proportion of the population, or on all Germans, respectively exemplified by psychobiographies of Hitler, case studies of the Nazi leaders or of SS troopers, and analyses such as those of Adorno et al. (1950) and Goldhagen (1996) that pertain to German society as a whole.
6. The role of intent and foresight, describing the Holocaust as being the consistently logical outcome of Nazi ideology versus attributing it to disorganized, almost chaotic, reactions as events unfolded in unexpected ways.

The explanations are by no means mutually exclusive. Each is convincing; all of the factors advanced by all of the theorists were operating. But which factors were necessary, which were sufficient, how important was each, and how did they interact? Can we somehow derive profiles of causal influences differing across time, or across individual perpetrators? Can we study other historical instances of mass ethnopolitical murder—in Anatolia, the Ukraine, Cambodia, Tibet, Rwanda, Indonesia, and Bosnia—and identify possible universal, or at least shared, factors as well as unique ones? If so, we may take some steps toward specifying the limits and mutual synergy between idiographic and nomothetic approaches and perhaps move from post hoc explanations toward an enhanced ability to predict and to intervene before the worst happens.

REFERENCES

Adorno, T. W., Frenkel-Brunswik, E., Levinson, D. J., & Sanford, R. (1950). *The authoritarian personality*. New York: Harper.

Arendt, D. H. (1977). *Eichmann in Jerusalem: A report on the banality of evil.* Harmondsworth, England: Penguin Books.

Barkai, A. (1994). *Volksgemeinschaft,* "Aryanization" and the Holocaust. In D. Cesarani (Ed.), *The Final Solution: Origins and implementation* (pp. 33–50). London: Routledge.

Bauer, Y. (1978). *The Holocaust in historical perspective.* Seattle: University of Washington Press.

Bauer, Y. (1982). *History of the Holocaust.* New York: Franklin Watts.

Bauer, Y. (1997). The trauma of the Holocaust: Some historical perspectives. In G. J. Colijn & M. S. Littell (Eds.), *Confronting the Holocaust: A mandate for the 21st century* (pp. 2–17). Lanham, MD: University Press of America.

Bauman, Z. (1991). *Modernity and the Holocaust.* Ithaca, NY: Cornell University Press.

Bernstein, M. A. (1994). *Foregone conclusions: Against apocalyptic history.* Berkeley: University of California Press.

Brannigan, A. (1998). Criminology and the Holocaust: Xenophobia, evolution, and genocide. *Crime and Delinquency, 44,* 257–276. (From *Psychological Abstracts, 85,* Abstract No. 20406)

Browning, C. R. (1992a). *Ordinary men: Reserve Police Battalion 101 and the Final Solution in Poland.* New York: HarperCollins.

Browning, C. R. (1992b). *The path to genocide: Essays on launching the Final Solution.* Cambridge, England: Cambridge University Press.

Bullock, A. (1964). *Hitler: A study in tyranny* (Rev. ed.). New York: Harper & Row.

Chirot, D. (1995). Modernism without liberalism: The ideological roots of modern tyranny. *Contention, 5,* 141–166.

Davis, P. J., & Hersh, R. (1986). *Descartes' dream: The world according to mathematics.* Boston: Houghton-Mifflin.

Elias, N. (1996). *The Germans.* New York: Columbia University Press.

Fischer, K. P. (1998). *The history of an obsession: German Judeophobia and the Holocaust.* New York: Continuum.

Foucault, M. (1980). *Power/knowledge: Selected interviews and other writings, 1972–1977* (C. Gordon, Trans. and Ed.). Brighton, UK: Harvester.

Frankl, V. E. (1963). *Man's search for meaning.* New York: Beacon Press.

Friedländer, S. (Ed.). (1992). *Probing the limits of representation: Nazism and the "Final Solution."* Cambridge, MA: Harvard University Press.

Girard, P. (1980). Historical foundations of anti-Semitism. In J. E. Dimsdale (Ed.), *Survivors, victims, and perpetrators: Essays on the Nazi Holocaust* (pp. 55–78). Washington, DC: Hemisphere.

Goldhagen, D. J. (1996). *Hitler's willing executioners: Ordinary Germans and the Holocaust.* New York: Knopf.

Gross, P. R., Levitt, N., & Lewis, M. W. (Eds.). (1996). *The flight from science and reason.* New York: New York Academy of Sciences.

Hiden, J., & Farquharson, J. (1989). *Explaining Hitler's Germany: Historians and the Third Reich* (2nd ed.). London: Batsford.

Hilberg, R. (1980). The nature of the process. In J. E. Dimsdale (Ed.), *Survivors, victims, and perpetrators: Essays on the Nazi Holocaust* (pp. 5–54). Washington, DC: Hemisphere.

Horowitz, D. L. (1985). *Ethnic groups in conflict*. Berkeley: University of California Press.

Irving, D. (1977). *Hitler's war*. New York: Viking.

Kaplan, H. (1994). *Conscience and memory: Meditations in a museum of the Holocaust*. Chicago: University of Chicago Press.

Katz, S. T. (1994). *The Holocaust in historical context: 1. The Holocaust and mass death before the modern age*. New York: Oxford University Press.

Kelman, H. C. (1972). Violence without moral restraint: Reflections on the dehumanization of victims and victimizers. *Journal of Social Issues, 29*, 25–63.

Kressel, N. J. (1996). *Mass hate: The global rise of genocide and terror*. New York: Plenum Press.

Langer, W. C. (1972). *The mind of Adolf Hitler: The secret wartime report*. New York: Basic Books.

Lanzmann, C. (1991). The obscenity of understanding: An evening with Claude Lanzmann. *American Imago, 48*, 473–495.

Lederer, E. (1979). Ende der Klassengesellschaft? Zur Analyse des Faschismus [The end of class society? Toward an analysis of Fascism]. In E. Lederer (Ed.), *Kapitalismus, Klassenstruktur, und Probleme der Demokratie in Deutschland 1910–1940*. Göttingen, Germany: Vandenhoeck & Ruprecht.

Levi, P. (1988). *The drowned and the saved*. New York: Summit Books.

Lindner, E. (1998). *The feeling of being humiliated: A central theme in armed conflicts*. Unpublished manuscript, University of Oslo, Norway.

Loewenberg, P. (1983). *Decoding the past: The psychohistorical approach*. New York: Knopf.

Mason, T. (1981). Intention and explanation: A current controversy about the interpretation of National Socialism. In G. Hirschfeld & L. Kettenacker (Eds.), *Der Führerstaat: Mythos und Realität* (pp. 21–40). Stuttgart, West Germany: Klett-Cotta.

Mayer, A. (1989). *Why did the heavens not darken? The "Final Solution" in history*. New York: Pantheon.

Mays, V. M., Bullock, M., Rosenzweig, M. R., & Wessells, M. (Eds.). (1998). Ethnic conflict: Global challenges and psychological perspectives. *American Psychologist, 53*, 737–794.

McCann, I. L., & Pearlman, L. A. (1990). *Psychological trauma and the adult survivor: Theory, therapy, and transformation*. New York: Brunner/Mazel.

Mosse, G. L., & Lampert, S. G. (1980). Weimar intellectuals and the rise of National Socialism. In J. E. Dimsdale (Ed.), *Survivors, victims, and perpetrators: Essays on the Nazi Holocaust* (pp. 79–105). Washington, DC: Hemisphere.

Müller-Hill, B. (1994). The idea of the Final Solution and the role of experts. In D. Cesarani (Ed.), *The Final Solution: Origins and implementation* (pp. 62–70). London: Routledge.

Nolte, E. (1984). *Theorien über den Faschismus* [Theories of Fascism]. Königstein: Atheneum. (Original work published 1967)

Rosenbaum, R. (1998). *Explaining Hitler: The search for the origins of his evil.* New York: Random House.

Smith, D. N. (1998). The psychocultural roots of genocide: Legitimacy and crisis in Rwanda. *American Psychologist, 53,* 743–753.

Speer, A. (1970). *Inside the Third Reich.* New York: Avon Books.

Staub, E. (1989). *The roots of evil: The origins of genocide and other group violence.* New York: Cambridge University Press.

Suedfeld, P. (2000). Reverberations of the Holocaust fifty years later: Psychology's contributions to understanding persecution and genocide. *Canadian Psychology, 41,* 1–9.

Waite, R. L. G. (1976). *The psychopathic god: Adolf Hitler.* New York: Basic Books.

Webster, R. (1995). *Why Freud was wrong.* New York: Basic Books.

Winter, D. G., & Molano, J. R. V. (1998, August). *Toward a psychological theory of ethno-political war.* Paper presented at Origins of Ethno-Political War, Persecution, and Genocide, a symposium conducted at the meeting of the 24th Congress of Applied Psychology, San Francisco, CA.

Yahil, L. (1990). *The Holocaust: The fate of European Jewry, 1932–1945.* New York: Oxford University Press.

5

ARMENIAN DEPORTATIONS AND MASSACRES IN 1915

FIKRET ADANIR

Why did the Armenian tragedy occur in 1915? Why is it viewed by many in the West as the first genocide of the 20th century, whereas the prevailing opinion in Turkey is that it resulted from legitimate state action in dire necessity against a rebellious people? An answer to these questions necessitates the clarification of further questions regarding the general conditions of the period, the nature of the Turkish–Armenian conflict, as well as the specific goals pursued by the actors chiefly involved.

Obviously, such an analysis should begin with a brief description of the place the Armenian community occupied within late Ottoman society. Armenians lived dispersed over a large territory partly within the Ottoman realm, and partly in the neighboring Russian and Persian Empires. Compact Armenian peasant populations could be found in the eastern and southeastern provinces of present-day Turkey. Moreover, substantial Armenian communities existed in urban centers such as Istanbul, Izmir, Bursa, and Adana. These groups were engaged mostly in handicraft production but also included merchants, commissioners for European companies, and bankers, as well as members of liberal professions such as physicians, lawyers, architects, and the like (Atamian, 1955).

The Armenian population within the Ottoman Empire was traditionally organized, just like other non-Muslim groups, in an autonomous religious community, called in the Ottoman context a millet (for further information on the millet system, see Braude & Lewis, 1982). This was a system that left not only the civil affairs of the Armenian community to be settled by its own institutions under the leadership of the Armenian patriarch of Istanbul, but also the developments within the cultural sphere, such as the education of children, fell under Armenian communal responsibility. In the course of the 19th century, significant changes occurred affecting the individual's civic status in society. Within the framework of a comprehensive program of reforms, the non-Muslim populations were granted legal equality with Muslims, including equal access to public office. Under these conditions, non-Muslim professional and commercial elites could secure by the last quarter of the century a predominant position in the socioeconomic life of the empire.

Conversely, the Muslim element became more and more concerned about their diminishing influence; in Istanbul, for example, where the Muslims represented the majority, they controlled only 25% of the retail trade, 15% of the wholesale business, and a negligible 3% of the transport companies. More interestingly, the non-Muslim elites of the period—and among these the most prominent the Armenians—also dominated Ottoman cultural life. Of the 47 newspapers and journals published in Istanbul in 1876, only 13—including official publications—were in Turkish; 9 newspapers appeared in Armenian. Of some 90 printing houses in the Ottoman capital at the end of the 19th century, only 23 were owned by Muslims, but 32 by Armenians. Also modern theatre and opera were introduced to the Turkish-speaking public by Armenian artists (Adanir, 1998).

EMERGENCE OF THE ARMENIAN QUESTION

In view of this successful integration, at least of the upper layers of the Armenian population in the Ottoman social fabric and of the growing Muslim awareness of their own inferiority, the question as to why and how it came to a shift toward a catastrophic development in Turkish–Armenian relations starting in the 1880s deserves careful consideration. A decisive factor was the upsurge of ethnic nationalism during the second half of the 19th century. The European romantic idea that a *Volk* was an organic community of shared destiny, a community, as it were, with a collective soul articulating itself through the medium of language, had become the focus of interest for educated circles in the Ottoman Empire as well. Intellectual energies were concentrated upon promoting "national awakening." Uprisings and guerrilla activity in the Balkans and especially the developments subsequent to the Ottoman defeat in the war with Russia in 1877–1878 were heavy blows to the fraternal union of Ottoman peoples, the slogan of the reform era. Hundreds of thousands of Muslims fleeing from the Russian armies or, later on, expelled by Christian successor states sought refuge in the empire (Dumont, 1980; Karpat, 1990; McCarthy, 1996; Turgay, 1991).

Impressed by these developments, Sultan Abdulhamid II (1876–1909) elaborated a new approach to the questions of Ottoman reform. He no longer stressed the idea of a multireligious and multicultural empire but instead the solidarity among his Muslim subjects as the basis for political loyalty. Parallel to this change of mood, a new concern about Islamization and/or Turkification of the empire could be discerned, which was reflected not least in efforts to shape the geographic pattern of settlement of Muslim refugees arriving in Asia Minor. Actually the sultan demanded nothing less than a reversal of the demographic balance, especially in strategically important areas, such as Thrace, the districts in the vicinity of the Straits, and from the 1880s on, also in the eastern and southeastern provinces of Anatolia. The problem of the refugees thus became a hotly disputed issue of nationalist politics.

A similar development directly affecting the sociopolitical fabric of the countryside was the sedentation of tribes, initiated already in the 1840s. A growing number of tribesmen occupied lands traditionally considered by Armenian villagers to be theirs. Local courts were unable to settle the conflicts, not least because it had always been imperial policy to turn the unruly tribesmen into taxpaying agriculturists. But also the fact that toward the end of the century a Cossack-type Kurdish militia was established, ostensibly to be used against the Russian enemy but in reality with the potential to exercise pressure upon the local population, and made the situation of the Armenians in the east more precarious (Deringil, 1998; Duguid, 1973; van Bruinessen, 1978).

The beginnings of Armenian revolutionary activity can be traced back to 1885, when local initiatives in the province of Van were coordinated in a resistance movement against Kurdish tribesmen (Nalbandian, 1963, p. 100). A more radical approach was taken by the Hunchakian Revolutionary Party that was founded in 1887 by Armenian students in Geneva. It propagated the need for the destruction of the Ottoman State by means of revolution; whatever the cost, the political and national independence of Turkish Armenia was to be achieved (Nalbandian, 1963, pp. 108–111).

The Hunchak Party viewed terror as a legitimate weapon. Terrorist actions would provoke retaliation by the Ottoman State and/or the Muslim population and thus induce the European powers to intervene on behalf of Armenian interests. Several spectacular actions were carried out, and rebellions instigated by the Hunchakist Armenian revolutionaries during the decade from 1887 to 1897 turned Ottoman urban centers as well as parts of the Anatolian countryside into a virtual battleground. More often than not the suppression of these activities was accompanied by large-scale massacres, because in many places the local Muslim irregulars participated in suppression campaigns and took revenge. It was the period when the dissolution of the Ottoman Empire appeared imminent, with the sultan insisting on his right to protect the territorial integrity of his realm. Among the liberal statesmen of Europe, however, the opinion was widespread that "every breach in the integrity of the Ottoman Empire was so much gain for mankind" (Langer, 1950, p. 360).

The most important Armenian political organization was founded in 1890 in Tiflis; it was called "Dashnaksuthiun" or "The Armenian Revolutionary Federation." The Federation aimed at uniting all Armenians within a single independent state, in other words, not only the Ottoman Armenians were to be liberated, but also those living in the Russian Empire (Nalbandian, 1963, p. 156). Another important difference from other Armenian organizations was that the Federation's program stressed the need for reconciliation with the Muslim populations who represented the majority in the prospective Armenian territory. The party made considerable efforts to persuade Kurdish opinion to take joint political action against the Ottoman State. This pragmatic approach to the national question in the Ottoman and Russian Empires explains also why the Dashnaksuthiun eventually found itself ready to cooperate with the "Young Turk Party of Union and Progress" (usually just called "the Young Turks").

Who were the Young Turks? By this term we understand an oppositional movement that had developed after the 1890s as an expression of the deep frustration and embitterment felt by Ottoman intellectuals. Politically, it was a desperate effort to halt the dissolution of the Ottoman State by means of a reconciliation of disparate nationalist strivings within the framework of a bureaucratically controlled constitutional regime. In their political thinking, most Young Turks were influenced by the positivism of Auguste Comte, as well as by social Darwinist ideas of the period. The positivist motto "*l'ordre et progrès*" found its way even into the title of the leading Young Turk organization, the Committee of Union and Progress (CUP). Under the influence of the positivists, the Young Turks had a mechanical concept of society. The solution to the basic problem of the Ottoman State, its backwardness, was to be sought in the establishment of a "scientific" form of government. The religious conservatism of the masses appeared in this perspective as an obstacle to such progress. A complementary influence in this regard emanated from Gustave Le Bon; consequently, the Young Turks believed that progress was to be expected only from the guidance by a select few—an elitist worldview that characterized their mentality well into the 20th century (Hanioğlu, 1995; Mardin, 1983).

The "Revolution" of 1908 was the result of an effective cooperation between the Young Turk movement and the Armenian Revolutionary Federation. Both groups were united in their aversion to the Islamist regime of the sultan. In their common program, which is a remarkable document of political compromise, the following points deserve attention: (a) The CUP promised, among others, to alleviate the distress of the Armenian peasantry, and, in a concrete fashion, the Young Turks pledged to return lands appropriated by Kurdish tribesmen; (b) as for the Armenian Federation, it pledged loyalty to the Ottoman Constitution and thus promised implicitly that it would no longer appeal to Europe for intervention on behalf of the Armenian national cause (Ahmad, 1982, pp. 401–434; Kansu, 1997, pp. 61–66, 78–81).

However, the liberal atmosphere of 1908 did not last long. Secessionist aspirations, especially in the Balkans, put their mark on politics. The government resorted to authoritarian measures, suppressing civic liberties, and even manipulated elections. Protracted uprisings in Albania and Yemen starting in 1910 undermined the trust in the future of the multiethnic empire further. Politically discredited and socially alienated from the masses, the CUP was totally deprived of its political influence by the time of the Italian invasion of Ottoman Tripoli (Libya) in 1911. It was the military debacle of the Balkan War of the following year, which resulted in the loss of practically all of "European Turkey," that signaled a new chance for the Young Turk cadres to seize power in Istanbul. In early 1913 the CUP staged a coup d'état, introducing a single-party dictatorship that was to last until 1918.

POLITICS OF CONFRONTATION

The Balkan Wars of 1912–1913 serve as a watershed in the development of the Young Turk–Armenian relations. Two shifts of policy seem significant in this regard. The first shift can be observed in the new approach of the CUP to the national question. Faced with a new wave of Muslim refugees from the Balkans, most Young Turks abandoned their Ottomanist egalitarian attitude and began to instrumentalize Muslim grievances in a campaign of defamation against non-Muslim populations. Thus, already in the first half of 1914 about 100,000 citizens of the Kingdom of Greece as well as Greek-Orthodox Ottoman subjects were compelled to leave Western Anatolia. Once World War I broke out, the deportation of Greek-Orthodox Ottomans continued, this time to places in the Anatolian interior (see Adanir, in press). The second shift occurred within the Armenian camp. In view of the catastrophic Ottoman defeat in the Balkan War as well as the fact that some Young Turk promises such as the one regarding the Armenian land issue had not materialized, the Armenian Revolutionary Federation decided to put the solution of the Armenian Question once again into the hands of the Great Powers (Hovannisian, 1967, pp. 30–32).

These changes led to a severe crisis in the Young Turk–Armenian relations in 1913 and 1914 when, upon a renewed great power intervention, the issue of the autonomy for the "Armenian provinces" became the subject of diplomatic bargaining. The Armenian insistence that only the sedentary population should be granted civil rights in the prospective autonomous region—a demand the fulfillment of which would have amounted in the CUP perspective to an unwarranted affront to the largely nomadic Kurds—

was the core of the dispute. The Armenians also wanted to keep the Muslim refugees out of the future autonomous province (Hovannisian, 1967, p. 33).

Already in December 1913, Djemal Pasha, the third man in the CUP leadership, warned his former Armenian colleagues that if they persisted in trying to get their way with the help of the Great Powers, "the Moslem population . . . will rise in arms, and three hundred to four hundred thousand Armenians will be massacred" (cited in Garo, 1990, p. 184), as was recorded in the memoirs of Garo Pasdermadjian, a member of the Ottoman parliament and the leader of the Armenian Revolutionary Federation in the Ottoman Empire. At the end of June 1914 the same Garo Pasdermadjian quarreled with the future Grand Vizier, Talat Pasha. Again the issue was the political rights of the nomadic Kurds. The Armenian leader shouted the following at Talat:

> Our national consciousness is so far advanced that we will prefer to demolish this great edifice called the Ottoman Empire, rather than permit you to see Armenia without Armenians. I know we shall remain under these ruins and suffer heavy losses. But in the last analysis, we shall emerge better off than you will . . . . We are the Armenian revolutionaries of yesteryear and we tell you what we have always said: We will not permit you to drive our working people out of our ancient land, for the benefit of nomadic Kurds. (cited in Garo, 1990, p. 191)

On the eve of the World War I, Armenian autonomy within the Ottoman Empire had become a reality; two European Christians were appointed as governor generals of the eastern provinces. But the internationalization of the Armenian Question boded ill for the future. The political leaders of the Armenian millet (the Patriarch, the Armenian communal assembly in Istanbul, the Armenian representatives in the Ottoman Parliament) were well aware of the gravity of the situation. Only a few weeks before the arrest of Armenian political leaders (April 24, 1915), Enver Pasha asked the Armenian Patriarch in a letter to use his influence with the nationalist leaders, so that these would show more moderation in such a critical time, as the Ottoman eastern front had collapsed, and the Entente navies were about to force their way into the Straits. According to what a close collaborator of the Patriarch reports, the matter was discussed in the Armenian communal assembly. But the majority disregarded the advice of the Patriarch and decided not to heed Enver Pasha's warnings of moderation. The prevailing mood was that the Armenian leaders could not afford losing favor with the Entente powers, whose entry into Constantinople was deemed a matter of a few weeks (Kévorkian, 1995, p. 286).

POLITICS OF "NATIONAL ECONOMY"

This catastrophic development should be seen against the background of Young Turk determination to replace the non-Muslim commercial groups with a Turkish national bourgeoisie, according to a policy inspired by the "national economy" of Friedrich List (see Ahmad, 1980, pp. 329–350; Alp, 1915; Landau, 1986, pp. 94–103). As early as 1904 a Turkish author, Akçura (see Akçura, 1981), had argued that Ottomanism as a viable policy had failed and that the future belonged to nationalism based on ethnic identity. Just as all other societies were involved in a "ceaseless conflict," the Turks too should aspire to increase their power even if this was detrimental to other groups (see also Georgeon, 1980, p. 21).

Such Darwinist perception of social relations became characteristic of mainstream Young Turk thinking, especially during World War I. It explains how a set of administrative measures could be elaborated as a comprehensive plan with a view to precipitating the Turkification of economic life: the compulsory use of Turkish as the language of business; a state-sponsored cooperative movement that worked against the non-Muslim merchant classes, state intervention in foreign trade, in currency transactions, in banking, and mass deportation of populations (see Göçek, 1996, pp. 108–116; Keyder, 1987, pp. 71–90; Toprak, 1982).

Thus in 1917, when the deportation of Armenians was an accomplished fact, Akçura expressed the view that

> just as the Jews and Germans constituted the bourgeoisie in Poland, in Turkey it was the native Jews, Greeks, and Armenians who were the agents and middlemen of European capitalism . . . . If the Turks fail[ed] to produce among themselves a bourgeois class. . .the chances of survival of a Turkish society composed only of peasants and officials [would] be very slim. (Akçura & Yurdu, cited in Berkes, 1964, p. 426)

However, we discern an equally Darwinist line of reasoning on the Armenian side as well. In the same year, 1917, Boghos Nubar Pasha, acting as the representative of Armenian national interests, demanded in a memorandum to the French government the creation of an Armenian state that should comprise the whole territory from the Caucasus to the Mediterranean. He justified this rather extravagant claim by using arguments that reflected the general intellectual, moral, and cultural climate of the era: Bogos Nubar pointed out that, before World War I, 2.1 million Armenians lived in the Ottoman Empire. Even though a relatively small minority (about 10% of the total population), the Armenians controlled 60% of the import business, 40% of the exports, and over 80% of the domestic trade. Hence one should not, he urged the French, be blinded by the quantitative aspect of population statistics but must rather recognize the "economic and moral" significance of the Armenian element (Beylerian, 1983, pp. 358–361).

THE ARMENIAN TRAGEDY IN RETROSPECT

The CUP decision to deport the Armenian population of Anatolia (Istanbul and Izmir being the only exceptions) was taken, to quote an American historian of Armenian background, "in desperation and panic. Not only were the Russians advancing in the east and the British and French navies threatening the capital, but the Armenians in Van had risen in revolt" (Suny, 1983, p. 16). As we have seen, there was also an ideological motivation behind that decision, as the Young Turk leadership was determined to preserve a territorial basis for the future Turkish nation-state. Muslim populations of Anatolia, in turn, feared expulsion; they could not help but be aware of the example of other Muslims who had been evicted from their Balkan or Caucasian homelands. In these circumstances, the CUP could rely on effective popular support, and consequently the deportation of the Armenians into the southern provinces of the empire was carried out under very hostile conditions. The deportees were plundered by local officials or antagonistic neighbors, were murdered by secret "Special Organization" agents, were attacked by bands of army deserters, or they fell victim to epidemic diseases. About half of the population deported perished on the way.[1]

What happened in 1915 is considered in retrospect as genocide. However, scholarly opinion is divided over the question of whether there was a premeditated plan to exterminate the Ottoman Armenians. The majority maintains that there was such a plan and that the genocide resulted primarily from racial and religious persecution of the Armenians by the Muslim Turks. If true, this would make the Armenian case appear quite similar to that of European Jewry under the Third Reich (see Dadrian, 1988b; Melson, 1992). A minority, however, is of the opinion that "the Genocide was, rather, a contingent event, initiated at a moment of imperial near-collapse," and that the catastrophe of 1915 "could be understood in the context of imperial decline, a fundamental re-conceptualization of the nature of the state along more nationalist and Pan-Turkish lines, and the radicalization of Young Turk policies in the fierce context of the First World War" (Suny, 1998, pp. 17–18; see also Dadrian, 1998a).

---

[1] Bogos Nubarian wrote in 1917, "Malgré le grand nombre des victimes des massacres et déportations, la majeure partie des Arméniens a pu s'échapper ou survivre à l'oeuvre d'extermination" [Despite the great number of the victims of the massacres and deportations, the majority of the Armenians managed to escape or survive the work of extermination.] (cited in Beylerian, 1983, p. 361).

The view taken in this chapter is obviously closer to this second interpretation. Looking at the matter from a historical angle, I have tried to focus on the progressive character of the development of Turkish–Armenian relations during the late Ottoman period. For those who espouse rather a postmodernist discourse, for those who consider history primarily the culture of remembrance whereby "memory has priority over what is remembered" (Ankersmit, 1989, p. 152), the approach of this chapter might seem inadequate.

REFERENCES

Adanir, F. (1998). Nicht-muslimische Eliten im Osmanischen Reich [Non-muslim elites in the Ottoman Empire]. In W. Höpken & H. Sundhaussen (Eds.), *Eliten in Südosteuropa: Rolle, Kontinuitäten, Brüche in Geschichte und Gegenwart* (pp. 49–68). Munich: Südosteuropa-Gesellschaft.

Adanir, F. (in press). The Greco–Turkish exchange of populations in Turkish historiography. In M. Cattaruzza, M. Dogo, & R. Pupo (Eds.), *Esodi. Trasferimenti forzati di popolazioni nei due dopoguerra: Europa centro-orientale, regione balcanico-egea, regione istro-dalmata.* Torino-Napoli: Edizioni Scientifiche Italiane.

Ahmad, F. (1980). Vanguard of a nascent bourgeoisie: The social and economic policy of the Young Turks, 1908–1918. In O. Okyar & H. Inalcik (Eds.), *Social and economic history of Turkey* (pp. 329–350). Ankara, Turkey: Hacettepe Üniversitesi.

Ahmad, F. (1982). Union relations with the Greek, Armenian, and Jewish Communities of the Ottoman Empire, 1908–1914. In B. Braude & B. Lewis (Eds.), *Christians and Jews in the Ottoman Empire* (Vol. 1, pp. 401–434). New York: Holmes & Meier.

Akçura, Y. (1981). Üç tarz-i siyaset [Three kinds of policy]. I. Fehmi, Trans. *Oriente Moderno, 61,* 11.

Alp, T. (1915). *Türkismus und Pantürkismus* [Turkism and Pan-turkism]. Weimar, Germany: G. Kiepenheuer.

Ankersmit, F. R. (1989). Historiography and postmodernism. *History and Theory, 28,* 137-153.

Atamian, S. (1955). *The Armenian community: The historical development of a social and ideological conflict.* New York: Philosophical Library.

Berkes, N. (1964). *The Development of Secularism in Turkey.* Montreal, Canada: McGill University Press.

Beylerian, A. (1983). *Les grandes puissances, l'Empire Ottoman, et les Arméniens dans les archives françaises (1914–1918).* Paris: Université de Paris I.

Braude, B., & Lewis, B. (Eds.). (1982). *Christians and Jews in the Ottoman Empire: The functioning of a plural society* (Vols. 1 & 2). New York: Holmes & Meier.

Dadrian, V. N. (1988a). The Armenian genocide and the pitfalls of a balanced analysis. *Armenian Forum, 1*(2), 73–130.

Dadrian, V. N. (1988b). The convergent aspects of the Armenian and Jewish cases of genocide: A reinterpretation of the concept of Holocaust. *Holocaust and Genocide Studies, 3*(2), 151–169.

Deringil, S. (1998). *The well-protected domains: Ideology and the legitimization of power in the Ottoman Empire, 1876–1909.* London: I. B. Tauris.

Duguid, S. (1973). The politics of unity: Hamidian policy in Eastern Anatolia. *Middle Eastern Studies, 9,* 139–155.

Dumont, P. (1980). L'Emigration des musulmans de Russie vers l'Empire ottoman au XIXème siècle: Aperçu bibliographique des travaux en langue turque [The immigration of muslims from Russia to the Ottoman Empire in the 19th century]. In *Les migrations internationales dela fin du XVIIIe siècle à nos jours* (pp. 212–218). Paris: Editions du CNRS.

Garo, A. (1990). *Bank Ottoman. Memoirs of Armen Garo: The Armenian Ambassador to America from the Independent Republic of Armenia* (H. T. Partizian, Ed. and Trans.). Detroit, MI: A. Topouzian.

Georgeon, F. (1980). *Aux origines du nationalisme turc: Yusuf Akçura (1876–1935).* Paris: Ed. ADPF.

Göçek, F. M. (1996). *Rise of the bourgeoisie, demise of empire: Ottoman westernization and social change.* New York: Oxford University Press.

Hanioğlu, M. S. (1995). *The Young Turks in opposition.* New York: Oxford University Press.

Hovannisian, R. G. (1967). *Armenia on the road to independence 1918.* Berkeley: University of California.

Kansu, A. (1997). *The revolution of 1908 in Turkey.* New York: E. J. Brill.

Karpat, K. H. (1990). The Hijra from Russia and the Balkans: The process of self-definition in the late Ottoman State. In D. F. Eickelman & J. P. Piscatori (Eds.), *Muslim travellers: Pilgrimage, migration, and the religious imagination* (pp. 131–252). Berkeley: University of California Press.

Kévorkian, R. H. (1995). R. P. Yervant P'erdahdjian: Événements et faits observés à Constantinople par le vicariat (patriarcal), 1914–1916 [Events and actions observed at the patriarchal vicariat]. *Revue d'histoire Arménienne Contemporaine, 1,* 247–287.

Keyder, Ç. (1987). *State and class in Turkey: A study in capitalist development.* London: Verso.

Landau, J. M. (1986). Munis Tekinalp's economic views regarding the Ottoman Empire and Turkey. In H. G. Majer (Ed.), *Osmanistische Studien zur Wirtschafts und Sozialgeschichte, in memoriam Vančo Boškov* (pp. 94–103). Wiesbaden, West Germany: O. Harrassowitz.

Langer, W. L. (1950). *The diplomacy of imperialism 1890–1902* (2nd ed.). New York: Knopf.

Mardin, Ş. (1983). *Jön türklerin siyasi fikirleri 1895–1908.* [Political ideas for the Young Turks, 2nd ed.]. Istanbul: Iletişim Yayınları.

McCarthy, J. (1996). *Death and exile: The ethnic cleansing of Ottoman Muslims 1821–1922.* Princeton, NJ: Darwin Press.

Melson, R. (1992). *Revolution and genocide: On the origins of the Armenian genocide and the Holocaust.* Chicago: University of Chicago Press.

Nalbandian, L. (1963). *The Armenian Revolutionary Movement: The development of Armenian political parties through the 19th century.* Berkeley: University of California Press.

Suny, R. G. (1983). *Armenia in the 20th century.* Chico, CA: Scholar's Press.

Suny, R. G. (1998). Empire and nation: Armenians, Turks, and the end of the Ottoman Empire, *Armenian Forum, 1*(2), 17–51.

Toprak, Z. (1982). *Türkiye'de Milli iktisat (1908–1918)* [National economy in Turkey, 1908–1918]. Ankara, Turkey: Yurt Yayınlari.

Turgay, A. Ü. (1991). Circassion immigration into the Ottoman Empire, 1856–1878. In W. B. Hallack & D. P. Little (Eds.), *Islamic studies* (pp. 193–217). Leiden, Germany: Brill.

van Bruinessen, M. (1978). *Agha, Shaikh and state: On the social and political organization of Kurdistan.* Utrecht, The Netherlands: Rijksuniversiteit.

6

THE ETHNIC ELEMENT IN THE CAMBODIAN GENOCIDE

BEN KIERNAN

The surrender of two of the last Khmer Rouge leaders, Nuon Chea and Khieu Samphan, to the Hun Sen government in December 1998, again brought the Cambodian genocide to international attention. What happened in Cambodia from 1975 to 1979 is less controversial than explanations for why it happened. It is now widely accepted that the death toll under the Khmer Rouge regime was closer to 2 million than to 1 million (for the most recent estimates, see Heuveline, 1998; Heuveline, chapter 7, this volume; Sliwinski, 1995). It is less widely known that over 800,000 peasants perished in the genocide, along with around the same number of urban dwellers (Kiernan, 1996, p. 458, Table 4). But it is now acknowledged that the total toll represented over 20% of Cambodia's population in less than four years. A recent legal study has noted the scholarly unanimity concerning the applicability of the term *genocide* in this case (Ratner & Abrams, 1997, p. 244). But the Cambodian tragedy is unique in its criminal intensity, except in the case of the Rwandan genocide, when possibly a similar number of victims were murdered in just a few months in 1994.

VARYING INTERPRETATIONS

Beyond that, there are widely differing interpretations of the nature of the Khmer Rouge regime and of the ideology that presided over this disaster. These interpretations tend to come in contending pairs, which may share a philosophical framework but conflict on matters of fact or interpretation. I will consider three pairs of viewpoints here (for recent analyses of the regime's practices, see Phim & Hinton, 1998).

The regime itself, which took the name Democratic Kampuchea (DK), considered that it was the "No. 1 Communist State" years, even 30 years, ahead of the other Asian Communist regimes (Kiernan, 1996, p. 25). Another view is that of historian David P. Chandler (1992) who, from an anti-communist political perspective, nevertheless has agreed that the Khmer Rouge were "the purest and most thoroughgoing Marxist–Leninist movement in an era of revolutions" (p. 3) and that the "socialist practice" of DK, "though more intense" (p. 4) was "standard operating procedure" (p. 49) in other communist revolutions. Here, two quite similar interpretations spring from opposing political standpoints.

In the second contending pair of interpretations, both sides have likewise agreed about the importance of China's role in DK. Hanoi has described the regime it overthrew as an example of Beijing's export of the Chinese Cultural Revolution and its imposition on Cambodia. This Maoist deviation from orthodox Marxism–Leninism (to which Hanoi proclaims adherence) proves the key role, in Hanoi's eyes, of China in the Cambodian tragedy ("Kampuchea Dossier II," 1978; Simonov, 1979). This mattered more to Hanoi than did other, possibly contradictory, analyses of DK, such as a Cambodian description of the "extremist and chauvinist tendency" of the Pol Pot group ('Surya' as cited in "Kampuchea Dossier I," 1978, p. 37). The main target of Hanoi's criticism, the Beijing regime, agreed with the assertion of its importance to Cambodia. But China predictably saw its own influence as positive. Beijing has described the Pol Pot period in Cambodian history as "the period of economic reconstruction."[1]

Historian Michael Vickery (1984), disagreeing with all four of these viewpoints, has described the Khmer Rouge as "a peasantist revolution of the purest sort" (p. 287)—in contrast to Chandler's view of it as "the purest" Marxism–Leninism. Not only did DK bear little resemblance to Marxism in Vickery's interpretation, but foreign influences more generally were "very nearly irrelevant." He saw DK as an indigenous peasant product, although its leaders exhibited "a peculiar hyper-chauvinism" (p. xii), particularly against Vietnam. Vickery was critical of the violence of the DK regime, but not for being communist or genocidal. In pointing to the "chauvinism" (p. 196) of DK (even while disputing the case for genocide against minority groups), Vickery was for long one of the few writers to give any attention to ethnic issues in the Cambodian genocide.

He was right to do so, although wrong to dismiss the Stalinist and Maoist influences on the Khmer Rouge. The "peasant revolution" thesis is hard to defend in the light of DK's deprivation of Cambodia's peasantry of their land, religion, and family life—three key features of peasant life anywhere. And the parallels with Maoism and Stalinism are clear, even if

---

[1] I am grateful to Penny Edwards for her translation of this phrase, which appeared in *Chinese in Cambodia* (1985).

Chandler incorrectly saw differences only in degree. But Vickery's description of Khmer Rouge "hyperchauvinism" is on the mark—even more so in places where he did not detect it. Other authors have failed to see it altogether (Heder, 1980, p. 1, for example, wrote merely that in DK "foreign influences and impingements were minimized").

What made the Cambodian revolution unique is the specific combination of communism and racism that led to genocide. The racism of DK, missed by all four previous analyses, is the variable that explains that uniqueness. I will now outline my view of these issues, in contrast to that of Vickery, but acknowledging his contribution along with that of other historians like Chandler.

POL POT'S RACISM

In 1949, Pol Pot was awarded a French government scholarship to study radio electricity in Paris. With a colleague, Mey Mann, he set out for France, traveling overland to Saigon to board ship. In the bustling, largely Chinese and Vietnamese city, Mey Mann later recalled that the two Cambodian youths felt like "dark monkeys from the mountains" (T. Sadler, personal communication, 1991).

As a student in Paris in the 1950s, Pol Pot (whose real name was Saloth Sar), used another revolutionary pseudonym: the "Original Khmer." The racialist and historical connotations of this term contrasted with the names chosen by other young revolutionaries in his circle: modernist, political, or class-based pseudonyms like "Free Khmer" or "Khmer Worker" (*Khemara Nisit*, 1952). Although he was a member of the French Communist Party, Pol Pot's ideology differed from that of many of his peers.

But Pol Pot was not unique. For instance, he was not the only one raised in the sheltered, conservative, mono-ethnic environment of Phnom Penh's royal palace. As I have argued elsewhere, the small circle of Khmer students in Paris who later formed the dominant core of DK leaders were mostly as feudal in their conceptions of Cambodia's territorial and demographic destiny as they were nationalist and anti-colonial, as preoccupied with issues of racial and national grandiosity as they were with communism, and as much anti-Vietnamese as anti-French. The four Thiounn brothers, for instance, descendants of two of the most powerful court families in Cambodia, complained in the 1940s that "Vietnamese intellectuals spoke of Angkor as their own." The Thiounns refused to even meet Ho Chi Minh, when invited at the time of the Fontainebleau conference in 1946. Their reason, given to the Yugoslav Communists at the time, "It is not right that a country as fertile as Kampuchea should have such a small population" (Kiernan, 1985, p. 30). This non sequitur is explicable only if these palace proletarians already saw Cambodia's population as a weapon against Vietnam. It would be many years before all four Thiounn brothers became leading officials of a regime that devastated that population by throwing it against their Vietnamese enemy and destroying the lives of a million fellow Khmers who did not share their policy priority.

These Khmer students in Paris trusted the Yugoslav Communists more, because of their independence from the Soviet Union. They saw this as a model for their own future relationship with Vietnam. In mid-1950, Pol Pot spent a month of his holidays participating in a work brigade near Zagreb. Although at the time he was a secret member of the French Communist Party, which had sided with Stalin against Tito in 1948, the national question intrigued Pol Pot as much as the ideological one. At that point, Yugoslavia was pursuing severe and voluntarist economic policies, including massive labor mobilization, the favoring of agricultural prices at the expense of urban living standards, and (in 1949–1950) enforced rural collectivization. Although this mixture of Stalinist and non-Stalinist policies may resemble those of DK a quarter century later, the point is that when Belgrade quickly reverted to fostering private peasant farming, Pol Pot, already back in Paris, appears not to have taken much notice. Yugoslavia was not so much an ideological as a national model (Kiernan, 1985, p. 120).

Similarly, while in Paris in the early 1950s, Pol Pot's future brother-in-law, Ieng Sary, made a close study of Stalin's writings on national minority policy as well as his technique of controlling the organizational structure of the Communist Party by "holding the dossiers" (Kiernan, 1985, pp. 120–121). The young Khmer Rouge had begun picking and choosing their future policies, irrespective of regime, on the basis of both racial/national and ideological priorities.

STALINISM AND RACISM

I was one of the first Westerners to publish an analysis of the Khmer Rouge death camp Tuol Sleng. In 1980, I likened it to the Lubyanka under Stalin and its inmates to Bukharin and Tukachevsky (Kiernan, 1980a). I had also earlier noted that "the ideology of the Pol Pot group drew upon Marxism-Leninism" (Kiernan, 1980b, p. 16). Others, however, discerned a Khmer Rouge "fascism" resembling Nazi ideology. Becker (1986), for example, noted that "fascism . . . led racial pogroms under Khmer Rouge rule" (p. 16), adding that "the Khmer Rouge adopted a philosophy of racial superiority and purity that resembled that of Nazi Germany" (p. 253). It is indeed impossible to explain the extraordinary virulence and violence of DK merely by reference to its Stalinist or Maoist antecedents. (In the 1995 book *Century of Genocide*, I called Khmer Rouge ideology an "amalgam" of

"Khmer elite chauvinism, Third World nationalism, the French revolution, Stalinism, and some aspects of Mao Tse-tung's Great Leap Forward . . . . The motor of the Pol Pot program was probably Khmer racist chauvinism, but it was fueled by strategies and tactics adopted from unacknowledged revolutionary models"; p. 449). No other communist regime eliminated one fifth of a nation's population in less than four years. It is necessary to take into account not only the social and political targets and ambitions of the Pol Pot group, but their racial and territorial preoccupations as well. The uniqueness of their revolution lay in its division of the population into categories that were both racial and political (for an earlier consideration of this issue, see Kiernan, 1998).

First, the Cambodian people were divided into two major groups: the "base people," the ethnic Khmer peasants of the rural areas long held by the revolutionaries, and the "new people" of the towns, contaminated by foreign influences. This fundamentally geographic distinction barely resembles Marxist–Leninist class analyses, which place importance on urban workers as well as rural peasants and distinguish workers from other urban classes such as the bourgeoisie. Moreover, onto this geographic division the Khmer Rouge grafted a racial and ideological hierarchy. The deportees, or "depositees," comprised the urban evacuees and the dispersed national minorities like the ethnic Chinese and Cham Muslims. The "candidates" were the rest of the new people conquered in 1975. And those with "full rights" were the base people, minus the rural ethnic minorities like the Cham.

The Cambodian case is notable for its combination of totalitarian political ambition and a racialist project of ethnic purification. DK was the only communist regime never to formally establish "autonomous zones" for its national minorities or even to publicly acknowledge their existence by name, and it was the only communist regime systematically to disperse its minorities by force and to forbid the practice not only of religion, but also of minority and foreign languages. Racial and ideological strands intertwined. The Cham Muslims, an ethnolinguistic group whose members belonged to a variety of social classes (peasants, artisans, workers, traders), fell victim to a purportedly social classification. This ethnic group was implicitly labeled by the Pol Pot group in 1973–1974 as uniquely unproletarian or petit bourgeois: "All nationalities have laborers, except for Islamic Khmers, whose lives are not so difficult." This nonsense was a clear-cut case of racial stereotyping in the interest of a policy of exclusion and ethnocide of the Chams. The Communist Party of Kampuchea (CPK) officials were ordered to "delay having them join the cooperatives" set up by the Party. "It is necessary to break up this group to some extent; do not allow too many of them to concentrate in one area" (Kiernan, 1996, p. 260).

Conversely, the liquidation of political opponents or potential dissidents of majority Khmer origin was often justified by a slogan with strong racialist connotations, in the name of wiping out those with "Khmer bodies and Vietnamese minds." Thus, political repression and ethnic cleansing went hand in hand. The minorities suffered a disproportionately high toll. One hundred percent of the Vietnamese who remained in DK after 1975, 50% of the Chinese, and 33% of the Cham all perished by 1979, compared to the national toll of around 20%. The toll among the ethnic Khmer was thus probably below 20%, even though, in absolute numbers, the majority of the DK regime's victims came from the Khmer majority (Kiernan, 1996, p. 458, Table 4).

THE ETHNIC PURGES

The first purges of the Khmer Rouge revolution were conducted against leaders and members of the CPK itself. During the 1970–1975 civil war, the Pol Pot leadership not only purged royalists and dissident Khmer revolutionaries, but also ruthlessly Khmerized the three ethnic minority branches of the Party apparatus. These were the ethnic Thai-dominated CPK branches in Koh Kong province on the border with Thailand, the tribal minority-dominated Northeast Zone branch on the borders with Laos and Vietnam, and the ethnic Cham "Eastern Zone Islamic Movement" sponsored by the CPK's Eastern Zone branch. From 1973 to 1975, the Koh Kong and Northeast party branches were purged of their minority leadership, who were replaced with ethnic Khmers loyal to the CPK Center. In 1974, the Eastern Zone Islamic Movement was disbanded. In all three cases, the repression provoked ethnic-based insurgencies, which sprung up along Cambodia's borders. (These resistance movements continued for several years and eventually provided many of the leaders of the post-Khmer Rouge regime; Kiernan, 1996, chapter 3.)

A major Cham rebellion broke out along the Mekong River, beginning in the Northern Zone in 1974 and reaching a peak in the Eastern Zone in July–September 1975. On November 30, 1975, a leading cadre in the Eastern Zone reported personally to Pol Pot that he had been unable to deport 150,000 people from the East as Pol Pot had ordered. The Cham people had been ordered dispersed into the Northern and Northwest Zones. The report to Pol Pot stated, "This withdrawal is the dispersal strategy according to the decision that you, Brother, had discussed with us earlier." However, officials in the two riverbank districts of the Northern Zone, where 50,000 deportees had been ferried from east of the Mekong, refused to take any "Islamic people," preferring "only pure Khmer people." The cadre reported that the Cham deportees had then been sent back to their own villages and that the Eastern Zone "will continue to do our best to keep charge of the Islamic people. This is not a problem." But, the cadre then asked, how did Pol Pot plan to reach the target of 150,000 deportees (Telegram No. 15, 1975)?

Here we see three different ethnic visions, as views of the place of the Chams in DK. First, Pol Pot (as in 1974) wanted the Chams "dispersed," that is, broken up as a community. Second, the Eastern Zone had agreed to deport 150,000 of them from the East "to keep them away from the Mekong River to help ease the atmosphere" along the river, that is, for political reasons. Third, Northern Zone officials took a racialist position and "absolutely refuse[d] to accept Islamic people," even after they had been shipped across the Mekong to reception points in the North. There was to be no place for Chams there, even dispersed across the Zone in small groups as Pol Pot had ordered. In the face of this refusal, the cadre in the East, pointing out the big problems experienced by the Cham deportees, had ferried them back to the Eastern Zone and "advised the Region and districts to take the Islamic people back to their villages" in Krauchhmar, Peamchi-leang, and Chhlong districts of Region 21. Moreover, "Over one hundred thousand additional Islamic people remain in the Eastern Zone. We only withdrew the people in important places along the river and at the [Vietnam-ese] border. We did not withdraw the people from Tbaung Khmum," a rice-growing district in the interior of the Zone. There was as yet no move to "disperse" the major concentration of Chams in the Eastern Zone, despite Pol Pot's instructions.

The East thus treated the Chams differently than the North, a Zone run by Ke Pauk, Pol Pot's warlord ally (until 1997). The official in the East speculated that "Comrade Pauk probably is not aware of these problems." But two months later, Ke Pauk himself sent Pol Pot a "report on the enemy situation." Pauk complained of "propaganda that the revolution is too strict." Enemies had "propagandized against the cooperatives." And "contradictions" had broken out in Chamkar Leu district of his Northern Zone. "The enemies were former [Lon Nol] soldiers, Islamic people, and former chiefs of the cooperatives," he explained. It is unlikely that Pauk would have welcomed "enemies" such as Islamic Chams to his Zone. And it is even more unlikely that both reception points in two different districts in Pauk's Zone would have refused to take them without his knowledge or approval (quotations are from Telegram No. 94, 1976).

Ethnic politics was a litmus test for the Khmer Rouge leadership. In 1978, in a brutal campaign directed by the Center and spearheaded by Pauk's Northern Zone units, the Eastern Zone was purged both of Chams and of the local CPK branch, which had failed to deport most of them and had accepted the rest back.

Meanwhile, the Khmer Rouge victory of April 1975 had brought Cambodia's cities under CPK control for the first time. The cities were seen as the strongholds, not only of the defeated Lon Nol regime, its protector the United States, and other foreign influences, but also of various Cambodian social groups. These included the Khmer feudal, commercial, and intellectual classes, and also the ethnic Chinese and Vietnamese minorities who in fact were a majority of the urban population and especially of the commercial and working classes of Phnom Penh. Evacuating the cities, as the Khmer Rouge did in 1975, effectively Khmerized the urban areas, as well as destroying any chances for a political resurgence of the supporters of Lon Nol or Sihanouk. The towns henceforth became the home of a small number of ethnic Khmer CPK cadres and army units (cleansed of their Cham fellow combatants in 1975; Kiernan, 1996, pp. 263–264).

In the first official meeting of his new Cabinet, held on April 22, 1976, Pol Pot announced that "Vietnam is a black dragon" that "spits its poison" (Kiernan, 1996, p. 111). As the final conflict with Hanoi broke into open warfare in January 1978, Pol Pot urged his forces to "kill the enemy at will, and the contemptible Vietnamese will surely shriek like monkeys screeching all over the forest" (Kiernan, 1996, p. 387). On May 10, 1978, DK radio broadcasted an appeal to "purify our armed forces, our Party, and the masses of the people"—ironically, "in defence of Cambodian territory and the Cambodian race." The radio added,

> [Each] one of us must kill thirty Vietnamese. . . . So far, we have succeeded. . . . Using these figures, one Cambodian soldier is equal to 30 Vietnamese soldiers. . . . We should have two million troops for 60 million Vietnamese. However, two million troops would be more than enough to fight the Vietnamese, because Vietnam has only 50 million inhabitants. We need only two million troops to crush the 50 million Vietnamese, and we would still have six million people left. (*BBC Summary of World Broadcasts*, 1978)

REFERENCES

BBC Summary of World Broadcasts. (1978, May 15). FE/5813/A3/2, translated text of Phnom Penh Radio broadcast, May 10, 1978.

Becker, E. (1986). *When the war was over*. New York: Simon & Schuster.

Chandler, D. P. (1992). *Brother number one*. Boulder, CO: Westview.

Chinese in Cambodia. (1985). Guangxi, China: People's Publishing House.

Heder, S. (1980). *From Pol Pot to Pen Sovan to the villages*. Bangkok: Chulalongkorn University.

Heuveline, P. (1998). Between one and three million: Towards the demographic reconstruction of a decade of Cambodian history (1970–1979). *Population Studies, 52*, 49–65.

"Kampuchea Dossier I." (1978). *Vietnam Courier*, p. 37.

"Kampuchea Dossier II." (1978). *Vietnam Courier*, pp. 8–9.

Khemara Nisit (Paris), No. 14, August 1952.

Kiernan, B. (1980a, May 2). Bureaucracy of death: Documents from inside Pol Pot's torture machine. *New Statesman*, pp. 649–650, 669–676.

Kiernan, B. (1980b). Conflict in the Kampuchean communist movement. *Journal of Contemporary Asia*, 10(1/2), 16.

Kiernan, B. (1985). *How Pol Pot came to power*. London: Verso.

Kiernan, B. (1995). The Cambodian genocide, 1975–1979. In S. Totten, W. Parsons, & I. Charny (Eds.), *Century of genocide*. New York: Garland.

Kiernan, B. (1996). *The Pol Pot regime: Race, power and genocide in Cambodia under the Khmer Rouge, 1975–1979*. New Haven, CT: Yale University Press.

Kiernan, B. (1998, May 14). Penser le génocide au Cambodge. *Le Monde, p. 17.*

Phim, T. S., & Hinton, A. L. (1998). *Anthropologies of the Khmer Rouge* (Working Paper No. 6). New Haven, CT: Yale Center for International and Area Studies, Genocide Studies Program.

Ratner, S., & Abrams, J. (1997). *Accountability for human rights atrocities in international law: Beyond the Nuremberg legacy*. Oxford, England: Clarendon Press.

Simonov, V. (1979). *Kampuchea: Crimes of Maoists and their rout*. Moscow: Novosti.

Sliwinski, M. (1995). *Le génocide Khmer Rouge: Une analyse démographique*. Paris: L'Harmattan.

Telegram No. 15, To Comrade Brother Pol with respect, signed Chhon. (1975, November 30). Original held at Documentation Center of Cambodia, Phnom Penh, DC-Cam Document No. N0001045 (01 bbk).

Telegram No. 94, To Brother Pol with respect, signed "Comrade Pauk." (1976, February 4). Original held at Documentation Center of Cambodia, Phnom Penh, DC-Cam Document No. N0001187 (02 bbk).

Vickery, M. (1984). *Cambodia 1975–1982*. Boston: South End.

7

APPROACHES TO MEASURING GENOCIDE: EXCESS MORTALITY DURING THE KHMER ROUGE PERIOD

PATRICK HEUVELINE

One does not take on a commissioned title such as "Measuring Geno-cide" without a wave of doubt. At first, there is a seeming contradiction in juxtaposing the two terms: between the punctilious, detached, and slow process of measurement and the collective, empathic, and urgent response due to the victims of genocide. Thus, the merit of this mildly provocative title is perhaps to raise a few questions before embarking on measurement issues. Before even wondering how, should we question measuring genocide at all? A first issue is whether the respect due to the immense suffering of the victims makes genocide an improper subject of scholarly investigation. A second issue is whether a measurable dimension of genocide exists.

The former issue has often been answered by historians and other scholars pointing out that silence only benefits the perpetrators and that the moral obligation to the victims is to precisely and indisputably document the crime of genocide. However, the issue for scholars is rarely to break the silence; more often it is to challenge previous accounts. My argument—here and in all of this chapter—rests on examples drawn from my experience in Cambodia and my research on the Khmer Rouge period (1975–1979), but I hope my points are relevant not only to that time and place. When I first went to Cambodia in 1992, journalists' accounts routinely referred to the 1 million victims of the Khmers Rouges. Demographers are trained to be skeptical about data, and my uninformed suspicion was that such a figure must incorporate a generous amount of rounding, most likely upward, given the tendency to select the more sensational as newsworthy. Results from my research turned out to be about twice the 1 million mark; but what if the numbers had been much lower than the consensual figure of the time? Is the moral obligation then to revise downward?

The title I chose to first describe my research, "Between One and Three Million in Cambodia" (Heuveline, 1998) bears the mark of these early doubts. Borrowed from a phrase in Margaret Drabble's (1991) beautiful novel, *Gates of Ivory*, this title was not meant to summarize my results but rather to refer to the incredible disparities among existing estimates. This novel is only one of many representing the symbolic shift of Cambodia in Western imagination from an idealized peaceful society to infernal labor camps, and from the construction of Angkor to the devastation of Angka. That Cambodia was not simply called upon to evoke recent atrocities, but also to symbolize a place where people and information disappear is what made it relevant to a demographic perspective. The narrator expresses dismay not just at what happened, but at our uncertainty about perhaps the most basic: How many people died in these tragic years? To add another figure to the set of disparate estimates already available thus seemed to matter less than to understand how such different figures could have been produced by good-faith scholars.

Appreciating the necessary uncertainty of any estimation approach is essential to understand this disparity, and I believe that documenting it largely addresses the above-mentioned moral issue. Thus, my discussion of the different approaches will concentrate as much on margins of error as on estimates. Another reason for past estimates to differ leads us to the second issue raised: What should be measured? In Cambodia, differences across estimates came in part from different criteria being used to define the deaths attributable to the Khmers Rouges. Whereas an increase in the number of deaths is perhaps the most tangible effect of an attempted genocide, the total number of deaths is not the most appropriate measure, because "normal" mortality is included, that is, mortality that would have occurred even under more favorable circumstances.

Most authors agree to concentrate on excess mortality. The reference period for that excess mortality is often less clearly delineated. Mortality typically returns to normal levels several years after a mortality "crisis." In Cambodia, many died in a severe famine immediately after the Khmers Rouges were overthrown. Should these additional deaths be attributed to the Khmer Rouge regime that had ended some months earlier? And should *all* additional deaths contribute to a measurement of genocide?

In Article 2 of the 1946 declaration of the Convention on the Prevention and Punishment of the Crime of Genocide adopted by the United Nations in 1951, *genocide* is defined as acts committed with the intent to destroy a population. In Cambodia, many people were executed, but many also died because of increases in malnutrition and disease. These deaths were the results of drastic changes in the conditions of life inflicted to the population of Cambodia (forced migration, overwork, and starvation) reflecting perhaps as much the incompetence of the Khmer Rouge leaders as their intent to kill massively. To classify deaths in such a way is probably impossible, and although I will discuss the estimation of the main causes of deaths, deciding what constitutes a genocide is eventually beyond a demographer's expertise. In addition, the "legal" definition of genocide opposes the deliberate targeting of some subpopulation (e.g., ethnic minorities) as opposed to the general population. Although Ben Kiernan (1996) has documented the ethnic dimension of mortality during the Khmer Rouge years, my discussion will remain at the level of the general population and global death toll. The same estimation techniques can be applied to subpopulations, however, as long as they are defined by individual characteristics that are fixed at birth. If group membership depends on characteristics that may change over the life course, the matter becomes much more complicated.

In the first part of this chapter, I present different approaches to estimating the total number of excess deaths between 1975 and 1979, including during the 1979 famine. The approaches are lumped into two categories: the sample approach and the residual approach. The *sample approach* consists of estimating excess mortality from a sample and extrapolating it to the entire population. The *residual approach* compares the total size of the group projected under "normal" conditions to the actual size of the group after the mortality crisis. The difference, or residual, is assumed to represent excess mortality. (Mortality estimates cited throughout this chapter are summarized in Tables 7.1 and 7.2.) In the second part of the chapter, I discuss how the different causes contributing to excess mortality can be disentangled. Clearly, mortality increase is only one of the effects of an attempted genocide. But as will be illustrated, some issues are already intractable when dealing with death, one of the most basic human events; the

TABLE 7.1
Estimates of Excess Mortality in Cambodia, 1975–1979,
by Type of Approach

Reference	Mortality Estimate
Sample Approach	
Sliwinski (1995)	1.864–1.869 million
Kiernan (1996)	1.5–1.7 million
Heder (1997)	1.5 million
Residual Approach	
Ea (1981, 1987)	1.0–1.2 million
Vickery (1984, 1988)	700,000–1 million
Banister & Paige Johnson (1993)	1.05 million
Heuveline (1998)	2.2 million
	[= midpoint of a range of estimate from 700,000–3.2 million]

TABLE 7.2.
Estimates of the Number of Executions in Cambodia, 1975–1979,
by Type of Approach

Reference	No. of Estimated Executions
Sample Approach	
Sliwinski (1995)	727,000–840,000
Heder (1997)	750,000
Residual Approach	
Ea (1981)[a]	120,000
Vickery (1988)[a]	350,000–500,000
Heuveline (1998)[b]	1.1 million
	[= midpoint of a range of estimate from 600,000–2.0 million]

Note. [a]Estimates derived from ancillary data, not from the residual approach. [b]Includes other violent deaths, from warfare in particular.

measurement of other potential dimensions of genocide is likely to be even more challenging.

MEASUREMENT OF EXCESS MORTALITY

Complete vital registration systems—the continuous recording of births and deaths—provide the most suitable data for mortality analyses. To the extent that such systems are maintained by a central authority, these data are unlikely to be usable in a case of genocide. In many situations, an attempted genocide would take place in a context of political turmoil and of a general failure of the central authority. When the perpetrators are capable of accurate record keeping of such acts (for the Khmers Rouges, see Kiernan, 1996), however, the records available for objective analysis will typically be too partial or too incomplete to provide a reliable basis for measurement.

The discussion will thus focus on indirect techniques to measure events, that is, deaths that could not be directly observed at the time. The different approaches have been lumped into two groups depending on the data being used. The sample approach uses survey data, such as interviews, which provide fairly detailed information on a small segment of the population. The residual approach uses census data that provide much more basic information but for the entire population.

The Sample Approach

The sample approach consists of collecting data on a small segment of the population and extrapolating measured proportions from the sample to the whole population. In Cambodia, several scholars have conducted interviews with survivors of the Khmer Rouge regime and estimated mortality among their family members. Because genocide is characterized by the targeting of specific ethnic, racial, or religious groups, it is essential to include people from different groups in the sample and to weigh the excess mortality risks in each group in order to represent the average risk in the original population.

Ben Kiernan was probably the first to use this approach, interviewing about 100 people in France in 1979 and 400 in Cambodia in 1980. His first estimate was 1.5 million excess deaths, later revised upward to 1.671 million (Kiernan, 1996, pp. 456–460). Stephen Heder (personal communication, 1997) obtained a similar estimate from 1,000 interviews in different parts of Cambodia and at the Thai border in 1980 and 1981. Respondents were asked about the survival of each parent, child, and sibling alive in 1970. They were divided into urban versus rural groups, and further into Khmer versus Chinese groups for the former, or by geographical origin for the latter (zone under governmental control in 1975 or not), in order to obtain separate mortality risks for these four groups. These risks were applied to the estimated population size of each group to obtain the number of deaths in each group and in the 1970 population of Cambodia. An estimate of the normal number of deaths since 1970 was subtracted then to obtain a number of excess deaths, slightly over 1.5 million.

In the most recent attempt following this approach, Marek Sliwinski (1995) conducted interviews between 1989 and 1991 with about 60 families living in France, 600 in refugee camps in Thailand, and 600 people living around Phnom Penh. Again, the survival of each parent, child, sibling, and spouse was recorded, from which sex- and age-specific mortality risks were estimated. An estimated population by age and sex for 1970 was then used to derive the total number of deaths. The author estimated at 25% the proportion of excess deaths between 1975 and 1979, leading him to a low estimate of 1.864 million and a high estimate of 1.869 million.

While adding credibility to these figures, the near agreement of these estimates is quite surprising. Uncertainty is inherent to any estimation process. The margin of error cannot be assessed in the examples just given, but it is probably quite higher than suggested by the proximity of the central estimates (1.5, 1.7, or 1.9 million). The foremost concern is the representativeness of the sample, or to which extent the proportion estimated on the sample population can be applied to the entire population. This common concern in statistics is typically addressed by looking at how people are selected and how many people are interviewed. The above-mentioned samples are small but not unusually so. If people had been randomly chosen from the population of interest, sample sizes of that order would lead to a margin of error of only a few percent. Unfortunately, in Cambodia, as in probably many places where genocide is being investigated, the ideal conditions of the underlying statistical model cannot be met.

The authors' efforts to stratify their sample into different subpopulations clearly show that they appreciated that the individual probability to be interviewed were not even. Yet, we may still doubt that the interviewed people are representative of their subpopulations, and critical information of selection procedures are often lacking to prove otherwise. I certainly would not want to sound too harsh about the possible shortcomings of early attempts to collect some data in post–Khmer Rouge Cambodia. One can only imagine the formidable constraints on doing research there and then. These data are rare and invaluable. My point is only that, for measurement purposes, one cannot assess their applicability to the entire country. Sliwinski's more recent research appears methodologically more sophisticated, yet he interviewed mostly people living around the capital city, Phnom Penh, who might not represent the rest of the country. In any event, although a margin of error cannot be computed for these estimates, we cannot reasonably expect them to be accurate within the traditional limits of a few percentage points.

A second common concern is data quality. People exaggerate, people forget, and sometimes they simply do not know. About the exaggeration, nothing can be done but to acknowledge that victims—especially refugees or emigrants—are susceptible to providing a more dramatic version of facts. Omissions might be rare for such traumatic events but still should increase over time (Sliwinski's interviews were conducted 10 to 16 years after the facts). In the earlier interviews people may not know what happened to their immediate family members. In Cambodia, it often took several years for people to trace lost family members back through programs such as the International Red Cross.

These problems are nothing but classic statistical issues common to all surveys, but there are made more critical by the context of the investigation. A more important concern is how the sample is being constituted. Even if interviewees were randomly selected from the surviving population in Cambodia and abroad, the described approach imposes a strict filter on the probability of being drawn into the sample population. At least one of the immediate relatives of a person must be alive at the time of the survey for that person's experience (death or survival) to have a chance to be recorded. In other words, the sample is not drawn from the population alive in Cambodia before the Khmers Rouges took the power, but from those who had a parent, child, or sibling still alive at the time of the survey. In particular, this approach would not record an entire family "disappearing" during these years. For that filter not to bias the estimates, one would have to hypothesize that the probabilities of survival of the relatives are independent. When we expect members of certain groups to have been specifically targeted, this assumption cannot be made. The longer after the events the interviews are conducted, the more the sample comes from a "selected" group (the interviewees had to survive longer).

To summarize, a margin of error cannot be estimated for the probability of dying that is computed from samples of survivors' relatives. Some aspects of the data collection tend to overestimate the true probability, some others to underestimate it. Overall, the estimated proportions might not be incorrect, but they cannot be very precise either. Furthermore, the estimates of the number of excess deaths depend not only on the earlier cited proportions for each subpopulation, but also on the respective population sizes in 1975. Even these figures are highly uncertain in a country like Cambodia where the last census was conducted in 1962. To take a numerical example consistent with the cited interviews results, a survey may yield an average probability of dying—in excess of normal mortality—of 25% for the entire population, while the population size of Cambodia is estimated at 7.5 million in 1975. The corresponding figure is then 1.875 million excess deaths. In my view, we only have some confidence about the probability of excess death being between, say, 20% and 30% and the population size between 7 and 8 million, which in fact allows for estimated numbers of excess deaths of anywhere between 1.4 and 2.4 million. As I discussed earlier, this is speculative, because there is no way of assessing the sampling error for nonrandomly selected samples, but it seems to me that the several gray areas in this approach should prevent us from attaching too much confidence to any of the figures derived from the sample approach without an interval at least that wide.

The Residual Approach

The residual approach rests on the basic identity of population accounting (Preston, Heuveline, & Guillot, 2001), using the following equation where $P(t)$ and $P(t+n)$ are the population size at time t and $t+n$ respectively, while $B(t,t+n)$, $D(t,t+n)$, $I(t,t+n)$, and $O(t,t+n)$ are respectively the number of births, deaths, and migrations in and out between time t and $t+n$:

$$(1)\ P(t + n) = P(t) + B(t, t + n) - D(t, t + n) + I(t, t + n) - O(t, t + n)$$

The narrator of the *Gates of Ivory*, Liz, is right: People do not disappear. There are only two ways to leave a population, death and emigration, as there are only two ways to enter a population, birth and immigration. Typically, this identity is used to estimate population over time, from an earlier census and estimates or records of the number of births, deaths, and migrations in and out. When two population censuses are available, the same identity is used to check the consistency of those and the estimated number of births, deaths, and migrants between the two census dates. Such a check does not indicate that the figures are correct but simply that they are internally consistent. The process of gradual adjustment toward internally consistent figures has been used most in historical demography and is known as *demographic reconstruction*.

The same process can be used to estimate excess mortality during any past period. To the extent that we know the population size at the beginning and at the end of the period of interest, and the number of births, number of deaths under normal conditions, and number of migrations in and out during the period, we could attribute any inconsistency or difference to excess mortality, using the following equation where $D^*(t,t+n)$ is now the number of deaths that would have been expected under normal conditions between time t and $t+n$, and $E(t,t+n)$ is the number of excess deaths between time t and $t+n$ defined as the difference between $D(t,t+n)$ and $D^*(t,t+n)$:

$$(2)\ E(t, t + n) = P(t)–P(t + n) + B(t, t + n)–D^*(t, t + n) + I(t, t + n)–O(t, t + n)$$

The number of excess deaths comes as residual element of the demographic reconstruction, unaccounted for by other components of population change. The possible errors come from census figures and other estimates, because any deviation from actual values is attributed to excess mortality.

This method has been applied to estimate the number of excess deaths caused by the Khmers Rouges, and it typically provided lower figures than those obtained by the sample approach—about 1 million or less. Ea (1981) was possibly the first to use this framework with a first estimate at 1.0 million, later revised upward to 1.2 million (Ea, 1987). The lowest estimate, I believe, is 740,000 from Michael Vickery (1984), who also slightly increased his estimate over time and later suggested the range of 700,000 to 1 million (Vickery, 1988).

Judith Banister and Paige Johnson (1993) used a finer approach than the basic identity for total population, the cohort–component projection model. This model simply disaggregates by age and sex, using the accounting framework in equation 1, which is an improvement in two respects. First, because the risk of dying and giving birth are strongly age- and sex-dependent, a model that incorporates the age-and-sex structure of the population over time should provide better estimates of the total number of deaths and births in that population. Second, the residual number, the estimate of excess mortality, is derived by age and sex. Banister and Paige Johnson's results are not very different, however, from previous residual estimates: 1.05 million excess deaths between 1975 and 1979.

Again, the near agreement of these authors is comforting at first but equally puzzling. These figures may seem to indicate that this approach provides robust estimates of excess mortality in the period whereas our demographic knowledge of Cambodia suggests otherwise. As was mentioned earlier, the last census was conducted in 1962. Jacques Migozzi (1973) analyzed this census and prepared different population projection scenarios that provide a plausible interval for the 1975 population size. Another demographer, Georges Siampos (1970), had also checked the census figures and provided quite different estimates of mortality and fertility than Migozzi had used in his projections (Heuveline, 1998). Even a small difference in the estimated rate of population growth in Cambodia in the 1960s and first part of the 1970s could amount to a 5% or larger difference in the estimated population size for 1975. Furthermore, neither of these careful demographers could anticipate the civil war and the disruptions of the early 1970s. Several hundred thousand Vietnamese were expelled or fled the country in the early 1970s. According to an often-quoted estimate—whose source I have not been able to trace—600,000 people died as a result of the civil war and the American bombings between 1970 and 1975. Banister and Paige Johnson argued that this figure is much too high, and a comparison with estimates of Vietnamese casualties during the "American" war suggests so as well (Barbieri, Allman, Pham, & Nguyen, 1995; Hirschman, Preston, & Vu, 1995). Finally, the impact of the civil war on births is unknown. For all these reasons, I have suggested that the 1975 population size might be anywhere between 7 and 8 million.

The most problematic element of past reconstruction efforts, however, is the size of the population after the Khmers Rouges. In short, one finds estimates of the 1980 total population size ranging from 5.7 million (U.S. Bureau of the Census, 1991, A-5) to 7.0 million (Banister & Paige Johnson, 1993, pp. 91–93). If we accept the ranges of population size as plausible, 7 to 8 million in 1975 and 5.7 to 7.0 million in 1980, the actual population change between 1975 and 1980 can be anywhere between 0 and −2.3 million. The residual number of excess deaths between 1975 and 1980 depends on that difference between the actual population change and the expected population change (equation 2), so the uncertainty about the estimated residual is at least as large as 2.3 million.

To improve the precision of the residual estimates, I have suggested the use of registration data collected by the United Nations in preparation for the 1993 elections (Heuveline, 1998). These data are usually not suitable for demographic analysis because they are too incomplete. Having participated in the electoral registration process in Cambodia and witnessed the determination to register most eligible voters, I felt, however, that these data might not be so incomplete and that given the paucity of our data on the current demographic situation in Cambodia, they could actually be quite useful. The most serious limitation of electoral data is its coverage of only people age 18 and older. Fortunately, that was not a problem for the estimation of excess mortality in the 1975 population, because these people were already 18 in 1993.

Another problematic feature of electoral data turned to an advantage in this exercise. Eligibility to vote is often restricted to a segment of the population, and electoral registrars can then be quite different from the de facto population of the country at the time. But the criteria used in these elections (see United Nations, 1995) made the registered population much more comparable to the 1975 population. Recent (post-1980) immigrants from Vietnam were not able to register, whereas Cambodians abroad were, in particular those still in refugee camps at the Thai border. This largely reduces the impact on the estimates of the large and undocumented migration flows across Cambodia. As for the quality of these data, the intuition of a decent coverage was confirmed by the analysis of the 1996 demographic survey, suggesting that the electoral registrars might have missed about 6% of the eligible population (Huguet, 1997), a rate that is not very far from typical census undercoverage in developing countries.

I have insisted somewhat more than strictly necessary for my present purpose on the potential values of United Nations data because, in many other contexts, similar, less conventional sources of data might be available but as yet unused. U.N. missions are often among the first to collect data after political turmoil, in the context of peace keeping or electoral assistance. Although they might be willing to provide these data for scholarly investigation, they will not make the effort to advertise those.

To investigate the uncertainty of residual estimates of excess deaths, I attempted to reconstruct demographic changes in Cambodia between the 1962 census and the 1993 electoral lists. As I have discussed, there are many sets of internally consistent parameters that will provide different residuals. For each parameter of the reconstruction, I thus assigned not only a most likely value, but also a minimum and a maximum value. By combining these minima and maxima, one can obtain the largest and the smallest possible residuals. The extreme values thus obtained for the number of excess deaths between 1975 and 1979 are 700,000 and 3.2 million, and the central value is 2.2 million. One may find the results inconclusive, given the very large range of estimates. They do explain, however, the dispersion of previous estimates. Given the little we know about critical parameters, by choosing low values or high values, different people could derive estimates as different as 700,000 or 3.2 million and still be consistent with available data.

The central values yield an estimate that is above 2 million and is higher than previous assessments. Although the interval of possible values around this central estimate is large, not all values within the interval are equally likely. This is somewhat difficult to quantify because the interval is not a confidence interval in the statistical sense. Each possible demographic reconstruction involves a purely deterministic simulation, and no random process is involved. Nevertheless, to derive an extreme figure such as 3.2 million would require selecting each parameter at the extreme of its plausible range. In that sense, extreme values are stretching available data to the limits, and the corresponding residuals appear much less likely than central values, whereas anything outside the minimum and maximum estimates must be extremely unlikely.

Having insisted so far on the necessity to provide some idea about the confidence interval in any estimation process, even I realize that too large an interval is of limited interest for many and could not long resist the pressure to provide at least a narrower range. There are two ways to attempt doing so. The first one is to think about the minimum–maximum range as a very, very likely confidence interval, say 99%. For a normal distribution, a 99% confidence interval is obtained by taking 2.6 standard errors on each side of the mean. Two standard errors still provide a 95% confidence interval, and a single standard error leaves a 68% confidence interval. Applying this analogy, the minimum–maximum interval suggests that an interval from 1.0 to 3.0 million would still include the exact value with a 95% chance, and even an interval from 1.6 to 2.6 million would still have a two thirds chance of including the exact value. Interestingly, this pseudo 68% confidence interval is similar to the 1.5 to 2.5 million interval suggested in the discussion of the sample approach.

The second way to reduce the interval is more demographic in nature. Because the range of each parameter contributes to the increase in the residual range, the latter can be decomposed by demographic components. Not surprisingly, doing so suggests that the largest factor of uncertainty is international migration between 1970 and 1980. An examination of the data sources for these migrations clearly indicates the limits of uncertainty reduction. These data are so poorly documented that we cannot attach any confidence to net migration estimates, give or take 300,000 people. This implies that the range of 1.5 million to 2.5 million excess deaths cannot really be further narrowed from a purely demographic perspective.

To summarize before moving on to specific causes of death, neither the sample approach nor the demographic approach can provide precise estimates in the context of Cambodia. If the residual approach has yielded lower figures, that is not intrinsically due to the different methods. The benefit of the residual approach is to provide an estimation range, although here the interval is made extremely wide by the demographic uncertainties about Cambodia since 1970. There is no reason to believe, however, that the estimates yielded by the sample approach are any more precise. In post–Khmer Rouge Cambodia, the practical conditions of sample selection are simply too far from those who would validate the extrapolation of sample results to the entire population.

MEASUREMENT OF SPECIFIC CAUSES OF DEATHS

In a context such as the post–Khmer Rouge Cambodia, the uncertainty concerning the population of interest hampers the extrapolation of sample results to the entire population and the assessment of the precision of the estimation. The benefit of the sample approach is to provide much more information than a simple count of events. Respondents' characteristics can be used to study how the probability of survival varies in the population (for an example on Vietnam War mortality, see Merli, 1988). Although the demographic techniques of the residual approach might be more appropriate to measure the total number of deaths in certain difficult contexts, they provide little further information. I discuss these features of the two approaches with respect to the assessment of the different causes of death responsible for the excess mortality in Cambodia from 1975 to 1979.

The Sample Approach

Interviews with relatives permit us to ask directly about causes of death. This common strategy has often been used and discussed in the epidemiological and demographic literature. The validity of the relatives' assessment is often questionable, but here I will limit myself to the main large categories of causes of death in Cambodia—warfare, execution, famine, and natural death—which reduces the risk of misclassification of death by witnesses. Misclassification remains quite possible, however, because many families were separated, and even relatives might not have witnessed the death they are reporting.

The data from interviews suggest that executions by the Khmers Rouges and famine were the main causes of death during the period and roughly to the same extent. Heder (personal communication, 1997) found that about 50% of the excess deaths were due to executions perpetrated by the Khmers Rouges. Sliwinski (1995) provided a finer breakdown from his interviews with executions still representing 36% of those deaths; famine, 33%; natural death, 10%; and combat, 2%. The remaining 13% were people who were reported to have disappeared.

The fact that these proportions cannot be confidently extrapolated to the entire population of Cambodia need not be repeated here. The critical issue is no longer the existence of potential biases making the sample population unrepresentative, however, but whether any of these biases affects some causes of death more than some other causes. For example, if a certain subpopulation that has been particularly targeted by the Khmers Rouges is overrepresented in the sample, the mortality estimates would be pulled upward, but that might not affect the relative distribution of causes of death.

Although the results should be accepted only with an ample margin of error, these authors seem again to concur. Heder's proportion corresponds to 750,000 deaths from execution. Sliwinski's estimate is 727,000, using 39% of his lower total estimate. That some of the disappeared people were actually killed is likely, and the estimate might be increased to around 840,000, using a proportion of 45% and his higher total estimate.

The Residual Approach

The balancing identity of population change does not provide any further information on the residual. Scholars who used that approach to assess excess mortality resorted to ancillary data to separate those deaths by causes. Vickery (1988) used oral accounts and came up with an impressionistic 50% estimate of total excess deaths as being the result of executions. The proportion is thus similar to those cited earlier but lead to estimates of only 350,000 to 500,000 executions, because his estimates of all excess deaths is significantly lower. Ea (1981) felt that even these figures are too high. Adding up annual estimates of executions, he argued that any estimate higher than 120,000 for the entire Khmer Rouge period would be "totally unrealistic" (p. 211).

If the balancing identity of population change is used for each age cohort (i.e., in a cohort–component population projection framework), some additional information is available to the analyst: the age structure of these excess deaths. Demographers have long studied age patterns of mortality, and Preston (1976), in particular, showed that an age structure of mortality reflects the relative prevalence of the different underlying causes of death. An examination of the age structure of excess deaths for males and females clearly suggests some unusual causes of deaths. Notwithstanding important geographical variations, typical age patterns of mortality are characterized by a J shape, that is, with highest mortality at extreme ages, decreasing very fast after birth, and increasing more gradually at older ages. When normal mortality increases, age-specific death rates tend to increase proportionally so that although they are higher in all age groups, the overall structure continues to follow a J pattern. Even in historical cases of famine, the youngest and the oldest were found to be most affected (Lebrun, 1971). For Cambodia, the age structure of the death from the famine recorded by Sliwinski (1995) suggests likewise.

The age structure of excess mortality resulting from increases in natural causes of death and famine is thus expected to also follow a J pattern. In Cambodia, the age structure for women nearly follows such a pattern, except for an unusually high mortality in the late adult ages. The age pattern for men is completely unlike the usual pattern: Late adult mortality is too high as well, but mortality actually peaks in early adulthood. These age patterns clearly reveal that excess mortality in Cambodia was not simply the result of an increase in natural causes of death as a result of exceptional hardships between 1975 and 1978 and the 1979 famine.

The residual approach thus permits the decomposition of excess mortality into two categories. The first one is the above-described mortality increase caused by the exceptional conditions inflicted on the people of Cambodia at the time, mostly famine and infectious diseases, malaria in particular. This increase can be modeled by using a model life table from a very high mortality population (Preston, McDaniel, & Grushka, 1993) in the population projection of the period. The new residual now corresponds to the other causes of death. In Cambodia, those were the executions and some war-related deaths. The decomposition can be adjusted by choosing a level of mortality from normal causes that would leave only a few deaths from other causes in some age and sex groups. For Cambodia, I assumed that death rates from executions and warfare were lowest for women in their 20s.

The results from this decomposition suggest that mortality from natural causes and famine might have increased to a level corresponding to a life expectancy at birth of 12 years for both sexes combined. In addition to that, 1.1 million deaths could not be accounted for by that increase and were attributed to violent deaths, executions, or warfare. Again, I sought the limits of this estimation procedure and obtained 600,000 for the lowest estimates and 2.0 million for the highest estimates.

Although higher, these results are compatible with those of Heder and Sliwinski because they reflect not only executions, but also deaths that could not be accounted for by a typical age pattern of extremely severe mortality. Other deaths can be expected to have been included in this crude decomposition, deaths from warfare in particular, but also possibly other causes poorly represented in model life tables as well. Notwithstanding, these results permit us to rule out some low estimates of the number of executions as conflicting with the age structure of excess mortality in the period.

As the introduction warned, the discussion has focused on estimation and error margins rather than on finding a best estimate of the number of excess deaths resulting from the Khmer Rouge rule of Cambodia. Yet, we have not been able to address the haunting question posed by Liz, the narrator of *Gates of Ivory*, and we will have to live with the unbearable uncertainty of a number "between one and three million."

Although the benefits and shortcomings of the different approaches were discussed in the context of Cambodia, the goal was not to select a particular approach as being more appropriate than others. In fact, in such situations where no single approach could provide reasonably precise estimates, some sense of confidence or likelihood might eventually come from several independent but compatible assessments. Even if each single estimate should come with a large confidence interval, the consistency of multiple estimates is the best test of validity.

Notwithstanding the uncertainty about the exact number of deaths, the intensity of excess mortality in Cambodia during these four years is staggering. Because of the population size of Cambodia, the number of Khmer Rouge victims remains smaller than those of several other 20th-century crises. By its proportions, however, the Cambodian drama might be unique in this century, reminding us of the Great Famine in Ireland. In a country of similar population size (8.2 million in 1841), 1.5 million people might have died between 1846 and 1851, while millions more emigrated.

In this chapter, I have documented the difficulties of measurement in Cambodia and difficulties likely in any context of presumed genocide. Will it ever be possible to put the issue to rest? Unfortunately, the power of the sample approach decreases over time, because the survivors are fewer and more selected over time, and their memory less accurate. The residual approach can be improved when better data sources become available and allow reducing the uncertainty about the size of the survivors' population. The population has to be estimated backward to end of the period being investigated, however, which adds more uncertainty the longer it takes to obtain the suitable data. Fortunately for the Cambodian people, the demographic marks of the 1975–1979 period on the population of Cambodia will gradually fade away.

REFERENCES

Banister, J., & Paige Johnson, E. P. (1993). After the nightmare: The population of Cambodia. In B. Kiernan (Ed.), *Genocide and democracy in Cambodia: The Khmer Rouge, the United Nations and the International Community* [Monograph Series 41, pp. 65–139]. New Haven, CT: Yale University, Southeast Asia Studies.

Barbieri M., Allman, J., Pham, B. S., & Nguyen, M. T. (1995). La situation démographique du Viêt Nam [The demographic situation of Viet Nam]. *Population, 50*(3), 621–652.

Drabble, M. (1991). *The gates of ivory.* London: Penguin Books.

Ea, M. T. (1981). Kampuchea: A country adrift. *Population and Development Review, 7*(2), 209–228.

Ea, M. T. (1987). Recent population trends in Kampuchea. In D. Ablin & M. Hood (Eds.), *The Cambodian agony* (pp. 3–15). New York: Sharpe.

Heuveline, P. (1998). "Between One and Three Million in Cambodia": Toward the demographic reconstruction of a decade of Cambodian history (1970–1980). *Population Studies, 52*(1), 49–65.

Hirschman C., Preston, S., & Vu, M. L. (1995). Vietnamese casualties during the American War: A new estimate. *Population and Development Review, 21*(4), 783–812.

Huguet, J. (1997). *Population of Cambodia: 1980–1996, and projected to 2000.* Phnom Penh, Cambodia: United Nations Population Fund for the National Institute of Statistics, Ministry of Planning.

Kiernan, B. (1996). *The Pol Pot regime.* New Haven, CT: Yale University Press.

Lebrun, F. (1971). *Les hommes et la mort en Anjou aux XVIIe et XVIIIe siècles: Essai de démographie et de psychologie historique* [Humankind and death in Anjou in the 17th and 18th centuries: Essay on demography and historical psychology]. Paris: La Haye, Mouton.

Merli, G. (1998, April). *Socioeconomic status and Vietnamese War mortality during the Vietnam War.* Paper presented at the meeting of the Population Association of America, Chicago, IL.

Migozzi, J. (1973). *Cambodge: Faits et problèmes de population* [Cambodia: Deeds and problems of population]. Paris: Editions du Centre National de la Recherche Scientifique.

Preston, S. H. (1976). *Mortality patterns in national populations.* New York: Academic Press.

Preston, S. H., Heuveline, P., & Guillot, M. (2001). *Demography: Measuring and modeling population processes.* Oxford, U.K. and Malden, MA: Blackwell Publishers.

Preston, S. H., McDaniel, A., & Grushka, C. (1993). New model life tables for high-mortality populations. *Historical Methods, 26*(4), 149–159.

Siampos, G. S. (1970). The population of Cambodia, 1945–1980. *Milbank Memorial Fund Quarterly, 48,* 317–360.

Sliwinski, M. (1995). *Le génocide Khmer Rouge: Une analyse démographique* [The Khmer Rouge genocide: A demographic analysis]. Paris: L'Harmattan.

United Nations. (1995). *United Nations in Cambodia* [The Blue Book Series]. New York: Author.

U.S. Bureau of the Census. (1991). *World population profile, 1991.* Washington, DC: U.S. Government Printing Office.

Vickery, M. (1984). *Cambodia, 1975–1982.* Boston: South End Press.

Vickery, M. (1988). How many died in Pol Pot's Kampuchea? *Bulletin of Concerned Asian Scholars, 20*(1), 70–73.

8

GENOCIDE IN RWANDA

GÉRARD PRUNIER

The discussion in this chapter is divided into three parts. First, I describe the Hutu and Tutsi and how they relate to the nation-state in Rwanda. Second, I discuss the monoethnic state that existed from 1959 and 1963 to 1994. Third, I explain the war that started in 1990, how it coalesced old problems and, to some degree, how foreign intervention made things worse.

The Tutsi and the Hutu are not tribes. An ethnic group, a tribe in Africa or in other parts of the world, is a small nation that may have its own religion, its own territory, its own culture and way of doing things, and its own language. The Hutu and Tutsi have none of these things.

They are not castes either—they do intermarry. For a long time I thought about what to call them. I think I would call them "orders"—in the sense of the German word *Stand*. When we speak of orders in premodern societies, we speak of occupational groups with a certain level of prestige attached to them. The Tutsi used to raise cattle, and there was much prestige associated with this. Of course, the Tutsi do not raise cattle anymore—they do not have the space to raise cattle. Therefore, the Tutsi became peasants like the Hutu, or they worked in the towns.

What was the relationship between Tutsi and Hutu before colonial times? Obviously the Tutsi were on top of a very complex system of patron–client relationships. The patron was responsible for the welfare of his clients, and the client had to give allegiance and obedience, especially in times of war. This was a kingdom that was permanently at war—either civil wars or foreign wars. But the civil wars never involved Hutu against Tutsi. They followed a vertical model, with powerful Tutsi lineages consisting of both Hutu and Tutsi clients fighting against other such lineages. A "small" Tutsi

For more in-depth information on the Rwanda crisis, including research resources, see Gérard Prunier, (1995), *The Rwanda Crisis: History of a Genocide (1959–1994)*, London: Hurst.

could be the client of a more powerful Tutsi, but the Tutsi were never the clients of Hutu lineages. When war occurred, which was very frequently, it was always a lineage of Tutsi with its Tutsi and Hutu clients against another lineage of Tutsi with its Tutsi and Hutu clients.

The civil wars were usually a struggle for the control of a certain group of hills. Rwanda consists of clusters of hills all over the country—there is no flat ground—the whole 20,000 square kilometers is all up and down. And so the hill is the basic economic and social unit. When people ask you where you are from, you say the name of the hill. So there were fights for control of a hill or group of hills, and at the top level it was a fight for the control of the monarchy. When the country was more or less peaceful inside it was usually at war with one of the small kingdoms that surrounded it—those that are now part of Uganda, eastern Zaire, and western Tanzania. This was a monarchic cluster with many kingdoms frequently at war with each other.

It is easy to understand why were there were monarchies here. This was a particularly fertile area, and there was usually a surplus of grain. The state was born very early and was very centralized, although it was small. This whole eastern area of Africa was a cluster of kingdoms in the 16th and 17th centuries, and there were very complex relationships between the Tutsi and Hutu with regard to this question of allegiance and clientship.

The Tutsi overlords used three chiefs on each hill. One was the chief of the pastures and was in charge of making sure that people grazed in the place that they were supposed to graze in (in those days the population density was much lower). The second was the chief of the land who made sure that people cultivated in the place that people were supposed to cultivate in. Usually the first one was a Tutsi and the second one was a Hutu, but not always. The third chief was called the chief of the men, whose job it was to generally oversee the administration and especially to raise men for war. He could be a Hutu, but his boss, the overlord, was always a Tutsi. The three chiefs on each hill were always chosen from a variety of lineages so that power could not be geographically concentrated.

This was a system that was wonderfully described by the first German resident, Richard Kandt, who was one of the most important observers of Rwandese culture. He called it a system of "intertwining fingers." This social system kept a balance, could reproduce itself successfully, and in war—which was part of African society—contributed to the maintenance of its institutions.

The Germans did not have much time to intervene, because their administration was very light. In 1914 when the Belgians attacked Rwanda and Burundi, there were 96 Germans on the 45,000 square kilometers of both kingdoms. There are times when we forget how colonialism was administered. Just as a matter of comparison, the British in their part of

Somalia had only 900 people at the time when Mussolini attacked it in 1940. So we see colonialism at times on the model of places like India, Nigeria, or South Africa, but there were also enormous expanses of land that hardly had any colonial presence.

The Belgians had a different, much heavier form of colonial impact on Rwanda. Basically, to make a long story short, they destroyed the intertwined fingers for reasons of administrative expediency. They did not like the system of having three chiefs per hill; it was much too complicated. In 1924 the governor just abolished the whole system. He centralized everything. He made one chief an administrator of each hill, and because the Tutsi had been the overlords, this man was automatically a Tutsi. So, a system that was deeply inegalitarian, which was not peaceful but which worked, was dismantled in favor of a much more peaceful, simpler system that was also much more centralized.

It worked in the short term. All of the social conflicts inherent to the old system had remained in balance through complex, divided hierarchies and nearly perpetual wars of one kind or another. Under Belgian rule, the system came to be balanced, instead, by a powerful arbitrator from the outside, the White man. But in terms of the relationship between the Tutsi and the Hutu, the balance and the complexities were changing, and the new system that was introduced in the 1920s could not work without an outside referee. The tensions between these different orders, with their different levels of prestige and power, and between hills and lineages could be managed only as long as somebody was on top to control them. But making the system work did not reduce the extraordinary tensions that existed, and the colonial institutions did not have the capacity of the pre-colonial ones to work both from the bottom up and from the top down. There was no allowance for any response from pressure that might arise from discontent at the bottom of the society, as there were no more Hutu elites among the top ranks of Africans who ran things under the Belgians.

This is basically the situation that prevailed in the 1950s at the time of independence. The Tutsi had been granted all the privileges by the Belgians. They received educational benefits, greater prestige, more power, and recognition as the only genuine elite. But naturally, it was among the Tutsi, with a higher level of education, that the anti-colonial movement for independence began after World War II, as in many parts of colonial Africa. The angry Belgians, at the last moment, three years before independence, switched their sympathies from the Tutsi to the Hutu.

Why? The Hutu, being much less educated, were much less interested in ideas of independence. In order to try to perpetuate colonial domination (which was a lost cause by the 1950s), the Belgians gave power to a group that had been a majority but had been totally marginalized. In other words, they put together a very nice bomb and then, when it turned out that they could not keep control over Rwanda or Burundi or the adjoining vast Belgian Congo, they walked away. The fact that the bomb exploded is not a surprise at all. In fact, it began to explode even before they left.

The first massacres started in 1959. The people who had known about the intertwined fingers were all dead. Life in Africa is short, and in those years it was even shorter. So the memory had faded of the different forms of systems that they had known before colonial time. The Hutu's hatred of the Tutsi was enormous and was, in many ways, understandable. The Tutsi had been despots under the protection of the White administration. They had been given absolute power over their people and told that they were the darlings of the administration. The Belgians had proclaimed the Tutsi to be racially superior to the Hutu; they had said they were more beautiful and so much more intelligent. There was in fact a whole literature concerning the beauty and intelligence as well as the high administrative ability of the Tutsi. The Tutsi loved it, and the Hutu lived with the idea that they were ugly and stupid and that God had created them to labor under the leadership of the Tutsi. This is not exactly something that makes you happy, and it is not good for social cohesion.

Beginning in 1959, the violence lasted about four years. In those days the population was smaller, so the number of deaths was limited to about 50,000. A lot of Tutsi ran away to the surrounding countries such as the Congo, Uganda, Tanzania, and Burundi. The Hutu created a monoethnic state, and it seemed to the outside world that this was democratic because the Hutu were 85% of the population. However, some Hutu were more equal than others. What democracy there was existed purely in ethnic terms. There was no internal democracy, because those in power constituted a tiny fraction of the Hutu in whose name they ruled. Those who inherited power from the Belgians told the other Hutu that it was good to support them because if they lost power, the Tutsi would come back into power and wreak terrible vengeance.

This ethnic state lasted from independence in the 1960s until the 1990s, for about 30 years and was explicitly based on ethnic discrimination. People had to have their ethnic membership written on their identity card, and everybody carried an identity card. People could not live somewhere without proper registration. Rwanda, with a very high and rapidly growing population density, was a pressure cooker. It was run as a highly centralized state, and people were totally obedient. Rwandans are German-like in their obedience to power. The government exercised a level of control over the population that was closer to that of a totalitarian state than of what is usually thought of as rather loose administrative control in much of the rest of Africa. One could not move to a small village without police authorization, and everybody was registered—which is why the genocide went like clockwork in 1994. Good genocides are always organized by governments, and the better organized the government, the more successful the genocide.

This ethnic state, when it was unchallenged, did not persecute the Tutsi. It marginalized them and kept them out of politics, the army, and the administration. But because they were better educated, dating from Belgian times, Tutsi often had quite a bit of economic clout. It is important to remember that in pre-genocidal Rwanda the Tutsi often held the best jobs in the private sector. Now the private sector in Africa is usually limited, but what there was in Rwanda tended to be dominated by Tutsi. The best jobs in the sub-Saharan Africa are often things like being a driver for an nongovernmental organization (NGO) or being an interpreter for an embassy. In local terms, in a poor economy with few opportunities, these were prestigious and well-paid positions, and they nearly always went to Tutsi. Foreigners tended to trust Tutsi more, partly because of the old image they had, but also because they were, on average, better educated. So there was a strange situation in Rwanda before the war. The Hutu were on top in all formal institutions. But within informal ones, it was a free-for-all, and the best man could win, usually a Tutsi. This created a lot of tension because, even 30 years after independence, the old elite was still, in some ways, dominant, and it retained its old prestige.

Many foreigners who were living in Rwanda and working for NGOs married local girls, but almost all of these spouses were Tutsi. I have never seen a foreigner marry a Hutu girl. The Hutu believed that the Tutsi were using these women to speak ill of them to foreigners, and this created a high level of paranoia. This is why I think that the genocide that took place in 1994 had a lot to do with culture and with the way people perceived themselves and perceived others rather than with purely objective factors such as language (which was not an issue at all) or even money.

In 1990 a group of Tutsi exiles in Uganda, who by a fluke of history had gained entrance into the Ugandan army as allies of Yoweri Museveni, attacked their country, or at least the country of their parents, to regain what they considered their lost land. This exiled community had joined Museveni during his struggle to gain control of Uganda, and when he became president, they found themselves with a powerful friend. They attacked from Uganda because for the past 10 to 15 years, the Tutsi exiles had been asking to be allowed back. All of these people are strong nationalists. They thought of themselves as Banyarwanda and had never considered themselves Ugandans. The question was, and remains, who is going to run Rwanda, for whom, and in what way? There can exist extraordinary violence with a common language, a common culture, and a deep common feeling of nationalism. But the Tutsi had been excluded from belonging to their nation-state under the post-colonial regime. When the exiles attacked Rwanda, it was like a catalyst for all these tensions that had built up over the past 30 years: the discrimination on one side, the economic success and cultural superiority of the Tutsi on the other. The accumulated resentments and fears were let loose by the attack.

But added to these there was also the fact that the Hutu elite was in deep economic trouble. The population in Rwanda was growing at the rate of close to 3.5% a year, and every single square inch of available land was being used. The population had multiplied 2½ times since independence. In 1986–1988 coffee prices had started falling, and the bottom dropped out of the tin market. These were Rwanda's only real exportable resources. The tin mines were closed. International aid, partly because of the shifting of priorities, started to dwindle. Thus, Rwanda became a country with a lot more people and a larger elite, and the pie they could share among themselves was shrinking.

The Hutu started killing each other—this was the first sign. The political elite started killing each other for well-paid jobs, mostly to be in the position where one could siphon off aid or what was left of the coffee money. The state had also cleared large tracts of land and introduced new "exotic" breeds of cattle, a project financed entirely by the World Bank. Some people made a lot of money for themselves in that process. The World Bank developed a new special economy in northern Rwanda, and some of the Hutu elite were fighting to be part of this development project. The intra-Hutu tensions kept rising internally at a time when one-party states were becoming less and less acceptable internationally.

The years 1988 to 1990 were very tense, and suddenly a lot of Tutsi started to come in from the outside, many with guns. To make matters even worse, there were the French, who had become the protectors of French-speaking former Belgian Africa, thus extending their area of influence well beyond the borders of their own former colonies, which had remained, for the most part, economic, military, and political protectorates. This led them to be the last big power defenders of Mobutu in Zaire (now, once again, the Congo) but also of the Rwandan regime. The French now felt that because the Tutsi coming from Uganda spoke English as their European language rather than French, they were Anglophones who threatened French influence in Africa. French paranoia about an Anglophone threat to their dominant position in much of Africa has been a constant theme of French policy for 30 years, and when the Tutsi came from Uganda, that was the last straw.

I believe that had the RPF (the Rwandese Patriotic Front) dominated by the Tutsi coming from Uganda been Francophone, this would not have been the same problem, and the French would have acted differently. After all, it was only by a fluke of history that these exiles came from Uganda.

They might have come from Zaire (Congo) and been Francophones. In any case, the French sent troops to protect the Hutu government and gave all the wrong messages to this monoethnic, embattled, scared dictatorship. They gave them the message that they would back their security, that they would stand by them.

Of course, the Hutu government tested this French commitment. They did a bit of massacring in October 1990, then again in 1991—small massacres of about 300 people at a time, nothing much compared to what would happen later. Each time, they watched to see how the French were going to react. The Hutu were pleased by France's tolerance and understanding, and they began to raise the level of violence. Had the French made it clear that they did not support this extremism, the situation might not have deteriorated so badly.

The final, terrible element was the internationally brokered peace agreement that was supposed to end the growing war between the RPF and the Hutu government. The Hutu elite realized that strong international pressure in 1993 obliged them to sign this agreement, which guaranteed some power sharing with the Tutsi. Given their historical feelings of inferiority to the Tutsi, and the fact that the Tutsi were returning with their status and reputation intact, one can imagine Hutu feelings. On top of that, aside from France, the rest of the international community seemed to be granting the Tutsi exactly what they had long sought and now considered them deserving underdogs. To the Hutu elite this seemed like a terrible, deadly solution that would end their power.

The Hutu elite felt that they had made a mistake by sparing the women and children in 1963. Too many exiles had been allowed to flee, and now they were returning to take vengeance. Too many Tutsi had survived within Rwanda, and now they were taking too many resources and acting as a potential fifth column within the country. This time, the Hutu elite decided, they would deal especially with the women and children so that there would be no third round, no continuing threat from the outside. As for international opinion, the French would protect them.

The genocide was a perfectly planned and executed operation by a people who felt that this was their last chance of staying in power. It went from the top to the bottom—from feelings of wanting to retain government jobs and to steal foreign aid to the small man who felt that he would lose his land if the Tutsi regained control. There was also the fear of revenge. The sentiment seemed to be, "We killed some of their parents, and they will somehow come and try to reclaim their possessions and avenge old scores." And then, "If we kill those who are inside the country, we can also take their land." So, the government could count on the loyalty of everybody, from top to bottom, to kill the Tutsi for a variety of reasons. These went from a feeling of inferiority, to the idea of getting land, to the idea of avoiding being ruled again by the old feudal system that would come and take over again.

Because the French had given the regime the impression that one major foreign power was supporting them in all their little internal massacres, they thought they could count on France to support them in the big one, too. Little did they realize that the French would reach their limit and could not publicly support an operation in which hundreds of thousands were going to be liquidated.

The whole thing was like a machine. In a different way, it reminds me of the start of World War I and the years of 1912–1914, except that it all took place in a much smaller place. It was like a Greek tragedy—all of the little things fall into place one after the other, and the ultimate catastrophe seems to be unavoidable. The situation of Rwanda from 1990 onward was exactly like that, and the peace agreement was in fact what finally triggered the catastrophe. The Hutu elite decided that the game was up; without a drastic solution, the monoethnic state could no longer be maintained, and the Hutu were going to lose everything.

And so it happened in early 1994, and the international community did nothing. But the RPF won the war, and the French did not intervene to change the outcome. That military victory eventually stopped the genocide, but even now, with the Tutsi in charge of Rwanda, nothing has been solved.

III

MAJOR ETHNOPOLITICAL WARFARE THAT STOPPED SHORT OF GENOCIDE

9

FROM ETHNIC COOPERATION TO VIOLENCE AND WAR IN YUGOSLAVIA

ANTHONY OBERSCHALL

Four explanations for ethnic violence are common.[1] In the *primordial* view, ethnic attachments and identities are a cultural given and a natural affinity, like kinship sentiments. They have an overpowering emotional and nonrational quality. Applied to the former Yugoslavia, the primordialist (e.g., Kaplan, 1993) believes that despite seemingly cooperative relations between nationalities in Yugoslavia, mistrust, enmity, and even hatred were just below the surface, as had always been true in the Balkans. Triggered by fierce competition for political power during the breakup of Yugoslavia and driven by the uncertainties over state boundaries and minority status, these enmities and hatreds, fueled by fear and retribution, were activated and turned neighbor against neighbor and district against district in an expanding spiral of aggression and reprisals.

Although the primordial account sounds plausible, much evidence on the nationalities in Yugoslavia and on the Bosnian civil war contradicts it. Ethnic cleansing was seldom neighbor against neighbor. In an analysis of

This research was supported by grant 3-USIP-126-975 from the United States Institute of Peace. In addition to published sources and documents, the findings are based on a content analysis of news stories on nationality issues in *Oslobodjenje* for 1990; on a content analysis of collective violence from U.N. reports and human rights nongovernmental organizations; and some 50 interviews with informants interviewed in Serbia, Bosnia, and Croatia in May–June 1998.

I thank Dr. Ivana Vuletic and students in my collective action course for research assistance with the content analysis. I particularly want to thank interviewees in the former Yugoslavia who generously gave me their time and very important information. The views expressed in this work are my responsibility alone.
[1]I use the words and concepts *ethnic*, *ethnonational*, and *nationality* interchangeably to refer to the Serbs, the Croats, the Albanians, the Muslims, and other similar large groups of peoples in Yugoslavia, selecting one or another term to conform to English usage (e.g., one writes "ethnic cleansing" and not "nationality cleansing").

17 assaults against villages during the ethnic cleansing of Prijedor district in May–June 1992, in all of them the perpetrators were military and uniformed paramilitary formations. In 14 assaults, the survivors did not recognize any of the aggressors, who did not even bother to wear masks or disguises. In 2 assaults, the victims recognized some faces and voices despite disguises. The primordial theory omits that ethnic hatreds can subside as a consequence of statecraft and living together. DeGaulle and Adenauer managed to reconcile the French and German people. Why no conciliation in Yugoslavia?

In the *instrumentalist* view, ethnic sentiments and loyalties are manipulated by political leaders and intellectuals for political ends, such as state creation (Rosens, 1989). For the former Yugoslavia, the instrumentalist explanation highlights Serb nationalists' goal of a Greater Serbia (Cigar, 1995) and a similar Croat nationalism in Croatia (Djilas, 1995). Ethnic cleansing resulted from a historical longing by Serbs for a Greater Serbia, with deep cultural roots. Milosevic and Serb nationalists tried to implement it when the opportunity arose in the late 1980s and early 1990s. Greater Serbia required ethnic cleansing of non-Serbs from areas inhabited by a majority of Serbs and the corridors linking Serb population clusters. Although there is evidence that ethnic cleansing was a state policy, orchestrated by the highest authorities in Serbia and the Bosnian Serb leadership, this explanation ignores that many Bosnian Serbs did not want secession, that many Serbs in Croatia at first backed moderate nationalists, and that only a minority of men of military age participated in violence. As for Serbs in Serbia, they refused to serve in an army that was realizing the dream of Greater Serbia and was protecting their brethren from non-Serbs. According to the chief of staff of the JNA (Yugoslav Army), the army was 18 divisions short at the start of the Croatian war because of draft resistance (Milosevic, 1997, p. 109). The instrumentalist view assumes an ethnic consensus that does not exist. But how did ethnic extremists then prevail over the moderates?

The *constructionist* view was originally formulated by Kuper (1977) after studying collective violence in societies deeply divided on ethnicity, race and/or religion. It does not deny the insights of the primordial and instrumentalist views. Religion or ethnicity are very real social facts, but in ordinary times they are only one of several roles and identities that matter. There is a lot of variance in a population on ethnic attachments and identities. In the words of Linz and Stepan (1996), "political identities are less primordial and fixed than contingent and changing. They are amenable to being constructed or eroded by political institutions and political choices" (p. 366).

Ethnic and religious issues can be manipulated by politicians and intellectuals to spread fear and insecurity. Yet the outcome is not inevitable. The constructionist view offers insights but is incomplete. How is nationality and ethnicity constructed and eroded by political mobilization and mass media propaganda? Which rival constructions emerge victorious? Extreme nationalism wins not by persuasion alone, but by violence: violence against the moderates in one's own ethnic group and violence against other ethnic groups. The constructionist view has to be complemented with a model of ethnic polarization and conflict escalation and the parallel failure of conflict resolution.

A fourth model of ethnic violence (Gagnon, 1997; Posen, 1993) centers on *state breakdown, anarchy,* and the *security dilemma* that such conditions pose to ethnic groups who engage in defensive arming to protect their lives and property against ethnic rivals, which then stimulates arming by other ethnic groups like an arms race between states. The driving motivations are not ethnic hatreds but fear and insecurity:

> Those who lived peacefully together under a central government suddenly view each other with suspicion; but efforts to make one's group more secure by arming create insecurity for others, who in turn arm, and in the end all are less secure. (David, 1997, p. 558–559)

In the Yugoslav crisis, Ignatieff (1993) put it thus:

> Once the Yugoslav communist state began to split into its constituent national particles the key question soon became: will the local Croat policeman protect me if I am a Serb? Will I keep my job in the soap factory if my new boss is a Serb or a Muslim? The answer to this question was no, because no state remained to enforce the old ethnic bargain. (p. 42)

There is a security dilemma in ethnic conflict, but why does deterrence fail? And why state breakdown to begin with? Can insecurity and fear be spread by propaganda even when daily experience contradicts the allegations of ethnic hostility and threat? One may well explain ethnic conflict, even violent conflict and still have to further explain why violent conflict in Yugoslavia targeted defenseless civilians on a vast scale, why horrible atrocities were committed, and what motivated such aggressors. In Holocaust studies similar questions were raised about the machinery of extermination and "ordinary men" who complied with leaders' orders to kill innocent and defenseless human beings (Browning, 1993).

PRIJEDOR: A CASE STUDY

To get a sense of the gap between the broad theories I have described and an explanation for conflict and collective violence at the grassroots, I examine Prijedor district in Northwest Bosnia in 1990–1992 from before the civil war to immediately after its outbreak in April 1992, when major ethnic violence and cleansing took place there. In the 1991 census, Prijedor district was 42.5 percent Serb and 44 percent Muslim. It was surrounded by districts that had either a slight Serb majority or were close to even, as Prijedor was. Prijedor Serbs were not an isolated Serb minority island surrounded by a sea of Muslims.

Having read through many pages of testimony on ethnic relations in Yugoslavia, I did not come across any Serb complaints of mistreatment, discrimination, or intimidation in Prijedor by non-Serbs or indeed discrimination of non-Serbs by Serbs. On the contrary, as a bewildered Muslim refugee from Prijedor stated,

> In Prijedor there were no conflicts between nationalities. We didn't make the distinctions. My colleague at work was an Orthodox Serb, we worked together. When we were children we went to the Orthodox church or the mosque together . . . . I don't understand. Before there were never any problems between us. We lived together. My sister is married to a Serb, and a brother of my wife is married to a Croat. (as cited in Mazowiecki, 1993, §24)

According to the Bassiouni Report (United Nations Security Council, 1994, Annex 5: Prijedor), Serbs had the leading positions in Prijedor in 1991, as they had during communism. Among the leading Serbs were the director of PTT (post office and telecommunications), the managers of the radio station and the newspaper, the managing directors of the largest employers and state enterprises—the mining company, the paper mill, the bank, the agricultural supply company, the electric supply, the mill and bakery, the cooperative store, the hospital, and the outpatient clinic—as well as political and police positions. In the 1991 elections, the Main Muslim Party (SDA) won 30 seats; the Main Serb Party (SDS) 28, and 32 went to several other parties including the successors to the communists. The Muslims refrained from taking over a number of leading official and economic posts to which their electoral victory entitled them because they believed in power sharing and cooperation across nationality. Even so the SDS blocked the work of the Prijedor Assembly and organized a parallel governance for Serbs in Prijedor, in alliance with the SDS leaders in nearby Banja Luka.

In Bosnia as a whole, the main Serb political party, SDS, had come in second behind the Muslim SDA, and the 35% Serbs in the legislature exceeded the 31% Serbs in the population. Although the SDA could have formed a coalition with the main Croat party (HDZ), its leaders decided on a unity government that included Serbs, Muslims, and Croats (Malcolm, 1996, p. 222). The military at this time was in the hands of the still existing Yugoslav federal government, which itself was controlled by the Milosevic regime. After the Croatian war, many units of the JNA transferring from

Croatia to Bosnian bases came directly into the hands of Bosnian Serb leaders. Thus, not just in Prijedor, but in Bosnia as a whole, the Serbs shared political power and controlled the most important military force.

As in other towns and cities in Bosnia, the SDS in Prijedor organized the Serb plebiscite on November 9–10, 1991, for the Serbian people to remain in the state of Yugoslavia with Serbia, Montenegro, the Krajina, Slavonia, and Baranja—a vote for Greater Serbia. In Bosnia as a whole, it is estimated that 85% of the Bosnian Serbs turned out and that 85% voted for Greater Serbia. A parallel Serb governance, called the "Crisis Committee," secretly created an armed force of Serbs with weapons obtained from Serbia and the JNA. The code name for the distribution of weapons to Serbs in Bosnia was "RAM" and was publicly revealed in July 1991 by the release of a tape-recorded telephone conversation between Slobodan Milosevic and Radovan Karadjic, the Bosnian Serb leader (Malcolm, 1996, p. 225). The Crisis Committee consisted of the deputy mayor, a retired police commander, the district secretary of the former Communist party, two retired police officers, a teacher, a driving instructor who was also the head of the local Serb paramilitary (Chetniks), several businessmen, and local politicians. Serb crisis committees were also formed among Serbs in some of Prijedor district's towns and villages.

On the night April 29, 1992, without any provocation or a shot being fired, 1,775 well-armed Serbs seized the city of Prijedor in a coup d'etat. That number was about one quarter of the Serb men of military age, 20–45, in Prijedor. By this time the Prijedor local government had completely lost power to various Serb groups. Paramilitaries had seized the radio and television transmitters and cut off all but Serb transmissions. The JNA managed to have its demobilized soldiers absorbed into the Territorial Defense Forces, a military reserve that came to be dominated by Serbs. By mid-April, Serb paramilitaries from Serbia had erected roadblocks in the district and controlled all movement. The Serb leaders later claimed that they had preempted an impeding Muslim seizure of power, but no evidence was provided. The Serb coup d'etat in Prijedor is similar to what happened in Northern Bosnia.

In Prijedor, the non-Serb leaders were arrested and shortly thereafter disappeared, presumed executed. Muslim police officers and other officials were fired from their posts. Schools closed; the newspaper ceased, and a Serb paper was started. Non-Serbs were harassed, intimidated, and fired from their jobs. A Muslim journalist wrote: "The streets were full with strangers, armed to the teeth. And everyone knew that only Serbs were armed . . . [the new authority] embarked on a systematic instigation of hatred toward . . . non-Serbs" (Hukanovic, 1996, p. 65). Amid incessant house searches, the weapons, mostly hunting guns, of non-Serbs were rounded up. After a May 30, 1992, an attempt by the Patriotic League of Croats and Muslims—an armed formation of 150 fighters—to retake the old city, many non-Serb inhabitants were arrested and shipped to the infamous Omarska camp (Helsinki Watch, 1992, Vol. 2, p. 405ff). Some fled to Croatia and became refugees.

Among the first batch of 3,000 prisoners were some Serbs who tried to help non-Serbs in Prijedor. At Omarska, prisoners were tortured and brutalized, starved, and killed. The guards were rural Serbs from nearby villages; the interrogators were Prijedor police inspectors. The beatings and tortures were meant to extract confessions from Muslims about hit lists, secret militias, and attacks on Serbs, which was a mirror image of what Serbs had done to the non-Serbs in the district. The Serb police chief Simo Drljaca claimed that in 6,000 interrogations of prisoners, much evidence of genocide and terrorism against the Serb people had been uncovered (United Nations Security Council, 1994, §148).

The villages and small towns in the district were also ethnically cleansed. Helsinki Watch (1992, Vol. 2) collected information from dozens of refugees who escaped from the town of Kozarac, about 10 km from Prijedor. On May 9, 1992, Serb authorities in Prijedor gave the Kozarac town leaders seven days to sign a loyalty oath to the newly proclaimed Bosnian Serb Republic. The townspeople formed a civilian defense council and tried to negotiate with the Serb authorities, but they were attacked on May 26–28 by the army and paramilitaries, and many townspeople were killed. One prisoner who was sent to remove corpses later counted 610 dead. Although there were a few defenders, most civilians surrendered with white flags; some fled into the forest. The attackers looted and burned the houses. People were rounded up, and some were executed. Those shot were Muslim leaders whose names were on a list: members of the Bosnian legislature, judges, police officers, managers, a local sports hero. About 20,000 people were forced to march in a line 5 km long to various detention camps. Of the about 300 aggressors, the victims recognized some from Prijedor and even a few from Kozarac itself, but the majority were not local Serbs.

Similar atrocities occurred in other villages and small towns in Prijedor district (United Nations Security Council, 1994, Annex 5). The Serbs in these places had been warned of the assault and usually left by the time it took place. Some Serbs warned their non-Serb neighbors that an attack was imminent, but people did not anticipate the magnitude of violence nor did they have anywhere to go that was safe. Not only Muslims were targeted. In Prnjavor, the houses of a large Ukrainian community were regularly shot at, and they were threatened with "When are you planning to leave, you Ukrainians?" In August 1992, all 1,100 of them decided to leave (Mazo-wiecki, 1993, §23). Much of the property looted during ethnic cleansing was distributed among the paramilitaries and local Serbs. A year later, of 50,000 Muslims, only an estimated 6,000 remained in Prijedor district, and these lived in fear and misery.

CAN THE THEORIES ACCOUNT FOR WHAT HAPPENED?

In view of the explanations for ethnic—and for the Yugoslav nationality—conflicts in particular, several observations should be made about the events in Prijedor. Muslims and Serbs had lived in peace before the conflict erupted. The Serbs, the later aggressors, were neither a numerical minority nor discriminated against. They not only had a share of power, they had the biggest share. Why did Serbs fear their fellow citizens in Prijedor? A cartoon from this period expresses the puzzle well. It shows a bearded Serb paramilitary armed to the teeth with guns, hand grenades, ammunition belt, and knives; waving a machine gun; with a worried look and yelling at the top of his lungs, "I am being threatened!" (Monnesland, 1997, p. 460).

There was no anarchy in Prijedor. Serbs may have had apprehensions about their future in an independent Bosnia, but even in Bosnia they had a big presence—numerical, military, political, and economic. There was no spontaneous popular rising of Serbs against non-Serbs, nor vice-versa, in Prijedor. Instead, there was a highly organized, secretly prepared coup d'etat, which reminds one of the 1917 Bolshevik seizure of power in Russia. The arming of the Serbs in Prijedor was straightforward. Vojislav Seselj, the head of the largest paramilitary and an extremist rival to Slobodan Milosevic, boasted in a BBC documentary, "Milosevic organized everything. We gathered volunteers and he gave us special barracks. . . . .all our uniforms, arms, military technology, and buses. All our units were always under the command of the Krajina, or the Republika Srpska, or the JNA" (as cited in Silber & Little, 1995, p. 230). As in the Russian revolution with the Soviets, the Serb parallel government was not only an instrument for seizing power from non-Serbs but of stripping the moderate Serbs of any influence and authority.

Contrary to the state breakdown and security dilemma view, the fact that Muslims in Bosnia abstained from arming actually sealed their doom. According to Bugajski (1996), the Muslim leadership put its faith in diplomacy and international support:

> The Bosnian government was clearly caught unprepared for armed conflict. Indeed Sarajevo was advised by Western governments that military initiatives would only serve to provoke Serb militants. It calculated that under the umbrella of international recognition, Serb leaders would desist from open warfare and a political compromise would be reached under EC auspices. (p. 133)

Woodward (1995) concurred: "members of the Republic's political and cultural elite and government leadership were still hopeful that war could be averted . . . . Izetbegovic's government did not prepare for war" (p. 195).

What was the reaction of ordinary Serbs in Prijedor to these events? Although there is no information on them, one can learn from what observers recorded nearby. Peter Maas (1995), a journalist, reported that in Banja Luka, a Serb lawyer estimated that 30% of Serbs opposed ethnic cleansing, and 60% agreed or were confused and went along with the 10% who "have the guns and control the television tower." That strikes me as the right proportions. An armed, organized 10% who control mass communications can have its way when the majority supports it overtly or tacitly and when the opposition is unorganized, divided, confused, and scared.

WHAT IS TO BE EXPLAINED?

One can take for granted that in a multinational state such as Yugoslavia, nationality will be a salient dimension of political contention and that there will be leaders and intellectuals with a nationalist ideology and agenda. The Yugoslav constitution and its political institutions were delicately balanced and crafted to deal with nationality. A nationalist challenge would inevitably zero in on stateness, minority rights, and power sharing: If accepted boundaries of political units are renegotiated or remade, who decides which peoples and territories belong to new and old political entities? Will all peoples in the new units be equal citizens for governance, or will majority ethnonational affiliation become the admission ticket for full citizenship?

Once unleashed, nationalism in Yugoslavia set on a collision course the two largest nationalities, the Serbs and the Croats. With a quarter of Serbs living outside Serbia, a centralized Yugoslav state was a guarantor of Serb well-being. For Croats and their long history of opposition to Hapsburg rule, a decentralized state and weak federation meant control of their own destinies, unencumbered by inefficient bureaucratic state agencies and enterprises staffed and controlled by Serbs. Nevertheless, nationality issues could have been sorted out with strong democratic institutions: nondiscrimination in employment and education, more collective rights for minorities on access to mass media and other cultural rights, systems of political representation in elections, and collective decision rules in assemblies that would protect minority voice and favor coalitions rather than majority domination (Sisk, 1996). Minorities everywhere in Yugoslavia would have felt secure; nationalities would not have been so apprehensive about the fate of their fellows in other republics. Nationalist leaders would have found it difficult to rally the citizenry to the nationalist cause.

One can also take for granted that in a country with great differences in economic development and standard of life between the republics there will be disagreements over economic policies, taxation, transfers, subsidies across regions, and abandoning socialism for a market economy. But all republics had experienced dramatic economic gains since World War II. It was not obvious that the Yugoslav Federation was beyond economic repair.

The Soviet Union had as great if not greater liabilities on nationality and on economic troubles, but except for the Caucasus, there was no war and collective violence. What then defeated conciliation and conflict resolution in Yugoslavia?

As in other Communist states in the late 1980s, the Yugoslav Communist leaders wanted to remain in power. Some reprogrammed as Reform Communists and hoped to transition into European-style social democracy, but they had no experience and credibility on democracy and on a market economy. They were vulnerable to challenge. Some communists instead chose ethnonationalism as the issue that would carry them to power and create a new principle of legitimacy for the post-Communist regime. Others earlier persecuted by the Communists for nationalism saw a new opportunity to advocate what they had believed in all along. Thus the Pandora's box of ethnonationalism and reactive nationalisms was opened.

Moderate nationalists stood for conciliation among nationalities; extremists were willing to pursue their goals with force and violence. Extremists prevailed, but why and how? Why did populist nationalism resonate with the citizenry? How is it that when the media wars unleashed the war of words before the war of bullets, so many believed the exaggerations, distortions, and fabrications on nationality that belied their personal experiences? Why did fear of others grow when, as Franklin Roosevelt so well expressed it in the Great Depression, "the only thing we have to fear is fear itself?" Why did the citizens vote for political leaders whose views and policies on nationality were more extreme than their own? Why did so many cheer, approve, or simply stand confused and silent, when nationalists purged and ethnically cleansed their fellow citizens? Why did the moderate opposition get disorganized and discouraged, reduced to silence and exile? How did ordinary soldiers and militiamen become killers of unarmed civilians?

A polarization and escalation model of ethnic strife helps organize a set of interrelated answers to these questions (Oberschall, 1973, chaps. 7 and 8; 1993, chap. 4). *Polarization* refers to the loosening and severance of social relations between two groups in both interpersonal relations and in organizational affiliation and the diverging of opinions, beliefs, and ways of thinking between them. Polarization describes the change from ethnic cooperation and integration to hostility and encapsulation. Ethnic polarization starts when a public controversy makes ethnicity more salient, that is, political and economic changes make ethnic competition for political positions and economic benefits more intense. In a crisis, even moderate leaders call for unity and ethnic solidarity and make appeals to ethnic loyalty, although they favor conciliation. We know from social psychological studies that any repeated categorization of people, be it religious, ethnic, or racial, or even an innocent division of summer campers into activity groups with distinct names and identities, will engender we-feeling and in-group preference, and a corresponding distancing from and bias against out-groups (Tajfel, 1970). In the Yugoslav political rhetoric of extreme nationalists, nothing else mattered but nationality, and other nationalities were the "enemy." Ethnic categorization solidarity in one nationality calls forth reactive categorization and solidarity in others. Unless steps are taken to stop polarization, it feeds on itself.

How are rank-and-file citizens influenced by extremist propaganda from the news media? Mass communication studies show that ordinary people check media messages with work mates, neighbors, family and kin, and opinion leaders. When media messages are contradicted in microenvironments, they will not be believed (Wright, 1959). In ethnic polarization, microenvironments become ethnically homogenous as people avoid interpersonal disputes. People will selectively expose themselves to their ethnic media and to social milieus that confirm partisan media messages. Many citizens will now believe the "big lie" of extremist leaders. Experiments have shown that people tend to judge that whatever has been repeated is true— even when the repetition is only the words of the assertion (Dawes, 1994, p. 202). And because of selective media exposure and agreement in microenvironments, the "big lie" keeps getting heard and is not challenged.

When nationalist propaganda awakens ethnic divisions, fears, and hatreds, individuals' actions become more uniform than their preferences and dispositions. Nationalists running for office persuade their ethnic peers that other nationalities will vote as a bloc to gain power, and in a self-fulfilling prophecy the majority of citizens vote as ethnic blocs. Strategic voting produces perverse effects (Schelling, 1978). The political leaders elected are more nationalist than their voters.

As in the great revolutions, extremists will gain at the expense of moderates (Brinton, 1957). Extremists form ethnic organizations and assemblies, and in these bodies, as is known from social psychological research (Dawes, 1994, p. 166), a group of people reach judgments more extreme than their individual opinions expressed before group discussion. These assemblies and organizations become the parallel governance that challenges the legitimacy of existing government and are the instrument of its overthrow.

Moderate leaders and activists meanwhile participate in assemblies and organizations that include several ethnic groups and all points of views: These bodies lack unity, deliberate slowly, delay, and compromise rather than take decisive action. Moderates are in charge of governing, but as is well known from revolutions, in a crisis, when the protection of life and property and the delivery of basic services are problematic, control of government becomes a liability. Thus extremists gain on moderates.

Extremists use coercion and violence as instruments of power. Ordinary people recruited through peer pressure and peer organizations get indoctrinated in extremist ideology and organized into armed groups. They intimidate, harass, and assault both moderates in their own ethnic group and other ethnics. It has been shown by Milgram (1974) that ordinary people have a tendency to accept authority even to the point of inflicting pain and harm on fellow human beings. After injuries and deaths, retaliation and preemptive strikes fuel the violence (Oberschall, 1973, pp. 284–291). Apply now ethnic polarization and escalation of violence to Yugoslavia.

FROM LATENT TO POPULIST NATIONALISM

Except for the Albanians and Serbs in Kosovo, nationalism was not a grassroots political force in the mid-1980s; it was a latent sentiment mobilized into populist nationalism by political leaders, intellectuals, and the mass media. Nevertheless, the latent sentiment was present and preceded the fall of communism in Eastern Europe. Albanians were the only major nationality without a republic, although they numbered more than the Montenegrins and the Macedonians. In November 1968 there were huge demonstrations for a republic, resulting in long prison sentences for nationalist leaders. Although they achieved an autonomous provincial status within Serbia in 1974, with a constitution and a separate legislature, Albanians resumed protests in 1981, and nationalist opposition to Serb domination continued after then using peaceful and sometimes violent means.

In the early 1970s, Croat nationalism led to severe conflicts in the League of Communists. Nationalists contended that Croatian revenues were subsidizing Yugoslav and Serb enterprises; that Serb immigration and Croat emigration were producing a Croat demographic decline; and that Croatia needed to protect its language, revive its culture, and rewrite its history. Some even advocated a separate army and national bank. According to Monnesland (1997, p. 290), "Croat nationalism was definitely anti-Serb." Zagreb University students engaged in strikes to back the Croat nationalists. Marshal Tito called on the police and military to break the strike. Nationalism was condemned. Student leaders and nationalists like Franjo Tudjman were sentenced to prison. Croat nationalism was then revived in 1989 and became a mass movement.

In Serbia, after Tito's death in 1980, some Serb intellectuals charged that with the 1974 constitution Tito had made Serbia "weak" in order to make Yugoslavia "strong." Dobrica Cosic (cited in Monnesland, 1997, p. 314) wrote that "Serbs won the war but lost the peace." It was alleged that outside Serbia the Serbs were being assimilated (especially in Croatia), that Kosovo Serbs were threatened with genocide, and that the Cyrillic alphabet was under attack. The 1986 Academy of Sciences manifesto of Serb nationalism asserted that Yugoslav policy and politics were calculated to "totally erase the unity of the Serb nation" (cited in Monnesland, 1997, p. 315).

Nationalist claims played loose with historical truth and contemporary fact. Croats alleged that Serbs in Croatia (12% of the population) were increasing through immigration and occupied a disproportionate share of the police, the army, the judiciary, and the state bureaucracy and were an instrument of Serb influence and domination. Serbs, to the contrary, contended that Serbs in Croatia were pressured to assimilate. Both beliefs cannot be true. There is a simple social science explanation for the occupational distinctiveness of Serbs in Croatia. They had a historic military and state service tradition since their settlement in the Krajina frontier, and they lived in a poor region with few entrepreneurial opportunities.

The plight of the Kosovo Serbs was twisted by nationalist politicians and intellectuals to unleash populist Serb nationalism. Everyone agreed that because of a higher Albanian birthrate and higher Serb out-migration, Kosovo changed from 23% Serb in 1971 to 10% in 1989. But Serb nationalists alleged that Albanians were threatening and pressuring Serbs to leave and that the police and judiciary were not protecting Serbs against Albanian violence. In 1986 a 2,000 strong delegation of Kosovo Serbs descended on Belgrade to demand protection from Albanians. A survey by the Serb Academy of Sciences of 500 Serb migrant households found that 25% reported violent incidents or intimidation (e.g., bullying their child at school). Many reported discrimination in employment and strained interpersonal relations with Albanians (insults, threats, and quarrels). Although widely believed by Serbs, the more extreme allegations were false. A social science researcher could not find one instance of Albanian rape of Serb women in 1987 (Pesic, 1998, p. 30). But those who questioned the "forcible migration" frame of the nationalist ideologues "were mercilessly attacked and branded a foe of Serbia." There must have been some threats and intimidation of Kosovo Serbs, but was it "genocide"?

A push–pull migration model can explain differential migration from Kosovo. It was the most underdeveloped region of Yugoslavia. Serbs there had an incentive and the opportunity to move to the richer neighboring central Serbia where their language was spoken and they were in the majority. Research also showed that they sold their homes and farms at good prices and could afford to buy an equivalent home and farm in central Serbia (Blagojevic, 1998, pp. 85–86). Albanians, with lower education, less knowledge of Serbo-Croatian, and heading into a minority status, had fewer incentives and opportunities. This commonsense and social science explanation was rejected. Serb mass media abounded with stories of rape, crime, violence, arson, the destruction of cemeteries, and other outrages by Albanians on Serbs.

The Kosovo crisis was fanned by Serb nationalists. With a "save the Serb nation" platform, Slobodan Milosevic ousted reform communists within the communist party—Ivan Stambolic and Bogdan Bogdanovic were accused of cowardice and opportunism and were expelled from the Central Committee, together with a purge of other moderates. Milosevic seized power, gained control of the state broadcasting organizations, and created a broad-based nationalist movement that gave him a populist, post-Communist legitimacy. In the summer of 1988, a series of mass meetings were organized by the Serb nationalists. High on the agenda was the "retaking of Kosovo." In a dozen cities, crowds of 10,000 to 200,000 demanded the resignation of incumbents and their replacement with Milosevic nationalists. At the core of these assemblies were professional demonstrators dressed in folk costumes, carrying placards and banners rich with Serb national and Orthodox religious symbols, for example, the names of Serb kings and saints, and of course "Slobo." The coverage in the mass media became a vast nationalist learning experience and legitimated the manifestations of Serb nationalism suppressed under Tito. Nationalist propaganda termed these events a "democratic" mass movement—thus confounding populism with democracy. In fact, the movement was a coalition of dogmatic communists, extreme Serb nationalists, the Orthodox Church, and Chetniks (shortly to become ethnic cleansers) (Monnesland, 1997, p. 319).

Populist nationalism worked. The Vojvodina and Montenegro party leaderships resigned and were replaced by Milosevic loyalists. To every Albanian demonstration in Kosovo there was a bigger Serb counter-demonstration in Belgrade: Nationalism begat reactive nationalism in what foreshadowed the dynamics of polarization and escalation in the rest of Yugoslavia. Latent Serb nationalism took a year and a half of intense mobilization and mass movements to revive and spread. It could not have happened without the eager complicity of intellectuals. As one observer put it, "Whenever the [Serb] government needed it, there were academicians ready to make factual pronouncements on current affairs and a scientific justification of the correctness of the politics" (Milosavljevic, 1998, p. 171). How was the man in the street to think otherwise when political leaders, members of the Academy of Sciences, church leaders, literary intellectuals, and news commentators all agreed on the urgency to "save the Serb nation"?

Abolishing the autonomous provinces of Kosovo and Vojvodina precipitated a constitutional crisis. According to Djilas (1995), "Kosovo and Vojvodina had their own representatives in the federal, state and party bodies where most of the time they voted against Serbia. The two provinces also had the right to veto any change in the Serbian constitution" (p. 92). The nationality balance in Yugoslav politics was thus disturbed. Serbia gained control of over half the votes in all federal bodies and institutions. For Slovenia and Croatia, this meant that Serbia might block the reforms necessary for joining the European Community and other international institutions. To other Yugoslavs, especially Albanians, Slovenes, and Croats, the Serb nationalist revival was threatening and dangerous and boded ill for a restructured Yugoslav state in which Serbia had a heavy hand. For Milosevic and Serb nationalists, riding the crest of nationalism saved them from the perilous politics of change from communism to democracy and from socialism to a market economy. Slovenes and Croats reacted with their own nationalism.

There was grassroots resistance to nationalism in Yugoslavia. A content analysis by my research team of news stories in *Oslobodjenje* for 1990 indicates that municipalities, youth and veterans' organizations, and trade unions repeatedly protested ethnic polarization and hatreds. In January, the municipal council of Vojnic organized a rally of brotherhood and unity to counter a Serbian unity rally; in Mostar, the Youth Association and a trade union issued the statement that "there is no place for the ghosts of the past . . . we condemn the spread of nationalist hatred," in response to a nationalist speech by Franjo Tudjman; in Glamoc and Kladanj, the Socialist Association of Working People sent a message to nationalists Franjo Tudjman, Vuk Draskovic, and Vojislav Seselj that it would not participate in civil war. The municipal committee of Nevesinje declared that interethnic relations in Nevesinje were good and called for a "decisive struggle against national divisions and territorial claims in Bosnia Hercegovina," whereas veterans organizations in Novi Pazar, Kladanj, and Banja Luka condemned "attempts to break up Yugoslavia." Thousands joined a huge rally and concert in Sarajevo against nationality divisions.

Important as it was, the resistance against nationalism was through Communist organizations that were being discredited, whereas populist nationalism was spreading at the grassroots. *Oslobodjenje* in 1990 is full of grassroots affirmations of nationality symbols and identities: the renaming of localities; the reburial of bones of World War II atrocity victims; the painting of nationalist graffiti on churches, mosques, monuments, and cemeteries; the disputing over flags; the singing of nationalist songs that result in fights; the hurling of verbal ethnic insults; and the spread of ethnic vandalism. But in 1990, violent fights were still few. Rumors circulated about weapons and arming, which led to armed patrols and night guards. Populist nationalism gained, and resistance to it waned.

Even so, for the majority of Yugoslavs, nationalism in the public arena did not translate into strained and hostile interpersonal relations across nationality. In May–June 1998 I interviewed several former managers of large state enterprises about workplace cooperation among their employees in 1990 and 1991: a chemical plant in Tulsa, a metalurgical factory in Banja Luka, a construction company in Zadar, a national park where hundreds camped, a law department of a large state enterprise, a music school with several hundred pupils in Sarajevo, a high school in Knin, and a university faculty in Sarajevo. With one exception, none reported any hostile incidents, fights, or noncooperation among workers, employees, clients, pupils, or campers of different nationalities—right up to the time the war broke out in Croatia and in Bosnia. The one exception was a Serb research assistant who was spreading false stories about a Muslim faculty member, alleging he was planning to set up an internment camp for Serbs. It is telling that such an incident occurred only in an academic setting, among culture producers, and not among ordinary workers and employees.

Others report confirming evidence on good relations among nationalities before the wars started. When journalist Misha Glenny visited Knin, later a hotbed of extremist militia activity he wrote, "Before May 1991 Croats and Serbs lived together [in Knin] in relative contentment . . . nobody in their wildest fantasy would have predicted that within 12 months . . . Croat soldiers would massacre innocent Serbs while Serb fighters would mutilate innocent Croats" (1992, pp. 19–20).

Indeed, most ordinary people were stunned by the violence that descended upon them unexpectedly. Jeri Laber (1993), a human rights activist, talked to refugees in a camp: "How was it before the war?" A young man whose wife was raped before his very eyes by a Serb he knew replied, "Yesterday we were friends . . . . I shake when I think of it. I can't believe it happened . . . overnight we became enemies; I don't know why." Another refugee said, "Before the war it was super . . . my neighbors were Muslims, Croats. We celebrated our holidays together. A few months before war broke out, people started separating. It was after Bosnia's independence was recognized. Our neighbors avoided us" (p. 6).

There is survey research on ethnic relations from mid-1990 when the constitutional crisis was already in full swing. Of a national sample of 4,232 Yugoslavs, only 7% believed that the country would break up into separate states, and 62% reported that the "Yugoslav" affiliation was very or quite important for them (Cohen, 1993, p. 173). On ethnonational relations, in workplaces, 36% characterized them as "good," 28% as "satisfactory," and only 6% as "bad" and "very bad." For ethnonational relations in neighborhoods, 57% answered "good," 28% "satisfactory," and only 12% "bad" and "very bad." Although rating interpersonal relations positively, respondents were apprehensive about deteriorating relations in their republic and the federal level, that is, about politics and public affairs ("Public Opinion Survey," 1990, pp. 25–26).

CRISIS: NATIONALISTS WIN THE 1990 ELECTIONS

The biggest boost for nationalism and the linkage of elite and populist nationalism was the founding of political parties and the election campaigns of 1990. Every town and city experienced the founding of political parties, often at a huge rally in a public building or a sports stadium, during which speaker after speaker gave vent to exaggerated nationalist rhetoric and hostile pronouncements and attacks against other nationalities. Drawing on the *Oslobodjenje* content analysis, one finds that in Bosanska Gradiska on June 9, 1990, the local extremist Croat party HDZ handed out flags that read "Serbs are swine, Serbs should leave," whereas three days later in Novi Pazar, Vuk Draskovic, the Serb firebrand, proclaimed at an election rally, "all those who like Turkey [i.e., Muslims] should go to Turkey," and that he would personally cut off an arm that raised the green (i.e., Muslim) flag.

This rally precipitated a fight that ended with tear gas and arrests by police. Such rhetoric and political fights created insecurity and fears about social stability. Nationalist extremists bested the moderates. In Bosanski Brod at the founding of the local HDZ on September 15, 1990, its moderate leader Ilija Kljujic was prevented from speaking because he was in favor of the sovereignty of Bosnia–Hercegovina. Moreover, he was ousted from the party by his peers. In the election campaigns, bigotry, hatred, and misinformation about nationality circulated freely and reached millions of people nightly on television.

The introduction of a multiparty system in communist Yugoslavia was flawed (International Commission on the Balkans, 1996, pp. 26–33). In the elections of 1990, citizens of the various republics had no chance to vote for maintaining the federation, despite the fact that most wanted it continued. In a 1990 public opinion survey ("Public Opinion," 1990, p. 16), 24% wanted the federation to continue as it was, 12% wanted it modified, 21% wished for a weaker confederation, and only 7% wanted Yugoslavia broken up into independent states. Only 8% agreed that "being a Yugoslav today no longer means anything." In another survey of over 4,000 respondents (Cohen, 1993, p. 172), 84% of Muslims and 71% of Serbs agreed that "Yugoslavia was quite important" to them, and a similar percentage agreed that federal institutions should remain paramount over the republics in a new constitution.

As happened elsewhere in Central Europe, there was a proliferation of political parties: 17 in Slovenia, 33 in Croatia, and 41 in Bosnia. The voters lacked information, the news media engaged in "patriotic journalism," and political parties and leaders had limited time and resources to organize and campaign. According to Woodward (1995), campaigns centered on "symbols and personalities":

> In a world of competing symbols and personalities, at a point of political transition, nationalism has a particular advantage. The message is simple, relies on the familiar, takes little resources, does not have to develop a new political language and explain the complexities of democratic institutions and market economy . . . nationalist appeals thus provide

the easiest route to politics for politicians without established constituencies and party organization. (p. 124)

Even so, the most nationalist parties did not win large majorities of the vote. In Croatia, the HDZ won 41.5% of the popular vote, but that translated into 58% of seats in the legislature. In Serbia, Milosevic and the main Serb nationalists, the SPS got 47% of the eligible voters, 65% of those voting, and 78% of the seats (Woodward, 1995, pp. 119, 121, 225, 228).

Despite the nationalist revival and political rhetoric, it is not obvious why as many voters supported nationalist parties and politicians as actually did. It should be remembered that in 1990 many moderate nationalists stood for office in the same parties as the extremists. More important was an explanation provided by several political analysts in interviews in 1998. Politicians warned their own nationality not to split their vote among several parties because other nationalities were bloc voting for their nationality candidates and party and thus would win the election. There was no prior evidence about nationality bloc voting, but its repeated assertion became a self-fulfilling prophecy.

Many voters came to believe the hostile rhetoric on nationality that contradicted their daily, personal experience with other nationalities. How could this be possible? Most of what we know we do not know from personal experience but accept as the truth from authorities and experts that we respect and from knowledgeable fellow citizens we trust. Who could really tell how many Serbs had been massacred by Ustasha in World War II? Franjo Tudjman admitted only one-tenth of what Serbs claimed. Who was right? Was a bomb that demolished a house in a distant village planted by one group or another? According to a media analyst, "In Serbia and Croatia, TV fabricated and shamelessly circulated war crime stories . . . the same victim would be identified on Zagreb screens as a Croat, on Belgrade screens as Serb" (Milosevic, 1997, p. 119). Politicians were making threats: Serbs go home to Serbia: Turks go to Turkey! The content of the mass media scared people, and rightly so.

The outcome of the 1990 elections and the actions of nationalist leaders unleashed apprehension, uncertainty, and fear about the future form of the Yugoslav state, the boundaries of successor states, and the security of ethnic minorities (Oberschall, 1996). Lake and Rothchild (1996) have written that "intense ethnic conflict is most often caused by collective fears of the future," and "when central authority declines, groups become fearful of their survival . . . state weakness . . . is a precondition for violent ethnic conflict to erupt" (pp. 41–43). Strong states in intense ethnic conflict— the United Kingdom in Northern Ireland, the Republic of South Africa, and the state of Israel—experienced ethnic riots, small insurgencies, and terrorism, but they managed to stop the escalation of collective violence. In Yugoslavia, the state failed as a guarantor and enforcer of ethnic peace. Just the opposite. Agents of the state instigated ethnic violence.

HATE AND PROPAGANDA THROUGH THE MASS MEDIA

After the elections of 1990 in the republics, the nationalist parties who won gained control of the news media, and especially television, which used to be under Communist party control (Milosevic, 1997). This control intensified what had already become a massive campaign of ethnonational mobilization based on negative ethnic stereotyping, falsification of history, lying about current events, and hate mongering. According to Helsinki Watch (1992):

> By the end of the 1980s, political debate at the federal level had declined to merely a politics of resentment between the various national groups . . . history has been used as either an opportunity to merely express resentment toward other ethnic groups or to excuse mistreatment. The constant invocation of history to bolster ethnic nationalism has impeded the search for lasting and equitable political solutions to ethnic strife in Yugoslavia. (p. 82)

Milosevic (1997) agreed that "For 70 years, Yugoslavs regardless of ethnic background lived daily in a multiethnic environment . . . a mental conversion was necessary before the majority of Yugoslavs could tolerate nationalist slogans" (pp. 108–109). Woodward (1995, p. 232) noted that much propaganda was meant to persuade of the impossibility of nations living together. Cigar (1995) thoroughly examined and documented the stream of negative stereotypes about Muslims in Serbia put out by intellectuals, parties and leaders, academies, orientalists and historians, and church leaders, whose purpose and consequence was to "dehumanize" the Muslims, always a necessary step before the unleashing of genocidal violence, according to studies by Fein (1979) and Kuper (1977). Both *Forging War: The Media in Serbia, Croatia, and Bosnia–Herzegovina* (Thompson, 1994) and a special report on the media during the civil war published by the United Nations (United Nations Security Council, 1994) concurred on essential points. As for the print media, privatization of state property and state licensing "provided a means and a cover for dismissing editorial boards, closing journals and newspapers, and imposing state control . . . as well as to squelch opposition" (Woodward, 1995, p. 231). Although the Serb movement for media freedom mobilized hundreds of thousands of demonstrators in Belgrade in the spring and summer of 1991, it was suppressed by force (Oberschall, 1996).

Propaganda poisoned ethnic relations. Glenny (1992) reported conversations with people of all sorts, who picked up the phrases and arguments and stereotypes from the media and dished it up for him, sometimes as the "undisputed truth" and sometimes more polemically. Especially telling is how the moderates in Knin a year later had vanished, in part under the influence of the local radio station:

> Without a doubt one of the most important actors on the Knin stage which transformed the consciousness of this dozy town was . . . Serbia Radio Knin . . . the people of Knin were extremely dependent on this radio station . . . Radio Knin is an accomplice in the dissemination of falsehood and the perpetuation of divisive myth which has turned one hapless narod [people] against another equally innocent one. (p. 20–24)

We know from mass communications studies and in particular the two-step flow of communication (Wright, 1959) that in ordinary circumstances crude propaganda tends to be discounted because people are exposed to a variety of broadcast messages and because they check media messages against the beliefs and opinions in their social milieus in interpersonal relationships and conversations. Ethnic polarization broke down such structural protection against propaganda. According to several informants, when politics became contentious, it strained friendships across nationality. Thus either one avoided public affairs and politics, or one stopped being friends and turned to a fellow ethnic with whom agreement was more likely. Such behavior follows from Festinger's theory of cognitive dissonance. In either case, homogeneous nationality clusters for political information exchange and opinion formation were formed, and these became aligned with nationalist journalists and nationalist leaders. A Muslim lawyer told me she did not talk politics with her Serb peers, although they maintained good professional relationships and after-work socializing. She was dumbfounded and felt betrayed the first week of the war in Sarajevo when she discovered that Serb lawyers had enlisted in the Serb army: "One of them brought me a rabbit from his hunt, and a week later he was shelling me from the mountain; I just don't understand it." (personal communication, June 2, 1998)

In an interview, a broadcast manager in Sarajevo explained the growth of "patriotic journalism" that played such an important part in the growth of populist nationalism. Why is it that newscasters and journalists broadcast and printed the politicians' exaggerations, unconfirmed rumors, and misinformation, when they knew they were rumors and misinformation? Unlike the Communist era, by the late 1980s the news media had achieved much autonomy from political masters. News people would have preferred to remain objective and professional and free of political oversight. But some started slanting the news to favor their own nationality, and others then did the same because they did not want their nationality to suffer in comparison. With no one to stop it and restore professionalism, news reporting and analysis became a competitive spiral of propaganda and misinformation.

Other methods of producing patriotic journalism were openly coercive. Milosevic (1997, p. 115) wrote that even musical program editors were fired by Radio Belgrade for airing too much Croatian and Slovene music. In an interview I had with a Sarajevo news reporter stationed in Banja Luka in 1991, he described how he was offered 3,000 German Marks for favorably reporting on the Serb National Assembly and how he was beaten when he refused.

In explaining the impact of the mass media on popular beliefs and emotions, remember that conditions in Serbia, and later in Croatia, approximated wartime rather than peacetime: The regime acquired media monopoly in television; intellectuals and experts were enlisted in the propaganda effort; patriotic journalism superseded professionalism; a sense of great threat and danger diffused—the Serb nation is under attack, as in a war; opponents and skeptics were branded traitors; and the mass audience had no means of verifying media content. Populist nationalism turned xenophobic, paranoid, and aggressive. What could have prevented such wartime media conditions would have been an independent broadcast authority not vulnerable to regime dismissals, threats, and manipulation.

Ordinary people responded favorably to the flood of nationalist propaganda even absent any economic and political threat from another nationality. A Croat-American young man whose family originated from the island of Olib in Dalmatia, and who has since 1979 spent three weeks every summer on the island, has written on the growth of Croat nationalism there (Pulsic, 1998). Only a few hundred people live on the island permanently, and 90% are Croats. Before the war in 1991, many people from all over Yugoslavia would come for summer holidays. There had not been any conflicts among the islanders, many of whom were related, nor between islanders and summer people. There was no competition over scarce resources, no fear of any nationality, no possibility of any military engagement, and never any doubt that governance remained in islander Croat hands. Yet the extreme nationalist Croat Party, the HDZ, won 103 of 111 votes in 1990.

Among new manifestations of Croat nationalism that Pulsic observed in the 1990s were using "Croat" words in preference to local Olibski dialect; singing Croat and Ustasha songs in taverns and on roads; saluting drinking pals in a new "Croatian" way; removing Tito's portraits from bars, restaurants, and stores and replacing them with the Croat crest and flag; vandalizing local World War II partisans' graves and memorials; singing the Croat national anthem during Catholic mass; looting and squatters' occupying Serb summer homes; replacing village-oriented leaders in the Olib government by HDZ members and sympathizers; sending anonymous threats in letters to ex-communists and moderates; and being rude to non-Croats, especially Serb visitors and summer people, who then stopped coming to the island.

Pulsic believed the nationalist surge was media driven, because there were no island events that otherwise could account for the change. The mass media, especially TV that everyone watched, were extremely nationalist. To ensure audience monopoly for Croat TV, the local station broadcast the non-nationalist YUTEL programs at 1:00 AM when everybody was asleep: "During three weeks watching television news, I did not observe a single critical opinion of President Tudjman or the HDZ" (Pulsic, 1998, p. 41). Even sports coverage was patriotic. When a Zagreb soccer team lost to a Belgrade team, none of the goals scored by the Serbs were shown in the sports summary.

STATE BREAKDOWN OR STATE REPRESSION?

With populist nationalism rampant and nationalists victorious at the polls, it still is not obvious why state formation became massively violent in Yugoslavia. The absence of democratic institutions was critically important, as was the blending of nationalism with the Communist political culture. That culture legitimated the purging of one's opponents from party and state positions. A large portion of the total economy was in state and party control, not just political offices such as mayors and legislators. When the Croat nationalists won in 1990, they purged the police, the media, and the state enterprises of Serbs and of their political rivals. It was a tremendous patronage opportunity for a new political party. Those ousted were not protected by nondiscrimination laws and constitutional rights, nor could they argue their case before impartial judges or enterprise management.

To get public support for mass expulsions, the targets were charged with treason, disloyalty to the state, subversion, and plotting armed rebellion, hence the office and house searches for weapons and "subversive" literature. The Serb manager of a Zadar construction company told me how his office was repeatedly ransacked and searched for weapons and for a short-wave radio transmitter he was allegedly hiding for staying in touch with accomplices in Knin. His house was also searched, and he was detained. One morning he found a letter of resignation on his desk, drafted by the board of directors. He signed it. In Banja Luka, many forced resignations of Muslims and Croats were made to look like refusals to serve in the Serb army, the very army that was attacking Muslims and Croats. A 45-year-old Croat I interviewed was fired from a state position, detained, and immediately "assigned" to military labor service, which meant digging trenches, building fortifications, and removing mines for Serbs while being exposed to crossfire from both armies. Such stories are legion.

The political winners created state breakdown for their victims, with state repression. In an interview with a former Serb judge in Zadar, who supplied documentation, I learned that after the HDZ victory Croat national-ists harassed Serbs and pressured Zadar police to conduct house searches and arrest Serbs on phony charges. On November 5, 1990, 142 police officers, of all nationalities, protested the unprofessional and illegal use of police for political purposes and sent a four-page letter of protest to high officials in Croatia and the still-existing federal government. The Serb police officers were all fired, the non-Serbs were suspended and disciplined. New police were hired, some with criminal records who the judge remembered sentencing to incarceration. With the police thus brought under HDZ control, the purge got into full swing. There was an organized night of breaking the shop windows and the looting of Serb stores in Zadar when teenagers and wrecking teams were told in advance that "the police will arrive late" (Pulsic, 1998, p. 33; Thompson, 1994, p. 246). Serbs received anonymous threat letters, such as "Order to leave! We are fed up with communist Serb dictatorship; leave or you will disappear!" (May 26, 1990 addressed to a Serb dentist) (personal communication, May 22, 1998). In nearby Biograd, flyers were posted with "Chetniks, it is forbidden to go to the medical center; signed: People of Biograd." The authorities refused to intervene because the HDZ (i.e., the authorities) approved the purge of Serbs. Uniformed HDZ militias operated in public and camped in the Zadar police station courtyard. As for the moderate Croats, my informant said only "no one was bold enough to help us [Serbs in Zadar]."

The purges were similar in Serb-dominated areas, and the moderates were similarly scared to intervene. I asked a Muslim business leader from Banja Luka what the moderate Serbs did when non-Serbs were fired from their positions, many evicted from their homes, and the mosques were dynamited. "They [moderate Serbs] were scared; even death threats were not uncommon," he replied. It was confirmed by a moderate Serb academic in Banja Luka who refused to join the SDS (the Serb party) and serve in the army: He was fired from his faculty position and was totally marginalized. Former friends crossed the street when they saw him approaching. He made a living as a petty trader. Thus nationalists, through control of the state and its agents, intimidated moderates, repressed their opponents, and created chaos for other nationalities.

MILITIAS TAKE OVER

Without protection from laws and the authorities, in fact frequently persecuted by the authorities and held collectively responsible for alleged past, present, and future sins of their nationality, victims and targets of persecution and aggression fled, submitted, or organized armed self-defense. Already in 1990 when ethnic vandalism got started, some villages and towns organized night watches and defense guards. Later in Croatia as the new Croat State tried to exercise sovereignty in Serb-majority districts but was resisted, local Serbs formed militias that resisted, sometimes with force and often with barricades and logs that blocked roads. Disputes between neighboring villages or neighborhoods within a village could also lead to clashes and arming. A Serb farmer near Knin told me that "during the election campaign we listened to TV, radio and the politicians, and it was scary because there was talk of revenge for the World War Two massacres, and that could mean war was coming." Incidents started with nearby Croat villagers: "They blocked the highway and we blocked the highway." They formed an armed village militia. Weapons were gotten from a Serb paramilitary operating in the district (personal communication, May 26, 1998).

In contrast to local defensive militias, offensive militias and paramilitaries roamed far and wide and perpetrated ethnic cleansing, massacres, atrocities, and other war crimes, as in the Prijedor district. One huge recruitment pool for militias were soccer hooligans. The largest and most criminal militia, Arkan's Tigers, was founded in May 1990 from the Red Star fan club in Belgrade. Arkan had been its president and had paid for members' trips to European cup matches. The fans popularized Serb symbols, flags, colors, and chants during games and rallies and engaged in violent clashes with other fan clubs. One of their chants paralleled the political program of the extreme Serb nationalists: "We are the fans from proud Serbia, Slobo [Milosevic] you Serb, Serbia stands behind you; come out on the bleachers, greet the Serbian race; from Kosovo to Knin Serb is united with Serb" (cited in Colovic, 1998, p. 269). The Tigers set up a military training camp visited by Red Star soccer stars. When they became ethnic cleansers, as in Prijedor in 1992, they "worked" on weekends and transported huge cargoes of loot back home to Serbia after each "operation." An informant told me that shoppers in Belgrade purchased such looted goods at bargain prices knowing well their origins.

Another pool of recruitment for militias were prisons and jails. It was a fantastic deal. In return for signing up and becoming draft exempt, one got not only freedom, but also a uniform and weapons, and unlimited opportunities to loot homes, steal automobiles, and extort German Marks from scared refugees—at little risk, because the victims were mostly unarmed civilians. Secondary schools were also recruitment pools. A young man from Knin told me that "my older classmates were recruited by both Serbs and Croats to join the military and to join militias, and threatened that we wouldn't ever get jobs if we didn't join" (personal communication, May 26, 1998). Peer pressure and intimidation also factored into making reluctant young men join.

We do not have to assume that militiamen were fanatics to start with, filled with ethnic hatred. Tim Judah (1997) described how a Serb militiaman was recruited by his peers from the local SDS (the Serb party) who pressured him for weeks: "We've all got to take up arms, or we'll disappear from here." He had Muslim and Croat friends. Would they protect him against extremists of all nationalities? It was not likely if it got serious. So he "took out a gun." Another Serb kept being asked in his café, "What are you going to do? Which side will you be on?" His peers divided all Serbs into "good Serbs" and "Alija's Serbs" (a compromiser with the Muslims, a traitor). In the end he, too, "took out a gun" (p. 194).

Peer pressure and fear, not only of Muslims but also of extremist Serbs who might finger him as a "traitor," were the major causes for a man to join a militia. Some of these men were unemployed and expected a job in the coming Serb government as militia or police. All were influenced by the incessant anti-Muslim propaganda from the Serb media that spewed forth ethnic hatred. Arkan's men were indoctrinated to kill civilians. According to a Russian mercenary who trained at Arkan's Erdut militia camp, he was startled by the "brutality drummed into the heads of the fighters: 'a Serbian patriot is merciless toward the enemy; he does not have the right to spare the latter's children, women, or aged' " (cited in Cigar, 1995, p. 64).

Once the young man "took out a gun," he became encapsulated in a quasi-military unit with peer solidarity and ethnic loyalty that trained him, indoctrinated him, and put him under a command. From an ordinary man, he changed into a potential killer. Helen Fein (1993) has scanned the 20th-century record on atrocities and genocide and has concluded that "killing on state order needs no special explanation" (p. 44). It was true of the "ordinary Germans" who became killers of Jews in Poland and the Ukraine in World War II (Browning, 1993). Note that it does not matter to the final outcome that many young men and adults refuse to participate in violence; in Bosnia and Serbia many deserted the Yugoslav army, refused to serve when called up by the army, and fled abroad to escape the draft. As long as 10–20% are willing to serve in police, militias, paramilitaries and the army, and as long as the other 80–90% are not organized, the extremist nationalists will prevail.

There were many militias and paramilitaries in the Bosnian war and in Croatia. A *militia* or *paramilitary* is a volunteer quasi-military group that is not directly under a military chain of command and not accountable to a military or civilian authority. The Bassiouni report (United Nations Security Council, 1994) listed some 83 known paramilitaries in Bosnia alone, 53 for Serbs with an estimated total of 20,000–40,000 members; 13 Croat militias, with 12,000–20,000 members; and 14 Bosnians, with 4,000–6,000 participants, operating between June 1991 and late 1993, at which time many were absorbed into the regular armies or had disbanded. There were also foreign volunteers and mercenaries, in unknown numbers, who added to this body of irregular military. In the Krajina part of Croatia, there were an estimated 12,000 paramilitaries. The largest militia was Milan Martic's "Marticevci," who not only terrorized Croats but also silenced the Serb moderates.

The Bassiouni report (United Nations Security Council, 1994) and Helsinki Watch (1992) have detailed atrocities committed by the militias as well as others. Robert Block (1993) managed to interview a Bosnian Croat killer from Tuta Naletalic's notorious militia that provides insight into the mentality of war criminals. They had perpetrated a massacre of Muslims at Ahmici, a village without a military target, when fleeing villagers were ambushed after shelling and executed at close range. The others were blown up when hand grenades were tossed into houses. A total of 190 civilians, including women and children, were butchered in a few minutes. Tuta's men called themselves a death squad or special punishment unit. The men "look as if they had been cast as thugs by a movie director." One of them admitted that they attacked a village and had come across 12 civilians hiding in a house: "We killed them. There was no other way. There was no one behind us who could take prisoners . . . very often they shoot you in the back. Even the old people." He also said: "I really don't hate Muslims . . . but because of the situation I want to kill them all." When asked to explain why such militias kill civilians, Mate Boban, leader of the Bosnian Croats merely said, "The Muslims did it to themselves" (p. 9).

When all is said and done, how could these militiamen commit atrocities? In any conflict there are moderates, usually the majority at the start, who condemn and oppose the violence of extremists and who stand for norms of civility, for compromise, for boundaries in conflict. But in the former Yugoslavia the moderates were marginalized, intimidated, threatened, expelled, and even killed. Several normative principles and beliefs were drummed into the hearts and minds of the people that lowered inhibitions against killing ethnic outsiders, even civilians. These principles and beliefs are as follows:

- Collective guilt—"they" act in unison; children grow into adults, women give birth to future warriors, even old people stab you from behind; "they" will never change.
- Revenge and retaliation—"they" massacred "us" in the past and are about to do it again; in fact they have already started. A settling of scores is justified: "an eye for an eye."
- Deterrence/first strike—disable them before they strike, which is what they are about to do, despite appearances, because they are secretive and treacherous.

- Danger/survival—these are extraordinary times, one's entire nationality is threatened, and extreme measures are justified.
- Legitimacy—ordinary people and militias are justified in taking extreme measures because the constituted authorities have not come to the defense of our people.

These are the rationalizations and the justifying norms of unrestrained collective violence. Other motives for collective violence were economic gain, peer pressure, and lack of accountability.

In accounting for the motivations and actions of the militias, it should be remembered that they were a small though not negligible part of the population. In the 1991 census, there were 1.4 million Serbs in Bosnia. If half were women, that leaves 700,000 men, and an estimated 200,000 men between the ages of 15 and 35. The United Nations estimated 20,000–40,000 Bosnian Serb militiamen. If we assume that every militiaman was involved in some atrocities, the perpetrators were 10–20% of the males of prime military age. Unfortunately, 10–20% of the men in militias was more than enough to spread death and destruction on a massive scale.

THE EXTREMISTS ELIMINATE THE MODERATES

The demise of the moderates was due to a combination of electoral defeats, loss of credibility in public opinion, and intimidation and threats from extremists. In the Croatia elections of 1990, the nationalist HDZ, which at this time still included some moderate nationalists, got 1.2 million votes, whereas the Reform Communists got almost 1 million, and the Serb nationalist party, the SDS, got very few, mostly in the vicinity of Knin. Not only did many Croats not vote for HDZ and the majority of Serbs not vote for SDS, the two most nationalist choices, but SDS itself, under Dr. Jovan Raskovic, was a moderate party that wanted a compromise with the Croat leadership, not independence from Croatia and joining a Greater Serbia. Yet a year later, on May 19, 1991, almost all Croats voted for independence, and almost all Serbs boycotted the vote and favored an independent Serb Krajina region.

What had occurred in the meantime to polarize the electorate toward extremes was the massive purge of Serbs in Croatia, the Serb seizure of power in Serb majority areas, and the fleeing and expulsion of Croats from there. The citizenry had been armed, militias were formed, and there was increasing resort to force and violence in contested districts. When they gained no concessions and could not stop ethnic clashes, moderates like Raskovic lost credibility (Silber & Little, 1995). In Zagreb, which had a strong liberal democratic tradition, a human rights activist told me how small groups of intellectuals and ad hoc committees, some 100 activists in all, advocated Serb–Croat conciliation in 1990 and 1991 and went on peace missions to villages and towns with a mixed population, but they became discouraged for lack of results: "Moderates just vanished; some joined the nationalists." Milar Pupovac, a Serb party leader who stood for Serb–Croat dialogue and conciliation, was vilified by both sets of extremists: "Both Belgrade and Zagreb did everything to neutralize and physically eliminate all those who stood in the way of war," wrote Stitkovac (1997, p. 159).

In Osijek, which was 40% Serb and about 60% Croat, a Serb economist who was also the vice mayor and had been elected as an independent moderate to the Zagreb legislature in 1990 described to me the rise of extremism and ethnic violence. "It was safer to take sides than being for peace in the middle," as her own case testifies. Former students avoided her in the street; one later told her "it was dangerous to be seen talking to you in public." While she was attending the legislature in Zagreb, her house was bombed. When she asked the mayor for police protection, he told her she had been targeted because "snipers probably used it" and added "What are you still doing in Osijek anyway?" When she herself was targeted by a sniper, she joined other refugees out of Osijek (personal communication, May 26, 1998).

Even the Bosnian Muslims who remained the least nationalist in the former Yugoslavia experienced a nationalist trend already before the war. For instance, in January 1990, according to *Oslobodjenje*, an Islamic group demanded separate food preparation in the JNA for observant Muslims. In the 1990 election the Muslim party (MBO) and leader (Ali Zulfikarpasic) who advocated the most conciliatory approach with other nationalities got a mere two seats in the legislature (Monnesland, 1997, p. 340). I interviewed a Muslim business leader from Banja Luka about organizing the local branch of a non-nationalist businessmen's party: "I promoted the politics of compromise, but the voters listened to the nationalists." Before he was purged, he managed to emigrate to Austria. Powerlessness, emigration, and detention were the fate of the moderates.

Knin is a good example of how moderates were purged by the extremists. Ethnic relations between Croats and Serbs had been good. But as Croatia was moving toward independence, the Krajina Serbs became apprehensive. A local dentist, Milan Babic, became a political leader, backed by a militia under a local police inspector, Milan Martic. According to Glenny (1992, pp. 19–21), these two and their men went around town intimidating the moderate Serbs in Knin who believed that Babic was driving them toward a senseless war, and they pressured them to enlist for volunteer duty in the militia. A similar fate befell Glina, another initially moderate city in the Krajina:

Babic had been sending emissaries from Knin in an attempt to under-mine the social-democratic forces in Glina in favor of the militant nationalist line. The Serbs in Glina resisted Babic's bloody entreaties until June [1990], but by then they felt that they had no longer a choice—it was Croats or Serbs, and they were Serbs. (Glenny, 1992, p. 93)

In a Bosnian example reported by Mazowiecki (1992, §8–11), "Accord-ing to a witness [from Bosanska Dubica], the elected authorities who were moderates or who tried to prevent acts of violence were dismissed or replaced by Serbian extremists." And then ethnic cleansing got started in the city. Other methods were killing moderate leaders, such as the murder of Josip Rheil-Kir, the regional Croat police chief of the Slavonian part of Croatia, a moderate who had negotiated cease fires between villages and towns, between Serbs and Croats, and who was gunned down by an HDZ (Croat) extremist.

The overthrow of moderates by extremists or radicals is well-known in the great revolutions: Girondins were overthrown by the Jacobins in the French revolution, and all groups were overthrown by the Bolsheviks in the Russian revolution.[2] The means of seizing power are similar. The radicals create parallel governance to the state and come to exercise de facto authority in many institutions, and militias and mutineers execute a coup d'etat. Then the remaining moderates are purged (Brinton, 1957). It happened in the mixed ethnic districts of Croatia and Bosnia. The extremists prevailed for the same reasons they win in the great revolutions. When there is a major political crisis, to govern is a disadvantage. Extremists create ethnic inci-dents, yet the moderates are not capable of protecting the life and property of the citizenry. The economic crisis feeds unemployment, but the moderates lack the resources for a recovery program. The extremists are united and willing to use force; the moderates are tolerant and democratic and lack unity. The extremists train and arm militias; the moderates count on negotia-tions and on international diplomacy.

The moderates need be overthrown by the extremists only in one ethnic group for the polarization and a spiral of violent conflict to get started, although it will be more rapid and intense if it occurs in both or all ethnic groups. Restraint by one ethnic group is not enough to check the violence, and restraint will weaken as casualties mount. The overthrow

---

[2] The overthrow of moderates by extremists has also been observed in other ethnonational conflicts. It happened in Rwanda before the genocide when Hutu extremists targeted and attacked Hutu moderates (Prunier, 1995). Similarly, in the Palestinian intifada, after 1987, there were few Israeli casualties compared to many Palestinian moderates assaulted by the insurgents—typically merchants' stores were burnt when they refused to join a strike, and "collaborators" were condemned in secret tribunals run by Hamas fundamentalists. Kuper (1977) has provided examples from other ethnonational conflicts.

of the moderates is not a single event but diffuses through cities, towns, and villages over a period of time. In some localities there are no extremists; in others, the moderates hold them in check, at least for a time. But extremists fan out from centers of strength with organizers and militias to gain control elsewhere, as Babic and Martic did from Knin. Help for extremists comes from outside in the form of weapons, volunteers, emigrés, and mercenaries. After the moderates have been overthrown by extremists, collective violence and war between nationalities is unleashed on a vast scale.

My account is not a narrative of events but an analytic explanation for the breakup of Yugoslavia. No explanation of such a complex event is complete and comprehensive, and mine is no exception. My explanation combines structural conditions such as Serb–Croat differences on federal governance, with agency, the contest of rival elites for power in post-communism. I highlight the linkages of elites to the citizenry, as in the growth of populist nationalism, the effects of the mass media, and the outcome of elections. I describe within-nationality differences, between moderates and extremists, as well as conflicts between nationality; and finally I describe concrete causal mechanisms of polarization and escalation, as the purging of minorities and opponents by the extremists.

Up to the 1980s two strong integrative institutions kept Yugoslavia united and its nationalities balanced: the League of Communists and the Yugoslav army, the JNA. Before his death, the personal prestige and authority of Marshal Tito was even more crucial. The 1980s economic crisis and the collapse of communism in Eastern Europe forced on the Yugoslav agenda major political and economic change. The solution to this challenge that it shared with other states in Eastern Europe was complicated by the nationality issue. Still, the breakup of Yugoslavia in wars and collective violence was not inevitable.

The explanations I started with have some merit, but they are incomplete. "Primordial attachments and ancient hatreds" were present in so far as there was a latent nationalism, but it was latent, and "ancient hatreds" were not part of it. Hatred came later, as a consequence of the ethnic cleansing and other outrages. Fear and insecurity were the dominant sentiments driving much political behavior, but politicians and ideologues had to labor mightily to open the Pandora's box of populist nationalism.

The instrumentalist view gets it right that nationality was manipulated by politicians and intellectuals for state creation and for fulfilling personal ambitions and careers. But these goals could not have been fulfilled without populist nationalism having resonance and the discrediting and defeat of moderates in competitive elections. I agree with the constructionist view, but it is unspecific on the construction and erosion of ethnic identities.

"State breakdown and security dilemma" is right about fear and insecurity. But there was no anarchy and state breakdown in Prijedor, Banja Luka,

Zadar, and most other cities and districts. Anarchy and breakdown were engineered by extremists with ethnic cleansing and purges; the war in Bosnia was a unilateral aggression against a peaceful, functioning state.

My explanation rests on a dynamic model of ethnic polarization and of escalation from bounded contention to violent actions, a model inspired by familiar social science and historical knowledge. The model explains how elites created populist nationalism, how the mass media were the engines for the diffusion of false beliefs and myths, how extremists manipulated populist nationalism to discredit moderates and win elections, how extremists in power purged minorities and opponents and spread fear and insecurity, and how finally militias were formed and ended up by killing innocent civilians.

REFERENCES

Blagojevic, M. (1998). Der Exodus aus Kosovo: ein Serbisches Trauma im Propagandakrieg [The exodus from Kosovo: A Serbian trauma in the propaganda war]. In T. Bremer, N. Popop, & H. Günther-Stobble (Eds.), *Serbiens Weg in den Krieg* (pp. 75–92). Berlin: Berlin Verlag.

Block, R. (1993, October 21). Killers. *The New York Review of Books* (p. 9).

Brinton, C. (1957). *The anatomy of revolution.* New York: Doubleday.

Browning, C. (1993). *Ordinary men.* New York: HarperCollins.

Bugajski, J. (1996). Balkan myths and Bosnian massacres. In R. Thomas & H. R. Friman (Eds.), *The south Slav conflict* (pp. 115–144). New York: Garland.

Cigar, N. (1995). *Genocide in Bosnia.* College Station: Texas A&M University Press.

Cohen, L. (1993). *Broken bonds: The disintegration of Yugoslavia.* Boulder, CO: Westview.

Colovic, I. (1998). Fussbal, Hooligans, und Krieg [Soccer, hooligans, and war]. In T. Bremer, N. Popop, & H. Günther-Stobble (Eds.), *Serbiens Weg in den Krieg* (pp. 261–277). Berlin: Berlin Verlag.

David, S. (1997). Internal war: Causes and cures. *World Politics, 49*(4), 552–576.

Dawes, R. (1994). *House of cards.* New York: Free Press.

Deutsch, M. (1973). *The resolution of conflict.* New Haven: Yale University Press.

Djilas, A. (1995). Fear thy neighbor: The breakup of Yugoslavia. In C. Kupchan (Ed.), *Nationalism and nationalities in the New Europe* (pp. 85–106). Ithaca, NY: Cornell University.

Fein, H. (1979). *Accounting for genocide.* New York: Free Press.

Fein, H. (1993). *Genocide: A sociological perspective.* Newbury Park, CA: Sage.

Gagnon, V. P. (1997). Ethnic nationalism and international conflict: The case of Serbia. In M. Brown (Ed.), *Nationalism and ethnic conflict* (pp. 146–162). Cambridge, MA: MIT Press.

Glenny, M. (1992). *The fall of Yugoslavia: The third Balkan War*. London: Penguin Books.

Helsinki Watch. (1992). *War crimes in Bosnia–Herzegovina*. New York: Human Rights Watch.

Hukanovic, R. (1996). *The tenth circle of hell*. New York: Basic Books.

Ignatieff, M. (1993). *Blood and belonging: Journey into the new nationalism*. New York: Farrar Strauss.

International Commission on the Balkans. (1996). *Unfinished peace*. Washington, DC: Carnegie Endowment for International Peace.

Judah, T. (1997). *The Serbs*. New Haven, CT: Yale University Press.

Kaplan, R. (1993). *Balkan ghosts*. New York: St. Martin Press.

Kuper, L. (1977). *The pity of it all: Polarization in racial and ethnic relations*. Minneapolis: University of Minnesota Press.

Laber, J. (1993, March). Bosnia, questions about rape. *The New York Review of Books* (pp. 3–6).

Lake, D., & Rothchild, D. (1996). Containing fear: The origin and management of ethnic conflict. *International Security, 21*, 41–75.

Linz, J. J., & Stepan, A. (1996). *Problems of democratic consolidation*. Baltimore: Johns Hopkins University Press.

Maas, P. (1995). *Love the neighbor: A story of war*. New York: Knopf.

Malcolm, N. (1996). *Bosnia: A short history*. New York: New York University Press.

Mazowiecki, T. (1992). *Report on the situation of human rights in the territory of the former Yugoslavia*. New York: United Nations Economic and Social Council.

Mazowiecki, T. (1993, June). *Seventh periodic report*. New York: United Nations Economic and Social Council.

Milgram, S. (1974). *Obedience to authority*. New York: Harper and Row.

Milosavljevic, O. (1998). Der Missbrauch der Autoritat der Wissenschaft [The misuse of scholarly authority]. In T. Bremer, N. Popop, & H. Günther-Stobble (Eds.), *Serbiens Weg in den Krieg* (pp. 159–181). Berlin: Berlin Verlag.

Milosevic, M. (1997). The media wars: 1987–1997. In J. Udovicki & J. Ridgeway (Eds.), *Burn this house down: The making and unmaking of Yugoslavia* (pp. 108–129). Durham, NC: Duke University.

Monnesland, S. (1997). *Land Ohne Wiederkehr: Ex Jugoslavien, die Wurzeln des Krieges* [Land without return: The former Yugoslavia, the roots of the war]. Klagenfurt, Germany: Wieser.

Oberschall, A. (1973). *Social movement and social conflict*. Englewood Cliffs, NJ: Prentice-Hall.

Oberschall, A. (1993). *Social movements: Ideologies, interests, and identities*. New Brunswick, NJ: Transaction Books.

Oberschall, A. (1996). The breakup of Yugoslavia. *Research on Democracy and Society, 3*, 355–377.

Pesic, V. (1998). Krieg und Nationalstaaten [War and nation states]. In T. Bremer, N. Popop, & H. Günther-Stobble (Eds.), *Serbiens Weg in den Krieg* (pp. 15–42). Berlin: Berlin Verlag.

Posen, B. (1993). The security dilemma and ethnic conflict. In M. Brown (Ed.), *Ethnic conflict and internal security* (pp. 103–124). Princeton, NJ: Princeton University Press.

Prunier, G. (1995). *The Rwanda crisis.* New York: Columbia University Press.

"Public opinion survey on the Federal Executive Council's social and economic reform." (1990). *Yugoslav Survey, 31*(3), 3–26.

Pulsic, W. (1998). *Olib nationalism.* Honors thesis, Department of Sociology, University of North Carolina, Chapel Hill.

Pusic, V. (1998, January). Croatia at the crossroads. *Journal of Democracy, 9*(1), 111–124.

Rosens, E. (1989). *Creating ethnicity.* London: Sage.

Schelling, T. (1978). *Micromotives and macrobehavior.* New York: W. W. Norton.

Silber, L., & Little, A. (1995). *Yugoslavia: Death of a nation.* New York: TV Books.

Sisk, T. (1996). *Power sharing and international mediation in ethnic conflicts.* Washington, DC: United States Institute of Peace.

Stitkovac, E. (1997). Croatia: The first war. In J. Udovicki & J. Ridgeway (Eds.), *Burn this house down: The making and unmaking of Yugoslavia* (pp. 153–173). Durham, NC: Duke University.

Tajfel, H. (1970). Experiments in intergroup discrimination. *Science, 223*(11), 96–102.

Thompson, M. (1994). *Forging war: The media in Serbia, Croatia, and Bosnia–Hercegovina.* Bath, England: Bath Press.

United Nations Security Council. (1994). *Final report of the Commission of Experts* [Bassiouni Report]. New York: United Nations.

Woodward, S. (1995). *Balkan tragedy.* Washington, DC: Brookings Institution.

Wright, W. (1959). *Mass communication.* New York: Random House.

10

THE YUGOSLAV CATASTROPHE

MISHA GLENNY

Warkworth, Before Northumberland's Castle.
Enter Rumour, painted full of tongues
Rumour: Open your ears; for which of you will stop
The vent of hearing when loud Rumor speaks?
I, from the orient to the drooping west,
Making the wind my post-horse, still unfold
The acts commenced on this ball of earth:
Upon my tongues continual slanders ride,
The which in every language I pronounce,
Stuffing the ears of men with false reports.
I speak of peace, while covert enmity
Under the smile of safety wounds the world:
And who but Rumour, who but only I,
Make fearful musters and prepar'd defence,
Whilst the big year, swol'n with some other grief,
Is thought with child by the stern tyrant war,
And no such matter? Rumour is a pipe
Blown by surmises, jealousies, conjectures,
And of so easy and so plain a stop
That the blunt monster with uncounted heads,
The still-discordant wavering multitude,
Can play upon it. But what need I thus
My well-known body to anatomize
Among my household? Why is Rumour here?
—from the prologue to William Shakespeare's, *Henry IV*, Part II,
   "Induction."

One rare positive phenomenon is emerging from the wars in Yugoslavia and the current crisis in Serbia, Montenegro, Kosovo, and God knows where else. A disparate group of scholars of different persuasions from within and without the Balkans are making a concerted attempt to kill the demon Rumour and the inordinate influence that his slanderous tongues have exercised in and about the Balkans. Slowly but thoroughly the history of the Balkans is being reexamined and rewritten in an attempt to drown out the siren-like tunes of surmises, jealousies, and conjectures that Rumour plays so well.

Rarely has a region been so ill served by the uses of history as the Balkans. But I am not talking about the abuse of history, which the state builders of Serbia, Greece, Romania, Bulgaria, and Turkey indulged in, although there is still much research to be done in that department. I am talking about a vast body of popular literary and political work, again both within and without the Balkans, which perpetuates the myth that the region is inhabited solely by congenitally irrational and blood-thirsty mobs who are never happier than when slitting the throats of their next-door neighbors. This literature of denial would subvert geography, culture, and history by excluding the Balkans from Europe by dint of the inhabitants' alleged propensity for violence and political instability. I might say that among an ever-widening circle of academics and Balkans specialists, the idea that the violent fall of Yugoslavia was not a product of "ancient hatreds" has for a long time been a truism. That is not to say, however, that the members of this circle agree on what it is a product of. Far from it; their disagreements as to the causes of the crisis have been intense, not to say unpleasant.

But despite the academic opinion that dismisses the ancient hatred theory, the idea remains stubbornly rooted in the understanding of the Western media, policy makers, and, indeed, some academics and Balkan specialists, including many who have participated or are still participating in the crisis. Their influence is in turn decisive in perpetuating this popular view of the Balkans and, as long as it remains so, we will continue to fumble in the dark with regard to the nature of communal conflict in which civilians become prime targets for military, paramilitary, and irregular forces.

My remarks in this chapter deal with atrocities in the Balkans within a specific historical context. First, I cannot stress enough my conviction that the wars of Yugoslav succession are not harbingers of a new post-communist fever of nationalist struggle in Eastern Europe. Rather, they represent the end of a process begun in the second half of the 19th century at whose heart lay the collapse of the Austro-Hungarian and Ottoman Empires. The attempt to overcome the shattering impact of the collapse of multinational empires in the Balkans by creating Yugoslavia, a state based on constitutional principles of the nation-state but modified by a commitment to multinational principles, culminated in the unedifying spectacle of the Croatian and Bosnian wars. Regrettably, the events in Kosovo in 1999 suggest that we must in all probability witness a reprise of violence in the Balkan south, with a clash between Slav and Albanian pretensions centered both on Kosovo and on Macedonia. But the Albanian Question, that is, the political fate of the Albanian communities in Kosovo and Macedonia—but also the political fate of Serbia, Montenegro, and Macedonia—is the final substantially unresolved issue of irredentism in the Balkans. Once a solution is found, the chance of nationalist war recurring in the Balkans will be slim—not negligible but slim (I am excluding the possibility here of a Greek–Turkish conflict).

As a country, Yugoslavia lasted as long as it did in part because its very existence provided an apparently workable solution for two of the most insuperable problems to plague the Balkans. Assessing the Congress of Berlin, which was convened in 1878 to solve the Great Eastern Crisis, the British historian A. J. P. Taylor noted in 1954 that

> Macedonia and Bosnia, the two great achievements of the congress, both contained the seeds of future disaster. The Macedonian question haunted European diplomacy for a generation and then caused the Balkan war of 1912. Bosnia first provoked the crisis of 1908 and then exploded World War in 1914, a war which brought down the Habsburg monarchy. (p. 252)

It is no coincidence that both Bosnia and the most contested part of Macedonia found themselves in the one state that truly bucked the Wilsonian trend of self-determination after Versailles—Yugoslavia. And Yugoslavia, flawed though it was both in its first and second incarnations, provided protection for these two areas. As the collapse of communism posed unique questions for Yugoslavia (with its unusually harmonious multi-ethnicity, not to mention its bridging role between East and West), it rapidly became clear that from being in pole position in the race for advancement in Europe, Yugoslavia was sliding to the back of the starting grid. What is more, if, as seemed likely, Wilsonian principles of self-determination were applied to Yugoslavia in the late 1980s and early 1990s, then Bosnia and Macedonia would have the most to fear, as their respective presidents, Alija Izetbegovic and Kiro Gligorov, clearly understood. If you agree, they realized, to Croatia becoming a nation-state, a state identified explicitly with the Croat people, then do not be surprised not only that the Serbs of Bosnia demand to secede from Bosnia, but also that the Albanians of Kosovo demand to leave Serbia, and the Albanians of Macedonia demand to leave Macedonia. Often those people who most fervently supported the secession of Croatia from Yugoslavia and its transformation into a state identified specifically with Croats were also the loudest in supporting an independent Bosnia where harmony depended on all three nationalities actively supporting that secession, a harmony that patently did not exist at the time of independence.

The fears of presidents Izetbegovic and Gligorov were not borne of a belief that the Serbs, Croats, or Albanians were peculiarly inclined to gorge themselves on nationalist excess. They simply knew that in times of constitutional uncertainty, the strongest regional elites had a tendency to siphon off part of the large reservoir of cultural nationalism that had developed through the Balkans in the 20th century and then transform this into a toxic brand of political nationalism. This process of turning neutral nationalism into heavy nationalism involves a more complicated process of political chemistry than may at first be imagined. "Heavy" nationalism is highly unstable: It may dissipate and lose its toxicity unexpectedly, or it may blow up in the chemist's face. "Brutal" nationalism is by no means as deeply rooted in Balkan society as is popularly believed.

Let me be resolutely clear—the level of economic backwardness in the Balkans in the 19th and early 20th centuries ensured that modern nationalism experienced a rigorous uphill struggle establishing itself in the region. The Great Eastern Crisis of 1875, when the Ottoman Empire began its final journey toward crucifixion, was laid to rest in 1878 by the Congress of Berlin. This is when the modern history of the Balkans began and, incidentally, many of the practices that are erroneously assumed by people in the West to be the produce of ancient Balkan enmities. Through most of its history, the Ottoman Empire was not the fabled murderous despotism but a complicated, flawed, but stable form of imperial organization which, with regard to matters like religious tolerance, was by far the most liberal Empire in Europe. Its reputation for violence inspired by religious bigotry emerged during the 19th century when the Sultan's grip on the periphery of empire began to slip. (The power vacuums, which emerged in Serbia, Greece, Egypt, and elsewhere, were filled by ambitious regional despots under whose rule communal violence became unexceptional. The memory of this violence was then projected back quite unfairly onto the entire Ottoman experience.) At the Berlin Congress, the Great Powers decided that they now wished to regulate the disintegration of the Ottoman Empire. So, like every other decisive moment in modern Balkan history, including the Dayton Agreements, the outcome of crisis at the Berlin Congress was dictated by the Great Powers.

The fateful imperialist decisions made at Berlin did not merely define much of the modern history of the Balkan Peninsula. As well as beginning the often arbitrary carving up of the Balkans, which ensured that large chunks of mouth-watering territory would be disputed in the future, it also added the spice of romanticism by triggering "The Great Game" in central Asia and, with more brutal honesty, "The Scramble for Africa." It is, I think, worth noting that the origins of conflict in Bosnia, Afghanistan, and Somalia can all be traced back to decisions made at the Congress of Berlin.

The decisions made by the Congress of Berlin represented a profound shift in the attitude of the Great Powers to the ailing Ottoman Empire. Following all previous crises in the East, the Powers had collaborated to preserve the Empire and encourage internal reform. At Berlin, they decided that it was beyond salvation (although it is a moot point whether it was or not), so they should instead begin its dismemberment. The one great

European holding left to the Sultan in 1878 was Macedonia. Most politicians inside and outside the Balkans, however, assumed that at some point in the near future, the Ottoman Empire would lose Macedonia. In the event of Macedonia fragmenting, as it must, who would gain control to the most strategically valuable part of the Balkans?

The Macedonian Question still contains great potential for violence. But its nature has changed considerably since the last time it mattered during World War II, and it is barely recognizable from 90 years ago when it consumed more column inches in *The Times* of London than did any other single foreign policy issue (this appears even more astonishing, given that the British had relatively few commercial interests in Macedonia). The competing expansionist claims of Greece, Bulgaria, and Serbia built the complex engine of the Macedonian struggle, as the events of the first decade of this century are known. In turn, the Great Powers, especially Austria–Hungary and Russia, provided the fuel. The source of the appalling violence visited upon the inhabitants of Macedonia was thus external. It did not flow from irredentist desires of the various Macedonian communities to wrench the region from the Ottoman orbit and attach the area to either of three surrounding mother ships. One contemporary observer noted,

> Macedonia is racked by political intrigue without, and within by turbulent, ambitious, mischief-making factions, which are neither of the people, nor voice their legitimate aspirations. It is the saddest part of Macedonia's unhappy lot that its worst enemies are those whose professions of friendship are loudest. (Brailsford, 1906, p. 57)

Relations among the various peasant communities in the Macedonian hinterland were, until the turn of the century, defined by all sorts of markers, except, I would argue, by nationalism. By the end of the Second Balkan War in 1913, however, the complicated relationships of economic exchange, intermarriage, and linguistic fusion had been virtually obliterated and replaced instead by a crude and vicious nationalism.

Politicians, diplomats, writers, geographers, folklorists, and historians provided the flesh and organs of that nationalism, especially during the crucial period from 1878 to 1914. But the spine of this nationalism was the army. All parts of that body politic, flesh and bones, gazed north to Germany and westward to Italy for inspiration. The great military model that the Serbs, Bulgarians, Turks and, to a lesser extent, Greeks and Romanians looked up to was Prussia. Publications sponsored by the Serbian military, popularly thought to be hostile to all things German, devoted considerable praise to Prussia's military traditions and modernizing ability. Many Serbian officers received their training in Germany, as did Bulgars and Turks.

From the specific example of Italy and Germany, and from logic learned from the behavior of all Great Powers, the small circle of Balkan state builders learned one central lesson—force determines history. And force means a strong state, which means centralization and a powerful army. These were not Balkan traditions. They were Western traditions. Let us look at the First and Second Balkan Wars, widely believed to offer definitive proof of Balkan madness, within that framework. It is certainly true that the decision by Montenegro, Serbia, Bulgaria, and Greece to join forces and expel the Ottoman Empire from Europe in 1912 was made by those states in defiance of great power intentions. But Balkan nationalism and militarism, as expressed in the Balkan Wars, were in fact much more closely related to the practices and morality of great power imperialism than to local traditions. The Balkan armies were largely funded by Western loans. Western firms supplied them with weapons and other technology; their officers were schooled and organized by the French, Germans, Russians, and Britons. The armies were staffed and, in the case of Turkey, actually commanded by Westerners. Representatives of Krupp, Škoda, Schneider-Creusot, and Vickers participated as observers in the wars. Their reports on the effectiveness of their weaponry was used to advertise the superiority of their products over those of their competitors. The compulsion of the new states to grab territory, with scant regard to the facts of demography or history, merely reflected the practices of their great power neighbors whose arbitrary and foolhardy decisions at the Congress of Berlin had ensured that there was plenty of territory to dispute.

Inasmuch as anyone in the West knows about the Balkan Wars, they have learned it from the report published in early 1914 by the Carnegie Endowment's International Commission to Inquire Into the Causes and Conduct of the Balkan Wars. This is an important document, and the commission's members were serious and well-intentioned. But I would like to draw attention to a passage from the introduction:

> What finally succeeds in bringing armed peace into disrepute, is that today the Great Powers are manifestly unwilling to make war. Each one of them, Germany, England, France and the United States, to name a few, has discovered the obvious truth that the richest country has the most to lose by war, and each country wishes for peace above all things. This is so true that these two Balkan wars have wrought us a new miracle—we must not forget it—namely, the active and sincere agreement of the Great Powers who, changing their tactics, have done everything to localize the hostilities in the Balkans and have become the defenders of the peace that they themselves threatened thirty-five years ago, at the time of the Congress of Berlin. (Carnegie Endowment, 1914, p. 17)

Five months later, notwithstanding the commission's belief in the inherent wisdom of the Great Powers, imperialist rivalry celebrated its zenith by persuading the club's senior members to divert their enormous economic and technological resources into one vast industrial conglomerate of death. During the five months of the Battle of Verdun in 1916, for example "more than twenty-three million shells were fired by the two contending armies [French and German] . . . on average more than a hundred shells a minute" (Gilbert, 1994, pp. 299–300). This was war beyond all comprehension and recognition for the participants. The generals who now marshaled gigantic armies had never conceived of military action on this scale, and hundreds of thousands of young men paid for the inexperience of their military chiefs.

The vast massacres of World War I relegated the ruinous social and economic impact of the Balkan Wars to the penny place. But those who witnessed or participated in the two wars were afforded a unique insight into what the 20th century had in store. Several battles pitted forces against one another that were each larger than Napoleon's mightiest army. This is despite Serbia, for example, boasting a population of less than 3 million. The Bulgarians mobilized a full 25% of its male population, just under 500,000 men. The fighting was characterized by trench warfare and merciless sieges and by pitiless artillery assaults on unprotected infantry and civilians; all sides, except Montenegro and Romania,[1] deployed airplanes against the enemy, mainly for reconnaissance or dropping leaflets, but also for the occasional bombing raid. For the first time in modern warfare, technology enabled commanders to fight 24 hours a day as huge searchlights illuminated enemy defenses. This was not Balkan warfare—this was Western warfare.

World War I started in the Balkans and devastated the region, but it was a European war and not a Balkan War. The profound tensions between the Habsburgs and the Serbs over Bosnia and over the wider South Slav question that triggered the war had little to do with the almighty destructive force unleashed over Europe after the Serb government refused the Austrian ultimatum of July 1914. The Balkans was not the powder keg but merely one of a number of devices that might have acted as a detonator. The powder keg was Europe itself.

The war lasted much longer in one part of the Balkans than elsewhere.

Both the Central Powers and the Entente attempted to persuade the Balkan nations to abandon neutrality and join in the war—the only part of the world where the main warring powers actively hoped to expand the theater of conflict. The Balkans was the scene of the most horrific violence, comparable with both the Western and Eastern Fronts in the Balkans, but it was routinely ignored by most historians. (How many people are readily aware that Turkey suffered over twice as many casualties at Gallipoli as the combined Allied forces, or that the decisive offensive of the Great War

---

[1]Calling Romania belligerent is stretching a point, but Bucharest exploited the massive coalition against Bulgaria in the Second Balkan War to occupy and annex the southern Dobrudja in northeastern Bulgaria.

was opened on the Salonika front and was the product of Serbian military strategy and executed by a joint Franco-Serbian force?) It was during World War I (at the same time as Gallipoli) that the first mass atrocity of the 20th century was perpetrated—the expulsion and extermination of hundreds of thousands of Armenians (although this took place in Anatolia, not part of the Balkan peninsula, Turkish political culture is an integral part of the Balkans among other regions).

The pattern begun here whereby those members of a minority least able to protect themselves attracted the full force of the majority's wrath would repeat itself many times in Europe and elsewhere in the course of the century. The relatively high incidence of such persecution and massacre in the Balkans is largely due to the complex demographic spread bequeathed to the region by both the Austro–Hungarian and the Ottoman Empires. Henceforth, murder and expulsion became the two most overused instruments in dealing with nationality questions in the Balkans.

The role of the elite and the political environment in which such revolting phenomena occur have often been underappreciated in favor of a more emotive response that highlights a particular nation or community as being especially prone to blood-thirsty behavior. But those who emphasize the role of the mob in the pogrom have the effect of minimizing or obscuring the role of those who are politically responsive. All Balkan massacres this century have enjoyed the specific approval of state organs whose agents have usually been the instigators as well. This is not merely an army commander winking to his troops surrounding defenseless women. In Turkey during the Great War, in Croatia during World War II, and in the Republika Srpska during the Yugoslav wars of 1991–1995, the legal system was turned on its head—murder was encouraged and approved by the state and its propaganda apparatus. Not participating in murder, conversely, was regarded if not as illegal than certainly as hostile behavior. Such events are invariably accompanied by a historical justification that can usually be boiled down to the simple formula of "eternal enmity" between two communities. The construction of this justification by historians, and newspapers and other media under state influence, however, tends to mask the real intentions of the elite—economic and/or political consolidation or aggrandizement.

The Greco–Turkish war, the zenith of an almost unbroken pattern of warfare involving the two countries since 1912, finally ended in 1923 with the forced transfer of just under 1 million Greeks from Turkey to Greece and some 300,000 Turks from Greece to Turkey. This horrific example of Balkan barbarism was the result of the Great Powers maneuvering at the Paris Peace Conference as Britain, France, and even the United States, in the form of Mr. Non-violence himself, Woodrow Wilson, gave the Greek Army explicit permission to do their Great Power dirty work in Anatolia. This is not to let irresponsible Balkan politicians off the hook—I consider two men supremely responsible for this enormous catastrophe—Eleftherios Venizelos and David Lloyd George. The British historian of modern Greece, Richard Clogg (1992), has written that

> although the exchange of populations necessarily occasioned a great deal of human misery . . . it did ensure that Greece itself became an ethnically homogenous society . . . . The result was that Greece was transformed into a country virtually without minority problems, by Balkan standards at least. (p. 121)

Since then diplomats and politicians have faced this Faustian dilemma in many parts of the world—usually they choose exchange and partition.

This brief history of the Balkans in the 20th century is designed to stress that the impetus for violence in the region is both a modern phenomenon and one for which the Great Powers, or Russia and the West, bear a decisive responsibility. So when we shake our heads in confusing despair about the events in Kosovo or Bosnia, we are in fact shaking our heads in despair over our own history as much as Balkan history. Explosive divisions in the Balkans have always been triggered by tectonic shifts of an even greater magnitude in European politics.

But there are other reasons for the susceptibility to exceptional violence, some of which are culturally specific to the Balkans, such as the blood feud. But the most important local contributor to Balkan violence can be found elsewhere. This concerns the relationship between the elites, who direct violence in times of crisis without usually getting their hands stained, and the masses, who perpetrate that violence. Slobodan Miloševic and Franjo Tudman successfully manipulated millions of people into joining, passively or actively, a crusade of nationalist violence in order to consolidate their positions and further their political aims. To do this they required three instruments—a subservient bureaucracy, absolutely pliant electronic media, and control over the legal system. The Serb and then the Croat leaders first established unlimited administrative power in the areas they controlled; they then softened up their public by emitting an endless stream of violent images on television; they then ensured that the legal system was turned on its head—the murder of certain groups was sanctioned by the state, and attempts to prevent murder were regarded with at best hostility and at worst as treasonable. With these instruments to hand, it is child's play persuading people to commit atrocities in a region that has witnessed tremendous violence this century.

There is clearly a democratic deficit in the Balkans, which facilitates the pursuit of irrational nationalism (by elites, who on most occasions are entirely unmoved by nationalist goals and passions). Yugoslavia is, in fact, an exception to nationalist violence in the Balkans and not the rule. Should we be surprised? In Yugoslavia, the democratization of the country in the late 1980s did not see the emergence of just two competing national identities as was, say, the case between Bulgarians and Turks or Romanians and Hungarians. Suddenly Serbian nationalism was competing with Slovene, Croat, Albanian, Bosniak/Muslim, and Macedonia nationalism. Croatian nationalism was competing with Serbian, Bosniak/Muslim, and even Slovene nationalism. The Bosniak/Muslims were competing with Serbian and Croatian nationalism and, in their eyes, being betrayed by Macedonian nationalism. Albanians were taking on Serbian and Macedonian nationalism and so on and so on.

Yet this is not an immutable problem. Romania and Bulgaria have suffered tremendously since the revolutions of 1989. The leaderships of the two countries could both have grasped nationalist agitation as a means of deflecting attention from the severe social and economic difficulties which their populations face. They need to have an incentive *not* to resort to nationalism or populism. So far they have been offered precious little. Let us look at Bulgaria, which has suffered the trauma of change from a poorly functioning planned economy to an unregulated free-market system over which the state has lost control. The International Monetary fund insisted on the continued repayment of its $10 billion debt. Bulgaria then lost $2 million in Iraqi debt when sanctions were imposed on Iraq. But then when the Security Council (Britain, France, the United States, Russia, and China—a council of great powers) imposed sanctions on Yugoslavia in 1992, who carried the burden of those sanctions? With the loss of its main trading partner and its direct route to Western Europe, Bulgaria annually lost $2–$3 billion. Any compensation? No. Any debt relief? No. Inward investment, perhaps? Virtually none. (Foreign capital deemed it was too close to Yugoslavia for comfort.) Bulgaria becomes a gangster economy (which incidentally produces the most perfect replica CDs and CD-ROMS, much better quality than the Chinese fakes, on sale for a 10th of the market price in the West). For the moment, this bothers nobody, unless of course you have the misfortune to be Bulgarian. But if the struggle in Kosovo metastasizes to Macedonia, then there will be a problem. By the time Bulgaria becomes involved in a Macedonian war, were that to happen, it will be too late to do anything about it. Both Romania and Bulgaria have deserved much more sympathetic treatment from the West than they have received, but doubtless should Bulgaria mobilize over Macedonia, then we will be told it is because they cannot resist the lure of some centuries-old historical goal.

Scurrilous rumor has it that Balkan peoples are different—less sensitive to human life than others. The Balkans is a twilight world that has absorbed Asiatic values and so on and so forth. These cliches have been underpinned by a startlingly large tradition of English-language literature, fictional and nonfictional, from Byron via Bram Stoker through Rebecca West that provided extremely fruitful source material for Hollywood. The narrative peak of the American soap opera *Dynasty* occurred in far-off Moldavia (it is almost certain that the script writers did not realize that Moldavia is a real place, as this was before 1989), where one of their offspring was marrying a member of the Moldavian royal family. In the middle of the service, Balkanesque terrorists stormed the chapel and gunned everyone down. I would argue, however, that notwithstanding these chronic misrepresentations, modern Balkan nationalism and the violence associated with it has been fashioned and encouraged much more by the post-enlightenment Western World than a pre-enlightenment Orient.

REFERENCES

Brailsford, H. N. (1906). *Macedonia: Its races and their future*. London: Metheun.

Carnegie Endowment, International Commission to Inquire Into the Causes and Conduct of the Balkan War. (1914). *Report of the International Commission*. Washington, DC: The Endowment.

Clogg, R. (1992). *A concise history of Greece*. Cambridge, England: Cambridge University Press.

Gilbert, M. (1994). *First World War*. New York: H. Holt.

Taylor, A. J. P. (1954). *The struggle for mastery in Europe 1848–1918*. Oxford, England: Clarendon Press.

11

KURDS IN TURKEY: A NATIONALIST MOVEMENT IN THE MAKING

REŞAT KASABA

This chapter focuses on the war that has pitted the Turkish state against its Kurdish citizens for the better part of the past 20 years. The repeated claims of the Turkish government to have "broken the back of the terrorist organization" notwithstanding, this conflict shows no sign of abating any time soon. During the past decade and a half, in a well-established pattern, each assault on a military installation, police station, or government office by the Kurdish fighters has invited yet another "final offensive" by the Turkish military. This, in turn, has succeeded only in planting more seeds of resentment among the Kurds living in southeastern Turkey and in pushing them closer to the Kurdish guerilla organization, PKK (Partiya Karkara Kurdistan—Kurdistan Workers Party). (For further reading on various aspects of the Kurdish conflict in Turkey, see Barkey & Fuller, 1998; Gunter, 1997; Kirişçi & Winrow, 1997; and McDowall, 1997.)

This picture is neither pretty, nor does it inspire much hope for a quick resolution. The southeastern provinces of Turkey have been under some kind of martial law since the military coup of 1980. Approximately one third of the entire armed forces of Turkey has been permanently deployed in that part of the country, where both the civilian and the military authority wield extraordinary powers. The paramilitary "special teams" that are formed specifically to police the region and are staffed by the former militants of ultranationalist gangs further enhance this military presence. Throughout the 18 years that have passed, and despite the return to civilian rule elsewhere, the Turkish army has continued to have a free hand in determining the contours of what is euphemistically called Turkey's "Eastern Policy." The army has pursued scorched-earth tactics, killing close to 30,000 people, evacuating hundreds of villages, razing thousands of pastures, and relocating thousands of Kurdish communities, without any accountability to speak of.

During these years the Kurdish war has also become the single most important factor undermining an otherwise expanding Turkish economy. Just as the country was going through a fundamental reorganization by dismantling the rigid controls over foreign exchange and investment, the Turkish state has laid out $6–$9 billion every year to deal with this conflict. One could safely infer that the source of a significant part of the $100 billion foreign debt that Turkey amassed in these years was the expenditures related to this war. (For a very informative and engaging account of Turkey's recent history and contemporary politics, see Pope & Pope, 1997.)

That this conflict has come so far, to threaten not only the unity but also the very viability of the Turkish state, poses a challenge to our understanding of modern Turkey. If Turkey is in fact one of the two (admittedly imperfect) democracies in the Middle East, as it is usually claimed to be, then its political system should have already found a way of absorbing the demands and interests of its Kurdish citizens through regular representational procedures. After all, this is not the first Kurdish uprising that the Turkish state has had to deal with since its establishment as a modern Republic in 1923. Since Shaykh Said's revolt in 1925, the Kurds have become increasingly more persistent and effective in expressing their discontent. It is obvious that the Kurdish side of this conflict includes more than a coterie of terrorist desperados, and the Turkish state has found it particularly difficult to address the demands of these people in an imaginative way.

There are three different explanations for the intractable nature of this conflict. The first of these comes from the Turkish military and government sources, the second from Kurdish organizations, and the third from a vocal segment of the public opinion that is not directly linked to either of these two antagonists. The official Turkish explanation makes little, if any, concession to the idea that Kurdishness might constitute a separate identity and that the Kurds may have a legitimate right to demand autonomy, let alone to demand self-determination or independence. In the early days of the republic, the Turkish government funded "anthropological" and "ethnographical" studies in order to prove that Kurds were little more than wayward Turks. In a typical passage from such a study on the history of eastern provinces, one reads,

> The one and only ideal that motivated me to write this book was [the desire to liberate] these common Turkish and Turkoman tribespeople and these peasant villagers—who in reality are of Turkish blood and pure Turkish stock—[from] the suffering of speaking these half-baked [Kurdish] languages." (cited in Meiselas, 1997, p. 229)

Nowadays, nobody repeats these views seriously, but the official explanations continue to insist that for historical, cultural, and social reasons it is impossible for Kurds to form a credible movement on their own. For example, in the official publications of the armed forces, one still reads that Kurds "live in the mountains of eastern Turkey where there is too much snow. Those who walk on this snow create a . . . noise, and the name 'Kurd' is derived from the way this noise sounds to the ear" (cited in Yavuz, 1998, p. 14). Hence, the sources related to the Turkish state claim that the apparent power and endurance of the Kurdish challenge can be explained only by referring to external sources of mischief. Over the years, the list of the possible culprits who might have been behind Kurdish insurgents included the Soviet Union, Russia, Germany, Greece, France, Armenia, Iran, Iraq, the CIA, and most recently, Syria.

It is well known that the European governments devised various plans to carve up what was left of the Ottoman Empire at the end of World War I. It is also widely acknowledged that they lent their support to the idea of establishing independent states for Kurds and/or Armenians in eastern Anatolia during those years. In formulating these policies and expressing their intentions, Europeans were motivated primarily by their own strategic interests. Furthermore, in an environment that was changing so quickly, it was natural that Great Britain, France, Russia, the Soviet Union, and the United States adopted positions that were not always consistent. It is widely documented and freely acknowledged that during the Cold War, both the American and the Soviet sides tried to influence Kurdish insurgency to advance their respective interests and spheres in the Middle East. (For the CIA's involvement in the Kurdish uprising of the 1960s in Iraq, see Randal, 1997.) Syria became the latest power to use the Kurdish insurgency as a proxy to protect its interests and limit Turkey's growing influence in the region. The main reason for this was Syria's growing insecurity in the aftermath of the Cold War.

Syrians were also fearful that the southeastern Anatolian Dam Project would give Turkey exclusive control over the flow of the river Euphrates and strangle the Syrian agriculture. Last but not least, they perceived the burgeoning alliance between Israel and Turkey as a mortal threat to the balance of power in the Middle East. It was only when the Turkish military threatened to go to war that the PKK leader Abdullah Öcalan was expelled from Damascus, where he had been given shelter for over 10 years. Although it is unlikely that the PKK leadership could have survived as long as it did without Syria's protection, it does not follow from this that without Syria, there would not have been a Kurdish insurgency in Turkey. In ethnic conflicts, with their overt or covert support, foreign powers can embolden and strengthen one side or another. They may even play a determining role at crucial junctures, as both the French and the Soviet support did for Mustafa Kemal in the early 1920s. But such factors can be effective only if the groups involved are already acting or prone to act on the basis of factors that are indigenous to their circumstances.

The Kurdish sources and their supporters see the conflict between the Turkish state and the Kurdish rebels as a war of national liberation. According to this point of view, most of the territory that is defined as Kurdistan, which is a large swath of land covering not only large parts of eastern Turkey but also northern Iraq, parts of Iran, and Syria, remains under Turkey's military occupation. Even though the Kurds are the only truly indigenous community in this region, as this explanation goes, they have never been permitted to have a state of their own, and now they have been reduced to the status of a discriminated minority in all of the countries where they live, especially in Turkey. These circumstances force them to fight for their natural right to self-determination and to form an independent state in their historic homeland. Like all romantic nationalists, Kurds portray their struggle as having a long history and deep roots in Kurdistan and see all the previous conflicts between the Kurds and the Ottoman and Turkish states as phases of the same righteous struggle. They argue that this war will not and should not end as long as the Turkish state refuses to accede to the just demands of the Kurdish nation. (This thesis can be found in many publications and web sites associated with Kurdish nationalists. For example, see Kurdish Information Network, http://www.xs4all.nl/~tank/kurdish/htdocs/)

The 14 provinces that are claimed as part of Kurdistan are indeed among the poorest in Turkey. Here, according to some calculations, per capita income is as low as one-tenth of the wealthier western provinces, where the average figure is approaching $6,000. It is also true that the newly established Turkish republic spent the better part of the 1920s and the 1930s fighting an all-out war in eastern Turkey against insurgent Kurdish tribes. This region was pacified only with the deportation and dispersion of large numbers of people to other parts of Turkey, wiping out hundreds of Kurdish villages and towns from the map and redistricting and even renaming some old centers of Kurdish life. All of this was carried out deliberately, in order to erase these communities and their past from the historical memory of the nation. Even though the underpinnings of the Kurdish nationalist thesis are hard to dispute, these arguments contain plenty of generalizations and use very broad strokes to paint a picture where primordially defined Kurdish people have always been fighting a static and monolithic Turkish Republic. Rather than seeing such policies of the new republic as acts of aggression and invasion directed only at the Kurds, we should remember that in those years the new Turkish state tried to remake not only the Kurds but everybody who had remained within the borders of the new country.

Finally, in recent years, public opinion in Turkey has become increasingly skeptical and downright cynical about the reasons that are put forth by the Turkish and Kurdish sources for the persistence of the Kurdish war. A growing number of people from across the social and political spectrum have come to believe that this conflict has become intractable, not because of the strength of Kurdish nationalism or the unscrupulous nature of their terrorism, but because of the widespread corruption that has engulfed the government, the military, and the PKK. The source of this cynicism goes back to 1996 when a traffic accident in Susurluk, on the highway between Istanbul and Izmir, killed a carload of organized crime members who were discovered to be carrying bona fide diplomatic passports and whose car trunk was full of government-issue weapons and ammunition (Kinzer, 1996). The only survivor of the crash was a wealthy Kurdish landlord who was also a member of the Turkish parliament.

Each of the three governments that succeeded one another in Turkey since this incident has been very reluctant to pursue this investigation. This is not surprising, because the newspapers have been reporting that various elements within each one of these governments, the police, and even some members of the armed forces have worked with organized crime families and the Kurdish tribal chiefs in carrying out a covert war against Kurdish nationalism. It also appears that this alliance might have been ensconced at the very center of an extremely lucrative and clandestine network of narcotics and weapon trafficking that connected Turkey with some of its neighbors. To make matters more complicated, the PKK itself has found ways of benefiting from these illegal activities as well. Given these revelations, cynics suggest that it is best to dismiss the fiery rhetoric that comes from the two sides as mere posturing and realize that neither the Kurds nor the Turks can really be interested in ending the Kurdish war in southeastern Turkey.

Since the Susurluk accident, much has come into light about the unsavory links among the Turkish government, the army, and the criminal underworld. In terms of providing irrefutable proof that the various organs of the state have been so compromised as to be thoroughly incapable of acting for the common good, these revelations are probably the single most important development in Turkish politics in recent years. Nevertheless, important as it is, the story of how the state institutions were corrupted should be examined separately from the analysis of the Kurdish conflict. Although it is true that a series of venal institutions and individuals have ensconced themselves in the southeast and have become key players in the Kurdish war, they should be seen as taking advantage of the chaotic conditions there, not as causing the conflict between the Turks and the Kurds.

Of these three explanations, only the second one takes Kurdish nationalism seriously, and that is where we need to start in order to gain an accurate understanding of the war in Turkey. Yet, there are a number of complexities underlying this conflict that the radical nationalist explanations ignore. Foremost among these is the fact that after 14 years of sustained struggle, the Kurdish side does not have much to show except for a captured and now condemned leader. Today, after all this time and the overwhelming sacrifices of the Kurdish people, this nationalist movement stands farther than it has ever been from reaching its goal. This is somewhat curious, because the Kurds seem to possess all the requisites for staging a successful nationalist movement. They have a culture that distinguishes them from their Arab, Persian, or Turkish neighbors. There is a territory where most of them are concentrated. And their most distinct and common experience is one of collective suffering under the thumb of several oppressive states in the region.

Despite these factors, the Kurdish forces have never moved much beyond establishing an occasional stalemate in their struggle with the Turkish state. Even the capture, the trial, and the sentencing of their leader, Abdullah Öcalan, did not galvanize the Kurdish fighters. After the first week that followed his apprehension in Kenya, when there were simultaneous and centrally organized demonstrations across European capitals, the Kurdish side has been surprisingly silent. Öcalan's lengthy confessions, his expressions of remorse, and his apparent willingness to "serve the Turkish state" did not lead to any kind of regrouping among the Kurdish nationalists. Instead, there were repeated assertions of unity by the PKK and the determination of the fighters to continue to follow the orders of their leader. Both the long-term failure of the Kurds to mount an effective struggle of self-determination and their short-term meekness can be attributed to three sets of forces that are indigenous to Kurdish society and history and have worked to prevent the development of Kurdish nationalism as a coherent and consistent political project in the modern era. In their desire to project a clear sense of purpose, the nationalist arguments tend to overlook these factors, but it is essential that we understand them because it is likely that these will continue to play a decisive role in determining the future direction of the war in Turkey.

Foremost among these countervailing forces are the linguistic, religious, and tribal divisions that have separated various Kurdish communities from each other and have prevented them from consummating their nation-building in the modern era. Twenty-two million Kurds (Kurdish Information Network, 2000) who live in Turkey, Iran, Iraq, and Syria speak a multiplicity of local dialects. These are grouped under two major languages as Kurmanji and Sorani, which are as different from each other as German and Dutch (see Kreyenbroek, 1992; van Bruinessen, 1992). While Sorani has always been a written language that uses the Arabic script, Kurmanji has only recently become one and is now written in Roman script. Occasional attempts to develop a single Kurdish language have been frustrated by the opposition of the states in the region. Absence of a uniform way of writing and speaking among the Kurds and the limited access that Kurdish intellectuals have to technologies of communication continue to be formidable barriers in the way of creating a unified and enduring ideology of Kurdish nationalism.

In addition to speaking several different languages, Kurds are also fragmented into thousands of different tribes that are occasionally but only temporarily grouped under several confederations that hold only for limited periods of time. The diversity of their religious beliefs constitutes yet another axis along which the Kurdish communities are separated. Most Kurds are Sunni Muslims, but there are also Alevis and Shi's among them, not to mention those who follow one of the numerous heterodox sects in the region. Even though they are dwindling in number, Jewish and Christian Kurds add a further layer of complexity to the picture.

A second factor that has impeded the formation of a broad nationalist consciousness among Kurds has been their mobility in and around eastern Anatolia and, in particular, the long-distance migration that has always been part of their history. Some of the relocations of the Kurds were and continue to be involuntary, because both the Ottoman and the modern Turkish states have routinely moved large numbers of tribes across long distances as a punitive measure against these communities. But especially since the 1950s, millions of people have also moved voluntarily from rural to urban areas and from eastern to western provinces to take advantage of the growing economic opportunities created by Turkey's expanding industries.

Kurds constitute a very large portion of this continuing wave of migration. As a result, in the second half of the 20th century, the southeastern provinces of Turkey (the bulk of the area described as Kurdistan) ceased to be the only place in the world where Kurds lived in very high concentration. Between 1965 and 1990 the percentage of Kurds in Marmara region in northwestern Turkey (where Istanbul is located) increased from 1.2 to 6.09. It is estimated that there are over 500,000 Kurds living in Istanbul, making it the urban center with the highest concentration of Kurds in the world. Although the labor statistics are not kept according to the ethnic background of migrant workers, it is generally assumed that there are more than half a million Kurds in Europe, most of whom are from Turkey. In Germany alone, about one third of the workers from Turkey are estimated to be ethnic Kurds (Mutlu, 1996).

It is ironic that Kurds have contributed to the creation of economic wealth in western Turkey and are partly "responsible" for the discrepancy between the levels of development in the western and the eastern provinces. As I noted, this has been one of the key factors that has fueled Kurdish resentment. In a further twist, in the aftermath of the earthquake of 1999, a substantial number of these immigrants are now looking for ways of returning to their places of origin. If this return migration continues and accelerates, it will have an enormous impact not only on the dynamics of

Kurdish nationalism, but also on the overall social and economic structures of eastern Turkey that are still steeped in the traditions of previous centuries.

Finally, Kurds have not been helped by their leadership as they tried to articulate their discontent and formulate their demands in the 19th and 20th centuries. The leaders of various tribes and their confederations have been more prone to focus on their personal and local interests and get absorbed in intertribal rivalries than working toward an enduring resolution of the Kurdish conflict. In this century, early leaders of the Kurdish insurgency appeared more as religious than as national leaders. For example, Shaykh Said, who led the 1925–1927 revolt that almost destroyed the newly established Turkish republican state, was a Naqshibandi Shaykh. He parted ways with the Kemalists only when the latter decided to abolish the caliphate in 1924 and declare the new republic to be a secular state. Until his capture in February 1999, Abdullah Öcalan was the undisputed supreme leader of PKK and the Kurdish nationalist movement in Turkey. Öcalan's ideology included elements of third world socialism, which he embellished with a strong dose of ethnic nationalism, rhetoric of martyrdom, and even some messianic pretensions (see Volkan, 1986, pp. 168–180). Such unpredictable and, at times, opportunistic aspects of the Kurdish leadership have prevented the nationalist struggle of the Kurds from achieving widespread support and respect abroad, even though there has always been considerable good will in the West for this particular cause.

These countervailing forces and the sustained pressure applied by the Turkish state have made it impossible for Kurdish nationalism to grow as a focused, long-term project. Instead, the modern history of this movement has been one of frequent shifts, changing alliances, and a constant effort to redefine its goals according to the dictates of the time. During the Ottoman and early Republican periods, Kurdish discontent was organized and expressed by religious and tribal leaders and their followers, who were more interested in resisting the centralizing and secularizing tenets of the Ottoman and Turkish states than in advancing Kurdish nationalism. Later in the 1960s, Kurdish organizations became adjuncts of socialist activism, the goal of which was to destroy the feudal relations in the east and advance a peasant revolution. In this scenario, liberation of the Kurds would come as part of this greater historical process. Finally, in the 1980s and the 1990s, especially since the collapse of the communist states in Eastern Europe and the Soviet Union, Kurds have started to express their demands by using the language of identity politics. This has brought them closest to a clear articulation of their interests in terms of nationalism, albeit one that bases its claims on primordial, ethnic elements and not on civic ideals.

Hence, their internal divisions, their mobility, and the nature of their leadership have so far deprived the Kurds of an effective social movement. But under the right circumstances, these very forces may have exactly the opposite effect and work not to undermine but to strengthen Kurdish nationalism. Take the linguistic barriers, tribal rivalries, and religious polarization that have pitted Kurdish communities against one another during the 1980s and the 1990s. Given the long distances that separated these communities from the Ottoman and Turkish central authorities and the cascades of large mountains that cut across the region, there is nothing surprising about the depth and longevity of these divisions. It was natural that the Kurds had much closer and more meaningful ties to their Sufi Shaykhs and to their tribal leaders than any affinity they may have felt toward the vague notions of Kurdish nation or nationalism that excited the political and intellectual leaders. In fact, it is highly probable that Kurdish identity owes its survival not to those grandiose theories but to these everyday ties and relationships that have proven highly flexible.

This very fluidity however, also makes it conceivable that most of these lines could eventually disappear, and a unified Kurdish people can in fact emerge out of this history. In recent years, the stubbornly uncompromising stand of the Turkish state has accelerated this process significantly. For example, as part of their nationalist campaigns, in recent years, Kurds have been involved in a sustained effort to elevate Kurmanji to the status of the Kurdish language by using it in all of their broadcasts, propaganda material, and other official communications (van Bruinessen, 1998). The power of new methods of communication and the popularity of certain forms of media have given this policy a good chance of success in overcoming some of the linguistic barriers within the Kurdish community.

Similarly, what the long-term consequences of migration will be on Kurdish communal and national identity cannot be predicted easily. On the one hand migration disperses the Kurdish communities across Turkey and hence weakens their ties to their homeland and to each other. It reduces them to the status of individual workers struggling to eke out a living on the margins of big urban centers in western Turkey and in Europe. It is wrong, however, to see these groups solely as marginal elements, ready to separate themselves from their new environments. For one thing, we should not overlook the very large number of assimilated Kurds in Turkey. Just as it is unrealistic to insist that the Turkish workers in Germany can never be "real Germans," it is also unrealistic to regard the Kurdish immigrants in western Turkey as temporary appendages that can easily be lifted and mobilized for a separatist cause. On a more visible level, anybody who has the slightest familiarity with Turkey can easily name very visible political and cultural figures of Kurdish background who have become prominent in Turkey. Among them is Hikmet Çetin, a former minister of foreign affairs who also served as the speaker of the parliament; Bedrettin Dalan, a very popular former mayor of Istanbul; Yaşar Kemal, the most famous novelist of Turkey; İbrahim Tatlıses, one of the most popular singers in the country;

and even the late President Turgut Özal. The prevalence and prominence of assimilated Kurds show that just as the tribal lines that divide the Kurds are fluid, ethnic markers that distinguish a Kurd from a Turk can also be imprecise and malleable.

On the other hand, there is always the possibility that by bringing Kurd and non-Kurd into close proximity and interaction with each other, this same process may make Kurds even more starkly aware of their disadvantaged position and hence strengthen their resentment and provide fuel to separatist ideas and heighten nationalist consciousness. Also, we should remember that as is the case with most modern migrations, Kurds do not sever all their connections with their homes when they migrate to the west. They form extended households; become parts of a network; and mediate the circulation of people, money, goods, and information. It is remarkable, for example, that following the recent earthquake, many of these migrants have been able to move back to their places of origin and reconnect with their communities there. Hence, even though the large-scale movement and circulation of people may blur the coherence of the Kurdish communities, these can, at the same time, create opportunities for the assertion of the underlying identities on a much larger scale and hence in a more visible and forceful way.

In light of all this, it is best to think of the Kurdish insurgency in Turkey as a nationalist movement in the making; as a historical process whose outcome is far from certain. The forces that underlie the current impasse are such that the conflict can evolve in a number of different ways. One of these alternatives is the further hardening of various divisions within the Kurdish community. In addition to leaving the Kurds divided, this path guarantees that the military stalemate between the Turkish and the Kurdish sides will not be solved any time soon. The second path would bring some dilution of these divisions and create a more unified and hence stronger Kurdish entity, but such a scenario would lead to harsher and even larger-scale confrontations with the Turkish side and therefore not do much in the way of ending the war itself. The third alternative carries the second one further by creating links not only among the Kurds themselves but also across the ethnic divide between the Kurds and the Turks and by generating democratic and pluralistic syntheses within the context of a reconstructed Turkish society.

At the time of the writing of this chapter, armed struggle has lost some of its intensity and Turkey's war with the Kurds has somewhat quieted down. But, in the long run this conflict seems to be taking the second path, moving in the direction of becoming even more intractable. So much so that even Öcalan's calls for peace and reconciliation from his prison cell and his stated willingness to help to bring this about did not soften the army's hardened stand. That the Turkish side has been so blindly single-minded defies all reason, because this attitude continues to harm Turkey's standing in Europe and reduces its already slim chances of being admitted to European Union—the single most important goal of Turkey's foreign policy in the past 40 years.

The Kurdish side, however, has been more successful in adapting its strategy to the post–Cold War realities and has broadened its base of support in Europe to include liberal political groups, human rights organizations, and even some governments. Nevertheless, this support has failed to reach its full potential because, despite the changes in the international arena, the Kurdish side has been reluctant to drop completely its rhetoric of socialism and class struggle. As a result, for most of the past 20 years, their ideology has proven to be at least as immovable as that of the Turkish state and the army.

An important and often neglected source of this stalemate lies in the internal organization of the Turkish military and the PKK, the main parties to this conflict. Both the Turkish armed forces and the guerilla wing of the PKK have elaborate methods of recruiting, training, and indoctrinating their fighters. Either in the boot camps or in the mountains, these recruits are cut off from their families and isolated from the society at large. They are taught absolute obedience to the centralized command of either the army or the PKK. The ideologies that govern the two organizations are equally rigid. They both prefer the narrowest and the most carefully delineated path to their respective futures and are equally convinced that even the slightest sign of compromise can be interpreted only as weakness and should be shunned.

The framework within which the military approaches the Kurdish conflict today is primarily shaped by the extraordinary circumstances of the late 19th and early 20th centuries when the Ottoman Empire lost three quarters of its territories, some of which it had controlled for over 500 years. Among the causes of this collapse were the economic and political strengthening of the European states, the nationalist pressures in the Balkans, the indecisiveness of the Ottoman leaders, and clumsy interventions by the European states.

Under Mustafa Kemal Atatürk's leadership, the Turkish nationalist movement succeeded in reversing some of these losses and establishing a new state between 1919 and 1923. Kemalist ideology that was the mortar of this enterprise was rigid and uncompromising because its authors feared that any other approach would open the new state to renewed claims on its remaining territories. In particular, the Kemalists saw the imputed "homogeneity" of the Turkish nation and its need to develop as a secular polity as indispensable for protecting the new state from the fate of the old imperial system. In the early years of the new regime, with its religious overtones, the Kurdish insurgency put to test both of these ideals at once.

It is no wonder that the new Turkish state reacted to Shaykh Said and Dersim rebellions so brutally, killing tens of thousands of people, forcefully relocating an equal number, and evacuating and razing thousands of villages and pastures.

In these early months of the 21st century, Turkish state and especially the military respond to the demands of the Kurds in exactly the same way. To them, it is still the case that even the smallest compromise to the demands of the Kurdish leaders would put Turkey back on the slippery slope of losing more territories and might ultimately force her even to exit history! Today, this rhetoric resonates little with the interests and aspirations of most Turks, but it was at the center of the founding principles of the modern Turkish republic, which the Turkish army sees itself as the protector of. It is from this source that the military derives its sense of purpose to continue the war of attrition in the southeast. Between 1992 and 1997 alone, over 3,000 Kurdish villages have been evacuated, and since 1984, about 30,000 people, most of them Kurdish guerillas and civilians, have been killed ("Turkey's Kurds," 1998).

If the Turkish military's vision has been frozen in the 1920s, until recently, that of the PKK had not moved much beyond the late 1960s when it was reinterpreting the grievances of the Kurdish tribes in the southeast to serve its goal of achieving "national liberation" and building socialism. Over the years, PKK has relied on the romantic appeal of yet another third world nationalism and has succeeded to augment its ranks with supporters and even some fighters from as far away as Australia (see Ignatieff, 1993, pp. 202–204).

But for the most part, the PKK's fighting militants come from among unemployed and underemployed Kurdish youth. The rapidly growing Kurdish population, bleak circumstances in the east, and the shifting economic structures in Turkey make sure that there is virtually an unlimited pool of such fighters. For people whose future prospects are limited, the guerrilla organization and its struggle provide a structure and a sense of purpose. As guerillas who have little education and who spend most of their time in the mountains, PKK fighters are even more isolated than the conscripts in the Turkish military. Some accounts based on interviews with them suggest that most of them have only a superficial knowledge of the "enemy" they are fighting, or the general conditions of Turkey, or even of the lands they claim as their homeland (Gürsel, 1996). Not realizing the degree to which they are out of step with large parts of their own community, they express deep disappointment that they have failed to instigate a general uprising or draw more support from non-Kurdish groups in Turkey and elsewhere. The real tragedy occurs when these equally uninformed groups of youth engage each other and fight under the respective commands of the Turkish and the Kurdish sides. (For a detailed description of recruitment and training of conscripts in the Turkish army, see Birand, 1991; for stories of soldiers who fought in the Kurdish war, see Mater, 1998.)

As long as the two sides of this conflict are governed by institutions that are firmly closed to democratic input and accountability, this war can drag on for some time to come. It may eventually dissolve in intertribal, personal, or ideological disagreements, as has been the case with most of the previous Kurdish revolts in this century. In the months that preceded Öcalan's capture, there were plenty of signs that the PKK's uprising was unraveling in precisely such a direction. With his capture, we can expect such fissures only to become deeper and the movement to become less unified and less effective. But as long as the narrow framework of defining the nature of the Turkish society continues to shape the army's approach to the southeast, and as long as the civilian governments continue to remain subservient to such a framework, new organizations are bound to take advantage of the grievances and aspirations of Kurdish communities. In order for the conflict between the Turks and the Kurds to end, a new way of thinking will have to evolve and permeate all the institutions of the state, including the Turkish army. But how does this happen? How does one break free of constraining ideologies that give their adherents a degree of security? How can the uncertain and uncharted paths which a more liberal thinking would entail be made more appealing than the self-consciously certain futures that are central to the nationalist ideologies of the Turkish and the Kurdish variants?

One way of answering this would be to say that if we wait long enough, the failure of the current path will become indisputably clear, corrupt institutions will meet their demise, and the parties will eventually pull themselves out of the ruins by thinking in new and more imaginative ways. But there is a price to be paid for this prescription. If left unaddressed, discontent and cynicism may erode all trust and loyalty a people might feel toward their state, government and, ultimately, each other. If conditions deteriorate that far, it becomes very difficult, if not impossible, to rebuild these bonds and recreate a community and a legitimate state that are essential for survival in the modern world. The looming anarchy that characterizes some of the former communist countries provides a useful cautionary note against the advice of letting things unravel under their own inertia.

Hence we need a more imaginative approach that will involve rearranging the relations between the Turkish state and the people who live in Turkey. One part of this proactive approach has to do with reincorporating into Turkish politics the representatives of the Kurdish communities and political parties, most of whom are banned and imprisoned today (see Sakallıoğlu, 1996). These individuals and groups have to be permitted to join the public debate in Turkey on their own terms. At the same time, the rigid ideologies of ethnic nationalism of both the Turkish and Kurdish variety need to be questioned and rejected in favor of a much more inclusive and civic framework. Rethinking these ideologies will have to start with reappraising the construction of both the Turkish and the Kurdish identities and the Turkish and Kurdish nationalisms. Telling the truth about the histories of these ideologies should be a central component of any effort to create a democratic polity in Turkey. In the elegant formulation of Appleby, Hunt, and Jacob (1994), this is no less than a quest for creating a "revitalized public . . . with protected dissent, [that can] mediate intelligently between society and the individual, knowledge and passion, clarity and obfuscation, hope and doubt" (p. 309): We should see this as a challenge that awaits not only the Turks and the Kurds but also the parties to other ethnic conflicts in the world.

REFERENCES

Appleby, J., Hunt, L., & Jacob, M. (1994). *Telling the truth about history*. New York: Norton.

Barkey, H., & Fuller, G. (1998). *Turkey's Kurdish question*. Lanham, MD: Rowman & Littlefield.

Birand, M. A. (1991). *Shirts of steel: An anatomy of the Turkish Officer Corps*. New York: I. B. Tauris.

Gunter, M. (1997). *The Kurds and the future of Turkey*. New York: St. Martin's Press.

Gürsel, K. (1996). *Dağdakiler: Bagok'tan Gabar'a 26 Gün* [On the mountains: 26 days from Bagok to Gabar]. Istanbul: Metis.

Ignatieff, M. (1993). *Blood and belonging*. New York: Farrar, Straus, & Giroux.

Kinzer, S. (1996, December 10). Scandal links Turkish aides to deaths, drugs and terror. *New York Times*, pp. 1, 7.

Kirişçi, K., & Winrow, G. (1997). *The Kurdish question and Turkey*. London: Frank Cass.

Kreyenbroek, P. (1992). On the Kurdish language. In P. Kreyenborek & S. Sperl (Eds.), *The Kurds: A contemporary overview* (pp. 68–84). London: Routledge.

Kurdish Information Network. (2000). *Kurds and Kurdistan, facts and figures: Language* [Article]. Amsterdam, the Netherlands: Author. Retrieved September 4, 2000 from the World Wide Web: http://www.xs4all.nl/~tank/kurdish/htdocs/facts/language.html

Mater, N. (1998). *Mehmed'in Kitabı: Güneydoğu'da Savaşmış Askerler Anlatıyor* [Mehmed's book: Stories of the soldiers who have fought in the southeast]. Istanbul: Metis.

McDowall, D. (1997). *A modern history of the Kurds*. London: I. B. Tauris.

Meiselas, S. (1997). *Kurdistan: In the shadow of history*. New York: Random House.

Mutlu, S. (1996). Ethnic Kurds in Turkey: A demographic study. *International Journal of Middle East Studies, 28*(4), 517–541.

Pope, H., & Pope, N. (1997). *Turkey unveiled.* London: Overlook.

Randal, J. (1997). *After such knowledge, what forgiveness? My encounters with Kurdistan.* New York: Farrar, Straus, & Giroux.

Sakallıoğlu, Ü. C. (1996, Spring). Historicizing the present and problematizing the future of the Kurdish problem: A Critique of the TOBB report on the Eastern Question. *New Perspectives on Turkey, 14,* 1–22.

Turkey's Kurds: Down but far from out. (1998, August 1). *The Economist.* Retrieved September 4, 2000 from the World Wide Web: http://www.economist.com/tfs/aarchive_tframeset.html

van Bruinessen, M. (1992). *Agha, Shaikh and state.* London: Zed.

van Bruinessen, M. (1998). Shifting national and ethnic identities: The Kurds in Turkey and the European Diaspora. *Journal of Muslim Minority Affairs, 18*(1), pp. 39–52.

Volkan, V. (1986). *Blood lines: From ethnic pride to ethnic terrorism.* New York: Farrar, Straus and Giroux.

Yavuz, H. (1998). A preamble to the Kurdish Question. *Journal of Muslim Minority Affairs, 18*(1), 14.

12

EXPLAINING THE LONG PEACE: WAR IN LATIN AMERICA

MIGUEL ANGEL CENTENO

The dogs of war have rarely barked in Latin America.[1] Since independence in the early 19th century, the continent has been relatively free of major international conflict. In the 20th century, the record is truly remarkable, especially in light of the experience of other regions of the world. Latin America has experienced relatively low levels of militarization, that is, the organization and mobilization of human and material resources for potential use in warfare (Centeno, 1998, in press). Latin Americans have tried to kill each other, but the vast majority of the violence has been internal rather than international. The violence experienced in the continent has also been largely chaotic, lacking the organizational component so central to modern wars. These distinctions are not trivial. Clearly violence has played an important political role on the continent, but not in the relationship between states or as an expression of international politics.

Why is it that Latin America appears to have largely escaped the scourge of international war? How do we explain this apparent anomaly? Why has its state system enjoyed such incredible stability? To what extent does it have to do with historical and environmental factors? These are the questions addressed by this chapter. Why is this relevant to a volume on ethnic conflict? I would argue that while civil and international wars have different dynamics, they share enough critical characteristics as to merit the analysis of a set of societies that have avoided one or the other. Any strategy

---

[1] The larger study of which this chapter is a part uses data from all the countries in four of the five geopolitical zones in Latin America: La Plata Basin (Argentina, Uruguay, Paraguay, Brazil), Pacific Littoral (Chile, Peru, Bolivia), Northern Andes (Ecuador, Colombia, Venezuela), and Mexico. I have not included Central America and the Caribbean, as the addition of these additional cases would make the management of the narrative impossibly complex. Moreover, in the absence of even remotely reliable data on these countries during much of the relevant time periods, their inclusion would bring little benefit.

or conditions that have minimized one type of violence may be useful to avoiding it in other forms and/or other circumstances. The Latin American long peace may have much to teach us on how ethnic conflict is transformed into genocidal holocaust. If we can understand how states avoided conflict with one another (despite the extent of violence pervasive in their societies), then we may understand how the transformation of hatreds into ethnic cleansing may be avoided.

The Latin American case is particularly interesting because the peace has been accompanied by a strong tradition of military influence in politics and a tradition of nationalism. This apparently contradictory situation has also produced both a weak state and underdeveloped notions of citizenship. If the modern state is characterized by its penetration of society and, conversely, by the participation of its citizens in political life (Mann, 1996), then Latin America has only recently and sporadically developed such institutions. My central hypothesis is that these two phenomena, general peace and institutional underdevelopment, are causally linked. Simply put, Latin American states did not have the organizational or ideological capacity to go to war. The societies were not geared toward the logistical and cultural transformations required by wartime. Equally important, the definition of the enemy in the Latin American context has rarely been along territorial lines. The enemy, as defined by state elites, has been within and defined racially and along class lines.

The most significant exception has been in the case of anti-communism, but again the threat was largely perceived as coming from inside the society, not from the outside. Conversely, the relative absence of war "deprived" Latin America of one of the most common stimulants for the development of state organization and nationalism (Tilly, 1992). Wars did not leave the institutional residue of a stronger state. National conflicts did not help forge a common identity. External violence did not facilitate the monopolization of violence, nor did it distract from internal hatreds.

If my hypothesis is true, contemporary institutional and political development may have darker sides than we have ever imagined. The iron cage of the modern state may represent a threat to human survival. Behind the apparent chaos of war lies organizational sophistication and bureaucratic rationality. Simultaneously, democracy entails in part the massification of politics. This in turn involves much larger numbers of people in political conflicts. Latin America's underdeveloped state and exclusive politics made it difficult if not impossible to create international killing fields. While very much cognizant of the destruction and violence that has characterized Latin American political life, I contend that the absence of international strife makes the continent an interesting model. I argue that we can learn a great deal from the Latin American example. The foremost lesson is to concentrate on the institutional bases that allow hatred to degenerate (or develop?) into something much more violent. The questions we ask about ethnic and other conflicts should not be "Why do these people kill each other?", but the infinitely more useful "How are they convinced to do so?" and "How are they organized?"

CAUSES OF WAR

How to explain war? In the following section I discuss alternative hypotheses (see Levy, 1983, for an exhaustive review) and argue that the leading theories are not applicable to the Latin American case. I then move to a discussion of several important structural constraints on war and finish with a detailed discussion of two key dimensions: nationalist ideology and state capacity.

We may begin by distinguishing between short- and long-term developments, or what Wright (1965) referred to as immediate versus general causes.[2] Analyses of the former include those that emphasize diplomatic history, the process of negotiation, and (more recently) different game-playing scenarios. A variant of these, for example, would include theories of balance of power. This approach has been used to explain the outbreak of war in specific circumstances in Latin America (e.g., Abente, 1987). Perhaps the most promising of these types of approaches is geopolitical analysis that claims that the alliance structure of the continent provides an explanation for the long peace (Kelly, 1997). Latin America, for example, is a classic geopolitical "checkerboard" in which "my neighbor is my enemy, but my neighbor's enemy is my friend." These patterns have prevented the development of hegemonic rivalries and have ensured that a balance of power was maintained even as the capacities of the players changed. In contrast, "shatterbelts" are where international rivalries are transformed into local squabbles. Except in the special case of Cuba and in the internal wars of Central America, the continent has not seen those kinds of proxy conflicts on any significant basis.

Overall, however, these models appear to have limited value in explaining the long period of peace that has prevailed on the continent.[3] That is, unless we are prepared to accept exceptional diplomatic skill, and almost omniscient game playing on the part of all the relevant actors, as well as an enviable structural stability in the balance of forces, none of these explanations can account for the generalized absence of war. The geopolitical

---

[2] An alternative distinction is between domestic and international causes. While this debate is well suited to discussions of the causes of individual wars, I believe it is a less fruitful manner of analyzing such long stretches of time as are involved here.

[3] Given the very general nature of my remarks in this proposal, I have omitted specific cites to the historical literature on Latin America.

explanation requires that we accept a century of military and political stability as an endogenous factor without investigating the origins of that stability.

Another important type of explanation, which has enjoyed considerable popularity in Latin America and therefore cannot be ignored, is the elite or class conspiracy. According to this view, the outbreak of war can be traced to the machinations of capitalist elites in one or another of the countries involved or in an imperial power that stands to benefit from such a struggle. As relevant as these concerns may be for exploring the outbreak of individual wars, it is difficult to imagine how such an interpretation could be applied to 100 years of relative peace. A century-long continental "conspiracy of peace" would require that Latin American elites exhibit a class-wide rationality for which there is little evidence.

We can therefore turn to more general or systemic explanations. Why is it that some nations appear to be more and others appear less prone to warlike behavior? In her systematic review of a variety of regime, socioeconomic, and situational variables, Zinnes (1980) found little evidence for any consistent structural correlation. One exception is found in the work of Weede (1984), who linked liberal regimes and democracy with more peaceful behavior. Yet, Latin America as a whole would tend to contradict such a perspective, given that militaristic, authoritarian, and conservative countries have been so successful at avoiding conflict with each other.

Howard (1984), among others, has emphasized what he called a cultural predisposition to war. Thus, particular societies, regions, and/or epochs might be culturally predisposed to interstate conflict. As in many of the other generalizing theories of war, this view can easily degenerate into tautology, as measures of bellicosity may be products of war itself. Moreover, it is difficult to imagine a continent where cultural predispositions to violence have been more emphasized than in Latin America. Although we should always be careful with culturally deterministic arguments, it is undeniable that the general political culture in Latin America is not peaceful. The pervasiveness and extent of internal violence do not indicate some essentialist quality that would prevent Latin Americans from killing each other. If anything, we might argue for a negative correlation between international bellicosity and internal violence. Chile, the so-called Prussia of Latin America, has enjoyed relative domestic tranquility. Mexico and Colombia, two states characterized by international peace for over 100 years, have been the victims of practically genocidal domestic conflict.

A related explanation might rely on the relatively homogenous culture of the continent. Without the struggles between different elite cultures, there was no subsequent conflict between political claims over territory. Yet, similar cultures did not make Renaissance Italy or 17th-century Germany particularly peaceful. Moreover, as we have seen recently in the Balkans and in East Africa, competing political institutions can forge inimical hetero-geneity out of the most apparently uniform populations. In the following pages, I suggest a series of factors that might better account for the Latin American exception. I then go on to discuss how these may be applicable to the analysis of ethnic conflict.

Physical and International Constraints

Borders often make for uneasy neighbors, and that has been the case in Latin America. There is a clear correlation between sharing a frontier and likelihood of conflict (Kelly, 1997). Latin America appears to have had a significant number of border disputes (Diehl & Goertz, 1988; Gochman & Maoz, 1984), in large part because of the vagueness of the colonial territorial legacy. But few of these evolved into war (e.g., 5% vs. 62% for Europe). What accounts for the pacificity in light of the availability of conflict?

First, with some limited exceptions, most frontier zones feature forbidding conditions. Keegan (1993) has suggested that large-scale military operations can be conducted only in certain physical environments. In Latin America, much of the interstate violence has been concentrated in the La Plata River system and the South Central Pacific Coast, both of which are much more hospitable to military logistics than the Andes or the Amazon. Second, it is also possible that international intraclass conflict did not occur because the region was large enough to allow the creation of sufficient buffer zones. In general, frontiers have not abutted significant population centers or areas of great economic potential. Thus, international conflict was precluded because competing elites never came into contact with each other. It was precisely in those areas of concentration of resources or potential for wealth (e.g., La Plata or the Andean deserts) where we see the greatest conflict.[4] That is, uncertainty in borders translated into fighting only when there was something to fight about.[5]

We also cannot ignore the role of external powers, which may have guaranteed borders and the status quo, thereby removing many of the imme-diate stimuli of conflict. The Latin American peace may be thus the ultimate expression of *dependencia*. The presence of the European powers prevented a series of military events that may have created a very different geopolitical balance (Andreski, 1971). We should be careful, however, about resorting to explanations that might deny Latin American societies any control over

---

[4] My thanks to Tom Rudel for first suggesting this point.
[5] This would indicate that we might see some conflict in the future near the Plata Basin from either Itaipu Dam or the confusion and conflict stemming from transborder capital flows and property rights (e.g., Brazilians buying land in Uruguay and Paraguay).

their own fate. We might even reverse the causal order and suggest that it was the absence of war that produced a weak state, which in turn made intervention possible. To paraphrase Perry Anderson's (1979) comments on Italy, because Latin America was unable to create an empire from within, it had to suffer one from without.

Locating systematic evidence of foreign intervention (or the absence thereof) is difficult because the significance of such efforts will obviously vary a great deal by context. Clearly, the United States has had an overwhelming role in shaping contemporary Latin America. The 1948 Rio accords to a large extent helped shape the foreign relations of the continent. Nevertheless, it would seem that at least in terms of intracontinental relations, the United States has respected the autonomy of the various republics (below the isthmus of Panama). The case where we have the best documentation, the Falklands/Malvinas conflict would indicate that the United States had relatively little direct influence over Argentine decision making (Alonso Piñeiro, 1992). Although not an exhaustive record, the Foreign Relations of the United States (Department of State, 1932) series can provide insights into U.S. attitudes toward continental conflicts.[6] Looking at correspondence dealing with the War of the Pacific, the Chaco War, and the 1941 border conflict between Peru and Ecuador, the consistent position of the United States is as follows: (a) concern that European countries not become involved; (b) reluctance to be seen as an arbitrator or mediator (even when such a role is requested by belligerents); and (c) sponsorship of Latin American neutrals becoming involved, particularly Brazil. Again, this is not to deny the powerful U.S. influence on Latin American politics in general. But, it does not appear that we can hold the United States responsible for the absence of conflict. Although the "structural" constraints of physical and international environments may help explain some of the Latin American exception, I wish to focus on the ideological and material constraints on war. Simply put, Latin American countries have not been interested in or capable of destroying each other.

Fears and Threats

There are two conditions that seem absolutely necessary for conflict to occur. First, some significant segment of the elite or the population must see war as a favorable option. Even more basically, war must be part of the policy repertoire of leading decision makers. If war is not ever considered or is judged as too extreme a solution or not providing enough chances

---

[6]But note Schoultz's (1998, p. 390) problems with this source. His wonderful book, however, does not contradict my reading of American noninterference in Latin American wars.

for some "return" to the country, then even the most intense rivalries or disagreements are less likely to lead to armed conflict. Second, a significant part of the population must be supportive of the notion of war or at least be willing to accept the government's decision. This is not to deny the coercive capacity of states or that many soldiers would rather be anywhere but the front line. But, in order to incur the expense and sacrifice of war, states must be able to count on at least a base of popular support or at least acquiescence.

I argue that neither condition has applied in Latin America (with some exceptions) during the past century. The absence of war over time creates conditions in which countries can avoid the type of behavior (e.g., arms races) that is correlated with conflict. The long peace of the 20th century may be thus explained by the absence of revanchist myths or long-standing cultures venerating interstate conflict. My empirical research on nationalist symbols has demonstrated that Latin American political iconography is surprisingly peaceful and lacks both bellicose themes and collective identifications associated with mass warfare (Centeno, 1999). In order to explore this issue, I concentrate on both the military attitudes toward war and that of the civilian population.

The Military Mind

Attempting to define, much less understand, the mind-set of a particular institution or its leading members is always difficult. In the case of one as inherently secretive as the military it is even more so. Scholars with privileged access such as Robert Potash in Argentina and Alfred Stepan in Brazil have done an admirable job of describing these attitudes at particular points in time. To replicate such efforts with a sample of 11 countries across a century would be practically impossible. Yet, to answer the question of why so little war, we need to at least peer into the professional perspective of the respective militaries. Was there a proclivity for war that was frustrated by the lack of resources? Conversely, can we speak of an inherent abhorrence of interstate conflict that placed limits on the bellicosity of civilian authorities? What did the military think about the possibility of interstate war on the continent?

In order to answer that question, I analyzed the contents of the leading professional military journals of the relevant countries.[7] These journals often

---

[7]These include *Revista del Circulo Militar* (Argentina); *Revista Armas y Servicios del Ejercito* (Chile); *Ejercito y Fuerza Aerea Mexicana* (Mexico); *Revista de las Fuerzas Armadas* (Venezuela); *Gaceta Academica de la Academia Boliviana de Historia Militar* (Bolivia); *Revista del Ejercito* (Colombia); *Revista de la Fuerzas Armadas Ecuatorianas* (Ecuador); *Revista Militar de las Fuerzas Armadas de la Nacion* (Paraguay); *Gaceta Militar y Naval* (Uruguay); and *Revista do Exacta Brasileiro, Revista Militar,*

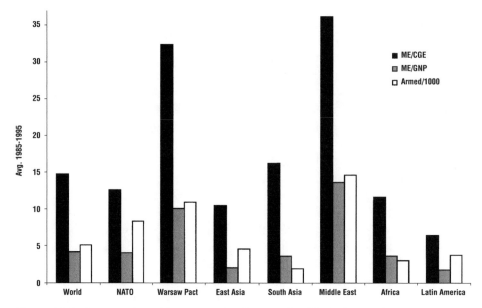

Figure 12.1. Comparative military capacity. Source: Stockholm International Peace Research Institute. ME = military expenditures; CGE = central government expenditures; GNP = gross national product.

serve as the professional platforms for up-and-coming junior officers. They also serve as a bully pulpit for retired personnel. Because these are public documents, they will not reveal the secret life of the military, but they do serve as a rough indicator of the spirit of the institution. What themes do they discuss? What enemies do they worry about?

Surprisingly, the respective militaries do not devote a great deal of attention or concern to interstate war (see Figures 12.1 and 12.2). The pattern is fairly consistent and remarkably similar across countries. When speaking with each other through these journals, the military like to dwell on (a) technical issues (e.g., ballistics and machinery), (b) organizational problems (e.g., how to train noncommissioned officers, pension plans, etc.), (c) historical reenactments (e.g., triumphs of San Martin), and (d) scholarly exercises (e.g., thoughts of Napoleon). Beginning in the late 1950s and early 1960s we do see the appearance of discussions of domestic issues (the economy) and especially concerns with national security and the threat of global communism (this trend began in Brazil and soon spread to every other military in the region). The one topic that is rarely dealt with is

Boletim Mensal do Estado Maior do Exercito, Nacao Armada, and *Revista do Clube Militar* (Brazil). The material available for Peru was limited, but came from the *Revista Militar del Peru.*

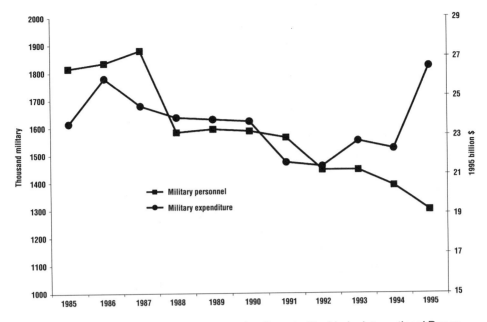

Figure 12.2. Latin American military capacity. Source: Stockholm International Peace Research Institute.

explicit strategic discussions about the region and possible battles between neighboring countries.[8]

Thus, at the very latest, beginning in the 1950s (if not before) the military gaze was largely turned inward. One could argue that this led to more violence and bloodshed than if the military had concentrated on its international mission. The link between a focus on the internal threat and the external peace is a tempting one, and it would be possible to argue for causal orders flowing both ways. As far as this chapter is concerned, however, the main point is to note the relatively limited role international conflict plays in professional military discourse.

This is not to argue that standard military considerations never play an important role in internal discussions, that each military might not have prepared contingency plans for a variety of scenarios, or that the military has not considered in excruciating detail the logistical needs of such operations. It is important however, to note how these are not part of the daily professional discourse.[9] An open, even if academic, discussion of such a

---

[8] This does not necessarily contradict the work of Kelly (1997) and Child (1985), who see a great deal of geopolitical thinking on the continent. This may go on, but it appears to take a very abstract form and does not seem to include "middle range" strategic planning.

[9] Martín González (1997) would even question the extent to which the militaries would be interested in fighting each other at all.

contingency is not an accepted part of the public dialogue. Contrast this with the much more open debate in NATO militaries concerning the likelihood of a conflict with the Soviet Union and possible strategies to deal with the threat or with the again "open secret" of planning for the next Franco–German war after 1871.

Obviously, different countries do express their own strategic interests in these magazines, but the possibility of war is rarely acknowledged.[10] Argentina's main military journals, for example, were, are, and probably will remain fixated on the Malvinas/Falklands. They also often feature articles on *"los hielos continentales"* or the glacier frontier between that country and Chile. Others discussed similar problems with the Beagle Channel. Their Chilean counterparts were less fixated on the Argentinean frontier than on the possibility of general "subversion," but in recent years, there has been much greater attention paid to protecting Antarctic claims. Peruvians discuss historical consequences of the wars between them and Ecuador and Chile. Given the continuing territorial tensions, the Peruvians may have the most developed tradition of explicitly recognizing likely enemies and discussing relevant strategies. Ecuador focuses on its claims to the Amazonian territories and the fear of Peru. Uruguayans express some trepidation of being squeezed between the two giants on their borders. The Brazilians formulate advanced treatises of the geopolitics of the continent. Alone among their neighbors, there is an intellectual tradition in the Brazilian military of discussing potential territorial expansion (usually regarding a link to the Pacific) and of geopolitical paranoia (stemming from Spanish/Portuguese colonial animosities; see Kelly, 1997, pp. 53–54, 84–134). What does not characterize any of these militaries, however, is a state of preparedness to go to war. It would appear that war is not considered an obvious viable option in strategic analysis.

This picture is consistent with the self-image provided through other military sources. A recent glossy publication by the Chilean Defense Ministry lists the following as "objectives of a national defense":

- Conserve the independence and sovereignty of the country.
- Maintain the territorial integrity of Chile.
- Contribute to preserve the institutional order and the state of law.
- Conserve and promote historical and cultural identity.
- Create the conditions of external security necessary for the well-being of the nation.

---

[10] There are exceptions of course. Chile, for example offered the British communication facilities during the Malvinas/Falklands War, and Brazil has explicitly stated its commitment to political stability in Paraguay and its willingness to intervene in order to preserve it.

- Contribute to the development of National Power ("that which supports the capacity of the nation to express its will").
- Strengthen the citizens commitment to defense.
- Support the international standing of Chile.
- Contribute to the maintenance and promotion of international peace and security in accord with national interest. (Ministerio de Defensa, 1997, p. 29)

Two points are worth noting from this list: first, the key role domestic issues play in defining the role of the armed forces and, second, the absence of bellicose sentiment. This is even clearer in a section devoted to war and crisis in which the discussion is kept on a purely abstract basis with no indication of where an external source of danger could or might originate. The section devoted to the rest of the continent emphasizes a system of "mutual confidence" by which the nations have institutionalized a process that is designed to lower perceived threats. With regard to neighboring countries, the document emphasizes Chile's defensive posture and the importance of recent steps toward integration. Even when referring to frontier zones with high economic potential but low population density, the emphasis is on potential economic development and even peaceful integration of immigrant populations, not on the construction of a military wall (Ministerio de Defensa, 1997, p. 126). This emphasis on "internal conquest" of peripheral zones runs throughout geopolitical discussions in the continent.

Again, the apparently nonbellicose professional military mind is an important, indeed vital, aspect of the explanation for the long peace. War was not featured on the strategic menu. It was not one of the first options discussed. It may have been even difficult to imagine as a policy outcome, and that conceptual impossibility may go far in explaining the long peace.[11]

Public Nationalism

Whether democratic or authoritarian, regimes need some element of support before engaging in war. As important as military proclivities may be for determining the likelihood of conflict, popular attitudes may be just as critical. To what extent have the various populations of Latin America learned to hate their neighbors? To what extent are they prepared to kill

---

[11] The military's view of the situation is supported by the reading of military experts. According to the Institute of International Strategic Studies, "The main challenge facing the security forces in the Caribbean and Latin America remains guerrilla groups, but with a less ideologically driven agenda and one more linked to organized crime and drug trafficking. Inter-state disputes remain few and are unlikely to provoke more than skirmishes over borders and illegal immigration" (see http://www.isn.ethz.ch/iiss/mb10.htm).

them or to die trying? Is there a public reservoir of bellicosity that regimes could tap in order to launch aggressive actions?

In the absence of systematic public opinion data, I have used newspapers as reflectors of public moods. There are several obvious limits to such a strategy. First, newspapers reflect their own editorial policies much more than popular sentiment. Second, they are often more concerned with elite opinions than with those of the masses. Third, they are often voices for the regime and may espouse a stronger patriotic line than might actually be felt by the majority. Nevertheless, they do serve as an imperfect mirror into the nationalistic ethos of the relevant countries.[12]

The most significant finding of this reading of the newspapers is the general and practically universal absence of nationalist sentiment expressed in ethnic terms. That is, although there are some clear cases of competition between countries reflected in speeches, public attitudes, and festivities, these are not marked by the expression of racial hatred.[13] The only exception I was able to locate was in the case of the Peru–Ecuador conflict. The analysis reveals the following major trends:

- There is a consistent mention of other Latin American countries as "sister republics" or with similar language. These indicate considerable diplomatic and interregime contact. The continent is seen as a larger community over and above the nation-state. One expression of this is the sharing of heroes and the tradition of giving statues to other cities commemorating one hero or another (the San Martin and Bolívar statues in New York's Central Park are part of this).
- An important subelement is use of the Latin American republics as coguarantors of treaties and deals on frontiers. There is often some resentment of this by the "losing" country, but there remains remarkable willingness to accept such meddling.
- Such celebrations of pan-continental unity are particularly strong on days of independence or celebrations of founding fathers that often include an emphasis on the commonalities

---

[12] I used the following: *La Prensa* (Buenos Aires), *O Estado de Sao Paulo* (Sao Paulo), *La Tribuna* (Asuncion), *El Telegrafó* (Quito), *El Mercurio* (Santiago), *El Comercio* (Lima), *El Dia* (Bogota), *Marcha* (Montevideo), and *Excelsior* (Mexico City). The choice was largely determined by the availability of newspaper archives. For each country, I selected a series of patriotic holidays during which one might expect the greatest public nationalistic sentiment. These were checked at five-year intervals beginning with the earliest available issue. I augmented these with coverage of moments of crisis in the history of the relevant countries.

[13] This is not to deny racist attitudes or unflattering characterizations of other nations. I would argue, however, that these rarely, if ever, take the form of "Bolivians must be eliminated" or "Kill Chileans before they kill you," and so forth.

of the countries established by them. These celebrations and conferences often include ex-enemies—for example, Peru participates in Bolivarian festivities in Ecuador.

- As was the case with monuments, the major celebrations are of the Independence Wars.
- Foreign policy is generally absent as a central political issue. It is common to read speeches given at major patriotic dates that make no references to external affairs or do so in the most general manner.
- Potential conflicts are generally muted. At least from the Colombian side, the frontier differences with Venezuela are not phrased in a particularly nationalistic way.
- There is a lack of public martial experience. The celebrations of national feast days—even in the 19th and early 20th centuries were relatively limited: "these days are reduced to simple holidays, to mere days of rest. Today should be what the 14th of July is in France, or what the 2nd of May is in Spain. Sadly, it is only an official holiday and the people do not come together to celebrate it" (cited in O Estado de Sao Paulo, 1899, p. 3). Another Brazilian journalist 15 years later noted that at a time when European countries were evoking the grand figures of their past, "it is good to remember a few of ours" (cited in O Estado de Sao Paulo, 1914, p. 7). The view of historical moments is also much more problematic. In 1887, a newspaper could make negative comparisons between Brazilian Independence and that of the United States—to the effect that in the United States, "liberty was planted with the blood of patriots" (cited in O Estado de Sao Paulo, 1887, pp. 1–2), while in Brazil a monarchy was established. Obviously, this reflects Republican sentiment prior to the end of the monarchy. The key issue here is that a normally sacrosanct date could be made problematic. Similarly, the celebration of the feats of Tiradentes in Brazil was abolished and reinstated depending on the extent to which such celebration fit with the political profile of the regime. Even when the moments to commemorate are not very distant, the celebration seems muted (e.g., the role of the Brazilian Expeditionary Force in World War II). Even in 1945, there appears to have been little effort to glorify this moment. Those celebrations that do exist often did not involve the masses but were seen as moments when the urban elite could demonstrate their patriotism. One could also read expressions of popular resentment of forced military service or patriotic propaganda:

"we are fed-up *(hartos)* with being told that one has to serve the fatherland, of heroism, of the national colors . . . It is all nonsense" (cited in *Marcha*, 1940, p. 5).

- Victory in wars is not always celebrated. In Brazil and Argentina, for example, there is a remarkable silence about the Triple Alliance: "[the war] interrupted once again the regular march of national progress" (cited in *O Estado de Sao Paulo*, 1913, p. 7). In neither country are the dates of exceptional battles celebrated. Paraguay, however, devotes considerable attention to "the National Epic" and to López, particularly beginning after the Chaco wars. The Panteón de Héroes becomes the site of celebrations of López's heroism and celebrations of patriotism and honoring the sacrifices of *"los caidos."* Yet, even in Paraguay, ex-enemies can establish good relationships. An account of celebration of Paraguayan independence noted a cocktail party held at the Brazilian embassy attended by members of the government and armed forces, while Bolivia held a similar feast to celebrate the end of the Chaco War (cited in *La Tribuna*, 1945a, p. 2; 1945b, p. 2).

Some conflicts do receive attention:

- We see evidence of tensions between Argentina and Chile going back to beginning of this century. There is considerable discussion of Patagonia, but the rhetoric is largely about Beagle Channel and *"hielos continetales."* What is most interesting is that neither country seems to engage in demonization of the other and that references are made to Chile and Argentina and rarely to *"los chilenos"* or *"los argentinos."* One reads some hyperbolic language such as "La cesión de las islas australes a Chile tendrá el significado de una deslealtad para la nación argentina, de una traición a su historia. . . . " [The cession of the southern islands to Chile amounts to a disloyalty to the Argentinian nation, a treason to her history. . . .] ("Alimirante Rojas," 1984, p. 3). The conflict over the Beagle Channel was particularly problematic and required the intervention of the Vatican. In the Chilean press, there is a regular discussion of the central importance of the Beagle Channel and its key role in the Antarctic claim. There is also conflict over the *"Laguna del Desierto."*
- Regarding the Malvinas/Falklands, there is a well-documented record of the national dementia that accompanied the announcement that Argentine forces had occupied the islands.

This was followed by exhibitions of Anglophobia in a country that had previously prided itself on its "Englishness." Even national icons and monuments were not spared. Yet despite the defeat and the horrible cost paid by Argentina, popular hatred of things British dissipated almost immediately after the end of hostilities and was largely transferred to the military that had created the absurd situation the first place.[14]

- The triangle of Chile, Peru, and Bolivia has had moments of tension (e.g., in the mid-1920s). The language here is often about the injustice of the Chilean conquest—Peru resenting the loss of Tacna (later recovered) and Arica, Bolivia resenting the loss of access to the sea.

- Chile actively celebrates the Battle of Yungay that defeated Peruvian–Bolivian Confederation in 1839. The central symbol here is the monument to the Roto Chileno, one of the very few monuments that celebrates the common soldier's bravery (and of course martyrdom).

- There is regular concern in Chile about Peruvian armed build-ups, specifically with greater population in Peru and its ability to recruit a much larger army (cited in *El Mercurio*, 1915, p. 3). But there is also awareness of the cost of the war and an often-expressed hope that it will not occur again (cited in *El Mercurio*, 1929, p. 3).

- There is an interesting mutual recognition of each other's heroes. The Chilean media, for example, constantly praise the Peruvian hero Miguel Grau. This is part of the general celebration of Arturo Prat's martyrdom at Iquique that is the central symbol in the commemoration of the War of the Pacific. Two things are of interest here: the emphasis on martyrdom and the willingness to recognize the heroism of the other side. For Peru, the martyrs are Grau and Francisco Bolognesi, whose line "tengo deberes sagrados y los cumplire hasta quemar el ultimo cartucho" [I have sacred obligations and I will fulfil them until the last card is played] is taught to every Peruvian schoolboy.

- In the late 1970s, some escalation of the "cold war" between Peru and Chile occurred. In part this was a reflection of the Peruvian military's use of the anniversary for a buildup of the armed forces and fears on the part of the Chileans that Juan Velasco

---

[14]The absence of such hatred took surprising forms. While living in Buenos Aires I never felt any tension when people on the street or bus would overhear my family speaking English. In a local toy store I bought some toy soldiers for my son, which not only had British uniforms, but also included a flag. When my son played with these in a nearby sandbox, no children commented on these except to ask to be included in the game.

would use the anniversary to strengthen his regime. Ambassadors were sent home, and Peru executed a noncommissioned officer accused of treason (cited in *El Mercurio*, 1979, p. 1). Bolivia and Peru were also tense during this period.

- Bolivia expresses continued frustration with the absence of an outlet to the sea. This is established as the "principal objective of the nation" ("President Paz Estensoro," 1963, p. 7).

- The Peru–Ecuador case is perhaps the most extensive and intensive example of popular participation. For February 1995, for example, there were reports in all the continental newspapers of "bellicose fervor" and popular demonstrations. Even the very limited conflict of 1995 was portrayed as an apocalyptic battle.

- At least on the Ecuadorian side (prior to 1941) there were expressions of hope that an agreement could be found to solve the border dispute ("President Isidro Ayora," 1930, p. 3). By 1940, one can detect a clearer martial air and claims that national territory will be defended, but still without the kind of racial language often seen in other conflicts. Yet, consistent mention is made of the fact that Ecuador and Peru share so much "history and blood" (cited in *El Telegrafó*, 1940a, p. 15; 1940b, pp. 8–10). Even when calling for buildup of its army in response to the Peruvian situation, the emphasis is on using the military to support development on the frontier rather than eliminating the enemy. The emphasis in anniversary speeches is not on martial posing, but instead on the need to pursue diplomatic efforts. Even a few years after the struggle, the Peruvian president could visit the frontier and be applauded by Ecuadorian citizens (cited in *El Tiempo*, 1944).

- Nevertheless, this is one of the few examples where the discussion of war brings in *"el pueblo"* and speaks of a nation at arms (cited in *El Telegrafó*, 1945a, p. 1). In the 1930s, wealthy citizens in Ecuador offered jewels to purchase arms with which to defend the national territory (cited in *El Comercio*, 1938, p. 9). July 1941 saw student demonstrations in both capitals in support of war, and the Ecuadorian president announced that "in each Ecuadorian there is a soldier, a hero. . . . ." (cited in *El Comercio*, 1941, p. 3). Anniversaries of the Rio Protocol (generally unfavorable to Ecuador and are seen as "atrociously mutilating the national territory") are celebrated with popular manifestations including student marches in Quito (cited in *El Telegrafó*, 1945b, p. 3; 1950, p. 1). Critiques of military juntas are often based on the supposed harm military governments do to the chances that Ecuador can reclaim lost territory (cited in *El*

Telegrafó, 1965). There is also the use of pejoratives, especially on the Peruvian side. Popular newspapers in Peru (*El Chivo, Aja!*) refer to Ecuadorians as *"monos."* The 1995 border incidents once again elicited great popular support for governments, but only limited amounts of xenophobia.

What do these press accounts tell us about war in Latin America? In general, when wars are celebrated, the liturgy is the same:

- The enemy had great superiority of numbers.
- National forces had courage, honor, dignity, and so forth. The enemy is not demonized but is characterized in a similar way.

I found no instance of a celebration of the "beauty of war." Overall, the population is not indoctrinated in a cult of war.

Defining the Enemy

In an earlier article, I analyzed the composition of nationalist symbols on the continent (Centeno, 1999). I argued that most Latin American countries have lacked the identification of an external enemy that encourages the development and solidification of a national identity. As far as state elites have been concerned, the greatest threat to their power has not come from a competing elite, but from the masses below. In some ways the internal war orientation of the military is partly a product of this ethnic division. The enemy to *"la patria"* was perceived not as the nation next door, but as those in the population threatening the social and economic status quo. This perception is particularly relevant in countries with significant Indian populations. It is important to recall that the "ethnic war" of the continent occurred prior to state formation. The Spanish Conquest and its consequences left deeper divisions within countries than could ever develop between them. Certainly in the case of Guatemala and perhaps in Peru, ideological and racial/class threats were clearly perceived as correlated. The external peace was therefore bought with internal hatred and divisions.

We also need to recall the distinction between a dominant and a ruling class. Latin America possessed the first, but arguably, not the second. Latin America lacked a coherent elite able to impose its will and organize the capacities of the state toward war. No faction of the dominant class was able to establish a strong enough hegemony so as to prioritize national collective interests (defined still in class terms). In the absence of that hegemony, the monopoly over the means of violence did not coalesce around any central actor, and subordinate classes were never totally vanquished. Simply put, each nation's military remained too busy killing its own peasants to bother with someone else's. (Conversely, the absence of wars may have also retarded national integration.)

In summary, whether analyzed from the point of view of the military professionals or the general populace, we see little of the culturalist basis for a creed of war. Latin American societies have not been trained to fight each other and to see in such battles the ultimate expression of their patriotism. We now turn to the institutional capacity of states to fight these wars.

MATERIAL LIMITS AND MILITARY CAPACITY

In explaining the Latin American peace, we also need to question the assumption that all states are capable of war. Singer and Small (1982) have explored the importance of "military capability" and found that there is a strong correlation between political and economic power and bellicose behavior. War requires basic organizational competence and access to resources that only certain states have. From this point of view, Latin America has been peaceful because the states in the region never developed the political capacity to have prolonged wars. No states, no wars.

The degree of internal violence that continues to dominate Latin America is both a cause and an indication of the relative inability of these states to fight each other. Perhaps the best evidence of this condition is the relative importance of civil as opposed to international wars during the 20th century. Clearly, Latin America was violent, but the large part of political conflict occurred within states, not between them. Again, some of this had to do with the definition of the internal enemy alluded to earlier. But, I would also argue that the search for an internal threat had something to do with the need of the military to define a mission it could handle. Whether one speaks of genocidal warfare in Guatemala or the disappearances of people in Argentina, the organizational and logistical demands placed on the respective militaries pales in comparison with what would have been required by external war. Faced with material constraints and already oriented toward suspecting the mass of the population, the military defined a mission it felt comfortable with and, equally important, felt that it could meet.

One of the most surprising trends in Latin America is that despite the fact that many of these countries spent much of he previous 50 years under military rule, the budget for the armed forces remained relatively low during the entire period (see Figure 12.3).[15] The pattern during the past 30 years shows remarkable stability in terms of relative importance of the military. We

---

[15] While I have used the best comparative information available, note should be made that Latin American defense budgets tend be opaque and are often spread over several ministries, making a full account difficult.

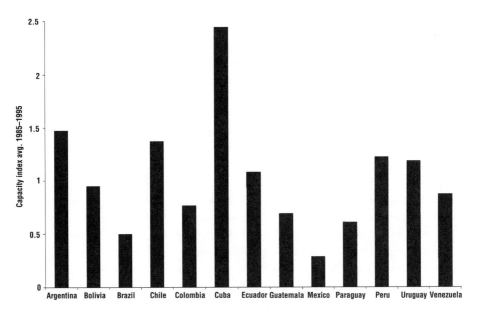

Figure 12.3. National military capacity. Index is based on average ratio to continental average of ME/GNP, ME/CGE, ME/per capita, ARMED/per capita. Source: Stockholm International Peace Research Institute. ME = military expenditures; GNP = gross national product; CGE = central government expenditures.

see some fluctuations in the military budgets as a percentage of government expenditures, but this is extremely sensitive to policy regimes that increase or decrease overall public spending. The biggest change seems to be the decline in overall military expenditures over the past few years (with an ominous rise beginning in 1993). Although the correlation between form of regime and military expenditure is difficult to measure exactly (but military governments appear to favor their own sectors), we have seen an apparent decline in the relative attention paid to the military after the democratic wave of the 1980s. Argentina may be the most extreme case, with a 30% decline in expenditures over the decade and an even more drastic reduction in the number of soldiers (60%). Even where civilians have been constrained by an institutionalized military "veto" such as in Chile, expenditures appear to have declined through the 1990s as a percentage of the gross national product (GNP) and government budgets (but increased in absolute terms; Ministerio de Defensa, 1997, pp. 194–196).

Certainly in comparison with other regions, the Latin American countries have spent much smaller amounts by any comparative measures. Expressing budgets as percentages of GNP or CGE (central government expenditures) serves to control for the massive differences in the resources available in terms of population or capital. The propensity to allocate moneys to the military is relatively low in Latin America, even if we control for the availability of resources. The gulf between the continent and other global regions is more extreme if we look at absolute amounts or on a per capita basis. Here, the combinations of smaller economies and less military concerns produce relatively minuscule military budgets (see Figure 12.1).

There is some logic to the geographical distribution of defense expenditures. The Southern Cone, which has seen the most intense geopolitical rivalries, tends to have spent more money on their respective militaries—at least as a percentage of the their total economic output. If we look at personnel and hardware, we again note that there is a geographical concentration of resources (see Table 12.1). Brazil obviously has the largest armed forces, but given the discrepancy in size, it appears to have devoted relatively less attention to military growth. Argentina, Chile, and Peru appear to have the most developed military capacity that may be explained both by the recent history of military involvement or by the geopolitical tensions between these countries and their neighbors.

The most important finding here is that these relatively small amounts of resources translate into severely constrained military capacity (cited in *Jane's Sentinel*, 1998). Even if we look at the countries with the most developed military, we note that both the numbers and quality of materiel would make prolonged warfare difficult if not impossible. Analyzing the composition of their military hardware indicates that it tends to be of less than mint vintage and with severely limited operational ranges. Moreover, with few exceptions, no country could afford the typical attrition one might expect in a naval or air battle. Without exception, the navies are designed primarily to guard the coast (Kelly, 1997, p. 29).

This situation, however, may be shifting. Although the region remains one of the smallest arms markets, spending rose in 1996 to $1.6 billion—its highest level since 1991. A major trade development has been the change in U.S. arms-sales policy that now allows U.S. companies to sell major conventional weapon systems to the region. Other competitors are also moving into the market. For example, Peru and Colombia have placed orders for combat aircraft and helicopters from Belarus and Russia.[16] Pressures to use the military for new tasks such as drug enforcement may have the unforeseen effect of creating arms races, for example, between a Chile alarmed by its neighbors' growth and a Peru partly financed by Drug Enforcement Administration money. A significant increase in the logistical and institutional capacity of the military unaccompanied by a clear delineation of a mission could produce a functional need to define potential conflicts outside of the borders and challenge the long peace.

---

[16] International Institute of Strategic Studies, http://www.isn.ethz.ch/iiss/mb10.htm.

TABLE 12.1
Latin American Military Capacity in 1996

Country	Active Armed Forces (in thousands)	Number of						
		Tanks	Combat Helicopters	Destroyers	Submarines	Fighters	Bombers
Argentina	36	460	41	6	4	100	6
Bolivia	25	36	18	0	0	22	0
Brasil	195	394	72	5	7	85	0
Chile	52	200	54	4	4	67	0
Colombia	121	12	0	0	4	27	0
Ecuador	50	153	54	0	2	37	3
Peru	85	410	59	1	8	67	19
Venezuela	34	261	20	0	2	62	0
Median	51	241	40	2	4	58	4

CONCLUSIONS

What are the lessons offered by the Latin American cases? I would argue that it is the absence of a consistent socially created hatred—whether inside the military or as part of civilian culture—and the limited capacity of the states that best explains the "long peace." These are not societies taught to go to war, nor are they societies in which extreme efforts have been made to facilitate military activity. The societies have not been taught to hate or given the capacity to destroy. What does this tell us about avoiding ethnic conflict? Again I would emphasize the ideological and organizational elements. Rather than assuming that "tribes will fight," we should identify those situations in which an effort is being made to create an "ideology" of hatred and where the organizational capacity exits to allow that hatred full expression.

The cases of Cuba and Guatemala may serve as indications that when these conditions are overcome, very different outcomes from the continental standard result. In the first case, the government has for all intents and purposes imposed a permanent state of war on the population since 1959. The situation is similar in Guatemala after 1982 when the Rios Montt government began a genocidal campaign in large parts of the countryside. Both countries (but especially Cuba) have expressed their commitment to armed force in two forms: extreme diversion of resources for the military and very high participation in the armed forces. Moreover, a language of war pervades public discourse. In Cuba, it is the threat posed by the United States (and earlier by international capitalism in general). In Guatemala there is the lethal combination of an ideological enemy (communism) with ethnic hatred (from Whites and Latinos toward Mayas). The violence that these two countries have seen (the Cuban forces in Africa, the Guatemalans in their own country) would indicate that it is not a generic cultural characteristic that helps explain the Latin American peace, but the very concrete manifestations of cultural and fiscal preparations for war.

REFERENCES

Abente, D. (1987). The war of the triple alliance: Three explanatory models. *Latin American Research Review, 22*(2), 47–69.

Almirante Rojas of Argentina. (1984, January 4). *La Prensa*, p. 3.

Alonso Piñeiro, A. (1992). *Historia de la guerra de Malvinas* [History of the Malvinas War]. Buenos Aires: Planeta.

Anderson, P. (1979). *Lineages of the absolutist state*. London: Verso.

Andreski, S. (1971). *Military organization and society*. Berkeley: University of California Press.

Bethell, L. (Ed.). (1987–1990). *The Cambridge history of Latin America: Vols. II, IV, V. 1987–1990*. London, New York: Cambridge University Press.

Centeno, M. A. (1997, May). Blood and debt: War and taxation in 19th century Latin America. *American Journal of Sociology, 102*(6), 1565–1605.

Centeno, M. A. (1998). The peaceful continent: War in Latin America. In G. Varona-Lacey & J. López-Arias (Eds.), *Latin America: An interdisciplinary approach* (pp. 121–136). New York: Peter Lang.

Centeno, M. A. (1999, June). War and memory: Symbols of state nationalism in Latin America. *European Review of Latin American and Caribbean Studies, 66*, 75–106.

Centeno, M. A. (in press). *Blood and debt: War stalemating in Latin America*. State College: Penn State Press.

Child, J. (1985). *Geopolitics and conflict in South America*. New York: Praeger.

Department of State. (1932). *U.S. foreign relations of the U.S.* Washington: Government Printing Office.

Diehl, P., & Goertz, G. (1988, March). Territorial changes and militarized conflicts. *Journal of Conflict Resolution, 32*(1), 103–122.

El Comercio. (1938, June 8). p. 9.

El Comercio. (1941, July 8). p. 3.

El Mercurio. (1915, January 21). p. 3.

El Mercurio. (1929, September 20). p. 3.

El Mercurio. (1979, January 20). p. 1.

El Telegrafó. (1940a, August 10). p. 15.

El Telegrafó. (1940b, August 11). pp. 8–10.

El Telegrafó. (1945a, January 29). p. 1.

El Telegrafó. (1945b, January 30). p. 3

El Telegrafó. (1950, January 29). p. 1.

El Telegrafó. (1965, December 17).

El Tiempo. (1944, December 18).

Gochman, C., & Maoz, Z. (1984, December). Militarized disputes: 1816–1976. *Journal of Conflict Resolution, 28*(4), 585–615.

Howard, M. (1984). *The causes of war*. Cambridge, MA: Harvard University Press.

Jane's Sentinel: South America. (1998).

Keegan, J. A. (1993). *History of warfare*. London: Hutchinson.

Kelly, P. (1997). *Checkerboards and shatterbelts: The geopolitics of South America*. Austin: University of Texas.

La Tribuna. (1945a, May 16). p. 2.

La Tribuna. (1945b, June 13). p. 2.

Levy, J. S. (1983). *War and the modern Great Power system*. Lexington: University Press of Kentucky.

Mann, M. (1996). *The sources of social power* (Vol. 2). Cambridge, England: Cambridge University Press.

Marcha. (1940, August 23). p. 5.

Martín González, F. (1997). *The longer peace in South America, 1935–1995.* Unpublished doctoral dissertation, Columbia University, New York.

McIntyre, D. (1995). *The longest peace: Why are there so few interstate wars in South America.* Unpublished doctoral dissertation, University of Chicago.

Ministerio de Defensa. (1997). *Libro de la Defensa Nacional de Chile* [Book of the national defense of Chile]. Santiago, Chile.

O Estado de Sao Paulo. (1887, April 21). pp. 1–2.

O Estado de Sao Paulo. (1899, September 7). p. 3.

O Estado de Sao Paulo. (1913, September 7). p. 7.

O Estado de Sao Paulo. (1914, September 7). p. 7.

President Isidro Ayora. (1930, August 11). *El Telegrafó,* p. 3.

President Paz Estensoro. (1963, August 7). *El Comercio,* p. 7.

Schoultz, L. (1998). *Beneath the United States: A history of U.S. policy towards Latin America.* Cambridge, MA: Harvard University Press.

Singer, J. D., & Small, M. (1982). *Resort to arms.* Beverly Hills, CA: Sage.

Tilly, C. (1992). *Coercion, capital, and European states, AD 990–1992.* Cambridge, MA: Blackwell.

Weede, E. (1984, December). Democracy and war involvement. *Journal of Conflict Resolution, 28*(4), 649–664.

Wright, Q. (1965). *A study of war.* Chicago: University of Chicago Press.

Zinnes, D. (1980). Why war? Evidence on the outbreak of international conflict. In T. Gurr (Ed.), *Handbook of political conflict.* New York: Free Press.

IV

LIMITED, CONTAINED, AND PARTLY RESOLVED ETHNOPOLITICAL WARFARE

13

THE NORTHERN IRELAND CONFLICT: PROSPECTS AND POSSIBILITIES

TONY GALLAGHER

In the early years of this century, it became clear that a majority of people in Ireland wished to achieve independence from Great Britain and that some measure of independence would be granted. However, a minority within Ireland wished to retain the link with Great Britain for reasons of culture, history, economy, and sentiment. Most of those so inclined lived in the northeast of the island, thereby providing a basis for a geographical solution to the competing desires. Thus was Northern Ireland born through the partition of the island into two political entities, one largely nationalist[1] and Catholic, the other largely unionist and Protestant.

Life is rarely so simple. Within Northern Ireland political stability was compromised by the fact that a substantial minority of Catholics remained on the "wrong" side of the border. Furthermore, because the evident desire of the nationalist minority was to move the border rather than themselves, unionists sought reassurance and security through the domination of political institutions and public life. Political life soon settled into a pattern of dull predictability on the confessional basis of political identity. John Darby (1997) described this situation as one where the elections were "less about casting your vote than voting your caste" (p. 58). The all-pervasive link among religion, politics, and nationality was realized in the practical sphere in a host of separate social activities including sports, education, culture, and commemoration.

It was hardly surprising then that a powerful zero-sum perception came to infect political calculations: Defense of unionism became synonymous with restricting the space accorded to nationalists, and any challenge, no matter how benign, was cast as a threat to the border. The nationalist

---

[1] In the political lexicon of Northern Ireland the more militant nationalists are termed *republicans*, and the more militant unionists are termed *loyalists*.

orientation differed only to the extent that there was less to defend and less likelihood of any victory. That victory of any kind was a finite resource, fought over by two immutable political bands, however, provided the taken-for-granted basis of what passed for politics in Northern Ireland.

The civil rights agitation of the late 1960s, the outbreak of widespread civil disorder, and the reemergence, in a new and more powerful form, of the Irish Republican Army (IRA) in the 1970s served only to reinforce once again this zero-sum calculation. Over the years of violence, this perception was to be strengthened still further by a sense of moral outrage driven by the mounting body count. The metaphorical heaps of corpses on all sides of the metaphorical battlefields provided the basis for in-group moral legitimacy. This was taken to justify a sense that to compromise was to "give in" and that to give in was to "give up." Each side focused on its losses, seemingly oblivious to the pain suffered and endured across all the divides in the society.

In the early 1970s, the British government tried to broker a deal between the main political parties and thereby isolate the extremists on either wing. Rather than bolstering the middle ground, however, this attempt foundered as a result of extremist reaction and its main manifestation, the power-sharing executive, lasted barely six months. Thereafter, the conflict settled into a seemingly inexorable battle between the security forces and the IRA. By the mid-1980s, the architecture of new possibility began to be put in place, with the signing of the Anglo–Irish Agreement in 1985. This provided a stable London–Dublin axis within which it was hoped that new political arrangements might evolve. This new context provided an important basis for widening the range of policy options in Northern Ireland. Politicians and civil servants from the Republic of Ireland had no executive authority in the North, but their contribution served to broaden the policy agenda and, in so doing, shored up a perception among some nationalists that incremental change for the better could occur.

In the mid-1990s the IRA and loyalist (unionist) paramilitaries declared cease-fires, although in the immediate period the peace process seemed to stall. Furthermore, this period also saw the emergence of a particularly virulent and unpleasant form of crude sectarianism. This was largely centered on the simmering and ongoing dispute over parades and marches. In the context provided by the cease-fires, many nationalists seemed to be saying that the new dispensation meant that their views must now be taken into account and that their permission would be required for Orange (unionist) marches in their areas. By contrast, many loyalists and unionists, suspicious in any case as to the full import of the peace process, felt that the defense of their traditional right to march anywhere was their "line in the sand." Many unionists felt that they were the ones who had comprised on all counts, and it was time to hold fast.

After 18 months the IRA cease-fire collapsed, only to be restored after changes in governments in London and Dublin and renewed impetus behind peace moves. The next few months saw a flurry of activity as a series of hitherto unimaginable goals were reached and achieved. Out of this came the Belfast Agreement, involving most of the local political parties and the British and Irish governments. The agreement received widespread popular endorsement on both sides of the Irish border following twin referendums. In Northern Ireland, 71%, in a high poll, supported the agreement, although unionist opinion was clearly evenly divided.

How can we best understand the process thus far, and what might be the prospects for the future? Sherif, Harvey, White, Hood, and Sherif's (1961) classic work on intergroup conflict highlights the relative ease with which conflict can be generated. In their Robbers Cave studies, Sherif and his colleagues demonstrated how competitive interdependence between groups leads to escalating conflict behavior (see also McCauley, chapter 21, this volume). Arguably, the zero-sum calculation provides an example of such competitive interdependence in that the two communities saw themselves as fixed within an enduring dispute over the most finite resource of all, territory. The apparent extension of this zero-sum thinking to other aspects of social and political life "proved" for many that the conflict was intractable and, ultimately, insoluble. That it does extend to other areas of social and political life should not be doubted.

As part of the "third way" politics being developed by social democratic politicians on both sides of the Atlantic, an emergent concept of interest is the notion of social capital. This is taken to refer to the network of contacts and communication that inspires confidence among a community of people and encourages a sense of in-group solidarity. In Northern Ireland there clearly exist social processes that promote social capital, but the outcome is dysfunctional to the extent that the processes are within the two main communities rather than between them.

Furthermore, there is a well-known social grammar of interpersonal interaction linked to perceptual cues. A variety of cues provide a reasonable estimate of a stranger's religious background—these include such indicators as name, area of residence, social and cultural interests, and school attended. It is not so much that people go out of their way to seek these cues in conversations with strangers, but that the emergence of one in a conversation is immediately recognized as providing important information. Once "cued" that the interlocutor is from the "other community," the interaction can proceed in a polite and sociable manner as long as certain taboo areas, such as religion and politics, are avoided. Thus the affluent middle classes can intermingle, safe in the knowledge that they do not share the fate of so many people from the poorer parts of town—which are almost invariably religiously segregated—but safe also in the knowledge that they will avoid dealing with the awkward and embarrassing realities of social division in Northern Ireland. The key point is that such resources of social capital as do exist in our society contribute to the reproduction of division rather than its amelioration. One striking consequence is that political discourses talk across each other rather than to each other: After all, if electoral politics is largely determined by a religious headcount, then what incentive or interest is there in appeals for support across the sectarian divide?

This was the context that faced the team led by the American, former Senator George J. Mitchell (D-ME), when the political talks process opened. The mediation team introduced two innovations that were to be crucial in providing a space for movement on both sides. First, they devised terms, the "Mitchell Principles," by which parties could enter into the talks process or on the basis of which they might be ejected. Second, they established criteria for "sufficient consensus" among the talks participants that provided the basis for decisions on contentious issues. On this basis a "sufficient consensus" was achieved only if a measure achieved support from a majority of the talks' participants, plus a minimum level of support from the political groups within both traditions. An additional factor was the establishment of a clear and unalterable deadline for the talks process, with the Mitchell team emphasizing over and over again that this deadline was for real.

These arrangements were crucial in a number of respects. They allowed the talks' participants to defer to rules of involvement that belonged to the process rather than to the decision of any individual group. These agreed-to rules provided a transparent basis for the inclusion of groups linked to paramilitary organizations and provided others with a justification for staying in the talks when the paramilitary parties entered the talks process. Once the parties were in the talks, it was important that the sufficient consensus criteria allowed them to circumvent the zero-sum problem that had constrained politics in the past, by encouraging coalition building and accommodation. Once the participants saw the beneficial effects of these rules—by confronting difficult problems and agreeing to decisions—the legitimacy of the procedures and the process were enhanced. Indeed, after the successful conclusion of the talks and the elections to a new Northern Ireland Assembly, a similar basis for decision making was enshrined in its rules. As with the talks process, the sufficient consensus requirements for decisions in the Assembly also work to promote coalition building and accommodation, as otherwise no decisions will be made.

An optimistic assessment would offer the hope that the effective implementation of these procedures should be cumulative in that cooperation, collaboration, and trust will grow in steady measure. Coalition politics, if it can be maintained, could produce the form of social capital that Sherif might have labeled as *cooperative interdependence*. Decisions taken by sufficient consensus could encourage a degree of shared ownership and responsibility. Indeed, these decisions might serve as superordinate goals for the politicians, even if they defend their compliance in certain decisions by arguing that the others wanted it, and they had to accept it if any decision was to be made.

Other aspects of the Belfast Agreement might reinforce this positive scenario. Alongside the elected Assembly, it was proposed to establish a Civic Forum in order to tap into the resources of civil society. The Civic Forum might help by sharing the responsibility further. It will have no executive or legislative authority, but this could give it the freedom to discuss issues and possible solutions that the politicians, with one eye of the electors, are loath to address until the issue has been aired at some length. The Civic Forum might also allow for more discursive freedom in the public sphere and could widen notions of participation and citizenship.

Further gains might be derived from the north–south bodies on the island of Ireland and from the east–west bodies between the two islands. These parallel structures might contain the basis for new and fruitful relationships between all the "imagined communities" of Great Britain and Ireland. No one much knows what to expect from these institutions, save that the nationalists seem to give most weight to the north–south bodies, while the unionists give most weight to the east–west ones. Both perspectives coincide with their desired futures, but their involvement in both might broaden their experience of practical politics.

In a somewhat longer time scale, the emerging European context may have an influence. Despite current English reluctance, it looks likely that the structures of the European Union are going to deepen and widen. The base for a more meaningful European community is being put in place at institutional, ritual, and experiential levels. There will be no European super state that subsumes particularistic identities: Unlike in the United States, assimilation to an agreed norm is not a European option, at least for the moment. The Union is therefore leaning toward a different version of sovereignty that accepts, indeed, celebrates (because it must), the dynamic that arises from pluralistic diversity. We are all Europeans, but we are also French, Italian, German, British, and Irish. The centralizing processes of the Union are paralleled by countervailing processes of localism. Key to this is the concept of subsidiarity, that is, the idea that decisions are taken at the most appropriate level.

Thus our identities do not stop at the national level because we are also, and are encouraged to be, South Tyroleans, Bavarians, Milanese, Catalans, and Scots. The Union works by the pooling of state sovereignty in order to achieve common and collective gains. But this implies also a different notion of sovereignty whereby our social identities comprise a variety of elements simultaneously. If this works, it could represent the sort of interlocking identifications that Henri Tajfel (1978) would have seen as a basis for social solidarity or, at least, reducing the possibility of social factionalism.

But that is for the future, and in 1999[2] the prospects for Northern Ireland do not appear to be so positive. After the referendums and the election of the new Assembly, a series of deadlines existed for the establishment of the institutional frameworks envisaged in the Agreement. Most of the deadlines have come and gone, few of the institutional frameworks are in place and, at the time of writing, none are functioning. The substance of the problem is analogous to the problems that have beset the Middle East peace process. In that process a number of crucial problems—perhaps most notably the status of Jerusalem—were circumvented without being resolved. The rational purpose in this was to maintain the momentum of the talks. However, in the Middle East these problems kept reemerging and contributed to the weakening of the process more generally.

In Northern Ireland the same thing has happened with the issue of the decommissioning of paramilitary weapons. The Belfast Agreement requires that full decommissioning will be completed within two years and that all organizations make and demonstrate a commitment to peaceful means of politics. Although the agreement does not provide for a starting point for decommissioning, unionists will not agree to the participation of Sinn Fein members in the executive body until the decommissioning process has begun. For many unionists the republican movement has not yet shown any concrete demonstration of its commitment to peaceful means. Sinn Fein, however, points to the fact that it has identified a liaison person with the Decommissioning Body and has publicly stated a form of words akin to an acceptance that the war is over. From the Sinn Fein perspective, the unionist position on decommissioning either shows that they will seek any excuse to halt progress or, alternatively, that they want the IRA to surrender. Many unionists are suspicious as to the intentions of the republican movement in general and the IRA in particular. They remain unsure that the IRA actually is reconciled to partition, and they fear that the IRA will continue to press its demands until such time as a united Ireland is conceded. Conversely, many republicans remain deeply suspicious as to unionist commitment to the agreement. Their concern is that unionists seek to reestablish majority rule and have no real commitment to equality between the two communities.

---

[2]Contrary to widespread expectations, the political parties managed to agree upon a basis for reestablishing the devolved government arrangements in May, 2000. This was linked to a process involving external oversight of IRA arms dumps. By August, 2000, the arrangements continued to operate even though the position of the Ulster Unionist leader, David Trimble, remained fragile. All paramilitary prisoners have been released but there is continuing controversy over proposals for reforming the police force.

This blockage provides us with a useful reminder of the depth of the problem in Northern Ireland and offers clear evidence of the continuing lack of trust and confidence, despite the progress achieved so far. Many of those outside the process seem to despair at the apparent attribution of responsibility and action as claimed by the political disputants. The main unionist party argues that Sinn Fein's lack of commitment to peaceful means is evidenced by the refusal of the IRA to hand over any arms. Sinn Fein claims that the unionists have not fundamentally changed and are trying to keep Sinn Fein out of the process by continually erecting new and unrealistic demands. Both seem to assume that the other is operating from a position of intransigence and strength, when to many outside the process both appear to operate from positions of weakness. In both cases the weakness follows from divisions in their own ranks over the appropriate course of action. The referendum showed that unionist opinion is evenly divided, while the republican movement remains an uneasy combination of those who support the peace strategy and those who would prefer to return to the certainties of war.

The zero-sum thinking referred to earlier has not so easily dissipated. At a prosaic level, the immediate problem will focus on the ability of the Ulster Unionist party to maintain its Assembly members intact. As we have seen, the rules of sufficient consensus require a defined proportion of each of the unionist and nationalist blocs to support a measure before it is passed. Currently the unionist parties who oppose the Agreement and who seem likely to try to block the Assembly are sitting just below the threshold they need to exercise a blocking role. If even only a few Ulster Unionists desert the party, then the Assembly could be stymied and unable to make any decisions. In this way the elaborate mechanisms designed to avoid zero-sum practice could founder.

As the practical problems accumulate, so too the emotional content of the debate is stoked. This is nowhere more evident than in the discourses of victimhood that have emerged. Unionists complain bitterly about the way paramilitary prisoners are being released early under the agreement, while little appears to be done for their victims. Some of the more militant unionist groups pursue this issue by explicitly differentiating between "innocent" victims and those who, presumably, deserved to die. Meanwhile, republican militants in the IRA and dissident groups wonder whether the limited form of north–south political structures are worthy of the sacrifice of their paramilitary colleagues. One Dublin journalist has encapsulated this thinking in the following mnemonic: ISWPPDF—Is this What Padraig Pearse Died For?

I have referred to Sherif et al.'s work on functional interdependence and how the particular form of contact between the political parties was used to try to promote cooperative interdependence: Contact alone, without other conditions, was an insufficient basis for attempting to reduce conflict. Tajfel's (1978) work on social identity theory extended this by highlighting the importance of social comparisons in the process of the construction of social identity. The main significance for the present is that, in certain circumstances, contact, even on an ostensibly cooperative basis, could be viewed by groups as a threat to identity. Cooperative interdependence, therefore, had to be underpinned by a context where the various actors approached each other on an equal basis and in a neutral context. The Mitchell Principles and the rules for sufficient consensus attempted to provide the context for both these conditions. And, of course, during the talks process the attempt seemed to work. However, in the post-talks environment they do not yet appear to have worked.

One way to try to understand this situation might be to draw on Michael Billig's (1976) commentary on the Sherif et al. studies. Billig pointed out the Sherif et al. used superordinate goals as the mechanism for creating positive functional interdependence between the two groups and thereby reducing intergroup conflict. However, despite the appearance to the study participants that the superordinate tasks had occurred by happenstance, Billig reminded us that these opportunities were deliberately created by the third group in the study, the experimenters. This echoes an important contribution to our understanding of the Northern Ireland conflict offered by the late Frank Wright.

Wright argued in 1987 that many conflicts in ethnic frontier regions were exacerbated by conflict between the neighboring states. However, not only are the two neighboring states for Northern Ireland—Great Britain and Ireland—not prepared to go to war over the region, but since 1985 they have worked together toward a solution. It was argued that this framework helped to provide a creative widening of the policy agenda in Northern Ireland in the 1980s and, in so doing, provided an environment within which moves toward political accommodation could take place. However, the role of the external states was even more evident in the final stages of the talks process when the Prime Ministers of Great Britain and Ireland both decamped to Belfast to cajole and persuade the talks participants to stay in the negotiating room until a deal was signed. And nor should we forget the considerable role played by U.S. President Bill Clinton in adding his weight to the pressure for accommodation toward the end of the talks and at points before and since.

The optimistic analysis just offered essentially suggests that the successful experience of the talks process, allied to the particular rules of engagement created by the mediators, helped to increase the mutual confidence of the talks participants and contributed to the success of the talks. This process might be understood as promoting social capital within the political process or as providing a psychologically powerful context for intergroup contact and engagement. Unfortunately, as events since then have demonstrated, the optimistic analysis may overstate the extent to which the political participants have, in fact, moved away from a zero-sum discourse of politics and identity. In the latter part of this chapter, I have suggested that the intervention of a *deus ex machina*, in the form of Tony Blair, Bertie Ahern, and Bill Clinton, may have been necessary to drag the talks to a successful close. Perhaps, by the same logic, the current logjam will be solved only by a last-minute intervention from outside. Even more worrisome, perhaps this is what the local political parties have come to depend on, convinced of their own inability to solve the problem. In this more pessimistic scenario, we have not so much moved away from zero-sum thinking as merely provided a crutch to deal with specific instances of its manifestation.

In Northern Ireland the key problem with identity has been the way so many social dimensions have served to reinforce a division centered on religion. This has rendered the religious dimension fundamental, if symbolic, and invested so many aspects of public life with its tone. This has led to the development of zero-sum thinking where politics, indeed much of social and political life, is experienced through a contemporary variant of premodern mercantilism. Psychologically this might be described as the normalization of competitive interdependence.

Through education, we strive constantly to remind our young people of the interdependence that actually exists between the communities. Through language, culture, humor, and social practice we have shared and borrowed across the sectarian divide as, inevitably, we must, given that we inhabit the same piece of earth and have done so for generations. Given the centrality of this division to our perception of ourselves, however, we tend to view interdependence as a threat rather than a resource, as a competitive necessity rather than a cooperative possibility. The experience of being European might allow us to break through to a positive interdependence that Sherif might have commended. The experience of the novel political structures envisaged by the Belfast Agreement could contribute to this process. If so, this would be to build on the foundations that our politicians had laid down in the process of breaking through to a new form of politics given their experience of negotiation and accommodation toward the agreement. Events since have reduced the vision and raised the possibility that the progress we have made has been due, in no small measure, to our dependence on others, rather than to creative interdependence among ourselves. But even this less optimistic analysis contains within it the seeds of hope, for tangible progress has been made: The experience of the past 5 years has been so unlike that of the previous 25 that it is quite difficult to countenance its dismissal. The journey out of conflict holds promise, but we have as yet only made the first few faltering steps, and the fear is that, having stumbled, we will turn back. For 25 of the past 30 years the tragedy of Northern

Ireland was that no road out of the impasse appeared to be available. Now that it has become available it would be an even greater tragedy if we choose not to take it.

REFERENCES AND BIBLIOGRAPHY

Billig, M. (1976). *Intergroup relations*. London: Harcourt Brace Jovanich.

Darby, J. (1997). *Scorpions in a bottle: Conflicting cultures in Northern Ireland*. London: Minority Rights Group.

Dunn, S. (1995). *Facets of the conflict in Northern Ireland*. London: Macmillan.

McGarry, J., & O'Leary, B. (1995). *Explaining Northern Ireland*. Oxford, England: Blackwell.

Ruane, J., & Todd, J. (1996). *The dynamics of conflict in Northern Ireland: Power, conflict and emancipation*. Cambridge, England: Cambridge University Press.

Sherif, M., Harvey, O. J., White, B. J., Hood, W. R., & Sherif, C. W. (1961). *The Robbers Cave experiment: Intergroup conflict and cooperation*. Norman, OK: Book Exchange.

Tajfel, H. (Ed.). (1978). *Differentiation between social groups*. London: Academic Press.

Wright, F. (1987). *Northern Ireland: A comparative analysis*. Dublin: Gill & McMillan.

14

CONTROL AND THE STABILITY OF JEWISH–ARAB RELATIONS IN ISRAEL

IAN S. LUSTICK

HISTORICAL AND LEGAL BACKGROUND

Arabs comprise approximately 18.5% of all Israeli citizens. They are the remnants and the descendants of the remnants of the Arab population of the territory that became the State of Israel in 1948. During approximately 15 months of fighting between November 1947 and January 1949, seven-eighths of the Arabs who lived in what emerged as Israel became refugees living outside of the state's boundaries. This massive displacement was due to the terror and confusion associated with a vicious war, aggressive actions by Jewish military units and policy makers seeking to "cleanse" the new Zionist homeland of non-Jewish inhabitants, and strict policies enforced after the signing of the Armistice Agreements that prevented all but about 30,000 Palestinians (illegal migrants and reunified family members) from returning to their homes. Most of the approximately 150,000 Arabs who did remain, mostly in scattered rural villages, in greatly reduced Arab enclaves in several cities, in the Arab town of Nazareth, and among Bedouin tribes, were granted Israeli citizenship and are the parents and grandparents of Israel's Arab citizenry.

Their citizenship status, including possession of both Israeli passports and official internal Israeli identity cards, distinguishes Israeli Arabs[1] from their relatives, friends, and compatriots living in the West Bank, the Gaza Strip, and expanded East Jerusalem—areas captured by Israel in the 1967

---

[1] Nomenclature is and always has been a difficult and sensitive subject. I will use the term *Israeli Arabs*, although I acknowledge that many Arab citizens of Israel prefer other terms, such as *Palestinians of 1948*, *Israeli Palestinians*, *Palestinian citizens of Israel*, and the *Arabs of 1948*.

"Six Day War." Legally, the Arabs of Israel proper are full and equal citizens and legally entitled to enjoy the same benefits, responsibilities, and protections of the state as do Jewish Israelis, including the right to vote in national elections. However, the more than 2.5 million Palestinian Arabs living in the West Bank (including expanded East Jerusalem) and the Gaza Strip do not have Israeli citizenship. These territories have been held under the international law of "belligerent occupation" as "occupied territories." Although Jews who have been permitted to settle in these areas are Israeli citizens and are subject, for the most part, to Israeli law, Arabs living in the Gaza Strip and the West Bank have not been made Israeli citizens. Although some now live under the jurisdiction of the Palestinian Authority created as a result of the Oslo Accords, even those who still reside in areas under the direct control of Israel do not have, and have never had, Israeli citizenship.

More complicated is the status of the 170,000 Palestinians living in expanded East Jerusalem, a 78-square-kilometer chunk of the West Bank that includes the Arab portion of Jerusalem (el-Kuds). Israel has given these residents of East Jerusalem and its surroundings not citizenship but "permanent resident status"—in accordance with Israel's official stance that it has administratively incorporated expanded "East Jerusalem" into the Israeli city of Yerushalayim, but without formally annexing the area or imposing citizenship on East Jerusalem Arabs. These permanent residents can vote in municipal elections (although most refuse to do so) but cannot vote in national elections.

My focus in this chapter is on those Israeli citizens who are Arabs, Arabs living within the "Green Line," which is to say within the boundaries of the state as defined, after the 1948 war, by the Armistice Agreements with Jordan, Syria, Lebanon, and Egypt. This is a population that has never played a significant role in any of the wars fought between Israel and the Arab states, and although close ties of national identification, support, and sympathy have arisen between Israeli Arabs and the Arabs of the West Bank and Gaza, Arabs in Israel have never operated as a political or military arm of the Palestine Liberation Organization or the Palestinian movement, even during the height of the Intifada, the Palestinian uprising in the West Bank and Gaza between 1987 and 1993. Yet the very existence of the Arab minority within Israel has had fundamental political importance. In its absence the sharp contradiction between Israel as a "Jewish State" and Israel as a democratic state for all its citizens would never have been as visible, as politically troubling, or as morally problematic.

Israel lacks a formal written constitution, but its Declaration of Independence does contain the basic and at least implicitly contradictory principles that ensured a multifaceted clash between Jewish–Zionist and democratic imperatives. On the one hand, the Declaration invokes the historical rights and struggles and religious faith of Jews to justify the establishment of "the Jewish State"—an expression of "the self-evident right of the Jewish people to be a nation, as all other nations, in its own sovereign state" (p. 14). But even as the state is designated as "Jewish" and as dedicated to achieving "the immigration of Jews from all countries of their dispersion," so does the document also promise that the state will

> promote the development of the country for the benefit of all its inhabitants; will be based on the precepts of liberty, justice and peace taught by the Hebrew prophets; and will uphold the full social and political equality of all its citizens, without distinction of race, creed or sex; will guarantee full freedom of conscience, worship, education and culture. . . . (p. 14)

The Declaration specifically calls upon "the Arab inhabitants of the State of Israel" to "play their part in the development of the State, with full and equal citizenship and due representation in all its bodies and institutions" (p. 15).

A law passed in 1985 was an important attempt to address this contradiction in formal, legal terms, but it succeeded only in reaffirming the fundamental ambiguity in the civic principles guiding operation of the Israeli polity. In response to the virulently anti-Arab and explicitly racist agitation of Rabbi Meir Kahane and his Kach movement, the Israeli Parliament passed an amendment to the Basic Law—Knesset, dealing with national elections, which allowed the election commission to bar groups from participating in national elections whose platforms were deemed racist. At the same time, however, the law gave the election commission the power to ban groups, specifically having in mind Arab political parties, from participation in the elections if their platforms implicitly or explicitly questioned the principle that Israel is the "State of the Jews" (Peled, 1992, pp. 432–443).

THE PUZZLE OF QUIESCENCE IN ARAB–JEWISH RELATIONS IN ISRAEL

The contradiction between the conception of Israel as a democracy for all its citizens and as a state with a peculiarly Jewish mission and Zionist ethos alone would suffice to create the expectation of discrimination against non-Jews in the state, of discontent on the part of the minority, and of tension in Jewish–Arab relations. But if one adds to this problem in political architecture the 120-year history of bloodshed and hatred that marks relations between Jews and Arabs in the country, then it would be a Pollyannaish observer who would imagine that relations between the two peoples, within

Israel, would be anything but tumultuous and fraught with violence or the possibility of violence. One might at the very least expect that the question of the status and future of the Arab minority would be one of the touchstones of politics in the country and at least as disruptive to its development and as central to its political history as the struggle of Black people in the United States (who constitute only about half the proportion of the American population as Arabs do of the Israeli population).

The puzzle posed by Israel's Arab population is obvious. Why, in light of its politically problematic status, the repeated wars that have raged between Israel and all her Arab neighbors, the population's severe discontent at the ill treatment it has received, and the full political rights it legally enjoys within Israel's vibrant democracy, the Arab minority's demands for equality, cultural recognition, equal protection under the law, and national expression have had so little effect on Israeli politics and society? Indeed internal Arab–Jewish relations have not led to chronic instability. Despite occasional acts of arson, stone throwing, murder, and lynchings, widespread violence or the threat of violence between Jews and Arabs has been absent. Although organized strikes and large-scale rallies have become regular features of Arab life in Israel since the early 1980s, massive and sustained civil rights or other protest movements have not emerged. For 50 years, there have been very few occasions on which the "Arab problem" within Israel has materialized as a dominant issue on the agenda of the Israeli polity, requiring and attracting sustained attention and debate by the public or its elected leaders.

ARAB DISCONTENT IN ISRAEL

Before considering a range of possible explanations for the relative political quiescence of a minority deeply divided from the country's ruling majority by national, religious, cultural, and political affiliations, let us consider some of the issues generating the Arab discontent that makes this state of affairs worthy of explanation. What distinguishes Israeli Arabs from most Palestinians who lived in what became Israel prior to 1948 is, of course, that they are still living in Israel. But a source of enormous discontent among the Arab population of Israel is that, despite their presence in the country and their citizenship, between 20% and 30% of the population has been classified and treated as refugees by the Israeli authorities. The legal anomaly of what are oxymoronically but accurately known as the present absentees is the result of an elaborately constructed "Absentee Property Law," designed to maximize the amount of land and other real property belonging to Arab inhabitants of the country that could be put at the disposal of the new Jewish state and its rapidly growing population.

The definition of an *absentee* was established as anyone who at any time after the U.N. Partition Resolution of November 29, 1947; has lived in or even visited Lebanon, Egypt, Syria, Saudi Arabia, Transjordan, Iraq, or Yemen; or who was, in any part of Palestine not within what became the borders of Israel; or who was a Palestinian citizen but who "left his ordinary place of residence in Palestine" for a destination outside of Palestine before September 1, 1948, or "for a place in Palestine held at the time by forces which sought to prevent the establishment of the State of Israel. . . ." (*Laws of the State of Israel*, 1949–1950, p. 68).[2] The effect of this convoluted but carefully designed law was to allow Arabs who fled or were expelled from their homes and villages and who took refuge in parts of the country that became Israel after the war, thereby remaining within Israel as Israeli citizens, to be classified as absentees. Once classified as absentees, their land and other immovable property was available for expropriation and transfer to the Custodian of Absentee Property and from there to the state "Development Authority," the "Israel Lands Administration," and the Jewish National Fund (a wing of the World Zionist Organization). This law meant, for example, that Arabs from the Christian villages of Ikrit and Biram in the Galilee, who collaborated with the Israeli army and who were evacuated under explicit agreements that they would be allowed to return after a matter of some weeks, were nonetheless classified as present absentees and saw their lands transferred to Jewish settlements (Al-Haj, 1988).

Despite court decisions in the early 1950s mandating their return and much more recent announcements by both Labor and Likud governments that the problem would be solved, these "internal refugees" are still prevented from returning to or rebuilding their villages. The single biggest obstacle to the solution to the problem is that, although the Ikrit and Biram cases are particularly poignant and particularly well-known, the legal basis for their classification as present absentees is identical to that used to separate tens of thousands of Israeli Arabs from their homes and lands in the post-independence period. These Arabs and their descendants now number in the hundreds of thousands, creating a fear within the bureaucracy, the government, and the Jewish agricultural settlements and villages who have been using and are now living on most of those lands, that a solution to the Ikrit and Biram problem would set the legal and political stage for demands for a large-scale return of present absentees to their villages and/or for massive amounts of compensation.

---

[2] The provisions of this law apply to the period beginning on November 29, 1947, but are not to end as long as the "State of Emergency" (declared on May 19, 1948) is in effect. Because that declared state of emergency is still in effect today, technically even the Israeli ambassadors to Egypt and Jordan, as well as other Israelis who visit parts of Palestine or the listed Arab countries, are liable to be classified as absentees.

In the larger context of Jewish–Arab relations in Israel, however, the legal conundrum of present absentees and its devastating impact on so many Arabs citizens is of most importance as an example of a wide variety of comparably complex techniques used by the authorities to expropriate, confiscate, or otherwise arrange the transfer of the Arab-owned land to Israeli Jews or to organs of the government and World Zionist Organization, whose institutional rules encourage or require the use of those lands for the exclusive benefit of Jewish Israelis. According to best-available estimates, Arab inhabitants of Israel have since 1948 lost between 40% and 60% of their land. A national survey conducted in 1988 reported that 58% of all Arab families were deprived of land as a result of government expropriations, including almost 75% of all land-owning Arab families (Smooha, 1989, 1992, pp. 152–153, 158). As a result of these land confiscations and transfers, 93% of the land area of Israel is jointly administered by the Israel Lands Authority (a government agency with a special and exclusive relationship to the Jewish National Fund) and the Jewish National Fund itself, which is the land acquisition and development arm of the World Zionist Organization.[3]

Aside from the actual loss of their property, the intensity of Arab discontent and resentment on land and other issues derive from the somewhat Kafkaesque character of the legal and political context of this deprivation—enforcing their loss of property without ever explicitly acknowledging a policy of discriminating in the treatment of Arabs as Israeli citizens. Consider, for example, the use of Article 125 of the Emergency Regulations to achieve "legal" land expropriations from Arab Israelis. From 1948 to 1966 most Arab inhabited areas of Israel were ruled by a military government (memshal tzvai).[4] The military government, or military administration, used an elaborate system of permits and denial of permits to limit and supervise virtually every facet of Arab life—from construction, to land use, travel outside of villages, political organization, and employment. The legal basis for the operation of the military government was the Emergency Regulations—a set of repressive laws imposed on Palestine by the British mandatory authorities, condemned by the Zionist movement at that time, but then maintained and made operative immediately following Israel's establishment by the declaration of a formal "state of emergency," which has yet to be lifted.

Article 125 of the Emergency Regulations empowered the military administration to prohibit entry of persons into designated "closed areas."

---

[3] Approximately half of the remaining 7% of Israel's land area is still privately owned by Arabs.
[4] Although technically all Jewish towns and villages within these areas fell under the military government's purview, in practice Jewish Israelis in military government areas were never subjected to its authority.

In combination with provisions of the Cultivation of Waste Lands Ordinance, held over by Israel from the Ottoman period, Article 125 served as the vehicle for substantial expropriations of Arab agricultural land. The process worked as follows. An area encompassing Arab-owned agricultural lands was declared a "closed area." The owners of the lands were then denied permission by the military officers in charge to enter the area for any purpose whatsoever, including cultivation. After the passage of three years, the Ministry of Agriculture then issued certificates classifying the lands as "uncultivated." The owners were then notified that unless cultivation was renewed immediately the lands would be subject to expropriation. The owners, still barred by the military government from entering the closed area within which their lands are located, could not resume cultivation. The lands were thereupon expropriated and transferred into the general land reserve for Jewish settlement under the control of the Israel Lands Administration and the Jewish National Fund. Finally, permission to enter the closed area was granted to Jewish farmers, or the classification as "closed" was lifted, completing the legal transfer of Arab land to Jewish control without invoking any statute that is explicitly discriminatory against Arab Israelis. Former Prime Minister Shimon Peres, who in 1962 served as director general of the Defense Ministry, revealed the conscious purpose behind this manipulative use of combinations of different laws by commenting that "by making use of Article 125 ... we can directly continue the struggle for Jewish settlement and Jewish immigration" (*Davar*, 1962, January 26; see also Lustick, 1980, pp. 177–178, 312).

Numerous other techniques and legal arrangements were used to orchestrate the mass transfer of Arab-owned land to Jewish ownership and control. None featured explicit discrimination against Arabs, but all were carefully implemented in the context of a fundamental ambiguity surrounding the notion of "public" or "national." Thus the Jewish National Fund, the Jewish Agency (which invests in settlement on developed lands and recreational and capital improvements in outlying villages), and the Histadrut (the Labor Party-dominated federation of labor) have, with others, been known as the "national institutions." When applied to the extraction or regulation of resources, such as land, labor, or water, these terms were used to mean "Israeli," thereby applying to Arabs, but when used as conduits for allocating these resources, through irrigation allotments, jobs in employment offices, or long-term leases on agricultural land, these terms were attached to the parochial "Jewish" meanings associated with their historical role and legal and political subordination to the World Zionist Organization or various Zionist political parties. The somewhat Kafkaesque result of this legal, policy, and institutional array was a thicket of legal barriers to Arab control over or protection of their resources—barriers made all the more impenetrable by never being acknowledged officially to exist.

The 1953 Acquisition of Land (Validation of Acts and Compensation) Law epitomized this overall technique. It retroactively removed the rights of anyone to sue in court for redress against illegal transfers of land accomplished through outright theft by neighboring villages or to gain access to lands that had been transferred to the "control" but not ownership of the state or the Jewish National Fund. The Law applied to any lands the government designated as currently "used or assigned for purposes of essential development, settlement or security. . . . " Although compensation for these lands was in principle available to Arab landowners, in fact the rules used to calculate the value of the land made monetary compensation financially irrelevant, and rules used to calculate the amount of substitute lands that would be made available were designed to create plots that would be too small to qualify for the exemption from real estate taxes that was attached to "agricultural land" (Lustick, 1980, pp. 174–178).

As noted, the land issue has been the single most important source of Arab dissatisfaction in Israel. However, the scale of discrimination involved and the complexity of the mechanisms accounting for its implementation have been more or less the same in virtually every sphere of Israeli life since 1948—in government spending and investment allocations to Arab versus Jewish localities, allotments of water and land for agricultural use, investments in infrastructure and industry, availability of public housing, access to education and professional training, availability of government social welfare services, construction of recreational facilities, participation in the civil service, entry into high-level posts in the political or judicial realms, control over content of school curriculum, and availability of approved zoning plans for residential and village expansion. According to the leading researcher of Arab sentiments in Israel:

> Most Arabs feel deprived: 87 percent hold that they do not enjoy equal job opportunities, 59 percent believe that Arab youth do not have reasonable chances of fulfilling their occupational aspirations, and 55 percent accuse the government of policies that widen the socioeconomic gap between Arabs and Jews. These widespread feelings of deprivation are even stronger among Arab leaders. . . . (Smooha, 1992, p. 158)

Although more equity has been achieved in some of these spheres in the 1990s, notably in allocations to municipalities, the indisputable and virtually undisputed fact of Arab life in Israel is that Arabs, although full citizens, have been severely discriminated against and have, as a consequence of that discrimination and of their national and political frustrations, harbored sentiments of anger, frustration, and severe discontent. In his 1988 survey, Smooha found that Arab Israelis believed their life chances in Israel and those of their children were severely restricted. Seventy-one percent (compared to 25% of Jewish respondents) answered in the affirmative when asked whether they agreed with the statement that "whatever one's personal efforts are in Israel, one will not get the education and job one is entitled to" (Smooha, 1992, p. 161).

What is puzzling about the case of Jewish–Arab relations in Israel is the relative quiescence of the Arab minority, in light of the seriousness of its grievances, the pervasiveness of the discrimination it has faced, the severity of its discontent, and the robustness of an Israeli democracy within which they have enjoyed full citizenship. (See the following resources for detailed accounts of Jewish–Arab inequalities and of the discontent and grievances of Israeli Arabs in almost every sphere of life: Al-Haj & Rosenfeld, 1990; Hareven, 1983; Kretzmer, 1990; Rabinowitz, 1997; Rouhana, 1997; Shipler, 1986; Yiftachel, 1992.) To be sure, even in the 1950s Arab elders regularly sought to present protest petitions to the authorities about the treatment their villagers or tribes had received. Until recently Arabs also exercised their right to vote in larger proportions than did Jews. Arab support for the politically ostracized and largely Jewish-controlled Communist Party did signal their fundamental opposition to state policies. In the 1960s, one small group of Arab intellectuals tried to form a political movement, El-Ad, although it never achieved a mass following. In the 1970s, groups of educated Arabs began raising issues of discrimination in government, in the press, and in government forums, and in 1976 the first general strike was called to protest Land Expropriations in the Galilee.

Since then a countrywide association of Arab mayors has helped to organize an average of one or two protest days a year on issues such as equality, peace, and land. Also, within the past decade, some small Arab political parties have emerged, and although none has yet participated in a governing coalition, they have had some significant influence on certain matters of policy and politics. But overall what is striking is the absence of mass protests, of civil disobedience campaigns, of significant levels of violence or terrorism and, most of all, what is striking is the failure of the Israeli Arab issue to sustain itself on the Israeli national agenda as a matter of importance or concern to most Israelis for more than a day or, at most, a few days at a time.

We may leave aside countries where ethnic and communal differences have contributed to the virtual disintegration of states and societies, such as Somalia, Lebanon, Bosnia, Cyprus, and Tajikistan. It is yet necessary to explain the contrast between Israel's experience—the apparent political irrelevance of a substantial and deeply discontented ethnic, national, and religious minority—and that of democracies with comparable or smaller minorities, such as the United States (African Americans), Sri Lanka (Tamils), Great Britain (Northern Irish Catholics, Scots, Welsh), Spain (Basques, Catalans), Canada (Quebecois), India (Muslims, Sikhs, Assamese), Turkey (Kurds), and Russia (Chechens, Tatars, etc.). The problem is all the more puzzling when one considers the well-supported argument that minority discontent weighs more heavily on states if the minority is linked to national, ethnic, religious, or linguistic majorities in neighboring states (Brubaker, 1996; Weiner, 1971). Israel, of course, immersed in conflict with its Arab neighbors for most of its existence, fits exactly into this category.

ALTERNATE EXPLANATIONS

Pluralist theory suggests one answer, an answer most likely to come to the minds of American observers. Pluralists have contended that the cohesiveness of the American social and political fabric comes not from a melting-pot-style blending of differences into an assimilative American cultural type, but from the crisscrossing of so many different economic, racial, cultural, ethnic, religious, and regional cleavages that (apart from the salient example of the Civil War and the associated problem of Black–White relations) most Americans have found themselves allying in some important issue areas with individuals and groups who appear as their opponents in other settings. This social and economic complexity is reinforced by a complex governing system of federalist institutions, each one built from divided and somewhat opposing branches of government and designed purposefully by the country's constitutional architects to discourage stable concentrations of power or uniform and reinforcing cleavages. American factionalism or "pluralism" and the myriad small but shifting conflicts associated with them, are, according to pluralist theory, seen to prevent the kind of polarized and stable oppositions that produce violent and sustained ethnic or communal violence.

To find this kind of pluralism in Israel, however, one would have to look inside the Jewish sector. Even there observers have found that many salient cleavages (religion, political affiliation, class, and ethnic background) often reinforce each other rather than crisscross one another. Still there are, for example, both Ashkenazi and Sephardi religious Jews and enough Ashkenazi and Sephardi members of the middle class that this kind of pluralist phenomenon is significant in maintaining cohesion within Jewish Israel. But such crisscrossing cleavages have not, except for unusual cases such as the Jewish–Arab Communist Party and fleeting alliances between Muslim and Jewish ultratraditionalists, spanned the divide between Jews and Arabs—a cleavage marked by reinforcing and in some cases virtually hermetic residential, religious, educational, linguistic, ethnic, and political patterns of Jewish–Arab segregation. Instead. the relationship between Jews and Arabs in Israel has been dominated by mutual perceptions of a categorical divide between the two sectors and of a zero-sum relationship between the interests of the two communities.

Another approach that might explain the relative quiescence of Arabs in Israel and the comparative nonsalience of the issue in Israeli political life is relative deprivation theory. In line with that theory, one might hypothesize, and indeed government publications on "minorities" in Israel have often argued, that Arabs have compared their standard of living and life chances in Israel to Arabs in other countries and to the way their parents and grandparents lived before 1948, rather than, contemporaneously, to the living conditions of Jewish Israelis. Considering the favorable comparisons to be made with these reference groups, high levels of satisfaction with what otherwise might be deemed discriminatory conditions could be explained. But although Israeli Arabs have sometimes favorably compared their fate to that of Palestinians living in the occupied West Bank and Gaza Strip, available evidence strongly suggests that most Arabs use Jewish Israelis as their reference group. In his 1985 survey of Arab opinion in Israel, Smooha (1989, 1992) reported that 61% of the Arab public in Israel compared their socioeconomic position to that of Jewish Israelis, with another 8% comparing themselves to inhabitants of "Western" countries. According to Smooha's 1980 survey, between 80% and 92% of Arab political leaders in Israel (except on the extreme fringe of Arab political opinion) compare themselves to Israeli Jews rather than to Arabs in the occupied territories, Arabs in Palestine before 1948, or Arabs in other countries.

Another approach, well known within the discipline of political science but hardly understood outside it, is "consociationalism." Consociational arrangements explain stability and political quiescence among competing ethnic or communal segments of a democratic polity by emphasizing coherent authority structures within each segment. Elites in charge of these structures, and representing their distinct communities, form a kind of "cartel," which designs and maintains a social pact under whose terms the political and economic pies are divided proportionally among the communities. Meanwhile, most issues likely to lead to conflict are kept off the agenda by decisions all round that the prospects of fighting for bigger shares would not be worth the risk of losing those fights. Versions of this arrangement are also labeled as "power-sharing" or "accommodation" (for a critical review of consociationalism, see Lustick, 1997). To an extent the relations between religious and nonreligious Jews in Israel have reflected these consociational techniques. But the elite bargaining and proportional division of political and economic resources that are the hallmarks of consociationalism have been almost completely absent from Jewish–Arab relations. Indeed no "all-Arab" organized structure of representation has ever emerged or been allowed to emerge (for a discussion of the difference between control and consociationalism, see "Stability," 1979). Indeed, every government in Israel has rejected what would be a consociationalist idea of Israel as a neutral state functioning to service the needs of, or maintain a balance between, competing communities in favor of the principle of Israel as a "Jewish state"—a state whose raison d'être is the promotion of the interests of the dominant community. (For details to this amendment to the Basic-Law Knesset, adopted in 1985, see Peled, 1992, p. 438.)

We may also reject, without extended consideration, the possibility that mechanisms of legal and extralegal repression and terrorism, such as enforced the quiescence of Black people in the American South between reconstruction and the civil rights movement, have been responsible for the unobtrusiveness of Arab demands and expressions of discontent in Israel. Although Arab literature and poetry in Israel contains many images of Arab citizens hemmed in by a suffocating apparatus of informers, ruthless and prejudiced officials, discriminatory practices, and an all-knowing secret police (the Shin Bet or "Shabak"), no opponents of Israeli policies, even the most radical critics, have portrayed Israeli policies as based on terrorism or fear, by ordinary Arab citizens, of imprisonment, lynchings, or torture (Habiby, 1985; Jiryis, 1969; Masalha, 1993; Zureik, 1988). Nor is there an apartheid system in Israel—a code of explicit discriminations, restrictions, and disabilities attached to nationality that mobilizes the entire formal judicial and police apparatus to enforce control over activities by members of a particular group. Yet the most effective explanation for the relative political quiescence of discontented Arabs in Israel, and the surprising unobtrusiveness of Arab political mobilization in the life of the Israeli polity, is control—but a systematic form of control operating beneath the formal–legal surface of the polity.

ISRAEL'S SYSTEM OF CONTROL OVER ARAB CITIZENS

The State of Israel was declared by the leaders of the Zionist movement in May 1948, in the midst of an unenforced U.N. decision to divide the former British colony into a Jewish State and a Palestinian Arab state. In May a raging civil war became a war between the fledgling state and several Arab armies, sent across the as yet undemarcated boundaries. Casualties were heavy on both sides. But as Jewish forces began to prevail, Jewish leaders and commanders realized that the state would survive. The questions then became how big would the state be, and how many Arabs would be left within it? Policies of boundary expansion and what today would be called "ethnic cleansing" were then vigorously implemented. When the dust settled, in 1949, the new regime found the country emptied but not quite empty of Arabs. Policies of some sort had to be fashioned toward this new minority, although virtually no thought at all had ever been given to this problem. Proposals to expel them or deprive them of citizenship were made but rejected.

As a de facto measure, a military government was created—a continuation of the rule of Arab inhabited areas by local military commanders during the war—to supervise the affairs of Arab Israelis. The original purposes of this step were to guard against any infiltration or return of Arab refugees to still-standing homes and villages and to prevent the emergence of a fifth column. But the government and the ruling Mapai (Labor) Party quickly determined that its control over the military government in Arab areas had much more important, if less publicly acknowledged, functions. Because it operated on the basis of the aforementioned "Emergency Regulations," which made local military governors virtual dictators in the areas of their jurisdiction, it could be used to negate the political and civil implications of Arab citizenship in Israel in all those areas and at those times when it would be convenient for the authorities to do so. Thus a system of pass laws kept Arabs limited to their own villages and towns—making Arab farmers wishing to market their produce and wage-laborers seeking employment in Jewish cities and settlements completely dependent on the favor of the military governor to secure their livelihoods.[5] This not only gave the Labor Party enormous leverage in securing an overwhelming majority of Arab votes in parliamentary elections, but also allowed the government to minimize unemployment among new Jewish immigrants by loosening travel restrictions for Arabs at times of low Jewish immigration and low unemployment in the Jewish sector and tightening those restrictions when Jewish immigration and unemployment rose.

This economic dependence of the Arabs on the Jewish economy and on the policies of government officials helped the military government, the Arab Departments of the different government ministries, the Shin Bet (secret service), and the Arab Department of the Histadrut to identify and co-opt leaders of village clans (*hamulas*), religious dignitaries, and tribal leaders. In these relationships, individual Arab elites at the local level were given assurances that they and their favored constituents would be granted travel passes, construction and other permits, protection against deportation, approval for family reunification requests, and so forth, in return for information about any "negative," "extremist," or "nationalist" behavior; delivery of the votes of their constituents in parliamentary elections; and help in the implementation of land expropriations, building demolitions, and so on. The co-optation of these traditional leaders and, later, more educated but still economically and administratively dependent younger elites, were

---

[5] It is worth noting that, officially and legally, the military government's authority was applied over geographical districts, thereby including within its compass Jewish as well as Arab citizens. Thus, there was nothing in the written regulations governing its behavior that distinguished between treatment of Arabs versus Jews. But the actual authority of the military government was never exercised with respect to Jews living within these areas, only with respect to Arabs.

both facilitated and enabled by policies of "divide and rule." These policies were based on both the segmentation of the polity into two almost completely separate Jewish and Arab sectors and on the fragmentation of the Arab sector itself.

Long-standing patterns of segregation between Jews and Arabs were reinforced by a press heavily influenced by the government in this area and by government policies in the housing, military, economic, and educational spheres. These policies suppressed the potential for cross-communal political identification latent in the legal circumstance that both Jews and Arabs were "equal Israeli citizens," leading the Jewish public to consider Arab citizens as nothing but a foreign, dangerous, and threatening enemy. Indeed only the Communist Party and some small left-wing or intellectual Jewish circles acted vigorously (but largely ineffectively) on behalf of real political, civil, and economic equality between Jews and Arabs. Furthermore, by maintaining separate Arab departments in each ministry and separate (minuscule) budgets for development projects in Arab localities, the government was able to maintain and even expand gaps in the infrastructural facilities (roads, power lines, water works, sewers, and communication networks) available to Jewish versus Arab communities. These expanding gaps in turn deepened the dependence of Arabs on the Jewish economy for jobs, markets, and investment opportunities.

To reinforce the parochialism and fragmentation already present in Arab society, the government and its representatives adhered to practices followed by the "Arabists" who had dealt covertly with Arab politicians and landowners during British mandatory period. Personal favors, bribes, and threats were used to play clans, tribes, and lineage groups against one another: Christians versus Muslims, Druse versus Muslims and Christians, Bedouins versus non-Bedouins, Galilee Arabs versus "Little Triangle" Arabs, and so on. Such divisions were easier to maintain and exploit because of the travel restrictions imposed by the military government, but even after its reform and eventual abolition (in 1966), the distrusts and intra-Arab jealousies and animosities it left as a legacy helped the Office of the Adviser to the Prime Minister on Arab Affairs (always headed by a senior figure from the Mossad or Shin Bet) to coordinate the continued fragmentation, dependence, and co-optation policies, which kept the Arab population politically invisible and ineffectively mobilized.

It was, indeed, the operation of these mechanisms—segmentation, fragmentation, co-optation, and dependence—in reciprocally reinforcing relationships within one another, that constituted an overall "system of control." It has been this system, well understood and appreciated in private by Israeli policy makers but seldom acknowledged in public and never recognized (as South Africa's Apartheid was) as existing within the legal framework of the state, that accounts for Arab political quiescence and the relative stability of Jewish–Arab relations in Israel, despite high levels of Arab discontent. Having evolved to correspond to preexisting patterns in the social structure, geographical distribution, and economic level of the Arab population in relation to the Jewish majority, this system operated both effectively and efficiently. That is to say, it required, at least until the late 1970s, very little in the way of human resources, money, international criticism, or the attention of high-level decision makers.

The key to understanding both the effectiveness and the efficiency of this system of control over Arabs in Israel is the network of interactions among these mechanisms at three different but reinforcing levels of analysis. These three levels are the structural level, where historical, developmental, and cultural legacies organize the two communities in relations of dependence and separation; the institutional level, where are produced normalized but enormously discriminatory standard operating procedures for distributing valued resources (housing for young couples, agricultural land, water for irrigation, capital improvement funds, etc.); and the policy or programmatic level, where relatively low-level officials and bureaucrats, without having to call often upon the attention or resources of the upper political echelons, can make adjustments and interventions when particular groups of so-called extremist, negative, or nationalistic Arabs tried to mobilize independently or beyond the boundaries of the acceptable.

In these synergistic ways, the mutually reinforcing effects of informal mechanisms of control associated with Arab dependence on Jews economically and infrastructurally, of multiple divisions within the Arab community and rigid segregation of Jews from Arabs, and of the co-optation of Arab elites conveniently produced a social structure emphasizing traditionalist villages and clans. Village elders, Bedouin sheiks, religious officials, and ambitious but dependent younger educated Arab "reformers" have helped to enforce and maintain a strikingly low political profile for Arab discontent and have prevented what otherwise might well have been a fierce and bloody history of communal struggle. (For a detailed analysis of the operation of this system of control up to the mid-1970s, see Lustick, 1980.)

CHALLENGES AND CHANGES: THE FUTURE COURSE OF JEWISH–ARAB RELATIONS

Jewish citizens have always enjoyed a rather vibrant democracy in Israel. Therefore, without explicit and legal separation of Arab from Jewish citizens, the democratic opportunities available for Jews have presented Arabs with opportunities to exploit their often irrelevant status as equal citizens to publicly (and sometimes effectively) assert their demands. Thus, in the 1960s and 1970s, small numbers of Arab students gained admission to Israeli, and overwhelmingly Jewish, universities—settings in which Arab students from across Israel and from different parochial and kinship units could form political organizations such as Arab student committees and produce activist, reformist, and politically aware leaders. The Communist Party (led by Jewish Israelis until very recently), with its links to the Soviet bloc, was and is largely ostracized from political life. But the party is legal and has always been represented in the Parliament. By serving as a vehicle for protest without demanding ideological loyalty, the Communist Party provided Arabs with opportunities to learn political and organizational skills; to get professional training (medicine, pharmacology, engineering, etc.); and even to build careers within party institutions, which were relatively independent of government influence or dependence.

Meanwhile, the rise of Palestinian nationalism and the free circulation of ideas and Palestinian workers from the occupied West Bank and Gaza Strip, following the 1967 war, encouraged many Israeli Arabs to view themselves as Palestinians, which helped them to overcome parochial (clan, village, and religious) loyalties. Altogether these aberrations in the system of control were reflected in the development of a country-wide association of Arab Local Councils, a substantially successful general strike against land expropriation in 1976, a suppressed but significant attempt by Arab intellectuals and the Communist Party to convene a national "congress" of Israeli Arabs in 1980, and a noticeable increase in international attention to the problem of the Arab minority in Israel.

Still, the major impact of these developments was to reduce somewhat the almost hermetic effectiveness of the system of control and to raise the cost of its operations—requiring more overt, and sometimes violent, intervention by higher echelons in the government in order to prevent independent Arab political organization or the intrusion of Arab demands upon the Israeli body politic. In the mid-1980s, however, some real change began to occur as the consequence of the deep, even, and polarizing struggle within the Israeli Jewish population between annexationists, who favored keeping the occupied West Bank and Gaza Strip under permanent Israeli control, and anti-annexationists, who favored trading most or all of these territories for peace with the Palestinians and the Arabs in general. With every election since 1981 decided by extremely narrow margins, and with the emergence of the Likud Party and its hawkish and religious allies as a coalition alternating in power with Labor and its liberal, secular, and dovish allies, the latter learned that it could not win elections unless the Arabs voted in large numbers and for parties willing to support them against the Likud in coalition bargaining.

Arabs thereby, for the first time, gained real bargaining power, and although they have yet to be invited into a governing coalition and although no Arab has yet been appointed to a ministerial post, small Arab political parties successfully competed in parliamentary elections. Polling and political calculations now regularly include the preferences and likely behavior of Arab Israelis. The votes of independently elected Arab Members of Knesset were crucial in replacing the Shamir government of the Likud with the Labor government led by Yitzhak Rabin, and on some issues of importance to the Arab population—such as funds for municipal development, limits on additional land expropriations, suspension of demolition orders against "illegally" built Arab homes[6]—substantial but limited progress has been made. (For a discussion of the "centripetal effect" of Jewish polarization on Arab political participation in Israel, see Lustick, 1989.)

Overall, however, the Arab minority still stands in a relationship of political subordination with respect to the Jewish majority. High-profile issues, symbolic of this control relationship, remain unresolved—including outstanding demands and unimplemented court orders for the return of illegally confiscated Arab lands; for an end to de facto discrimination in housing, industrial and professional development, education, and the civil service; for establishment of an Arab and Arabic language university; for Arab cultural autonomy; or for recognition of Arabs as a second national group within Israel as a state for all its citizens rather than as a "Jewish state." Although levels of Arab political activism are on the rise—including secular and Islamist groupings—and although the number of Arab citizens will soon surpass 1 million, the general impact of Arab political mobilization on Israeli politics remains marginal. No mass-based Arab civil rights movement exists. No unified Arab political party has succeeded in forming. In the press, in elite circles, and in Jewish public opinion, the same categories and conditioned responses to signs of Arab dissatisfaction predominate. It is recognized that the Arabs have problems that should be addressed, but also that substantial inequalities are inevitable in a Jewish state caught in a protracted conflict with its Arab neighbors and that Arab protests are dangerous signs of fanaticism and anti-Israeli, anti-Jewish hatred. Although most Arabs are excluded by the military from service in the army, the absence of Arabs from the military is used as a nondiscriminatory device to exclude Arabs from a host of crucial veterans benefits.

But the future of Arabs in Israel is no longer so easily predictable by the past. Nor is that future likely to be determined simply as a function of a Jewish majority's (unlikely) decision to "de-Zionize" the country, to formally relinquish its identity as a "Jewish state," or to grant Israeli Arabs some

---

[6]One important technique for enforcing political quiescence has been the refusal of the Interior Ministry to approve "master plans" for Arab localities. With rapid population growth occurring in overpopulated and land-starved villages and towns, this means Arabs must build houses without permits (available only once a master plan has been approved) on lands not formally designated as residential areas. The result is the issuance of thousands of demolition orders against Arab homes whose implementation is effectively at the discretion of the authorities.

special culturally autonomous status. Rather, with hundreds of thousands of non-Jewish immigrants accompanying the Jewish immigrants from the former Soviet Union and Ethiopia, with hundreds of thousands more non-Jewish "guest workers" finding ways to establish permanent residency in the country, and with Arabs perhaps playing a crucial political role in bringing the peace process with the Palestinians to a successful conclusion, it can be expected that the future will give a higher profile to the rights and role of non-Jews in Israeli society (see Lustick, 1999). Although this may lead to higher levels of tension and overt conflict between Jews and Arabs, it can also lead to deeper forms of cooperation, as secular Jews find common cause with non-Jewish citizens and inhabitants against politically powerful pietist, ultranationalist, and fundamentalist elements in the Jewish sector, or as Arabs and economically disadvantaged Jews of Middle Eastern or Oriental background find similar reasons to object to the extended largess of the state in its treatment of large numbers of European immigrants.

But given the deep divisions within the Jewish community and the intensity of anti-Arab sentiments, the heightened profile of the Arab minority will be likely to trigger substantially higher levels of overt Arab–Jewish conflict in the future than it has in the past. If this means that the demands of Arab Israelis begin to weigh much more heavily on the calculations of Israeli politicians and leaders, and if it means that much more of the country's resources will have to be devoted to coping with Arab dissatisfaction, this may, indeed, be a failure for the system of control. But in the long run it will be success for Israeli democracy.

REFERENCES

Al-Haj, M. (1988). The Arab internal refugees in Israel: The emergence of a minority within the minority. *Immigrants and Minorities, 7*, 149–165.

Al-Haj, M., & Rosenfeld, H. (1990). *Arab local government in Israel.* Boulder, CO: Westview Press.

Brubaker, R. (1996). *Nationalism reframed: Nationhood and the national question in the New Europe.* Cambridge, England: Cambridge University Press.

Davar. (1962, January 26).

Habiby, E. (1985). *The secret life of Saeed the Pessoptimist.* London: Zed Books.

Hareven, A. (Ed.). (1983). *Every sixth Israeli.* Jerusalem: Van Leer Jerusalem Foundation.

Jiryis, S. (1969). *The Arabs of Israel.* Beirut: Institute for Palestine Studies.

Kretzmer, D. (1990). *The legal status of Arabs in Israel.* Boulder, CO: Westview Press.

Laws of the State of Israel, Vol. 4. (1949–1950). p. 68.

Lustick, I. S. (1980). *Arabs in the Jewish State: Israel's control of a national minority.* Austin: University of Texas.

Lustick, I. S. (1989). The political road to binationalism: Arabs in Jewish politics. In I. Peleg & O. Seliktar (Eds.), *The emergence of a binational Israel: The second republic in the making* (pp. 97–123). Boulder, CO: Westview Press.

Lustick, I. S. (1997, October). Lijphart, Lakatos, and consociationalism, *World Politics, 50*(1), 88–117.

Lustick, I. S. (1999). Israel as a non-Arab state: The political implications of mass immigration of non-Jews. *Middle East Journal, 53*(3), 417–433.

Masalha, N. (Ed.). (1993). *Palestinians in Israel: Is Israel the state of all its citizens and "absentees"?* Haifa, Israel: Galilee Center for Social Research.

Peled, Y. (1992, June). Ethnic democracy and the legal construction of citizenship: Arab citizens of the Jewish State. *American Political Science Review, 86*(2), 432–443.

Rabinowitz, D. (1997). *Overlooking Nazareth: The ethnography of exclusion in Galilee.* Cambridge, England: Cambridge University Press.

Rouhana, N. (1997). *Palestinian citizens in an ethnic Jewish state: Identities in conflict.* New Haven, CT: Yale University Press.

Shipler, D. K. (1986). *Arab and Jew: Wounded spirits in a promised land.* New York: Times Books.

Smooha, S. (1989). *Arabs and Jews in Israel: Conflicting and shared attitudes in a divided society* (Vol. 1). Boulder, CO: Westview Press.

Smooha, S. (1992). *Arabs and Jews in Israel: Change and continuity in mutual intolerance* (Vol. 2). Boulder, CO: Westview Press.

Stability in deeply divided societies: Consociationalism vs. control. (1979, April). *World Politics, 31*(3), 325–344.

Weiner, M. (1971, July). The Macedonian syndrome: An historical model of international relations and political development. *World Politics, 23*(4), 665–683.

Yiftachel, O. (1992). *Planning a mixed region in Israel: The political geography of Arab–Jewish relations in the Galilee.* Aldershot: Ashgate.

Zureik, E. (1988, November). Crime, justice, and underdevelopment: The Palestinians under Israeli control. *International Journal of Middle East Studies, 20*(4), 411–442.

15

WHO PAYS FOR PEACE? IMPLICATIONS OF THE NEGOTIATED SETTLEMENT IN A POST-APARTHEID SOUTH AFRICA

BRANDON HAMBER

> But was it a miracle? Or was it an expression of one of those good moments that sometimes happen in history? That have happened in all histories. Fancifully, we believe such events happened more frequently in South Africa than elsewhere; these strange moments that are strange because of their goodness. Strange because mostly our context is not good. Mostly it is wretched. (Nicol, 1995, p. 91)

The transition to democracy in South Africa in April 1994 is heralded by many as one of the major achievements of 20th century. The transformation of the apartheid state to majority rule has been warmly (and at times, cynically) referred to as "a negotiated revolution," "a miracle transition," and "the birth of a new rainbow nation." It is true that South African society has changed. Power has been ushered correctly into the hands of the majority, overt racism has been outlawed, human rights policies are entrenched, a constitutional system that can rival any liberal democracy in the world has been established, and there has been limited delivery of socioeconomic change.

Despite these successes, the long-term impact of the compromises made by all parties to ensure peace (which have dexterously been grouped under the banner of "reconciliation") loom large. A highly politicized population remains trapped in an economy where the wealth differentials are staggering. Those brutally victimized by the security forces have witnessed ruthless

My thanks to Paul Arthur, Adrian Guelke, Roger McGinty, Gillian Robinson, and Sue Williams for their valuable comments on drafts of this chapter. The assistance of Damaris Hess is also gratefully acknowledged.

killers and their governmental accomplices walk free in exchange for their often meager confessions. The price for peace for some victims and survivors of apartheid has been high.

In this chapter, I focus on the legacy of the negotiated settlement in South Africa. I begin by outlining the events surrounding the South African transition, and I explicitly highlight the role of violence in the process. The reasons for the timing of the transition and the compromises that typified the peaceful settlement in South Africa are explored. The issue of amnesty is highlighted. The long-term consequences of the granting of amnesty and the economic concessions that forged peace are discussed with reference to their impact on the survivors of the political and structural violence perpetrated by the apartheid system.

THE TRANSITION TO DEMOCRACY IN SOUTH AFRICA

It is no coincidence that the formal transition to democracy in South Africa coincided with the demise of the Cold War and the collapse of the Soviet Union. Confronted with the ostensible failures of the communist system, political parties and liberation movements across the world, including the African National Congress (ANC), began rapidly to move away from the concepts of state centralism, nationalization, and the doctrine of violent revolution. At the same time, the West began to relax its commitment to prevent the spread of communism primarily through military means. Rather the West, particularly the United States, seized the opportunity finally to eradicate communism through injecting free-market reform measures into previously communist countries and through vigorously marketing its global free-market agenda as the only workable alternative to the fading communist ethos.

This is clearly demonstrated by the policy of the United States. Until the mid-1980s, the United States failed to discourage (and indirectly sponsored, some would argue) the South African armed conflicts in Namibia, Angola, and Mozambique under the guise of fighting communist insurgence in these states.[1] However, as the Cubans withdrew from Angola and Namibia and moved toward independence in the late 1980s, and as the socialist agenda of the ANC became increasingly unworkable and unthinkable within

---

[1]For example, from 1976, the United States supported Savimbi's National Union for the Total Independent Angola (UNITA) rebel movement, which was fighting against the government in Angola. South African forces fought alongside those of Savimbi. The South African destabilization activities in its neighboring countries caused the death of 1.5 million people and cost the country $45 million according to a *Commonwealth Report* released in 1989 (Sparks, 1997).

the context of the demise of communism, the United States began to be more vocal about the need for change in South Africa. In 1989 South Africa was urged to liberalize, and the U.S. government informed the South African President F. W. De Klerk that he had only one year to end the state of emergency, lift the ban on the liberation movement, and release all political prisoners (Landsberg, 1994, also cited in Wilson, 1997).

Toward the end of the 1980s, the National Party (NP) concurrently realized that the so-called communist-inspired *rooi gevaa* (red danger) was declining. As Johnson and Schlemmer (1996) noted,

> De Klerk too was quick to understand that it no longer greatly mattered whether or not the South African Communist Party controlled the ANC: the Communists were now toothless tigers and the "Communist menace" no longer existed. Negotiation was now possible on terms never before possible. (p. 5)

This recognition also took place within a context where the South African government was under significant and increasing economic pressure. International economic sanctions, particularly those imposed by the European Union in 1985 and the U.S. Comprehensive Anti-Apartheid Act of 1986, began to take their toll by the late 1980s. In addition, the border wars, the maintenance of an extensive internal security apparatus, large-scale civil unrest, and highly organized strikes and boycotts were draining an already shrinking domestic economy throughout the 1980s. The result was that big business and government steadily began to comprehend that there was more to gain by being part of the international economy than by being on the outside. The only proviso being, from their perspective, that the rights of the White minority could be protected and their economic interests secured. The more enlightened sectors of big business opened discussions with the ANC in exile from the mid-1980s onward, and by the late 1980s the NP government too had realized that a political settlement might be the lesser of the potential evils they faced.

In February 1990 the NP unbanned the liberation movement parties and released Nelson Mandela and other key ANC leaders from jail. Thereafter hundreds of liberation movement prisoners were released in May 1990 and others over the course of 1991. Indemnity was also granted to the returning "liberation movement" exiles. Almost two years after Mandela's release, all-party talks began in December 1991 and were followed by more talks in May 1992.

The primary NP strategy was to use the negotiations to force power-sharing and the protection of minority rights on an unprepared ANC who was struggling to make the transition from a revolutionary movement to a political party. Below the NP's dramatic liberalization and enlightenment also lurked a more sinister strategy that was to have a determining effect on the negotiations process and the final settlement. This strategy comprised mainly of the establishment of a third force of state security operatives and the funding of Inkatha Freedom Party (IFP) paramilitaries to carry out attacks on the liberation movement and civilians. The third-force elements within the security forces allowed (and at times directly supported) campaigns of terror to be carried out by IFP warlords and others. In some instances, covert violence was directly sponsored by the government. The NP government itself was also complicit in the violence through acts of omission. De Klerk largely turned a blind eye on violent renegade elements within the security apparatus.[2]

By the early 1990s, the situation had spiraled out of control, and a cycle of murder and retribution permeated most of the South African townships. Multifarious forms of orchestrated and seemingly random violence proliferated across the country. Violence flared between the ANC and the IFP, paramilitaries from all sides armed themselves in the name of defending their communities, targeted assassinations and massacres left hundreds of fatalities, drive-by shootings became commonplace, violence against commuters on trains and at taxi ranks ensued, and the White extreme right vocally threatened armed insurrection if minority rule were ended. This created a context of instability and terror.

Johnson (1994) captured the mood at the time when he wrote,

> It is hard to know what would count as normality in a society where scores of Africans can be shot down in the street by other Africans and no one even dreams of apprehending their killers. Where Eugene Terre'Blanche can appear on TV and boast that AWB [Afrikaner Resistance Movement] raid into Bophuthatswana[3] was a "victory" because his men killed a hundred innocent Africans, and no one even suggests that in that case he should be arrested for murder. Where taxi wars rage, leaving scores dead. Where men with Kalashnikovs board commuter trains shouting *"Bulala abathakathi"* (Kill the witches) and then proceed to hurl any "witches" they find off the moving train. Where a disturbed woman with a criminal record can be elected head of her

---

[2] See Sparks (1997, pp. 153–178) for a discussion on the degree to which De Klerk and others sanctioned this strategy and the third-force activities of those in the security forces. Sparks concluded that the evidence is now overwhelming that there was indeed a third force, consisting of elements of the IFP, the police, and Military Intelligence. He also concluded that, although De Klerk had an interest in weakening the ANC, he did not want to destabilize the negotiations and the country considerably. An explanation for his half-hearted attempts to stop the violence, according to Sparks, lay with his uncertainty of the extent of his control over Botha's old securocrat establishment and fears of his armed forces turning against him. Arguably, this does not free De Klerk (and others) from complicity in the violence by acts of omission.
[3] This incident is discussed in a later section of this chapter.

party's women's section, an MP, and ... to the Cabinet. Where Afrikaner conservatives insist, under the threat of war, on a *volkstaat*[4] but cannot for the life of them tell you where they want it to be. (pp. 93–94)

Once the violence had begun in the early 1990s, the exact sources of it were difficult to place. State security forces were certainly complicit in the violence, but a range of political opportunists from across the spectrum also used violence to strengthen their hand at the negotiation table and to increase their personal power at the local level. As with so many conflicts, the competition over access to scarce resources was a further component that sparked the violence and created opportunity within many impoverished communities.

Simpson and Rauch (1993) argued that during the negotiations period of 1990–1994, the competing claims to limited resources became less constrained by the repressive apartheid mechanisms that had historically entrenched limitations on people's aspirations. This caused heightened levels of conflict. Ethnic identity was also manipulated as a recruitment tool, mainly by IFP paramilitary groupings, but also at times by the ANC. Once mobilized, these ethnic-based groups were generally volatile, defensive, and extremely difficult to demobilize (National Crime Prevention Strategy, 1996).

In the mid-1970s, political violence resulted in an average of 44 deaths a month, in the mid-1980s it had risen to 86, and by the 1990s it was 250 (South African Institute of Race Relations, 1993, p. 7). The violence itself also changed in nature from what can be termed "vertical violence" (i.e., the state against its citizens and the citizens against the state) to "horizontal violence" (i.e., fellow citizens against one another). In the 1970s and 1980s the police were responsible for many of the deaths, but by the 1990s intracommunity and intraorganizational conflict in the townships and rural areas (some covertly sponsored by the state and its agents) accounted for the greatest number of fatalities.[5] Over the entire period of the negotiations from February 1990 to April 1994, as South Africa was supposedly normalizing, 14,807 people were killed, according to the institute. This is starkly

---

[4] One of the demands of the far right (mainly the Freedom Front and the Afrikaner Resistance Movement [AWB]) was for an independent and separate homeland exclusively for Afrikaners (and sympathetic White people) within the borders of South Africa.

[5] The number of fatalities at the hands of the AWB and other extreme White right groups were minimal, comparatively speaking. The Human Rights Commission (Coleman, 1998) has reported that from July 1990 to June 1993, the extreme White right accounted for only 0.6% of fatalities, that is, 54 deaths of the total 9,325. Nonetheless, the AWB receives prominence in this paper because their violence had a significant impact on the negotiations process. They inflicted a number of deaths between June 1993 and the election of April 1994. In the 10-month build-up to the election, the right wing caused the deaths of 48 people and injured 279 more in 172 incidents, which included 85 bombings (Coleman, 1998).

comparable to the 5,387[6] people killed in political violence in the 1985 to 1989 period.

In June 1992, in the wake of the Boipatong Massacre[7] outside Johannesburg in which 48 people died at the hands of the IFP, the all-party talks collapsed. Clearly, a solution to the violence was urgently needed. In response, many civil groups took to the streets to demand an end to the violence and the reopening of negotiations. Across the country, 4 million people joined in two days of peaceful mass action. The National Peace Accord (NPA), a countrywide network of peace committees at the local, regional, and national levels, also stepped up its campaign to get political parties, labor leaders, local structures, and the business community to pursue the common objective of peace (cf. Gastrow, 1995). A mass mobilization campaign was organized by the ANC and its allies. Thousands of ANC supporters took to the streets at marches around the country, and rolling mass-action campaigns and a host of worker stay-aways threatened a decline into anarchy.

These actions reached an explosive head on September 7, 1992, when the Ciskei Defense Force killed 28 ANC supporters at a march in Bisho. Paradoxically, the incident served as a catalyst to get the talks back on track rather than derail them. As Johnson and Schlemmer (1996) noted,

> The "popular upsurge" implicit in mass mobilization was enough to frighten even the ANC moderates (who played little part in the mass mobilization campaign), but in the end all parties came to worry that the damage to society might be so deep that recovery would be impossible, whatever the political outcome. It was this worry, rather than fear of a military coup, which hung over all the negotiators and which underlay the implicit pact between the ANC and NP throughout the negotiations. (p. 9)

The Bisho massacre jolted people to their senses, as Aziz Pahad of the ANC commented at the time. The horror of the carnage, coupled with

---

[6] It should be noted that the divisions between what is labeled as "political" violence and what was termed "criminal" violence in South Africa over this period were blurred. This accounts for some discrepancies between different agencies' statistics on fatalities. In addition, relativizing (and approximating) the number of fatalities is also used cautiously, because this not only cheapens the lives of each individual killed, but also obscures other forms of repression. For example, between 1984 and 1986, the South African police shot dead 300 children, wounded 1,000, detained 11,000 without trial, arrested 18,000 on charges relating to political protest, and held a further 173,000 in police cells awaiting trial (Catholic Institute for International Relations, 1996). From the start of the negotiations in mid-1990 to the actual election, it is estimated that 22,000 people were injured (Coleman, 1998).

[7] See Sparks (1997, pp. 141–147) for a personal account of the massacre and the dramatic events that followed. These included the killing by the police of ANC protesters and the driving of De Klerk from Boipatong by an enraged mob when he tried to make a conciliatory visit. Mandela himself even came under fire from angry township residents, who yelled at him during a rally in nearby Evaton, "You are like lambs while the government is killing us" (p. 146).

the extensive civil protests and unrest, and the ANC concession (under considerable local and international pressure) to cancel two other marches, forced the negotiation process to realign. This incident highlights how violence can play the contradictory role of both "maker" and "breaker" of peace—a role it tragically fulfilled throughout the entire negotiations period in South Africa.

In September 1992, Mandela and De Klerk signed the "Record of Understanding" that outlined conditions for the talks to begin again and to bring an end to the violence. The negotiation process began once again, but with one fundamental difference. Compared to the preceding two years of negotiation, the balance of power was now leaning in favor of the ANC. This is evidenced by the fact that the NP was forced to concede to the release of several hundred ANC prisoners at this time. Given the show of support for the ANC, and progressive revelations of the covert strategies of the security forces, it was clear that the NP had a limited support base and its legitimacy was being eroded. This hampered the NP leaders' ability to enforce through negotiation the minority and economic rights they had initially hoped to secure through the negotiation process. Likewise, it became apparent to the ANC that it had to engage with the negotiations process to prevent further carnage, which was having a devastating effect at the local level. The ANC leadership undoubtedly realized that this would inevitably mean compromise and the possible alienation of the radicals within their ranks who wanted to see the complete capitulation of the apartheid regime.

Wilson (1997) captured the mood at this point when he wrote,

> Feeling the pressure from the international community as well as from a society tired of violence, fear and instability, both sides in the conflict in South Africa began to move from viewing negotiations as an extension of war by other means towards seeing peace as an end in itself. (p. 14)

With negotiators from both sides firmly entrenched in the process,[8] the realpolitik of compromise began to take shape. Ironically, within this context, it was the civil groups who had been responsible for demanding that negotiations be put back on track who were the first to be marginalized from the process. A compromised negotiation demanded a greater distancing by the political party negotiators from their constituencies. Constant report-back, ensuring consensus on every issue, and confronting the disagreement

---

[8]See Sparks (1997) for some fascinating accounts (some anecdotal) of how relationships were built (in and outside the negotiation chambers and in secret meetings) between the members of different parties and race groups during, and prior, to the negotiations. He specifically highlighted the positive relationship between Cyril Ramaphosa and Roelf Meyer, the ANC and NP chief negotiators, as instrumental to the successful outcome of the process.

of the more radical fringes would have frustrated and slowed the already haphazard progress of the negotiated settlement.

However, the process was again threatened with collapse in April 1993 following the assassination of the prominent ANC leader Chris Hani. The incident plunged the country once more to the precipice of disaster; violent revolution from the masses seemed imminent. In his 1996 book, *Letter to Daniel: Dispatches from the Heart,* the journalist Fergal Keane captured the uncertainty at the time when he wrote,

> This is a strange and frightening hour in South Africa: the voices of reason are being drowned, swept away in a wave of anger and bitterness. For the first time in my experience, naked hatred of Whites is in the eyes and speech of those I met on the township streets. I experienced it myself in Soweto yesterday. An angry crowd surged around my car and chanted the slogan of the radical left, "One settler, one bullet' . . . this was a crowd seething with hatred and only my Black colleague's calming voice soothed them. (p. 74)

Initially the ANC leadership seemed unable to control their supporters as riots broke out across the country. However, with time, Mandela, as shadow-president, managed to restrain the rising anger and stabilize the situation. Frost (1998) wrote that

> Effectively he was already acting as President when, on television, he called for calm and pointed out that it was a woman of Afrikaner origin who risked her life to get the necessary information which had led to the arrest of the assassins. How South Africans handled the pain, grief, and outrage would determine whether the country moved forward to an elected government of its people. (p. 7)

Paradoxically, and contrary to the intentions of the killers, his ability to control the majority at this point strengthened his leadership position considerably and made it unquestionable who was to be the next president of South Africa. Once again violence, and the threat of national chaos, had also served to push the negotiators further into the middle ground and toward settlement.

Again, in mid-1993, the process was threatened when the AWB (*Afrikaner Weerstandsbeweging* [Afrikaner Resistance Movement]) occupied the room where the talks were taking place after driving an armed vehicle through the front window of the negotiations venue outside Johannesburg. This incident was also weathered and served to undermine the credibility of the AWB and push them to the marginalized radical fringes. The event also disrupted the tenuous alliance that Buthelezi of the IFP had forged with the extreme right (Guelke, 1996), thus pushing the IFP back into a more moderate position.

As the process was cemented, macroeconomic factors also began to play a significant role. The NP engaged in a process of economic sabotage to ensure that the ANC would not inherit a very powerful centralized state. Riding on the back of the global neo-liberal climate, De Klerk began to privatize many parastatals and give away state land and facilities. The government handed 20 million hectares of land to homeland leaders in Bophuthatswana, Kwazulu, and Lebowa as an election sweetener, and 96% of White state schools were handed into the administration and ownership of the community (Catholic Institute for International Relations, 1996). The economy was also radically opened in a manner that would force the new government into a range of international and local alliance deals, guaranteeing some perpetuation of the old economic order.

The Western economic powers also began to assert their influence authoritatively. From behind the scenes they persuaded the ANC to adopt free-market economics and abandon their commitment to socialism (Wilson, 1997). Once the ANC accepted this, they started to find more common ground with the NP. This stabilized the negotiation process significantly, but this concession, in turn, gave the NP more power at the negotiation table. A common acceptance of free-market principles and the prioritization of economic stability above all else inevitably meant that the White-dominated economy could not be overhauled substantially.

Pilger (1998) asserted that economic factors were at the heart of the negotiated settlement:

> The most important "historic compromise" was made not with the apartheid regime, but with the forces of Western and White South African capital, which changed their allegiance from P. W. Botha to Nelson Mandela on condition that their multinational corporations would not be obstructed as they "opened up" the South African economy, and the ANC would drop the foolish promises in its Freedom Charter about equity and the country's natural resources, such as minerals, "belonging to the people." This meant the ANC agreeing to investment conditions that favoured big business. (p. 607)

In October 1993 it was announced that F. W. De Klerk and Nelson Mandela were to be awarded the Noble Peace Prize, oddly, on the same day as the death sentence was given to the murderers of Chris Hani.[9] The

---

[9]Nicol (1995) noted that on that day, across the street from where the Rand Supreme Court were judging the murderers of Hani, a memorial service was being held for five young people (two under the age of 12) killed by the South African Defense Force (SADF) in Umtata the previous Friday. The SADF attacked what they believed to be a PAC stronghold in a 27-minute assault resulting in some of the victims having as many as 18 bullet wounds. At the service mourners chanted "In the name of Jesus Christ . . . one settler, one bullet." Presumably, this would have meant De Klerk himself, a Nobel Peace Prize Laureate, who is said to have authorized the attack and was condemned by Mandela three days later in a radio interview. In 1998, Clive Derby-Lewis and Janusz Walus, both serving life sentences for the murder of Hani, applied for amnesty. They were both refused

final negotiated settlement was reached in November 1993 and the election date set for April 1994. The violence declined slightly but did not stop after these agreements. Fierce interorganizational conflict, mainly between the ANC and the IFP, continued in Kwazulu-Natal and the East Rand townships outside Johannesburg, several massacres took place, the peculiar phenomenon of violence against commuters continued and, finally, the extreme right's threats of violence were translated into action.

In February 1994, the AWB rushed to assist the president of Bophuthatswana,[10] Lucas Mangope, who was being deposed by his people largely because he was encouraging them not to vote in the upcoming election. After riding through the streets on the back of bakkie-vans firing on civilians and killing several, some AWB members were finally apprehended and wounded by soldiers. Shortly thereafter, while lying wounded and bleeding, two AWB men were executed at point blank range by one of Mangope's mutinous troops in the full glare of the press. This horrendous incident symbolized the collapse of the right wing in South Africa. Their threats of armed insurrection were suddenly eclipsed by haunting images of the powerless pleas of a previously menacing far-right fanatic for medical attention, before he was callously murdered in front of the entire country. Keane (1996) noted, "The belief that Blacks would melt away in the face of White firepower, that a White South African somehow carried an aura of untouchability when he confronted a Black in battle, was punctured forever" (p. 137).

The final, albeit devastating, grasp the AWB made at maintaining the old order was when they detonated a spate of bombs a week before the election.[11] Twenty South Africans lost their lives, and another 45 were injured—but at this point the process seemed unstoppable. Despite the violence and fears that a full-blown civil war would follow the election (many White South Africans had begun stockpiling their cupboards with basic provisions, fearing that war was imminent), the election passed peacefully. The first day of elections, April 27, 1994, was perhaps the closest

---

amnesty on April 7, 1999 for failing to fully disclose all of the information regarding their crimes and that they were not acting on the expressed authority or orders of the Conservative party, on whose behalf they claimed to be acting when they assassinated Mr. Hani.

[10] Under apartheid, Bophuthatswana was the "separate development" homeland for the Batswana tribe. Mangope ruled Bophuthatswana on behalf of the NP government as the "perfect puppet: a man who was quick to denounce racial discrimination but who was equally willing to praise the notion of separate development as means to achieving peace and prosperity" (Keane, 1996, p. 117). For a moving and personal account of the events of February 1994, see Keane, 1996 (pp. 115–141) and Sparks, 1997 (pp. 197–225).

[11] Five members of the AWB were sentenced to 26 years and two to 8 years each for the incidents; three received smaller sentences. When Mandela extended the cutoff date for amnesty to May 1994 (it was originally December 1993, when a settlement was reached), those found guilty of the pre-election bombings became eligible to apply for amnesty.

moment to a miracle in the entire process. Nicol (1995) captured the moment poignantly:

> On election day we switched on the radio at seven in the morning. We needed to know what was happening: that there had not been another bomb or . . . the sort of minibus taxi killing that fills me with horror. What we heard was how people had walked for miles through the dark and bush to get to the polling stations and how they stood there in a fierce autumn sun sometimes for seven hours without food, without water, without toilets as they waited to draw their crosses. We were told of people who broke into tears afterwards, how they sobbed in one another's arms at the simplicity of what they had done. (pp. 23–24)

On May 10, 1994, Mandela was inaugurated as president. It was at this point that the long walk down the difficult "road to freedom" that he was to mention in his inaugural speech was to begin. Political violence continued, albeit at much lower levels than during the negotiations process. In the course of 1995 the Human Rights Commission documented over 800 deaths that were due to political violence, the majority of deaths resulting from massacres of whole families. The worst of these was the massacre of 20 ANC supporters that occurred in the Shoba Shobane area in Kwazulu Natal on Christmas Day 1995. Political violence has continued to flare sporadically throughout 1996 and onward.

In 1997, according to the Human Rights Commission, more than 300 people were killed in Kwazulu-Natal and 151 in the rural Eastern Cape as a result of political violence; by the end of May 1998, another 368 people had been killed across the country. Although these figures remain alarming, political conflict in the immediate years following the elections was significantly lower, relative to the preceding years, and has been largely manageable. In South Africa today the number of deaths from political violence is dramatically overshadowed by the high levels of violent crime. (For more information on the causes and extent of the shift from political to criminal violence, see Hamber, 1997, 1998a; National Crime Prevention Strategy, 1996; Simpson & Rauch, 1993.

To all intents and purposes, the negotiated settlement did result in political stability in South Africa, and it brought about an end to large-scale political violence. It was also a powerful lesson in mutual dependency between former enemies who, within a context of continual crisis management and high levels of violence, were forced to accept compromise. In his book, *Tomorrow is Another Country: The Inside Story of South Africa's Negotiated Revolution*, Sparks (1997) captured this important ingredient in the South African peace process when he wrote,

> For this was always a crisis-driven process. From the moment De Klerk made his fateful announcement on February 2, 1990, there could be

no turning back. There was no way he could ban the ANC or any other Black movement again, return Mandela to prison, or revert to apartheid again. With his political opponents in the same boat, he had embarked on a one-way voyage, and they could either arrive at a new shore together or sink together. There were no other options. So as each new crisis reminded these squabbling voyagers afresh of their mutual dependency, they leaned on their oars with renewed effort and pulled for the shore. (p. 178)

The settlement in South Africa contained a range of compromises from the ANC's perspective,[12] including temporary power-sharing and job reservation for selected civil servants. Most notably, the ANC also agreed to the granting of amnesty to members of the old regime. The rationale was that, without such a guarantee, the country ran the risk of being plunged back into bitter political conflict. In this regard, amnesty was an essential and inescapable precondition to the negotiated peace settlement.

Although the ANC did not have sufficient power to demand prosecutions of former human rights abusers (and, in reality, the criminal justice system in South Africa probably did not have the resources or efficiency to prosecute large numbers of individuals anyway), it had sufficient power to prevent the NP from granting itself blanket amnesty. The balance of power tipped slightly in favor of the ANC, giving birth to a criterion-driven amnesty process. Amnesty would be granted only on the condition that the crime was political in nature and that the individual fully disclosed all of the details of the act for which amnesty was sought. In essence, truth was traded for formal justice. The function of deciding on amnesties was to fall on the Truth and Reconciliation Commission (TRC). The TRC was also to provide survivors with space to recount their traumas of the past, and the TRC was mandated to submit a reparations policy to the new government for implementation. (For more discussion of the mandate, structure, and operations of the TRC, see Asmal, Asmal, & Roberts, 1996; Hamber & Kibble, 1998; Simpson & van Zyl, 1995. For the full mandate of the TRC and the full text of the 1995 Promotion of National Unity Act, No. 34, see www.truth.org.za/legal/act9534.html.)

The TRC was seen as one of the components of the total transformation strategy. Other bodies and processes were set up to deal with additional

---

[12] I argue that the settlement was a compromise for the majority within the context of the power balances during 1990–1994. It is interesting to note that Guelke (1996) had a slightly different position. He argued that the settlement was not fundamentally different from the transfer of power to Black majority rule in Kenya, Zimbabwe, and Namibia and that there is a myth that South Africa came up with a political model new to Africa. He said that the temporary power-sharing arrangements in South Africa were similar to those in other countries and that, in their day, the transitions in Kenya, Zimbabwe, and Namibia were all hailed as miracles of accommodation and reconciliation.

issues. For example, the Human Rights Commission was established to deal with current and future human rights violations, a gender equality process was set in motion, a change management process was adopted in the police services, the ANC and Pan-African Congress (PAC) paramilitaries and military personnel were incorporated into the mainstream military and other security apparatus, and a Land Claims Court was established to settle land disputes. Arguably the most important new program was the Reconstruction and Development Program (RDP),[13] which aimed at redressing the structural economic imbalances in the country. In this way the transformation of the country was parceled into manageable pieces.

THE RELATIONSHIP BETWEEN RECONCILIATION AND TRANSFORMATION

To prevent any risk of fundamentally disturbing the frail economy and igniting conflict in the short term, the ANC agreed that change was to occur from "the inside out," rather than through rapidly dismantling the apartheid institutions. This approach ran contrary to their electorates' aspirations, but it opened the opportunity for gradual and lasting change. It gave the ANC-controlled government the power to begin to direct the trickle-down economic benefits of their liberal economic system, glean international investment, and follow a path of laggard transformation of the old apartheid institutions within a context of guaranteeing the basic civil liberties of the population.

Broadly speaking, reconciliation as a concept in South Africa became synonymous with the compromises and the pragmatic path to transformation. In a similar vein to the balanced approach that typified the new government's strategy, the TRC would also walk the narrow line between fundamental change and the maintenance of stability. The TRC held the promise of labeling responsibility and accountability and delivering reparations and truth to the survivors of apartheid violence. By not prosecuting, the TRC ensured that the fragile peace could be sustained.

Despite the portioning out of the transformation process into different components, the TRC, as the public face of the new government's reconciliation agenda, is criticized for not addressing the structural violations of the apartheid system. The TRC is criticized by some for defining the concept

---

[13] The RDP was largely subsumed by the growth, employment, and redistribution (GEAR) plan in June 1996. GEAR focuses on growth through fiscal and monetary stringency hinging on a massive increase in private-sector investment (Marais, 1998). The plan, which has failed to meet its target, has been dubbed by its critics as neoliberal and has been accused of pandering to global economic concerns at the expense of local priorities.

of victims too narrowly, that is, restricting its focus to only the victims of the so-called gross violations of killing, abduction, torture, or severe ill treatment. These criticisms are fueled by the reality that the majority of survivors who appeared before the TRC were victimized not only because of their political affiliation and activities, but also because of their structural circumstances including their gender, poverty, race, and general social marginalization (Hamber, 1998a).

When victims are too narrowly defined, the notions of direct perpetrators and victims can be weighted too heavily. The result is an overemphasis on direct perpetrators of gross violations and insufficient focus on the indirect beneficiaries of the apartheid system. The larger truth of the systematic oppression of apartheid is obscured when the truth is solely constructed from testimony of individual human rights victims and abusers (for an exploration of these criticisms, see Mamdani, 1996; Statman, 1995). It could be argued that the underemphasis on the complicity of the beneficiaries of the apartheid system in the TRC process mirrors the spirit embodied in the negotiated settlement. This approach exalts inclusiveness and stability at all costs, even if this means the maintenance of significant levels of economic privilege.

Despite these criticisms, the TRC has largely stuck to its mandate to focus only on the gross violations. To compensate, it has held a limited number of hearings on the sectors of the society (e.g., judiciary, business, and health sectors) broadly complicit in maintaining apartheid, and the TRC has argued that the broader context of apartheid is painted in their final report. In this way the TRC has touched on the link between the structural conditions of the victims and their experience of gross violations, but the TRC did not deal with the issue extensively.

However, it is incorrect to lay all the blame for a general underemphasis on structural oppression in the new South Africa solely at the doorstep of the mandate of the TRC. The mandate was established shortly after the negotiations at a time when most people were still elated by the euphoria of political change and largely unaware of the economic compromises agreed to by the ANC. It was assumed that the government was going to address the structural issues through the RDP; within this context of optimistic expectancy, it was not necessary for the TRC to focus on the question of structural violations.

With the benefit of hindsight, it is now apparent that it was a mistaken and simplistic assumption that truth-telling, public testimony, and confession would guarantee reconciliation. From the outset, the TRC should have been saying that truth alone does not equate with reconciliation and transformation, and that truth is just one of the components of the process. In contemporary South Africa, this is now a common and accepted discourse. However, in the beginning of the TRC process, truth was equated with reconciliation in the language of the TRC—a polemic position that the TRC was perhaps forced to adopt to offset rampant opposition from the right who was trying to scupper the entire process.

The negotiated agreements were made largely between the politicians and outside of the reach or influence of the average citizen; accordingly, the public did not absorb the pragmatic complexity of the process or the parceled-out approach to transformation. Rather, the majority experienced the peaceful settlement and the election as the first step to rapid change that would meet their high expectations of a better life. Truth recovery, and the work of the TRC, was simplistically viewed by many as the primary vehicle for reconciliation. As a result, and because of the intrinsic limitations of the TRC's remit of work, the fact that structural equality was integral to genuine reconciliation was ignored. It could be argued that, given the economic compromises made at the negotiation table, and given the legacy of apartheid inequality, economic imbalance clearly would not be addressed in the immediate future, therefore a blind eye had to be turned on the link between structural inequality and reconciliation in the short term.

A cynical view would be that reconciliation between the oppressor and the oppressed was merely a theatrical facade the new government used to perpetuate the inequalities of the past and build a new Black elite (Pilger, 1998). In this way, reconciliation was a tool used to consolidate the power of the new government and sell out the aspirations of the poor in the interests of the new ruling class made up of a sector of the Black population and their formidable White counterparts. A more generous view would be one that sees reconciliation as a pragmatic means to achieving gradual stable transformation and the redistribution of wealth in South Africa over an extended period of time. This is not to say that the situation has simply deteriorated under the new government. The progress to date is best summarized in the following words: "The real political transition is taking place in the long shadows cast by apartheid and popular opposition to it. Measured against the scale of the task, progress has been limited but nonetheless remarkable" (Catholic Institute for International Relations, 1996, p. 3).

It would be an injustice not to point out that many of the new laws and development strategies adopted by the ANC have had a positive effect on people's lives. For example, labor law now covers all workers, and basic constitutional rights have been guaranteed for all citizens. There are improved minimum standards, strong rights for trade unions and workers, and a powerful emphasis on collective bargaining. School nutrition programs have been introduced, and free school meals are provided to millions of students daily. There is free health care for children and for breast-feeding and pregnant women, as well as improved access to health care for some sectors of the population. New water legislation has essentially stripped historically advantaged companies and farmers of their privileged water rights; by 1996, 700,000 additional people had been supplied with water and another 1.7 million in 1997.

Nonetheless, the new government has not managed to meet many of its promised targets. The most notable example is with regard to housing. On coming to office, the new government promised it would build 1 million houses in five years. The government admitted in parliament in 1995 that only about 10,000 houses had been built, 50% fewer than in apartheid's last year (this program looked more positive in 1997, with 200,000 homes started or in line for construction; Frost, 1998). By 2000, the government had spent R10bn (equivalent to roughly 1.32 billion U.S. dollars) on housing subsidies with more than 700,000 low-cost houses built or under construction (Business Day, 2000). According to the National Housing Firm, 240,000 houses must be built annually merely to keep up with South Africa's population growth (Marais, 1998).

Economic disparity in South Africa still remains stark. According to U.N. Development Program figures (cited in Villa-Vicencio, 1998), the standard of living of Black South Africans is comparable to the 124th most wealthy nation in the world (after Congo); for White South Africans it is comparable to the 24th (after Spain). The average annual income of the poorer sections of the population is lower than what it was in 1975, and one quarter of households live on less than half the poverty line figure (according to the *Weekly Mail & Guardian*, cited in Frost, 1998). Even within White communities, the number of those below the poverty line has risen from 3% in 1975 to 7% in 1991 (Frost, 1998) and is getting worse.

The current economic policy (i.e., the Growth, Employment, and Redistribution Program) remains neo-liberal in its framework. It places emphasis on rapid growth within the worldwide capitalist system and essentially focuses on a trickle-down approach to development. The new government advocates a noninterventionist governmental approach to the functioning of the market with a focus on foreign investors, deregulation, and privatization. The bare bones of the policy was captured by Nelson Mandela when he said, "You can say [our policy] is Thatcherite, but for this country, privatisation is the fundamental policy of the government" (cited in Pilger, 1998, p. 606).

In the context of enormous inequality, and with economic growth not increasing in the past few years, it certainly remains questionable whether this approach, placing limited emphasis on state intervention, has any prospect of changing the economic landscape of South Africa. An acceptance of the new global economic order is perhaps an inescapable reality for South Africa at this point, but the question remains to what degree the implications of this acceptance are being considered and whether alternatives are being explored by the new government. Furthermore, if we accept its policy, then the delivery of the government needs to be evaluated within the framework of this system, and to date, socioeconomic progress for the poor is far from impressive under the new government. The current reality in South Africa is summarized by Frost (1998): "Those wishing for economic reparation to Africans will have to compromise . . . and come to terms with the implications of the ANC's acceptance of the market economy" (p. 178).

One danger is that, in order to divert attention from the economic inequality and to avoid the likelihood that wealth differentials will not improve in the short-term with the trickle-down economic approach adopted and the apartheid backlog, the government may attempt to divert attention from its own shortcomings. The classical deflective argument seen in many countries is that it is not the government that is reinforcing the gaps between rich and poor or the government's policy that is holding back economic change. Rather, it is specific people inside the country who are hampering progress—enemies of change.

At the level of economics, White communities do remain the enemies of change to a large extent and, as time passes, other South Africans who favor the maintenance of the present economic order are increasingly joining them. But there are dangers in this sort of labeling. This argument can be readily used by those in power to blame those controlling the wealth for all ongoing inequities and in so doing distract attention from their own internal problems, policy deficiencies, and the economic concessions. The White community will have to be challenged to a greater extent in the years to come in South Africa. However, the government, too, will have to take some responsibility for creating a post-apartheid economic environment that has been favorable to entrenching existing White economic privilege and simultaneously helped create a small but powerful Black elite.

But if there is no substantial economic change for the poor in South Africa, at least in the short term, has the entire South African reconciliation enterprise failed? One argument that has implicitly been posited thus far is that economic equality is the base of true reconciliation and that without economic change there is no reconciliation. In this sense, "reconciliation" as a concept in South Africa can cynically be viewed as the code word for perpetuating the divisions through the maintenance of an unjust economic system. Under the banner of reconciliation, those who always had power have been overly favored in the new dispensation—which has simply maintained old power imbalances. Reconciliation has been a smoke screen to obscure the fact that, given the government's acceptance of a range of compromises and their seeming commitment to neo-liberal economics, transformation will at best be gradual.

Perhaps more reasonably, it would be mistaken to see the entire reconciliation endeavor in South Africa as meaningless because the economic situation has not changed dramatically (and perhaps unrealistically) in the past few years. Value must be given to the other components of the reconciliation process embodied by structures such as TRC. This is best typified by the principles that Archbishop Desmond Tutu externalizes—principles such as non-racialism, unity, and the maintenance of peace at all costs (Frost, 1998, discussed the role that Tutu has played in achieving peace and reconciliation). The concrete outcomes of this approach include the limited but important mending of damaged relationships and the attitudinal change between conflicting parties effected by the inclusive and not overly punitive peace settlement. Such an approach has the potential for more positive relationships in the future, particularly among young people.

In addition, it is undeniably positive that many survivors have been given the opportunity to recount and discover the truth about the past through the work of the TRC. This has ensured that stories of the survivors and victims have become indisputable and that the silences of the past have been broken. The importance of the symbolic value of the TRC and other reconciliation endeavors also cannot be dismissed. A peace based on compromise has meant that many South Africans have been given the space to feel that they have been included in an important and symbolic process of healing, coming together, and moving on.

It could be argued, perhaps idealistically, that this approach has the most potential for guaranteeing that significant numbers of people are on board with the new social order. Bringing people into the process, rather than alienating them, has the greatest potential to address the economic impediments of the past. In this way, perhaps like the framework of South Africa's economic policy, the benefits of reconciliation take on a trickle-down effect in which the dividends accrue over time.

WHO PAYS FOR PEACE?

The extensive social processes of the TRC and the government's broader commitment to transformation through compromise and stability have represented a collective willingness to deal with the past and create a new future despite the relatively slow rate of social and economic delivery to date. Unfortunately, on an individual level, the compromises and the process of the TRC are experienced differently. On a purely psychological level, it is highly unlikely that individual processes of healing will coincide with national or collective strategies such as the TRC. To ensure stability, the interests of the nation have been placed before those of individuals. Even if the pragmatism of the various compromises was unavoidable to ensure peace, the impact of the process on an individual level cannot be ignored.

Amnesty provisions, whether unavoidable or not, have denied some individuals their rights to justice and civil recompense. The denial of access to these rights, even if they are only rights on paper which will never be exercised by the majority, is sharply juxtaposed with the spectacle of the perpetrators walking off with the prize of amnesty, in many instances with the golden handshakes of the past government still jingling in their pockets. This is further aggravated by the fact that these rights are being denied in a context of substantial and intractable personal loss, where, for the most part, survivors continue to live in poverty. The result has been that, in many cases, the TRC amnesty process has increased calls for justice rather than diminished them.

The double-bind when dealing with the aftermath of large-scale political violence is that acknowledgment, apology, recognition, and even substantial material improvement can never bring back the dead or be guaranteed to converge with and ameliorate all the levels of psychological pain suffered by a survivor (cf. Hamber, 2000). Nor is rapid economic progress a panacea to deal with the long-term effects of political violence. Unfortunately, the amount of distress, hurt, injustice, and anger experienced by the survivor is immeasurable.

The voices of the survivors will be heard for many years. On a purely psychological level, for a survivor to react in an overly forgiving way toward perpetrators or to simply let bygones be bygones is highly improbable in the short term (Hamber 1998b). The TRC has been a catalyst for successful resolution of this kind in some cases. However, when the TRC is complete, and reparations are granted, most survivors will not be ready psychologically to put the past behind them at that specific point.

It is critical that victims not be expected, either implicitly or explicitly, to forgive the perpetrators or forget about the past because some form of reparation has been made or a truth-recovery process has been completed. Ongoing space has to be provided for survivors to express their feelings of sadness and rage as they struggle to come to terms with the psychological and emotional impact of their loss—a loss that any strategy can only nominally acknowledge (Hamber 1998c). These spaces can take the form of private spaces (e.g., counseling and traditional mechanisms for storytelling and sharing) and the ongoing use of public space (e.g., media and exhibitions).

The population in South Africa remains highly politicized and expectant, and it is unlikely that large-scale inequality will go unnoticed. The tide of unmet expectations of a politicized electorate will remain a problem for the new government. It is likely that the populace will start to complain (and protest) about structural conditions if inequality persists. Survivors who appeared before the TRC may even start to feel that they were the pawns in the process of reconciliation and consolidation of new forms of power. They could then see the TRC as a process that ignored their poverty but used their voices to ensure greater levels of political coexistence between the elite in the name of reconciliation.

The poor may even ascribe their ongoing difficulties to the TRC, because it was the most visible element of the new government's strategy for reconciliation. Survivors may blame the inadequacies of the TRC's reparation policy for their ongoing poverty. Paradoxically this blaming of the TRC may serve the government, as it will deflect attention from the shortcomings of their macroeconomic policy and channel the frustrations of unmet economic expectations at the TRC, which is supposedly independent from the government.

The historic compromises that brought peace to South Africa in April 1994 were arguably a pragmatic prerequisite to peace, but on an individual level they were compromises that were personally costly and in some cases individually damaging. One should never lose sight of the fact that the majority had little say over the intricacies of the negotiated settlement and that they have had to carry the weight of the consequences of the settlement on top of the injustices that they experienced in the past.

The flip side of this argument is that the costs would have been much higher if peace had not been brokered in the way it was in South Africa. Still, the constant reiteration that the compromises were indispensable and that there was no alternative only serve to worsen the situation for those who have gleaned little concrete benefit to date. There may be small comfort, but acknowledgment nonetheless, in changing the public discourse from glib references to the sensible, pragmatic, and judicious compromises, to compromises that with the benefit of hindsight are considered unfortunate, individually unjust for many and, in some instances, blatantly incorrect considering their unforeseen consequences.

The problem of past violations, and the legacy of the compromises for peace, will not simply vanish with time or when reparations are granted to the victims. Although processes like the TRC have been collectively necessary, by their nature they can never be sufficient for the individual. Resolution depends on the individual personally working through the traumas of the past in the context of the present. Reparations and compensation, both material and symbolic, are useful markers in this process. Government strategies like truth commissions can help to open the door for the possibility of the individual and the country to begin the process of working through a violent and conflicted history. Socioeconomic development will naturally ease this process.

South Africa cannot afford to allow resentment to simmer among those individuals who feel their personal suffering was the price paid for peace in South Africa. The apartheid past has left a legacy of violence and mistrust within communities and not merely between the state and its citizens. These remain charged and have been defused by the TRC only to a limited degree. It is within communities, and at the local level, where future conflict will manifest itself. This will occur when new power struggles emerge, as leaders vie for the support of the majority, leaders who are the key determinants of political power in the new South Africa. In this context, disaffected individuals, and those who feel their rights were sacrificed for minimal return in the past, will become the first recruits of political entrepreneurs who will exploit past resentments.

The history of conflict in South Africa teaches us that, on the backbone of a fragile social fabric undermined by years of apartheid's destruction, political tensions often result in violence that spreads horizontally across communities. The compromises that resulted in peace in South Africa helped quell this type of violence once, but not before an excessive loss of life and violence. It remains to be seen whether a political system based on accommodation, compromise, and moderation will be able to hold frustrations at bay in a new political landscape, where real economic change for the majority seems unlikely in the near future and when the honeymoon of the "miracle" transition is merely a distant memory.

In retrospect, it is easy to look back on the negotiated settlement and argue that the settlement could have been different. Likewise, it is convenient to argue that there was no alternative to the route taken, without ever having explored an alternative. What is clear, however, is that the path to peace chosen by South Africa cannot be divorced from the context in which it was chosen. Smothered by a veil of violence and under the close scrutiny of international capital, South Africa arguably had little choice but to ensure, in the manner that it did, a peace based on compromise. The acceptance of this context, however, does not negate the need for an ongoing and realistic assessment of the consequences of the approach adopted.

Gabriel García Márquez (1972), in his novel *One Hundred Years of Solitude*, wrote that for those peoples condemned to 100 years of solitude, everything is unrepeatable, because they do not have a second opportunity on earth. It is true, South Africa will probably not have a second chance, and the time to seize the opportunities made available by the historic changes is running short. Within this context, complacency and a constant cry that there is no alternative to the current economic and international system (which clearly does not meet the needs of the poor in the developing world) is surely insufficient. However, South Africa did not operate in solitude. South Africa was not alone in its struggle for peace, nor was it alone in its violence or in its exploitation of those most in need. The world still watches and waits, hoping that South Africa can triumph, not against the odds, but in spite of them and on behalf of everyone. It appears that, across the globe, people (and governments) want to see an end to violence. But it is less certain that those who benefit most from the international global economic system (both in and outside South Africa) want to see the demise of the structural violence that perpetuates the system. In our so-called modern world, the solitude is felt in the empty calls for an economically just alternative.

For Nicol (1995), the unimaginable (and at times miraculous) tale of the South African transition seemed enough when he wrote,

> Perhaps it was because of the constitution, because of Mandela, because of the "reservoir of good will," that things happened the way they did. It was a high point in our history and probably nothing like it will occur again. But I think it was enough that it happened once, that at least there was this story that could be told in any future turned suddenly dark. (p. 92)

But, in our embattled world, one has to ask whether the moving story of the incomplete miracle in South Africa is all we will ever have. Or can we imagine ourselves into a just and equitable reality beyond the narratives of peace?

REFERENCES

Asmal, K., Asmal, L., & Roberts, R. S. (1996). *Reconciliation through truth: A reckoning of apartheid's criminal governance.* Cape Town, South Africa: David Philip.

Catholic Institute for International Relations. (1996). *South Africa: Breaking new ground.* London: Author.

Coleman, M. (Ed.). (1998). *A crime against humanity: Analysing the repression of the apartheid state.* Cape Town & Johannesburg, South Africa: David Phillip Publishers and Mayibuye Books & Human Rights Committee.

Frost, B. (1998). *Struggling to forgive: Nelson Mandela and South Africa's search for reconciliation.* London: HarperCollins.

Gastrow, P. (1995). *Bargaining for peace: South Africa and the National Peace Accord.* Washington, DC: U.S. Institute of Peace Press.

Guelke, A. (1996, Spring). Dissecting the South African miracle: African parallels. *Nationalism and Ethnic Politics, 2*(1), 141–154.

Hamber, B. (1997). Living with the legacy of impunity: Lessons for South Africa about truth, justice and crime in Brazil. *Unisa Latin American Report, 13*(2), 4–16.

Hamber, B. (1998a). Dr. Jekyll and Mr. Hyde: Problems of violence prevention and reconciliation in South Africa's transition to democracy. In E. Bornman, R. van Eeden, & M. Wentzel (Eds.), *Violence in South Africa* (pp. 349–370). Pretoria, South Africa: Human Sciences and Research Council.

Hamber, B. (1998b). The burdens of truth: An evaluation of the psychological support services and initiatives undertaken by the South African Truth and Reconciliation Commission. *American Imago, Vol. 55, No. 1*, Spring, 9–28.

Hamber, B. (Ed.). (1998c). *Past Imperfect: Dealing with the Past in Northern Ireland and Socieities in Transition.* Derry/Londonderry, Northern Ireland: University of Ulster & INCORE.

Hamber, B. (2000). Repairing the irreparable: Dealing with double-binds of making reparations for crimes of the past. *Ethnicity and Health*, 5(3).

Hamber, B., & Kibble, S. (1998). *From truth to transformation: South Africa's Truth and Reconciliation Commission* (Briefing paper). London: Catholic Institute for International Relations.

Johnson, R.W. (1994). Here for the crunch: R. W. Johnson in South Africa. *London Review of Books*, 16(8), 3–6.

Johnson, R.W., & Schlemmer, L. (1996). Introduction: The transition to democracy. In R.W. Johnson & L. Schlemmer (Eds.), *Launching democracy in South Africa: The first open election, April 1994.* New Haven, CT: Yale University Press.

Keane, F. (1996). *Letter to Daniel: Dispatches from the heart.* London: BBC & Penguin Books.

Landsberg, C. (1994). Directing from the stalls? The International Community and the South African Negotiating Forum. In D. Atkinson & S. Friedman (Eds.), *The small miracle: South Africa's negotiated settlement* (South African Review 7, 276–300). Johannesburg, South Africa: Raven Press.

Mamdani, M. (1996). Reconciliation without justice. *Southern African Review of Books*, 46, 3–5.

Marais, H. (1998). *South Africa limits to change: The political economy of transformation.* London: Zed Books and Cape Town, South Africa: UCT Press.

Márquez, G. G. (1972). *One hundred years of solitude.* London: Penguin.

National Crime Prevention Strategy. (1996). *Document by an Inter-Departmental Strategy Team of the Departments of Correctional Services, Defense, Intelligence, Safety and Security Justice and Welfare,* Pretoria, South Africa.

Nicol, M. (1995). *The waiting country: A South African witness.* London: Victor Gollancz.

Pilger, J. (1998). *Hidden agendas.* London: Vintage.

Simpson, G., & Rauch, J. (1995). Political violence 1991. In N. Boister & K. Ferguson-Brown (Eds.), *Human rights yearbook* (pp. 212–239). Cape Town, South Africa: Oxford University Press.

Simpson, G., & van Zyl, P. (1995). *South Africa's Truth and Reconciliation Commission.* Johannesburg, South Africa: Center for the Study of Violence and Reconciliation.

South African Institute of Race Relations. (1993). *Fast Facts*, No. 6, p. 7. Johannesburg, South Africa: Author.

Sparks, A. (1997). *Tomorrow is another country: The inside story of South Africa's negotiated revolution*. London: Arrow Books.

Statman, J. M. (1995, July). *Exorcising the ghosts of apartheid: Memory, identity and trauma in the "new" South Africa*. Paper presented at the meeting of International Society of Political Psychology, Washington, DC.

Villa-Vicencio, C. (1998, September). *The South African Truth and Reconciliation Commission: Some guiding principles: Justice, amnesty and reconciliation*. Presented at "Burying the past: Justice, forgiveness and reconciliation in the politics of South Africa, Guatemala, East Germany and Northern Ireland," a conference conducted at Oxford University, England.

Wilson, R. (1997). *The people's conscience? Civil groups, peace and justice in the South African and Guatemalan transitions* (Briefing paper). London: Catholic Institute for International Relations.

16

THE ACCOMMODATION OF CULTURAL DIVERSITY IN TANZANIA

AILI MARI TRIPP AND CRAWFORD YOUNG

In an era when ethnopolitical warfare appears a metaphor for the post–Cold War epoch, Tanzania stands out as an island of relative communal harmony. The low intensity of cultural conflict in a land harboring visible and conspicuous differences of ethnicity, race, and religion in its populace, which contrasts sharply with the salience of identity politics in most of Africa, invites reflection and beckons explanation. In this chapter, we explore the politics of cultural pluralism in Tanzania and possible reasons why an impressive degree of communal comity is evident, in contrast to nearby countries whose sociological parameters might appear similar.

By way of prefatory example, one may note the low level of public visibility of the ethnic antecedents of the current head of state, Benjamin Mkapa. Although he has been in office several years, and many know his region of origin (Rufiji), his Makua ethnicity is much less widely known. As one Tanzanian sociologist explained in response to an inquiry about Mkapa's ethnicity: "It is true that we never bother to find our where a person comes from generally, [and] we never ask what kabila [ethnicity] a person is. This is RUDE." (W. Mjema, personal communication, September 17, 1998). Can one imagine any citizen of Kenya, Uganda, or Rwanda being oblivious to the ethnic identity of the ruler?

If anything stands out clearly in the past couple of decades of intensified academic scrutiny of identity politics, it is the central importance of an ongoing dynamic of change. Cultural identities are not timeless, essentialized forms of consciousness, but they are in a continuous process of evolution, reformulation, quiescence, and arousal in response to the broader social and political environment in which individual and group interactions are

---

For more in-depth information on this subject, see Tripp, 1999, and Young, 1976, pp. 216–275.

embedded. We believe that the resolution of the enigma of low cultural mobilization that is our topic lies precisely in this domain. Accordingly, we propose a historical sociology of identity politics in Tanzania, examining six conjunctural moments in the political evolution of the country: the pre-colonial baseline, the German colonial period, the era of British rule, the de-colonization decade, the Nyerere single-party epoch, and the current moment of relative liberalization. Themes running through our analysis are the importance of historical sequences in identity dynamics, the degree of path dependency in shaping the range of outcomes in each successive period, the important element of contingency, and the complexity and multiplicity of identity forms.

PRECOLONIAL TANZANIA

Prior to colonial occupation, on mainland Tanzania there were a wide variety of social forms and related identities. In most places, descent-based groups (clans and lineages) were a core affective site for everyday life and social interactions. Also important was the local residential community, particularly in areas where village agglomerations rather than scattered homesteads were the norm. In some areas, especially in the north, substantial kingdoms existed, providing a political identity interwoven with those of descent and residence. To varying degrees, some *kabila* (the Swahili term for ethnic group) consciousness existed, not necessarily coincident with a political unit. This was often loosely bounded and weakly articulated. Only with a historical imagination overdetermined by contemporary identity mappings could one discover a specifically ethnic dimension to the ebb and flow of conflict and cooperation among the hundreds of groups inhabiting the Tanzanian mainland.[1]

Zanzibar, however, was a different story. Long an important base for the Indian Ocean trade, by 1840 Zanzibar became the seat of an Omani Arab mercantile state, ruling over a significant Indian merchant class and a populace of African origin. The Omani state was accompanied by a significant Arab influx, which by the colonial period constituted about 16% of the population; the Indians were about 6%. The subordinated African population tended clove plantations for Arab planters or were relegated to the more marginal zones of the Zanzibar islands. During the 19th century, a large number of slaves were imported as plantation labor, making up 20% of the African populace by the time of colonial occupation. As the immigrant

---

[1] "Tanzania" is a product of the 1964 amalgamation of the mainland territory previously labeled "Tanganyika," and Zanzibar, an offshore polity composed of two main islands, Zanzibar and Pemba. Hereafter we will use Tanganyika to refer to the mainland and Tanzania for the post-1964 state.

Arab ruling stratum became enrooted, a degree of racial mixing occurred, and Swahili became the dominant medium of communication.

In the immediate pre-colonial decades, Swahili-speaking Afro–Arab merchants rapidly extended ivory and slave trade routes deep into central Africa, planting outposts and forming alliances with some local rulers and trading groups who became military and mercantile auxiliaries. Some of the coastal zone came under Zanzibari rule, and the interior trading outposts became nodal points of Swahili culture. In this guise, Islam made its first appearance in the mainland interior.

In the period immediately preceding colonial occupation, Christian missions began operating in some coastal and interior locations, gathering around them small clusters of converts. Although the Afro–Arab traders were not primarily concerned with religious conversion, the magnetic effect of their power and wealth attracted a number of followers to Islam. Thus in embryo the pattern of religious division that obtains today was already visible in the closing pre-colonial years.

At this juncture, as the steel grid of German occupation was about to descend on mainland Tanzania in 1885, we may pause to reflect on a possible counterfactual scenario: What would the politics of cultural pluralism look like in the area now called Tanzania absent the colonial partition? One may speculate that the state-building dynamic of Zanzibar might well have continued, creating a large polity whose core identity was culturally Afro–Arab, linguistically Swahili, and religiously Islamic. The formative cultural influence of its exemplary center would have produced a very different identity map.

GERMAN COLONIALISM

The second historical moment was the German colonial period, from 1885 until World War I. The Germans organized hegemony primarily through African agents (akidas), who were not indigenous to the regions they administered. A large proportion were Swahili-speaking coastal Muslims. The association of Islam and Swahili with power in a new form fostered a continued growth of Islamic communities around the garrison towns and the further spread of Swahili. Christian mission activity, Catholic and Protestant, greatly expanded, under cover of the security provided by the colonial state. Although conversion was not massive, core Christian communities took root in a number of areas. By and large the Germans were hostile to the local leaders and tended to undermine their authority. German administrative geography, one may note, was not primarily shaped by an ethnic premise. A racial dimension to cultural cleavages took form as well, as White settlement was encouraged in some areas. In addition, an Asian trading community spread inland, from its initial Zanzibar and coastal base.

A second counterfactual interrogation invites contemplation at this juncture. German East Africa included the present states of Rwanda and Burundi, allocated to Belgian mandate after World War I. The exercise of German hegemony in these zones was much more indirect and operated through the existing kingdoms. The British would undoubtedly have preserved and strengthened indirect rule in these regions had an undivided German East Africa passed into their hands. Subsequently, the strongly integrative policies, which we will examine for the Nyerere period, could have encountered substantial difficulties in grappling with the Hutu–Tutsi polarization, which was codified and reinforced by indirect rule. Yet if the escalated Hutu–Tutsi tensions, which reached genocidal levels in both polities, had been contained within a larger political space, and if they had thus not catalyzed a life-or-death struggle for control of the sovereign state, they might have been more easily managed. Almost certainly the pattern of communal politics would differ from the current maelstrom, which draws into its turbulent vortex the entire Great Lakes region. We introduce these speculative thoughts to illustrate the critical importance of contingency rather than implacable historical destiny in the sequences of the politics of cultural pluralism.

BRITISH COLONIALIZATION

The third historical moment, British rule during the era of high colonialism in Africa, from 1920 to 1950, altered the cultural trajectory in several important ways. Most important was a different set of communal premises that informed the administrative organization of colonial domination. A long imperial encounter with south Asian societies and principles distilled from experiences elsewhere in Africa embedded an ethnic premise in the inner logic of colonial rule. In the administrative imagination of the colonizer, efficient organization of occupation necessitated imposing an ethnic template upon the territory. The "tribal" cartography involved discovery of the ethnic unit, using linguistic, customary law, and political criteria, investing an intermediary leadership with a delegated authority naturalized by linkage to a named group, and drawing administrative boundaries to conform to these entities. In the process, indigenous ruling groups and emergent elites themselves acquired an interest in as well as an attachment to the ethnic geography enshrined in the structures of rule (on the nature of such processes, see Vail, 1989; on the powerful impact of state classifications, see Scott, 1998). Although the categories were by no means simple "inventions," over time they produced a far-reaching reweaving of patterns of identity. For example, the important Chagga group is an amalgamation of 17 different identity categories; the Maasai belong to at least 10 distinct Maa-speaking groups.

In linguistic terms, the British chose to actively promote the diffusion of Swahili as a vehicular language for the territory. A standard version had been developed by 1930, and its use in schools was encouraged. Although in some neighboring colonial territories (especially the Belgian Congo), some powerful Christian missions opposed the spread of Swahili because of its purported association with Islam, in colonial Tanganyika no such antagonism emerged. This potent support by the colonizer fostered the rapid spread of the language; already by 1942, 52% of the population could speak Swahili.

Both Islam and Christianity continued to gain adherents; by 1938 Christians were 10% of the Tanganyika population (and 25% by 1957, compared to about 30% Muslim). A basic pattern solidified of a coastal zone where Islam was predominant, with scattered Christian communities and an interior with the reverse pattern: Christians were most numerous and influential, but dispersed Muslim clusters existed. However, compared to neighboring Uganda, the pattern of evangelization was less competitive, and the kind of Protestant–Catholic rivalry so important to Uganda played little role.

Finally, the colonial social geography favored distinct racial niches for Europeans and Asians, within a clear hierarchy confining Africans firmly to the bottom rung. Europeans were never numerous—only 21,000 in the 1950s (Young, 1976, p. 224)—but nonetheless insisted that their claimed racial superiority gave right to political voice. Asians in the late colonial period numbered 96,000, and they as well came to assume entitlement to representation in the colonial consultative machinery.

Zanzibar throughout the colonial period (1890–1963) was under British rule as a distinct territory. British hegemony fastened upon the existing Omani ruling house, transformed into clients of the colonizer, and consolidated the pronounced racial hierarchy that was to poison the politics of decolonization. At the top (in addition to a tiny British establishment) was a minority labeling itself "Arab," which over time became a status term. The use of Arabic—in comparative terms, the defining element in Arabhood—faded, as Swahili consolidated its linguistic primacy. The degree of racial intermingling between the Arab immigrant group and Africans (but not Indians) blurred the purely phenotypical markers of race, but the differentiation of status, expressed in a racialized discourse, remained sharp. Indeed, there was some permeability of the social boundaries of Arabhood, a standing that might be successfully achieved by some Africans.

Sharing a higher racial standing was the Indian mercantile community, dominant in trade and significant in the professions and public service, jealously preserving its racial boundaries but internally divided by caste, language, and sect. At the base of the pyramid were Africans, themselves divided in identity. The majority, established in Zanzibar before the Arab influx, came to use the status label of *Shirazi*, betokening (or imagining) a distant Persian connection and demarcating themselves from those of immediate slave antecedents. In turn, within the *Shirazi* framework three quasi-ethnic categories had gained currency: *Pemba*, for those dwelling on the adjacent island of that name; *Tumbatu*, for those native to another small adjacent island subordinate to Zanzibar, but with substantial settlements on Zanzibar island; and *Hadimu*, for those long native to the main island but primary victims of the Arab 19th-century land spoliations (the primary source of material on Zanzibar is Lofchie, 1970). Those of the 19th-century slave generation, and subsequent mainland immigrants, coalesced into a generic "African" identity category. Islam was the overwhelmingly dominant religion, as was the Swahili language.

DECOLONIZATION

The fourth historical moment was the period of de-colonization after World War II, leading up to independence in 1961. African nationalism became a significant challenge only in the mid-1950s, and the pace of change accelerated swiftly at that point. The cultural politics of colonial domination defined the initial framework for nationalist mobilization. However, there was a rapid transformation of the basic fabric of politics, brought about by a fundamental change in the rules governing access to power and the imperatives of political struggle to shape and exploit the structures of power transfer.

The first phases of de-colonization politics were dominated by the British theory of multiracial partnership as *passe-partout* formula for central and southern Africa. This bizarre concept constructed the polity as essentially defined by its three racial components (European, Asian, and Africans, whose population proportions were 1:4:430). Thus constituted, the challenge to institutional design was the embedding of a rough parity between the racial "partners," notwithstanding the huge numerical disparity. Although not finally abandoned until 1959, the looming menace of a multiracial master plan gave potent energy to shared African purpose in political organization. A unanimous insistence that the democratic institutions legitimating power transfer could be erected only on the basis of an equal weighting of all citizens found expression in two views of what human aggregate legitimately constituted a Tanganyikan body politic. The first, represented by Julius Nyerere and his Tanganyika African National Union (TANU), offered in lieu of racial partnership nonracial citizenship within a universal franchise majoritarian system. The second, a more radically Africanist perspective, argued for an exclusivist concept, with immigrant communities seen as alien to the political realm.

The TANU vision found vindication in the first national elections in 1958, still structured by racial partnership dogmas. After some hesitation, TANU agreed to participate, enlisting under its banner some European and Asian candidates. After a bitter parliamentary debate that focused on the economic and political allegiances of the Asian community in Tanganyika, the National Assembly passed the Tanganyika Citizenship Bill of 1961 granting citizenship to all British protected people (that is, mainly Asians) and citizens of the United Kingdom and colonies born in Tanganyika and with at least one parent also born in Tanganyika. Non-Tanganyikans could become citizens through registration or naturalization. The sweeping TANU victory, as well as accumulating evidence elsewhere in British-ruled central and southern African domains of the dysfunctionality of the racial partnership thesis, brought abandonment of this imposition in favor of universal suffrage balloting in 1960. Thus the politics of de-colonization were no longer mortgaged to preservation of the colonial racial hierarchy.

In the de-colonization era, as social spaces opened, a wide range of ethnic associations emerged, some of substantial influence (e.g., the Chagga Union and the Haya Union). In the early mobilizational phases of TANU, ethnic associations and religious bodies were welcome building blocs for the party. During this phase, when the primal struggle was for recognition of African paramountcy, the latent particularisms implicit in culturally constituted subentities seemed unimportant. Faced with the transcendent primacy of African rights, there was no conflict between religious or ethnic identity and the party vision of African unity. Once the incubus of racial partnership vanished overnight in 1959, however, identity dynamics changed, and TANU doctrine shifted to an uncompromising insistence on a single Tanganyikan nation as the sole identity bearing political legitimacy.

Ethnicity and religion thereafter became perceived as possible impediments to the dream of a united Tanzanian nation. In the process, there was the silent appropriation of a particular vision of "nation," entirely hegemonic in the final moments of the transition to independence. A state required the legitimating annointment of nationhood. In turn, "nation," according to then-dominant discourse, was unitary in essence. Although in a context such as Tanganyika one could not easily banish from citizens' consciousness an everyday ethnic and religious identity, proscription of their political expression seemed possible. The nation as a sacred vocation of unity was not ethnic, but territorial, political, and civic, to borrow a distinction which was not yet current in debates about nationalism. (The civic vs. ethnic nationalism debate assumed prominence decades later; see, e.g., Greenfeld, 1992.) Thus the challenge to leadership was not to obliterate less worthy forms of identity, but rather to wall them within a private realm. In the vision articulated by terminal colonial nationalism, the public realm was destined to be purely national space, with the overwhelmingly ascendant party, TANU, as its authorized interpreter.

The apparent realization of this vision, on the eve of independence, was greatly facilitated by some unusual features of the cultural geography of Tanganyika. The fertile, better-watered zones of the country, where denser populations are found, are strung around the rimland. Much of the central part of the country is dry savanna with unreliable rainfall and thus is more sparsely populated. The new patterns of social mobility created by the colonial economy thus did not place ethnic groups in direct resource competition to the same degree as elsewhere. Nor was there any obviously dominant group demographically in terms of the ethnic classifications in common use; the largest single group did not exceed 10% of the populace. Nor did social competition in emergent urban centers play a cultural mobilizational role. In the colonial capital of Dar es Salaam, the most numerous ethnic category, Zaramo, never developed a strong ethnic identity. Mainly Muslim, lacking political influence, and often disparaged by others, their social marginality did not find expression in an ethnic idiom of protest. The intimate symbiosis in the capital and surrounding coastal areas between ethnic consciousness and a broader syncretic "Swahili" culture doubtless partly explains the failure of an assertive ethnicity to emerge.

In addition, groups blessed with favorable ecological circumstance and well-developed mission school infrastructures, such as the Chagga and the Haya, did not develop aggressive ethnic ideologies comparable to the Ganda in Uganda or the Kikuyu in Kenya. Chagga elites, although they formed a Chagga Union, could never produce a unified language out of the distinctive dialects associated with the separate mountain valleys that shaped pre-colonial identities. They found ample economic and social opportunity in their Kilimanjaro homeland and were not driven to migrate elsewhere in large numbers in search of opportunity as were the Congo Kasai-Luba or the Nigerian Igbo.

A further intriguing counter-factual lies in the failure of a unified Sukuma–Nyamwezi consciousness to emerge. These two groups, very closely related linguistically and culturally, occupied a substantial area of central Tanganyika, and in terms of basic identity resources could easily have won classification as a single group, which would have numbered 17% of the population. However, the categorizations of the British ethnic template treated them as separate groups, a distinction internalized and naturalized during the colonial years.

Zanzibar, however, lived the fourth historical moment differently. Rather than evaporating, its distinct racial hierarchy, ranking Africans well below Arabs and Indo–Pakistanis, became embedded in a singularly contentious and bitter terminal colonial politics. The ascendant Arab elite was determined to preserve its sociopolitical dominance in the suddenly altered rules of de-colonization, when representative institutions grounded in universal suffrage elevated numerical strength to a determinative role. Demographics made imperative combining the discourse of anti-colonial nationalism with an alliance with elements of the African population. The accumulated resentments of racial subordination created a natural reservoir of solidarity for emergent African leaders to challenge the existing social hierarchy. However, animosity toward the Arab ruling elite was unequally experienced: intense among the mainland Africans and Hadimu, far more diffuse on Pemba and among the Tumbatu.

Thus, successive elections (1957, two in 1961, and 1963) produced intense, racially flavored polarization, between an Arab-led Nationalist Party and an Afro-Shirazi Party, forecasting a return to slavery should the Nationalist Party lead the country to independence. In the final colonial balloting, the Nationalist Party in alliance with a Pemba movement secured a narrow majority, after an election laden with racially inflammatory invective. In terms of communal comity at the opening of the fifth historical moment, the contrast with Tanganyika could not have been more sharp.

THE ZANZIBAR REVOLUTION OF 1964

One of the first dramatic events of the fifth moment occurred immediately following Zanzibar's independence at the end of 1963: the Zanzibar revolution of January 1964 and the subsequent incorporation of Zanzibar into what became Tanzania in April 1964. We will not recount in detail either of these events but note that the amalgamation altered the cultural destiny of both (see Lofchie, 1970). A tiny band of 250 seized power in Zanzibar and unleashed a wave of racial vengeance on the formerly dominant groups. It is estimated that up to 500 Arabs and Asians were killed during the rebellion, and both groups suffered heavy property losses. About a fifth of the Arabs fled, and 80% of the Asians left Zanzibar (Nagar, 1996). The unsettling prospect of prolonged disorder and communal violence, exacerbated by Cold War intrusions, led Nyerere and a coterie of Afro–Shirazi leaders to negotiate a jerry-built amalgamated state, granting a substantial role to Zanzibari figures in the central institutions, while accepting a very broad autonomy for Zanzibar.

This dramatic unification, secretly negotiated and promulgated without public discussion, was possible in good part because of a defining feature of the fifth political moment: the extraordinary charisma and leadership skills of Nyerere and his personal ascendancy. His charm, oratorical mastery, private austerity and integrity, and principled convictions sustained popular affection and admiration through most of his long tenure. His political movement earned overwhelming electoral backing before any legal barriers to opposition existed. And he began his post-colonial stewardship with some path-dependent assets: the relative absence of cultural groups with highly elaborated ideologies of identity, the low level of communal polarization in terminal colonial politics (except Zanzibar), and the wide acceptance of Swahili as the *lingua franca*.

The Nyerere regime (1961–1985) committed the ample political resources of the new state to a developmental program of which nation-building was a cornerstone. This comprehensive project was intimately interwoven with the overall development ideology of populist socialism. More broadly, nation-building was inscribed in an aspirational text of high modernity.

The strategy contained several institutional features. The move to a one-party state was premised on the axiom that, in a society lacking entrenched class divisions, multiple parties risked fastening upon the communal as the only available line of differentiation. Constituencies utilized for competition for party nomination were gerrymandered to avoid single-ethnic districts. Civil servants and political officials were assigned outside of their communities of origin. The ruling bodies of government and party were carefully balanced by region and religion. One of the worst accusations that could be leveled against a public official was that he or she was guilty of *ukabila* (tribalism). Letters to the editor in the government-owned paper *Daily News* and the party paper *Uhuru* would from time to time accuse various ministries and state-owned companies of hiring individuals based on ethnic favoritism rather than on merit and demand that authorities take measures to end such visible manifestations of tribalism (Jerman, 1997).

The one institutional sphere in which balance was not observed was in the top command structure of the security forces. Stung by a damaging mutiny in 1964, requiring a humiliating recourse to British military intervention, and alerted by the generalized phenomenon of the African military coup from 1965 on, Nyerere was always especially attentive to control of the armed forces. In his later years, like most other African leaders, he was influenced by an "ethnic security map" (Enloe, 1980), relying upon a network of key officers from his Zanaki ethnic group.[2]

---

[2] For some evidence, see *Africa Confidential* (1983). The military drew heavily from ethnic groups that had a tradition of enlisting in the army since colonial times, e.g., the Hehe, Tende, and Kuria. Thus, the ethnic balance, perhaps conveniently, tilted towards those from Nyerere's own Mara region in northwestern Tanzania when it came to top security posts within the security forces. The Zanaki are closely related to the Kuria. At the same time, after the 1964 mutiny highlighted the challenge of control over the military, Nyerere also made an effort to broaden the composition of the armed forces to avoid excessive preponderance of particular ethnic groups (Joan Wicken [personal assistant to President Nyerere], personal communication, March 3, 2000).

Beyond the positive institutional initiatives, nation-building proceeded as well by proscriptive measures. An ethnicity-free public environment was reinforced by banning use of ethnic terms in the media. Ethnic associations were also dismantled. The colonial chiefs, perceived as tainted in part by the ethnic cartography to which their office was beholden, were eliminated in several stages. Those culpable of advancing religious or ethnic claims were swiftly called to order.

Language was a core element of cultural statecraft. The colonial support for Swahili was elevated to a new level: promotion of the language as the primary vehicle for public sphere communication and as expressive instrument of the nation-in-becoming. By 1967, usage of Swahili was required for all government and national businesses wherever possible and convenient. By this time, well over 90% could speak Swahili, and a growing percentage, particularly among younger generations, used it as their first language (Whiteley, 1969, p. 3). Indeed, the Swahili diffusion dynamic led some to wonder whether the price of its success might be the disappearance of some local languages.

Permeating the modernization program of TANU was a political culture of egalitarianism. In cultural terms, this implied a priority for regional equity in development policy. Investment in social infrastructure consciously sought to focus resources on underserviced regions and even to prevent zones such as Chaggaland with unusually dense educational networks from using locally generated funding to further expand their schools. Such areas in practice were able to circumvent such restrictions, but the egalitarian national commitments doubtless dampened any potential resentments from disadvantaged regions.

The egalitarian creed found expression in the comprehensive application of a socialist project, codified in the 1967 Arusha Declaration. At first, the ethical attractiveness of this systematized egalitarian commitment won not only strong internal support, but also widespread adulation internationally, not only from doctrinally sympathetic Scandinavian social democratic governments, but also from the World Bank bureaucracy and American aid officialdom. However, over time the hypertrophy of the state joined to its deteriorating economic performance, and the burdens imposed by a huge, malfunctioning, and deficit-ridden state enterprise sector undermined the Nyerere populist socialist vision. The blockage of local community initiative, the expropriation of cooperative societies (a number of which were organized within ethnic boundaries), and related measures created a political economy impervious to local interests and concerns, yet unable to perform.

Particularly harmful was the 1971 Acquisition of Buildings Act, a virtual expropriation of real property. This measure followed a series of other Africanization policies that convinced Asians that they were a target; 97% of the nationalized buildings had Asian ownership. Within three months of this act nearly half the Asian population (over 40,000) had emigrated. The virtual criminalization of the formal private sector drove many of those remaining into assorted illicit activities such as smuggling and black market currency dealing of doubtful benefit to the country.

The Zanzibar union was a source of recurrent difficulties for Nyerere during the fifth moment. The constitutional amalgamation left in place Afro–Shirazi Party leader Abeid Karume, who presided over a notoriously thuggish regime stained by gross human rights abuses, particularly directed at Arabs and Asians. When Karume died in 1972, the reign of terror ended, but Zanzibar politics remained a special zone where the cultural integrative statecraft of Nyerere did not fully apply. A step toward further integration occurred in 1977, when the two ruling parties fused as the Chama Cha Mapinduzi (CCM, or "revolutionary party").

Overall, however, there can be little doubt that the nation-building project enjoyed significant success. By the time of his retirement in 1985, Nyerere's image was partially tarnished by his stubborn reluctance to abandon his socialist commitments long after their dysfunctionality was evident. But the integrity of his vision of "nation" drew little challenge, and the degree to which he lashed his own place in history to the creation of a affective engagement of the citizen with Tanzania played a large part in its consolidation. His own ethnic background, as son of a small community of limited social visibility, facilitated a career as icon of nationhood; no subtext of ethnic hegemony diminished its resonance. The sharp contrast in this respect with perceptions of Kenyatta or Moi in Kenya, Obote in Uganda, Habyarimana in Rwanda, or Mobutu in Congo/Zaire stands out.

LIBERALIZATION

The defining attribute of the sixth political moment, beginning in the middle 1980s, is liberalization, economic and political, however halting and incomplete. In 1984, yielding to strong international financial institution and donor community pressure and a growing domestic skepticism about a state-owned, operated, and managed economy, Tanzania moved to liberalize trade. Extension of liberalization to the political realm came a few years later; competing political parties were permitted in 1992. Nyerere retired from the presidency in 1985, ceding his post, as required by a principle of alternation adopted at the time of the 1964 amalgamation, to Zanzibari Ali Hassan Mwinyi. Mainlander Benjamin Mkapa then succeeded in 1995, easily winning the first multiparty election.

Economic liberalization has gone much further than its political counterpart. In reality, an underground economic liberalization had been under way for a number of years, as ordinary citizens struggled to preserve livelihoods the state appeared to undermine through the pervasive superstructure of socialist orientation (for a discussion of the significance of these phenomena, see Tripp, 1997). Economic reform created social space for a wide variety of local initiatives, based on a range of associational principles, of which local community was one (but far from the only); gender-based enterprises, formerly subordinated to the authorized party ancillary body, grew in importance.

The turn to capitalism is not without its debit side in the realm of communal comity. The most visible axis of tension involves the Asian community. Asians entered the era of liberalization with important advantages. Above all, they have well-honed commercial skills, acquired through generations of experience in the economic niches they have occupied. But they also continue to have advantageous access to capital, through several channels. The surreptitious modalities of accumulation in the parallel economy leave some concealed sources. Asian entrepreneurs can often submit more solid collateral and dossiers to the private banking system. Finally, a by-product of the 1971 exodus is a more strongly established diaspora community, within which capital resources exist.

As a consequence of these factors, by the 1990s openly expressed African resentment of the Asian business community became more frequent. Public debates about the Asian role and pointed questions about their loyalty and commitment to the Tanzanian economy highlight the risks of escalated racial tensions and the potential vulnerability of the Asian minority. In the fifth historical moment, such open attacks on the Asians were forbidden.

Political liberalization has been accompanied by a prohibition of parties based on religion or ethnicity. The ban has prevented the emergence of explicit sectarian or ethnic formations, but outside the bounds of political party competition a clear increase in religious tension is evident. Muslims, whose formal organization was placed under party tutelage during the fifth political moment, are now free to express accumulated frustrations about what they believe is the failure of independence to improve their access to education and leadership. Muslims are now at least a third of the population, but they point to 1995 figures showing that only four of 24 Principal Secretaries, eight of 113 District Commissioners, and five of 20 Regional Commissioners were Muslim. A 1993 study of the University of Dar es Salaam student body showed that 86% were Christian and only 13% Muslim (Tripp, 1999). In addition, Muslims argued that the secularity of the Tanzanian State was a sham, concealing a Christian inner essence. The uproar over a surreptitious 1992 Zanzibar application to join the Organization of the Islamic Conference (rejected by the OIC) was symptomatic of a Christian double standard; Tanzania, after all, was a member of the Red Cross, a body of Christian associations (Luanda, 1996).

Christians, however, perceived growing signs of undue Muslim influence and favoritism under President Mwinyi. Many Christians viewed with dismay what they took to be a rise in Muslim fundamentalism, associated in their eyes with sinister foreign finance and support. The furtive Zanzibar application to join the OIC confirmed these suspicions. In both religious communities, fringe extreme elements appeared to exacerbate the tensions. On the Christian side, Reverend Christopher Mtikila enjoyed a well-earned reputation for inflammatory attacks on the Muslim community in the mid-1990s. On the Muslim side, small but noisy integralist elements had also emerged.

The other dimension of increasing tensions surrounding diversity is the Zanzibar status question. The OIC affair; a sense among many mainlanders, especially Christians, that Zanzibar enjoys disproportionate representation in the union; and a belief that the mainland derives no benefit from the Zanzibar linkage brought serious questioning of the nature and future of the amalgamated state. Within Zanzibar itself, the older quasi-ethnonyms of Hadimu, Tumbatu, and even Shirazi have virtually disappeared; the distinctions that remain are between Africans ("Swahilis") and Arabs (including those of mixed ancestry associated with the Arab label). A regional distinction remains between Pemba and the main island of Unguja, which spilled over into serious violence and apparent fraud during the 1995 election campaign; the social vocabulary of identity has altered, but the potential for conflict remains strong. Indeed, the original Nyerere calculation seems to remain valid: Absent the union, recurrent and serious communal confrontations would mark the Zanzibar scene, threatening the stability of the mainland itself.

CONCLUSION

In conclusion, we need to return to the overall judgment with which we began. If we raise our gaze beyond the palpable racial, religious, and regional tensions which beset Tanzania, and especially if we place its experience in the accommodation of cultural diversity in comparative perspective, we are led to a largely positive conclusion. "Success," always in the eye of the beholder, is a singularly elusive notion to apply to the political management of cultural pluralism. The many contemporary cases of spectacular and indisputable failure illuminate the intrinsic difficulties of the task.

We need to return to the origins of mainland Tanzania as a culturally artificial product of the colonial partition. Although cultural calculus influenced imperial strategies for cost-effective domination, the idea of nation was entirely alien to the colonial state. Only in the fifth and sixth historical moments was there a conscious policy of constructing a concept of national community. The unintended cultural legacies of the colonial moments were ambiguous. An ethnic cartography without clear pre-colonial antecedents was imposed. However, cultural geography and historical sequence resulted in identity categories whose affective intensity was significantly less than in a number of other states. The particular trajectory of anti-colonial nationalism, and the towering personality of Julius Nyerere, made possible an extended fifth moment period of energetic inculcation of the national idea, which encountered neither challenge nor resistance.

Despite the frictions that have become more visible in the sixth moment, such a Tanzanian nation clearly does exist today, far more rooted in the popular consciousness than an idea of nationhood was in 1962. In the fifth moment, informed by a vision of unitary nationhood then globally dominant but now supplanted by more multicultural concepts, Nyerere doubtless plunged too far down the path of denial and proscription. But the present moment of liberalization opens the way to novel difficulties and new challenges. Notwithstanding the failings of his economic doctrines, as political architect Nyerere bequeathed a legacy of national community constructed to durable specifications.

REFERENCES

Africa Confidential. (1983, March 16). *24*(6).

Enloe, C. (1980). *Ethnic soldiers.* Athens: University of Georgia Press.

Greenfeld, L. (1992). *Nationalism: Five roads to modernity.* Cambridge, MA: Harvard University Press.

Jerman, H. (1997). Between five lines: The development of ethnicity in Tanzania with special reference to the Western Baramayo District. *Transactions of the Finnish Anthropological Society, 38,* 327–328.

Lofchie, M. F. (1970). The Zanzibari Revolution: African protest in a racially plural society. In R. I. Rotberg & A. A. Mazrui (Eds.), *Protest and power in Black Africa* (pp. 924–968). New York: Oxford University Press.

Luanda, N. N. (1996). Christianity and Islam contending for the throne on the Tanzanian mainland. In A. O. Olukoshi & L. Laakso (Eds.), *Challenges to the nation–state in Africa* (pp. 168–182). Uppsala, Sweden: Nordiska Afrikainstitutet.

Nagar, R. (1996). The South Asian diaspora in Tanzania: A history retold. *Comparative Studies of South Asia, Africa, and the Middle East, 16*(2), 62–80.

Scott, J. C. (1998). *Seeing like a state: How certain schemes to improve the human condition have failed.* New Haven, CT: Yale University Press.

Tripp, A. M. (1997). *Changing the rules: The politics of liberalization and the urban informal economy in Tanzania.* Berkeley: University of California Press.

Tripp, A. M. (1999). The political mediation of ethnic and religious diversity in Tanzania. In C. Young (Ed.), *Cultural diversity and public policy: Case Studies* (pp. 37–71). Basingstoke, England: Macmillan.

Vail, L. (Ed.). (1989). *The creation of tribalism in Southern Africa.* Berkeley: University of California Press.

Whiteley, W. (1969). *Swahili: The rise of a national language.* London: Methuen.

Young, C. (1976). *The politics of cultural pluralism.* Madison: University of Wisconsin Press.

17

WHY HAS THERE BEEN NO RACE WAR IN THE AMERICAN SOUTH?

JOHN SHELTON REED

American Southerners are not accustomed to having our region thought of as a good example—certainly not when it comes to race relations. But the question posed by my title may lower the bar enough that we can qualify. Of course we did have one race war, a protracted one against the American Indians, culminating in what was euphemistically called in the 1830s the "removal" of some 60,000 to Oklahoma.[1] But that was a long time ago, by American standards. So long ago that most Americans now think of the South as having always been essentially a biracial society, Black and White. And that is the race war that may not have happened. Let me sketch a cursory history of Black–White relations in the American South, emphasizing the violent conflict that did occur; then we can decide whether something needs to be explained.

THE SLAVERY ERA, 1661–1865

After slavery was legally recognized in Virginia in 1661, it soon spread to the other North American colonies, especially to the plantation colonies of the South and, by the turn of the 18th century, the wholesale importation of enslaved Africans was well under way. For the next 260 years Black people in the American South were ruthlessly and efficiently subordinated, first under slavery, then under the Jim Crow system of law and custom.

---

[1] All told, the Southern Indian population was reduced from a high of around 150,000 to something under 10,000. The ironic sequel to this sad story is that 40% of native White Southerners and half of Black Southerners now tell public opinion pollsters that they have at least one American Indian ancestor (Reed, 1997). If the "one drop rule" once applied to Negro ancestry were followed in this case, the Indians—*we* Indians—would be about to take the South back.

When legal importation of slaves ended in 1807, roughly a half-million Black people had been brought to what became the United States, and by 1860 the Black population of the South had increased to more than 4 million, over 90% of them enslaved.

Most slaves were agricultural field hands, especially on the cotton plantations of the Deep South, where many counties (and the states of Mississippi and South Carolina) had Black majorities. Slave rebellions and conspiracies were far from rare in the South—there were at least 250 of them—but most were small, and all were suicidal. The bloodiest and best known was that led by Nat Turner in Virginia in 1831: Turner's rebels killed some 60 White people; the 60 or 70 insurrectionists and at least 120 unimplicated Black people also died.

The demographics I mentioned earlier largely explain why there were not successful slave revolts in the American South. At emancipation, most Black Americans were at least three generations removed from Africa, and the age and sex distributions of the Black population were more balanced than elsewhere in the Americas. They lived in families, for the most part, not as gangs of young men. Also unlike elsewhere, slaves in the South were dispersed, usually outnumbered and always outgunned by the White population. When Black people had the opportunity to resist successfully, they seized it: During the Civil War over 200,000 joined the invading Union Army. And when their segregated units faced Confederate troops, we did see something like a race war, with all the usual atrocities. Confederates seldom took Negro prisoners.

RECONSTRUCTION AND JIM CROW, 1865–1958

With the defeat of the Confederacy and emancipation came a brief period of experimentation and uncertainty about the future of race relations, in some states even a period of Black political rule, but also a period of extensive and systematic violence directed against the Black population and White Republicans (Lincoln's political party). The year 1866 saw massive race riots in Memphis and New Orleans, and soon the Ku Klux Klan and dozens of similar organizations sprang up in every Southern state, acting as a secret paramilitary arm of the Democratic party to intimidate Republican voters and politicians and to kill hundreds of them. If this was not a race war, it often looked like one.

Weariness in the face of this determined and protracted resistance certainly contributed to the shift in northern public opinion that led eventually to the removal of federal troops from the South and the restoration of White Democratic rule. After 1878 conservative southern Whites moved swiftly to reestablish control of the Black population, and by 1900 southern Blacks were as effectively subordinated as they had been under slavery. Most were sharecroppers, in a condition of near-peonage. Stripped of the vote, segregated by custom and increasingly by law, without effective legal protection or even the protection slaves had as property, they were reduced to dependence on the good will of Whites.

It should be emphasized, however, that the Black population as a whole was an indispensable component of the Southern economy. Although the situation of individual Black people was precarious, the jobs to which most were relegated by segregation—especially field labor—were essential, as planters' later opposition to the activities of Northern labor recruiters attests. Under such a regime, violence was hardly necessary to maintain White supremacy, and too much violence could have had dire economic consequences. There was a good deal of it, nevertheless, especially in Southern cities, where most Black institutions were concentrated and where African Americans had established the greatest measure of independence from White control.

The decades around the turn of the century witnessed dozens of large-scale urban race riots (and not just in the South: over 20 cities across the United States experienced them in the summer of 1919). In 1898 one of the worst, in Wilmington, North Carolina, decimated that port city's flourishing Black middle class. (How to commemorate its centenary in 1998 presented an interesting civic problem for Wilmington. Atlanta faces a similar problem in 2006.)

That the segregation era saw virtually nothing in the way of violent Black resistance except in immediate self-defense surely speaks both to the effectiveness of the White majority's domination of the Black minority and to the obvious futility of such resistance. As the national success in 1915 of the racist film *Birth of a Nation* attested, Black Southerners could not look outside the South for politically consequential White allies. White Northerners by and large shared Southern White views of appropriate race relations, or at least they believed in allowing White Southerners to implement their views without Northerners' interference.

When individual acts of defiance did occur, they were dealt with brutally. (Lynching peaked in the 1890s but continued after the turn of the century at a rate of 50–100 cases a year, reaching a total of over 3,700 before waning in the 1930s.) A far more common response was emigration: Millions of Black Americans left the South in one of the great migrations of human history. In 1900, 90% of Black Americans lived in South; by 1965 only 40% did. In the 1950s one out of every four Southern-born Black Americans lived outside the South, and more than half of the non-Southern Black population was Southern-born.

THE CIVIL RIGHTS MOVEMENT

At mid-century, the segregationist regime of the South seemed to most observers simply an immutable fact, one that would have to be reckoned with by anyone concerned about improving Southern race relations. As late as 1942 only 2% of White Southerners had told a public opinion poll that Black and White children should attend the same schools (Black, 1979; Greeley & Sheatsley, 1971; Hyman & Sheatsley, 1964; Schwartz, 1967; Sheatsley, 1967). It appeared to be true, in the words of historian Ulrich B. Phillips, that a determination that the South "be and remain a White man's country" was "the cardinal test of a Southerner" (Phillips, 1928, p. 31). (For Phillips and others, "a Southerner" was simply assumed to be White.) As the civil rights movement picked up steam around 1960, it appeared to be headed straight into a solid wall of White opposition. Reporting on a study conducted in 1961, political scientists Matthews and Prothro (1966) concluded that "only a significant change in White racial attitudes, awareness, and expectations [could ensure] the prevention of a racial holocaust and the preservation of political democracy in the South" (p. 365).

Well, a few decades later, what do we see? There has been a significant change in White attitudes. Support for racial segregation has simply evaporated. Only about 5% of Southern White parents object to sending their children to school where "a few" of the children are Black, a figure no higher than that for the rest of the country. In most respects, White Southerners' racial attitudes are no longer appreciably different from those of other White Americans in communities with significant Black populations. The poverty rate for Black families in the South—twice as high as that elsewhere as late as 1970—is now comparable to that for the rest of the country. In fact, the Southern rate has now fallen below that for the North Central states.

In 1960, a mere quarter of the eligible Black voters in the South were registered to vote. (In Mississippi only 6% were registered five years after that.) The Voting Rights Act of 1965 changed that, and one consequence is that Black Americans are now more likely to hold elected office in the South than in any other region. In 1965, of the tens of thousands of elected officials in the South, precisely 78 were Black. Thirty-odd years later, two thirds of America's 8,015 Black elected officials were in the South, nearly 1,500 in Mississippi alone. Perhaps the most impressive statistics are those that show, since about 1970, more Blacks moving to the South than leaving it, reversing a population flow that once seemed a given in American demography. In the 1990s the rate of Black migration to the South was even accelerating. Once again a majority of Blacks live in the South.

Greeley (1974) has argued that the change these statistics reflect is "one of the most impressive social accomplishments of modern times" (p. 307;

for a similar argument, see Reed, 1984). Certainly the collapse of White Southerners' support for segregation is at least one of the most complete turnarounds in the history of public opinion polling. Moreover, in historical and comparative terms, this change happened very quickly, and it can be argued that it came about at remarkably little cost.

That last statement would strike many Americans as bizarre. The civil rights movement lasted for roughly a decade, from the Montgomery bus boycott of 1955 to the Voting Rights Act of 1965, and Americans remember these years as violent ones, a collective memory periodically reinforced by historical melodramas like the movie *Mississippi Burning*. Among the most conspicuous examples of violent opposition to the movement were the riots at the University of Mississippi in which two people died; the deaths of four young Black girls in the bombing of a Birmingham church; the assassination of Medgar Evers of the National Association for the Advancement of Colored People and later that of Martin Luther King himself; beatings and killings in connection with the Selma, Alabama, voting rights march; and the Mississippi Summer Project of 1964, which witnessed 80 beatings, 35 shootings, 35 church bombings, 30 house bombings, and 6 murders (Brown, 1981). We should not forget these events, nor should we forget the courage it took to confront this sort of thing.

But we must recognize that, as historian Richard Maxwell Brown has pointed out, the violence deployed against the civil rights movement, although brutal and terrifying (as it was meant to be), was seldom fatal. Brown estimated that the massive structure of Jim Crow law, designed to fix the shape of Southern race relations forever, was utterly destroyed at a cost of 44 people killed during the entire course of the civil rights movement (Brown, 1981, p. 52). Those deaths should not be forgotten or minimized, but they must also be assessed by comparison to the thousands of earlier deaths by lynching and in race riots, not to mention the ghastly toll exacted by intercommunal violence elsewhere in the world.

SOMETHING TO BE EXPLAINED

Here, if anything, is what needs explaining. Matthews and Prothro were not the only observers who feared "racial holocaust" in the South, yet it is simply a fact that the basic structure of Southern society was changed without anything near that description. How did this happen? (Much of the following discussion is based on Black & Reed, 1985.)

Part of the answer surely lies in the political and strategic genius of the civil rights movement's campaign of nonviolent civil disobedience. Organized and run largely through Black churches, the most powerful independent institutions in the Black South, the movement was able to enforce a remarkable level of discipline on its adherents. Its powerful ideology and charismatic leadership no doubt helped, too. That campaign resulted not only in concrete, immediate concessions, but (more importantly, I believe) in long-term sympathy from White Northern public opinion. Of course, to produce that result, White Southerners had to respond with enough violence to alienate non-Southern public opinion, which they—perhaps I should say "we"—obligingly did. The interesting question is why they did not respond with crushing counterforce, as their ancestors had occasionally done in the Reconstruction and Jim Crow periods.

One answer is that non-Southern public opinion, shaped by television coverage of the movement and translated into political support, guaranteed that when Southern White opponents of the movement confronted armed resistance, it came not from Black militias or guerillas but from federal marshals, "federalized" National Guardsmen, or the U.S. Army. This may largely explain why violent resistance came from such a small minority of the opposition, compared to the violence that had worked 90 years earlier to end Republican rule. Few segregationists were willing (as those in the movement were willing) to risk their lives, their freedom, their jobs, or even their comfort on behalf of their views.

But that is not the whole story. Why did the violent minority not receive the unqualified and near-unanimous support from the White community that the equivalent, and much larger, minority did in the 1870s? The political importance of ambivalence, resignation, and indifference should not be underestimated. As one observer noted during Little Rock's troubles, 124,500 of the city's 125,000 citizens went about their business, then went home at night and watched the other 500 on television (Macmillan quoted in Brown, 1981, p. 65). What produced this balance?

AN AMERICAN DILEMMA, AND A SOUTHERN ONE

All I can do here is to speculate, but let us return to the strategic wisdom of the civil rights movement's leaders. It is clear, in retrospect at least, that their appeal to basic Christian and American values not only won support outside the South, it also persuaded a few White Southerners and immobilized a good many others. Social psychologist Paul Sheatsley (1967) wrote in the mid-1960s that most White Americans knew "that racial discrimination is morally wrong and recognize the legitimacy of the Negro protest." "In their hearts," he concluded, "they know that the American Negro is right" (p. 323). It seems unlikely that most White Southerners knew anything of the sort, but enough did, and enough others suspected as much, that the facade of White racial unity was less solid than it had appeared.

A generation earlier, Gunnar Myrdal (1944) had written in *An American Dilemma* of the gross contradiction between the values embodied in America's founding documents and official creed and the nation's—especially the South's—treatment of its Black citizens. This contradiction was not immediately self-evident to many White Southerners; they had persuaded themselves and each other—and sincerely believed—that Black Southerners did not object to segregation, even that they preferred it. (Sheatsley, 1967, reported, for example, that in 1963 only 35% of White Southerners believed that "most Negroes feel strongly about [the] right to send children to the same schools as Whites," p. 317.) The movement's activities made it much more difficult to see support for segregation as a matter of endorsing a polite biracial consensus; it became more clearly support for the naked imposition of inferior status on an unwilling people. Some White Southerners did not shrink from that view of what they were about, but others did.

In addition, and perhaps even more importantly for the South, the movement appealed explicitly to the shared Evangelical Protestant heritage of Black and White Southerners. Cultural similarity is obviously not sufficient and may not even be necessary for harmony, but of the many similarities between Black and White Southern cultures, this one proved especially important. When the civil rights movement's opponents tried to paint it as alien to American and Southern values—in particular, when they tried to tar it as Communist inspired—they got no help from the movement itself. Led by Protestant clergy, its rhetoric filled with Biblical imagery, its songs (without exception, as far as I know) gospel songs, quoting Thomas Jefferson and Moses instead of Karl Marx and Frantz Fanon, asking only for what almost everyone agreed were the rights of American citizens and those made in the image of God—if nothing else, the movement put its opponents at a distinct rhetorical disadvantage.

COMPETING VALUES AND CONVENTIONAL ATTITUDES

A second factor is that most White Southerners, although committed to White supremacy and racial segregation, were not committed only to White supremacy and segregation. For many, commitment to other values—to law and order, to the good repute of their communities, to economic development—competed for primacy. In particular, I believe, the movement benefited from an American value fully as widespread in the South as elsewhere, that of materialism. Economic development is not everything, but it is closer to being everything in the South than anywhere else I know, and much of the region's economic growth in this century has been fueled by outside investment. Cities identified with racial strife—Little Rock in

1957, Birmingham in 1963—demonstrably paid an economic price for that identification. Atlanta, which proudly billed itself as "the city too busy to hate," is only the best-known case of a city whose business elite determined to make whatever concessions were necessary to avoid racial "trouble" because it would be bad for business. Another is Charlotte, North Carolina, whose motto was once "Charlotte: A good place to make money." (You cannot imagine the satisfaction many North Carolinians felt when Charlotte's school desegregation plan was held up as a model for Boston, Massachusetts.)

For other White Southerners, fatalism may have had the same result as avarice. A common cultural value among both Black and White Southerners, fatalism has been most common among rural, poorly educated, older people: in those sectors of the population who, if White, were most likely to oppose desegregation. (Matthews and Prothro, 1966, pp. 358–359, indicated that White segregationists expected more change, faster, than did other White Americans; Reed, 1983, examined the correlates of a constellation of "traditional Southern values" that included both fatalism and White supremacist ideology.) Confronted with the prospect of change, many segregationists believed that their cause was lost whatever they might do. They may not have been happy about what was going to happen, but did not believe they could prevent it.

Moreover, it is clear with hindsight that the segregationist attitudes of many White Southerners were merely conventional—that Pettigrew (1972, p. 162) was right when he argued in 1959 that many were simply conforming to community norms, endorsing existing arrangements and institutions. The rapidity of the subsequent change suggests as much: If attitudes are deeply rooted, embedded in a supporting ideology, or serving important psychological functions, change does not take place readily. To be sure, the destruction of an established and taken-for-granted social order is a disconcerting prospect, but it can be a relief simply to have matters settled. Once desegregation had taken place, its opponents were the ones who wanted change, and whatever contribution temperamental conservatism had made to the defense of segregation it now made to the defense of a new status quo.

It helped, of course, that desegregation was simply not as bad as many White Southerners had feared. That many had been genuinely frightened by the prospect—it meant an end, after all, to the South as they knew it—is indicated by the fact that the Supreme Court's 1954 school desegregation decision apparently produced a measurable deflection in the Southern White birth rate (Rindfuss, Reed, & St. John, 1978). Given that, perhaps it is not surprising that many of the most vociferous opponents of desegregation withdrew in the wake of its accomplishment to private schools, to private clubs, and the like—which, of course, allowed the process to proceed more smoothly (Nevin & Bills, 1976). (In some communities, that withdrawal has now proven to be temporary, although in others, of course, it appears to be more or less permanent.) In any case, I believe that all of these factors contributed to the frequent finding in the survey data from the 1960s that those White Southerners who had actually experienced desegregation were the least likely to oppose it (Sheatsley, 1967).

ARE THERE LESSONS FOR OTHERS?

Without glossing over the very real problems of race relations that remain, I believe we must conclude that we have a higher class of problems than we used to. We can treat the recent Southern experience of relatively peaceful social change and racial adjustment as something of a success story. Can that experience be replicated? A number of factors came together in the American South in the 1960s, and unfortunately I do not see many examples of that happy concatenation elsewhere in the world—or in human history, for that matter.

But let me try to avoid simply concluding with a variation on the tiresome theme of American exceptionalism by listing a few of the factors that helped to produce the result we in the South have seen.

- Important civic and religious values shared by the movement and its opponents, to which the movement could plausibly appeal to justify its activities.
- Opponents who held values that could be brought into conflict with their opposition (perhaps especially bourgeois materialism—as Samuel Johnson said once, "A man is seldom so innocently engaged as when he is making money").
- Aims that when realized proved to be less unpleasant for opponents than they expected.
- "Safety valves" that allowed the most determined opponents to avoid some of the consequences of its success.
- A movement for social change with leadership that recognized the futility of violence (at least in this case—I would not care to argue that violence is always futile).
- An organization capable of enforcing discipline, keeping its members committed to nonviolence in the face of egregious provocation, while isolating and immobilizing potentially violent dissenters.
- Potential outside allies for the movement who could deploy overwhelming deterrent force, without the movement's having to do so itself.

This last condition is particularly important, not only to prevent the escalation of violence in the course of the movement, but in its implications for whatever process of reconciliation takes place subsequently. But that's another issue.

REFERENCES

Black, M. (1979, Summer). The modification of a major cultural belief: Declining support for "strict segregation" among White southerners, 1961–1972. *Journal of the North Carolina Political Science Association, 1*, 4–21.

Black, M., & Reed, J. S. (1985, Fall). How southerners gave up Jim Crow. *New Perspectives, 17*(4), 15–19.

Brown, R. M. (1981). Southern violence vs. the civil rights movement, 1954–1968. In M. Black & J. S. Reed (Eds.), *Perspectives on the American South: An annual review of society, politics and culture* (Vol. 1, p. 54). New York: Gordon and Breach Science.

Greeley, A. M. (1974). *Building coalitions.* New York: New Viewpoints.

Greeley, A. M., & Sheatsley, P. B. (1971, December). Attitudes toward racial integration. *Scientific American,* pp. 13–19.

Hyman, H. H., & Sheatsley, P. B. (1964, July). Attitudes toward desegregation. *Scientific American,* pp. 16–23.

Matthews, D. R., & Prothro, J. W. (1966). *Negroes and the new southern politics.* New York: Harcourt, Brace & World.

Myrdal, G. (1944). *An American dilemma: The Negro problem and modern democracy.* New York: Harper.

Nevin, D., & Bills, R. E. (1976). *The schools that fear built: Segregationist academies in the South.* Washington, DC: Acropolis Books.

Pettigrew, T. F. (1972). Regional differences in anti-Negro prejudice. In J. C. Brigham & T. A. Weissbach (Eds.), *Racial attitudes in America* (p. 162). New York: Harper & Row.

Phillips, U. B. (1928, October). The central theme of southern history. *American Historical Review, 34*(1), 31.

Reed, J. S. (1983). *Southerners: The social psychology of sectionalism.* Chapel Hill: University of North Carolina Press.

Reed, J. S. (1984, Summer). Up from segregation. *Virginia Quarterly Review, 60*, 377–393.

Reed, J. S. (1997, Spring). The Cherokee princess in the family tree. *Southern Cultures, 3*, 111–113.

Rindfuss, R. R., Reed, J. S., & St. John, C. (1978). A fertility reaction to a historical event: White southern birthrates and the 1954 desegregation decision. *Science*, *201*(14), 178–180.

Schwartz, M. A. (1967). *Trends in White attitudes toward Black people*. Chicago: National Opinion Research Center

Sheatsley, P. B. (1967). White attitudes toward the Negro. In T. Parsons & K. B. Clark (Eds.), *The Negro American* (pp. 303–304). Boston: Beacon Press.

V

THE SOCIAL PSYCHOLOGY OF ETHNOPOLITICAL WARFARE AND PSYCHOLOGY'S CONTRIBUTIONS TO THE SOLUTIONS

18

ETHNOPOLITICAL AND OTHER GROUP VIOLENCE: ORIGINS AND PREVENTION

ERVIN STAUB

Genocide, mass killing, and lesser violence between groups of people is ancient, but they have reappeared and become widespread in the second half of the 20th century. What kind of violence are we talking about? *Genocide*, as defined by the U.N. Genocide Convention, December 9, 1948, consists of "acts committed with intent to destroy in whole or in part, a national, ethnical, racial or religious group." Political groups were not included because of the objections of the Soviet Union and other nations. They did not want interference in how they treated political dissidents and opponents. Some scholars consider such acts against political groups genocide, others call it *politicide* (Harff & Gurr, 1990) or *democide* (Rummell, 1994).

I regard *mass killing* as killing large numbers of people, usually members of some group, without the intent to destroy the whole group. But because genocide often evolves, mass killing can be a way station toward genocide. Often violence between groups does not reach the proportion of mass killing, or it does only if considered over a long time period. In the extended conflict in Northern Ireland "only" about 3,000 people were killed between the mid-1960s and 1998 (Cairns & Darby, 1998). Although the dividing line in such group violence is often ethnic, as already noted, it can be racial, religious, national, or political as well. Regardless of how group lines are drawn, there can be substantial communality in the influences leading to such violence. In this chapter I discuss the origins of group violence and briefly its prevention.

To understand the origins of group violence requires a multidisciplinary approach. It requires a conception that considers social conditions, culture, the political system, and group and individual psychology. I developed such a conception based on the analysis of four instances of group violence: the

289

Holocaust, the genocide of the Armenians, the "autogenocide" in Cambodia, and the disappearances in Argentina (Staub, 1989a). I later applied this conception to other cases, like the mass killing in Bosnia (Staub, 1996a) and the genocide in Rwanda (Staub, 1999).

I briefly describe this conception here, with some extensions and some specification of the role of psychological processes in leading to group violence. I only occasionally include examples of how principles or processes apply in particular instances. After a brief discussion of prevention (Staub, 1996b, 1999), I apply the conception to the understanding of instances in which instigators to group violence were present but did not lead to intense violence.

THE ORIGINS OF GROUP VIOLENCE

Social conditions within a group can be a starting point for group violence. Difficult life conditions, consisting of intense economic problems, political conflict and disorganization, or great social–political changes, often lead groups to turn against others. These conditions have important psychological consequences. They frustrate fundamental human needs, including the need for security (to feel that one's body will be free of harm and that one will be able to provide for oneself and one's family), for a positive identity, for positive connections to other people, and for a feeling of effectiveness and control over important events in one's life.

Difficult life conditions make people insecure and afraid; they make people ineffective and weaken their identity; they create disconnection as everyone focuses on the satisfaction of their own needs. Another fundamental need is to have a "usable" worldview or comprehension of reality. When societal chaos and great change frustrate this need, people will seek a new comprehension of reality. These needs demand satisfaction, and people will turn to any possible means to satisfy them. Severe life problems in a society tend to give rise to psychological and social processes that provide destructive satisfaction of these needs, in that they do not address the underlying problems, which may be complex and difficult to change, and they lead the group to turn against others.

In difficult times people tend to turn to some group for identity and connection. Although this is not inherently destructive, it becomes so as the group scapegoats some other group for life problems. Scapegoating provides an illusion of understanding the reasons for life problems, reduces a feeling of one's own and one's group's responsibility, and thereby strengthens identity and creates connection among those who scapegoat. There is usually also an ideology that the group turns to, a vision of the world that offers hope. People need positive visions, especially in difficult times. But the ideology becomes destructive as an enemy is identified who is seen as standing in the way of the ideology's fulfillment. The scapegoated group is usually this enemy.

There is almost always an ideology involved in group violence. Sometimes it is a "better-world" ideology (Staub, 1989a), like communism, which offers a vision for improving the life of all human beings. At other times it is a nationalist ideology, its focus the creation of a new nation or greater power, wealth, influence, or purity of the nation. Often the ideology has both components, as did the Nazi ideology. Its racial principle implied that eliminating lower races, like Jews, would improve not only the life of Germans but of all humanity beyond those who are destroyed. The principle of the Germans' right to living space, which meant the territory of others, was a purely nationalistic element.

Another starting point for violence is conflict between groups. This is likely to lead to group violence when it involves vital interests, like land to live on, as in the Israeli–Palestinian conflict, or develops out of a history of antagonism and violence. Frequently, both are present, which makes the resolution of conflict especially difficult.

A history of antagonism often creates an "ideology of antagonism" (Staub, 1989a). This refers to a view of the other as an enemy bent on one's destruction, a view of one's own group as an enemy of the other, and at least an implicit belief that the world would be a better place without the existence of the other group. An ideology of antagonism makes it difficult to negotiate with the other in good faith and makes groups unwilling to make concessions required for resolving conflict. It even leads groups to accept suffering in order to impose greater suffering on the other.

A very important source of group violence is conflict between superordinate and subordinate groups. Subordination can be based on ethnicity, religion, class, caste, political history, and so on. Groups have often peacefully lived for very long periods of time with discrimination that limited their rights, opportunities, and education and as a result their well-being. Historically, in many societies, ideologies, visions of life and the world, or "hierarchy legitimizing myths" (Levin, Sidanius, Rabinowitz, & Frederica, 1998) have been in place, held by those in power and to various extents accepted by those with less power. To be consistent with my other terminology, I call these *legitimizing ideologies*. Sometimes it is when repression in a society has eased (Staub & Rosenthal, 1994) that feelings of injustice intensify and give rise to demands for greater rights and opportunities. Superordinate groups tend to react to this with violence. According to one analysis, conflict between subordinate and superordinate groups has been the most frequent source of genocide since World War II (Fein, 1993).

Finally, at times the motivation for group violence develops out of self-interest. A dominant group may want the land of a minority. Often this minority is on the fringes of the society. However, even in these instances many of the elements that contribute to genocide that I discuss are present: devaluation of the group, the evolution of violence, and so on.

For example, Native Americans in the United States were seen as profoundly inferior to White people. As they responded to violence against them, they came to be seen as highly dangerous. There were many actions taken to change their culture, "civilize" them, and then to relocate them. As they resisted, increasing violence was used against them. The ideology of manifest destiny was an implicit and sometimes explicit underpinning of these actions (Sheehan, 1973).

The Evolution of Violence

Difficult life conditions, scapegoating and ideologies, group conflict, or self-interest turn a group against another. But individuals and groups change as a result of their actions (Staub, 1989a, 1989b). As members of a group begin to harm members of another group or there is mutual harm-doing, psychological and social changes make it more likely that harm-doing increases. Harming other people has to be justified. Supported by the widely held belief that the world is a just place (Lerner, 1980), perpetrators come to see the people they harm as deserving their fate, because of their actions, their character, or both. The "higher" ideals of the ideology are used to further justify actions against them. Devaluation becomes progressively more intense, until the victims are excluded from the moral and human universe (Opotow, 1990; Staub, 1990). The usual moral rules become inapplicable to them. Commitment by the perpetrators to their ideology and violent course also intensify.

Accompanying these psychological changes are changes in social norms that makes harmful action against the victim group acceptable or even praiseworthy. People who are especially hostile to the victim group move into dominant positions (Merkl, 1980). Institutions change or new ones are created to serve violence. With "steps along a continuum of destruction," the society moves toward increasing violence.

Cultural Characteristics

Certain characteristics of the culture and the political system make the process I described more likely. This is a probabilistic conception: The greater the number and intensity of the relevant characteristics, the more probable that instigating conditions will lead to group violence. An extremely important characteristic is cultural devaluation, a history of devaluation of a group of people in a society. The division between "us" and "them" is a profound human potential or even proclivity. The devaluation of particular groups frequently becomes embedded in a culture (Fein, 1979; Staub, 1989a). This in turn preselects groups as scapegoats or ideological enemies. Devaluation can vary in intensity and has the potential to lead to violence. Members of a group can be seen as lazy and stupid, as morally bad or even evil, or as an enemy bent on one's destruction. These make harmful actions against the other increasingly likely. Ideologies of antagonism embody the most intense forms of devaluation.

Other important cultural characteristics include a past history of the use of violence to deal with difficult life conditions and group conflict and certain kinds of group self-concepts. Both a feeling of vulnerability and weakness and a sense of superiority, which may hide vulnerability, strengthen the instigating power of life problems. Strong respect for authority is another important characteristic. Germans, Turks, and Cambodians (Staub, 1989a), as well as Serbs (Kressel, 1996) and Rwandese (Smith, 1998), have been characterized as having strong respect for and obedience to authority. This makes it less likely that people will oppose leaders who promote hostility and violence.

The same is true of a monolithic rather than pluralistic society, with a limited range of acceptable values and limited public participation in societal processes. This is consistent with the view that democracies, which are pluralistic and less authority oriented, are less likely to engage in genocide or mass killing (Rummel, 1994). But this view must be qualified, in that its seems mainly true of "mature" democracies. There are many quasi-democratic states, like Argentina before 1980, where the military frequently assumed power (Staub, 1989a), and other South American countries where many groups had been excluded from participation.

The presence of unhealed wounds from past victimization is another important predisposing characteristic. Members of victimized groups tend to have vulnerable, damaged identities and to see the world as a dangerous place. In the case of group conflict this makes it extremely difficult for them to consider the other's legitimate needs. Conflict and threat easily give rise to what they see as defensive violence (Staub, 1999).

Followers and Leaders

In analyzing the origins of group violence I have focused on the important role of followers (Staub, 1989b). There are always potentially extreme leaders, but it is the combination of instigating conditions, cultural characteristics, and the material and psychological needs they create in a population that makes members of a group especially open and responsive to scapegoating, destructive ideologies, and other violence-generating leadership. I still believe this. However, the role of leaders is also important. While the range of leadership accepted by a population will be restricted by culture and social conditions, including group conflict, except under the most extreme conditions leaders still usually have some room to move.

It is frequently leaders and the elite of a country who propagate scapegoating and destructive ideologies. They often create paramilitary organizations, which have been important in most instances of group violence, including in Germany, Turkey, Argentina, Bosnia, and Rwanda, or involve the military in such violence. They use extensive fear- and hate-generating propaganda, such as the radio programs in Rwanda depicting the Tutsi as ready to destroy the Hutus (des Forges, 1999; Kressel, 1996; Prunier, 1995; Smith, 1998).

Conventional thinking has been that leaders turn the group against others to gain or strengthen their leadership and to increase cohesion in the group (Allport, 1954/1979). But this seems only part of the story. Leaders are members of their group and, like followers, are affected by social and cultural conditions. They may also carry unhealed wounds both as members of their group and in their personal history. For example, family members of some of the Serb leaders in Bosnia were killed in the mass killing of Serbs by Croatia during World War II.

Fear, Panic, and Their Evolution *Rwanda*

At times a group and/or its leaders seem to develop intense fear of their intended victim. Fear and the strong belief that one needs to protect oneself from the other are among the psychological elements generated by the varied influences that contribute to group violence. Persistent, intensely difficult life conditions profoundly threaten security. They focus on the self they create, so that people do not support each other, and the general chaos and disorganization, make the threat even greater. A whole people may feel deeply vulnerable, and fearful. Scapegoating and ideology channel and further intensify this fear as they direct it toward another group. They also contribute to it by diverting attention and energy from working on real solutions to life problems. Positive visions that help people join in working for real solutions are likely to increase security and diminish fear. Ideologies not only intensify fear but add hate to them. The enemy stands in the way of creating a better life for the group and for all humanity.

In cases of group conflict, fear of another group may be present from the start. When there is mutual violence, the harm inflicted on one's group adds to fear and hatred. But even here ideology usually intensifies these. The Turks scapegoated the Armenians as they experienced intense losses during World War I. They also created a pan-Turkish ideology that envisioned the creation of a new, great Turkish state (Gokalp, 1920/1968). They saw the Armenians as standing in the way of the ideology's fulfillment, both because of the area they lived in within Turkey and by their demands for greater rights.

The psychological components of the evolution of increasing violence also intensify fear and hatred. As harm-doing is justified, devaluation of the victim becomes more extreme and more fear-generating. As violence intensifies, the possibility of retaliation may also increase fear.

The Role of Bystanders   *Difference of bystanders in India + Rwanda*

A final crucial influence on the development of intense violence is the behavior of bystanders. Over time, perpetrators become increasingly committed to their views and course of action. Only bystanders, witnesses who are not directly involved, can stop them.

Unfortunately, members of the population who are not themselves perpetrators usually remain passive. As they follow the dictates of the system, which at times include acts of hostility toward the victims, they also change and evolve. Increasing numbers of them become perpetrators (Browning, 1992; Staub, 1989b). Outside groups, including nations, often remain passive and continue with business as usual in relation to a perpetrator nation. This has important psychological effects. Perpetrators see it as affirmation and support (Taylor, 1983).

The passivity of nations is in part due to defining their "interests" in terms of power, wealth, and influence. It is also due to nations historically not seeing themselves as moral agents responsible for the welfare of people outside their borders. And it is due to an international system that since the treaty of Westphalia has stressed nonintervention as a way of avoiding war. But it also due to psychological factors. Like perpetrators, bystanders tend to devalue victims (Lerner, 1980), seeing them as having brought their suffering on themselves by their actions or character. As they remain passive, they tend to psychologically distance themselves from victims, in order to reduce their guilt as well as their empathic distress.

At times, because of long-term historical ties, or driven by their definition of national interest, bystander nations actively support perpetrators, as the United States and much of the world supported Iraq before its invasion of Kuwait. At other times nations create conditions that lead to ethnic violence or mass killing and then do nothing to reverse the consequences of their actions. An example of this is the U.S. invasion of Guatemala in 1954, which was followed by support for the extremely violent dictatorships there (Comas-Diaz, Lykes, & Alarcon, 1998).

HALTING AND PREVENTING GROUP VIOLENCE

Bystander Actions

Bystanders, especially the United Nations, international organizations, and the community of nations, has a central responsibility to halt violence once it begins. This requires early warning and agencies to gather and disseminate information. Conceptions like the one I advanced here, or others (Bond & Vogele, 1995; Charney, 1991; Harff & Gurr, 1990), can help to determine what is relevant information. However, early warning often does not lead to a response. Information by Human Rights Watch about impending violence and a report to the United Nations from the head of its peacekeeping operations in Rwanda about plans for genocide led to no action (des Forges, 1999; Smith, 1998). A system that activates responses to incoming information is essential.

A sequence of actions is required. The earlier the response, the earlier in the sequence can actions begin. First, there should be private communication to leaders, at times to leaders of both parties, offering help with mediation and material support, but also specifying consequences of further violence. If this is ineffective, public condemnation should follow, then sanctions and boycotts (focusing as much as possible on the leaders, such as freezing their foreign bank accounts—see the Carnegie Commission on the Prevention of Deadly Conflict, 1997) and, as a last resort, military action. However, early, sensitive, as well as resolute responses are likely to make the use of force unnecessary.

Healing and Reconciliation

Victimized groups tend to see the world as dangerous and others outside the group as hostile. They are likely to react to renewed threat with violence, which they see as defensive (Staub, 1996b, 1999, 2000). To make this less likely, to break a continuing cycle of violence, it is important to help victimized groups heal. Frequently, both parties need to heal. At times victimization is mutual, and even if it is not, perpetrators often feel like victims as well. This may be because they had previously been victimized, or because there has been some violence directed at them in response to their violence, or because inflicting violence on others is wounding (Staub, 1999). It is also the case that perpetrators need to justify their actions. They do this to others as well as themselves, by describing their victims as a perpetrator against them and a source of continuing threat.

Nonetheless, both parties may need to heal. Healing is furthered by the world acknowledging a group's suffering, showing empathy and caring. Members of a group joining to talk about their pain and suffering and participating in certain kinds of testimonials and ceremonies can also be healing. Truth commissions and tribunals that establish what was done to the group and the punishment of at least important perpetrators can increase feelings of safety and justice and promote healing (Staub, 1998, 1999).

Contact, Dialogue, Conflict Resolution, and Reconciliation

Significant contact between previously hostile groups can help overcome hostility. Superficial contact does not do this. But deep engagement can help people see the humanity of the other. Addressing prior hurts, pain, and violence that the groups have inflicted on each other, and members of the groups assuming responsibility for their group's actions and showing empathy to each other, can be extremely helpful (Volkan, 1988). Joint problem solving can lead to the resolution of real-life issues and further connection and trust (Fisher, 1997; Kelman, 1990). Setting shared goals and joining to fulfill them, ranging from rebuilding villages, to helping children heal, to joint business ventures, can be important sources of contact. All these activities can further reconciliation, which in turns facilitates healing.

CULTURE CHANGES AND DEMOCRATIZATION

Changing a group's culture is important for prevention. However, their culture is experienced as natural and right by people. They rarely set out to intentionally change it and rarely welcome efforts by others to do so. Still, at least some groups are open to intentional efforts at democratization. Promoting democracy is one possible avenue to significant cultural change. As democracy evolves and deepens, the culture becomes more pluralistic, more accepting of varied values and perspectives. Obedience to authority becomes less intense. As all groups are admitted to the public domain and participate in the life of the society, devaluation, and discrimination which maintains devaluation, diminish.

Following the collapse of communism, Eastern European societies have been open to receiving help in building the institutions of civil society, including the development of nongovernmental organizations (Sampson, 1996). Bystanders can help develop a group's justice system, free media (Manoff, 1996), even an effective system of political parties. They can help develop ways to educate children in responsible citizenship.

Whether with help from outsiders or through internal processes, it is important for societies to develop positive visions that connect rather than separate subgroups. It is important for them to help people experience community and connection in ways that do not generate enmity. To the extent that ethnic, religious, or political groups are not their only source of identity, people will be less likely to go along with violent practices by them. Helping groups with economic development that reduces poverty and suffering is also important. This is a focus of the U.N. development efforts (Carnegie Commission, 1997). However, although economic development is important, in a greatly changing world, it is not enough. People need at least minimum satisfaction of all their basic needs and support and connection in dealing with social and technological change.

WHEN INSTIGATION DOES NOT RESULT IN MASS MURDER

Ethnic, religious, political, or national groups can coexist, as they do in Switzerland and in the United States. In Tanzania, in contrast to the rest of Africa, ethnic groups have lived together harmoniously. This is in part because there are a number of groups, and none has been dominant. Also, the different groups live in the periphery of the country with relatively limited contact. In addition, until recently, government policy has actively prohibited ethnic association and organization (Young, 1998).

Inattention to past violence between groups and to the resulting wounds may be a serious problem, as in the case of the former Yugoslavia, where Marshal Tito maintained such a policy. Prohibiting ethnic association creates some danger when the policy is lifted and other circumstances change; the earlier prohibition intensifies the focus on ethnicity. In Tanzania, there has recently been such an increased focus. Probably the best policy is to create structures that protect each group's rights and interests, foster connections, promote shared goals, and provide education about each other.

The conception I advanced offers explanation for why instigating conditions at times do not lead to group violence. Less intense instigating conditions, weaker cultural predisposing characteristics, more positive behavior of leaders, and less use of scapegoating and destructive ideologies—partly perhaps because of the nature of cultural characteristics—all may have a role. Active bystanders seem especially important.

So are preventive efforts, whether naturally occurring or intentionally created, like the existence and creation of positive contact between groups as ways to overcome past antagonism, as well as societal healing. Given such efforts there can be a positive evolution, which prepares groups for creating agreements and developing structures for the resolution of conflict. Both with regard to causation and the avoidance or prevention of group violence, this is a probabilistic conception: The presence and intensity of certain conditions affects the likelihood of evolution either toward violence or positive relations. Important research is to be done in carefully evaluating the degree of presence of all these conditions both in cases of mass murder and their absence. Here I will briefly look at a few instances.

When instigating conditions exist and/or an evolution toward mass killing has already started, the role of bystanders appears highly significant in halting it. In South Africa, the international boycott had great importance. Preceding this, South Africans, who are very sports minded, were made constantly aware by the exclusion of South African athletes from international events that the world disapproved of apartheid. As the boycotts proceeded, the business community, unwilling to be ruined, supported the abolition of apartheid (Pogrund, 1991). The business community had been deeply engaged with the West and was therefore probably not only materially but also psychologically affected by the boycotts.

The actions of one particular bystander were also significant. The husband of a friend of Winnie Mandela, a White South African lawyer, took it upon himself to influence his friend, the justice minister Jacobus Coetsee, to see Nelson Mandela in a different light and initiate contact with him (Sparks, 1994). The character of Mandela, as it later showed itself to the world, and as it appeared to Coetsee on their first meeting, was also important. It is likely to have led to greater trust by members of the government in engaging with him and the movement he represented.

The role of positive leadership was also important, particularly the leadership of F. W. De Klerk, who started his presidency by legalizing Black liberation organizations and their sympathizers, which had been outlawed for 30 years. But such leadership in part depends on public attitudes and moods, as are affected by the behavior of bystanders and by the existence of like-minded others, like Coetsee.

In Bosnia, the limited military intervention by NATO stopped the fighting and killing. Continued involvement by NATO and the United States in peace negotiations and in peacekeeping efforts led to a peace agreement, giving Bosnia a chance to halt a continuing cycle of violence. There are ongoing efforts by outside groups to create positive connections among members of the different ethnic and religious groups, bringing them together for dialogue, problem solving, and other joint efforts. There are many efforts as well to help people heal from the effects of the violence and destruction. Mostly these efforts are directed at individuals: More group approaches to healing are required (Staub, 2000).

In Northern Ireland there have been centuries of violence between Protestants and Catholics. In 1921 the primarily Catholic Republic of Ireland was established. After that, many Catholics in the remaining Northern Ireland, which continued to be part of the United Kingdom, wanted to join the Republic, and many Protestants wanted continuing union with Great Britain.

The most recent cycle of violence began in the mid-1960s. Although the bombings, the destruction of buildings, and the killing of people was highly destructive to the morale of the society, "only" 3,000 people were killed and about 30,000 injured. A strong British military presence helped prevent escalation. So did a strong police presence, with a substantial increase in the number of police and with military personnel the police could call on (Cairns & Darby, 1998). Military, police, and other authorities also managed to control the inflow of arms. Restraint by the British military helped to not inflame the situation.

The nature of leadership, which in part emanated from London, was also very important. Inequalities have been reduced, with Catholics gaining improved housing and employment. Many efforts have existed at the community level and in schools to create contact between groups. All this prepared the ground for negotiations and the ensuing agreement in 1998.

Bystanders, third parties, had a very important role in this as well. The British Prime Minister was deeply engaged. Former U.S. Senator George Mitchell mediated talks between the parties, and President Bill Clinton provided support and encouragement. It was important as well that most of the parties, including those that had participated in the fighting, participated in the talks. They had a voice, they could represent their constituencies and then work with them on behalf of the agreement. It is instructive that the violence that followed on the agreement was primarily initiated by marginal groups not included in the negotiations (personal communication from the Director of Initiative on Conflict Resolution and Ethnicity to Mari Fitzduff, August 1998).

Although Jews and Arabs fought several wars, the violence between Jews and Palestinians in Israel and the West Bank remained limited in scale. The continuous involvement of the United States, its engagement, may have had an important role in this. Initially Israel and subsequently both Israel and Palestinians needed the United States for support and mediation. The watchful eyes of others is crucial in limiting group violence. Nations as bystanders, like the United States and the Norway in the Oslo accords, have also been crucial in bringing the parties together for peace negotiations.

In addition, Israel is a democratic country with a plurality of values and points of view. Many voices have urged peace and accommodation with Palestinians. Many groups have worked to create contact and educate the groups about each other (Rouhana & Bar-Tal, 1998). For example, in the Israeli village of Neve, Shalom Jews, Israeli Muslim Arabs, and Christian Arabs live together. This village brought many young people together for contact and shared education about the other. For many years outside parties have also brought Jews and Palestinians together, in dialogue groups, conflict resolution workshops, and the like. The best known, at least among psychologists, have been the problem-solving workshops of Herbert Kelman and his associates (Kelman, 1990; Rouhana & Kelman, 1994). Graduates of these groups have later been involved in the peace negotiations as advisers and even participants.

In the American South, at the time of the civil rights movement, bystanders were very important in limiting violence. The physical presence of the national guard and military was important in inhibiting violence, but so was their symbolic role as representatives of the U.S. government and its people. Contrast this with the history of the approximately 5,000 lynchings in the South in the second part of the last century and the first part of this one (U.S. Bureau of Census, 1960), with local people frequently watching and encouraging the lynchers, who would remain unpunished (Ginzburg, 1988).

Preceding the civil rights movement, contact with Black people within the military and around the military bases in the South began to diminish devaluation and hostility by many White people. The Supreme Court decision on desegregation and other national legislation began to change the national climate. Just as violence evolves step by step, so does the possibility of constructive, positive relations between groups.

TOWARD THE 21ST CENTURY

The pace of technological, cultural, and social change in the world is tremendous, deeply affecting people and frustrating basic needs. Without significant preventive and ameliorative efforts, people are likely to continue to turn to ethnic or other "identity" groups and to ideologies for identity, connection, and a hopeful vision of life. In addition, in the age of television and other telecommunication, people become aware of their poverty and relative deprivation, as well as the possibility of better lives. An expanding vision of individual and group rights strengthens their perception of injustice and their belief in their right to better lives. Because they are likely to see this in group terms, they are likely to demand greater rights and privileges for their group, threatening the interests and identity of dominant groups and their worldview or legitimizing ideology. The potential for group conflict leading to violence will, therefore, be great. The kind of preventive efforts I have briefly outlined are essential for the creation of a more peaceful century than the one we have left behind.

REFERENCES

Allport, G. W. (1979). *The nature of prejudice*. Reading, MA: Addison-Wesley. (Original work published 1954)

Bond, D., & Vogele, W. (1995). *Profiles of international hotspots.* Unpublished manuscript, Harvard University, Center for International Affairs, Program on Nonviolent Sanctions and Cultural Survival.

Browning, C. R. (1992). *Ordinary men: Reserve Battalion 101 and the Final Solution in Poland.* New York: HarperCollins.

Cairns, E., & Darby, J. (1998). The conflict in Northern Ireland. *American Psychologist, 53,* 754–760.

Carnegie Commission on the Prevention of Deadly Conflict. (1997). *Preventing deadly conflict: Final report.* New York: Carnegie Corporation.

Charney, I. (1991). Genocide: Intervention and prevention. *Social Education,* pp. 124–127.

Comas-Diaz, L., Lykes, M. B., & Alarcon, R. D. (1998). Ethnic conflict and the psychology of liberation in Guatemala, Peru, and Puerto Rico. *American Psychologist, 53,* 778–792.

des Forges, A. (1999). *Leave none to tell the story: Genocide in Rwanda.* New York: Human Rights Watch.

Fein, H. (1979). *Accounting for genocide: Victims and survivors of the Holocaust.* New York: Free Press.

Fein, H. (1993). Accounting for genocide after 1945: Theories and some findings. *International Journal of Group Rights, 1,* 79–106.

Fisher, R. J. (1997). *Interactive conflict resolution.* Syracuse, NY: Syracuse University Press.

Ginzburg, R. (1988). *100 years of lynching.* Baltimore, MD: Black Classic Press.

Gokalp, Z. (1968). *The principles of Turkism.* Leiden, Germany: A.J. Brill. (Original work published 1920).

Harff, B., & Gurr, T. R. (1990). Victims of the state genocides, politicides and group repression since 1945. *International Review of Victimology, 1,* 1–19.

Kelman, H. C. (1990). Applying a human needs perspective to the practice of conflict resolution: The Israeli–Palestinian Case. In J. Burton (Ed.), *Conflict: Human needs theory.* New York: St. Martin's Press.

Kressel, N. J. (1996). *Mass hate: The global rise of genocide and terror.* New York: Plenum Press.

Lerner, M. (1980). *The belief in a just world: A fundamental delusion.* New York: Plenum Press.

Levin, S., Sidanius, J., Rabinowitz, J. L., & Frederica, L. (1998). Ethnic identity, legitimizing ideologies and social status: A matter of ideological asymmetry. *Political Psychology, 18,* 373–404.

Manoff, R. (1996). *The mass media and social violence: Is there a role for the media in preventing and moderating ethnic, national, and religious conflict?* Unpublished manuscript, New York University, Center for War, Peace, and News Media, Department of Journalism and Mass Communication.

Merkl, P. H. (1980). *The making of a stormtrooper.* Princeton, NJ: Princeton University Press.

Opawa, S. (Ed.). (1990). Moral exclusion and injustice. *Journal of Social Issues, 46*(1).

Pogrund, B. (1991). *The transformation in South Africa.* (Lecture). University of Massachusetts, Department of Journalism.

Prunier, G. (1995). *Rwanda.* New York: Columbia University Press.

Rouhana, N. N., & Bar-Tal, D. (1998). Psychological dynamics of intractable ethno-national conflicts: The Israeli–Palestinian case. *American Psychologist, 53,* 761–770.

Rouhana, N. N., & Kelman, H. C. (1994). Promoting joint thinking in international conflicts: An Israeli–Palestinian continuing workshop. *Journal of Social Issues, 50,* 157–178.

Rummel, R. J. (1994). Democide in totalitarian states: Mortacracies and mega-murderers. In I. W. Charny (Ed.), *Widening circle of genocide* (Genocide: A Critical Bibliographic Review 3, pp. 7–9). New Brunswick, NJ: Transaction.

Sampson, S. (1996). The social life of projects: Importing civil society to Albania. In C. Hann & E. Dunn (Eds.), *Civil society: Challenging western models.* New York: Routledge.

Sheehan, B. (1973). *Seeds of extinction.* Chapel Hill: University of North Carolina Press.

Smith, N. S. (1998). The psycho-cultural roots of genocide. *American Psychologist, 53,* 743–753.

Sparks, A. (1994, April). Letter from South Africa: The secret revolution. *The New Yorker,* pp. 56–89.

Staub, E. (1989a). *The roots of evil: The origins of genocide and other group violence.* New York: Cambridge University Press.

Staub, E. (1989b). Steps along the continuum of destruction: The evolution of bystanders: German psychoanalysts and lessons for today. *Political Psychology, 10,* 39–53.

Staub, E. (1990). The psychology and culture of torture and torturers. In P. Suedfeld (Ed.), *Psychology and torture.* Washington, DC: Hemisphere.

Staub, E. (1996a). The cultural–societal roots of violence: The examples of genocidal violence and of contemporary youth violence in the United States. *American Psychologist, 51,* 117–132.

Staub, E. (1996b). Preventing genocide: Activating bystanders, helping victims and the creation of caring. *Peace and Conflict: Journal of Peace Psychology, 2,* 189–201.

Staub, E. (1998). Breaking the cycle of genocidal violence: Healing and reconciliation. In J. Harvey (Ed.), *Perspectives on loss: A sourcebook* (pp. 231–241). Philadelphia: Taylor & Francis.

Staub, E. (1999). The origins and prevention of genocide and mass killing. *Peace and Conflict: Journal of Peace Psychology, 5*(4), 303–336.

Staub, E. (2000). Genocide and mass killing: Origins, prevention, healing, and reconciliation. *Political Psychology, 21*(2), 367–383.

Staub, E., & Rosenthal, L. (1994). Mob violence: Social–cultural influences, group processes, and participants. In *Commission on violence and youth* (Vol. 2, pp. 281–315). Washington, DC: American Psychological Association.

Taylor, F. (Ed.). (1988). *The Goebbels diaries: 1939–1941.* New York: Putnam.

U.S. Bureau of Census. (1960). *Historical statistics of the United States: Colonial times to 1957.* Washington, DC: U.S. Government Printing Office.

Volkan, V. D. (1988). *The need to have enemies and allies.* Northvale, NY: Jason Aronson.

Young, C. (1998, June–July). *How has Tanzania maintained ethnic peace in a troubled region?* Presentation at the conference on Ethno-Political Warfare: Causes and Solutions, Derry/Londonderry, Northern Ireland.

19

PSYCHOSOCIAL ASSISTANCE DURING ETHNOPOLITICAL WARFARE IN THE FORMER YUGOSLAVIA

INGER AGGER

During the recent war in the former Yugoslavia from 1991 to 1995, the first armed conflict in Europe since World War II, psychosocial assistance was offered on a large scale to the population as part of humanitarian aid. Of relevance for the understanding of why psychosocial projects became important elements in the humanitarian aid package at that time is the change in the concept of humanitarian aid that happened after the disintegration of the Soviet Union and the end of the Cold War around 1990.[1] In the countries and regions that had formerly been within the interest sphere of the Soviet Union, conflicts emerged in which the rights and problems of ethnic minorities became a central political issue in connection with the building of new states, as we saw in the case of the former Yugoslavia and Caucasus.

In the post–Cold War situation, the United Nations began to take on a much stronger responsibility for the prevention and resolution of conflicts as well as for peacekeeping and peace building, as expressed in 1992 by the U.N. Secretary-General Boutros Boutros-Ghali in his 1992 report, *An Agenda for Peace*. The activities mentioned by the Secretary-General included preventive diplomacy, to resolve disputes before violence breaks out; peacemaking and peace building, to attempt to halt conflicts and

I wish to convey my gratitude to the Area for Gender and Social Inequality at the Center for Development Research in Copenhagen for providing me with office facilities and financial support during the writing of this chapter.
[1] Because of the widespread armed conflicts in post-colonial areas, the psychological and social dimensions of refugee populations were also addressed during the 1980s in Africa and South East Asia (Save the Children Alliance, 1996).

preserve peace once it is attained; and finally, post-conflict peace building, to prevent the recurrence of violence and strengthen peace. This meant a whole new agenda for the United Nations and international peace work, which also included working with a new "tool box" of interventions that could facilitate peace building and conflict resolution (Schultz, 1994).

This development can be seen as part of a process in which aid donors have moved toward an increasing involvement in the "gray zone" between emergency and development aid in an effort to link short-term, humanitarian aid to long-term development assistance with the inclusion of "soft" areas such as the promotion of human rights, democracy, and good governance in their programs in an effort to secure stability and conditions for post-conflict development (Sperber, 1998; Stepputat, 1994). Psychosocial projects should be seen in the context of this trend, and they also fit nicely into the new orientation in aid policy toward "human resource development."

The war in the former Yugoslavia had the characteristics of a civil war and also of an ethnopolitical war, with ideologies of ethnicity being played out as part of war propaganda during and after the conflict. This European war confronted international humanitarian aid organizations with a new "complex emergency" context, caused in part to the high prewar standard of health, social welfare, and education. "The unusual nature of this context has forced aid agencies to adapt the operational procedures which they have developed in conflicts in developing countries" (World Health Organization [WHO] & Médecins Sans Frontières [MSF], 1995, p. 1). Many relief organizations developed new and specific techniques and models for intervention and programs. Among these were much more individualized approaches to psychosocial assistance. This was in keeping with the tradition of European mental health practice that was already well developed in these areas. This type of approach, which was generally "considered to be a valuable development, was made possible by the level of knowledge present at the local level in former Yugoslavia on which to build the new programmes" (WHO & MSF, 1995, p. 9). The introduction of large-scale psychosocial emergency assistance during the war merits reflection and evaluation: How can we use this experience to learn more about ethnopolitical warfare, people in crisis, and methods for assisting them?

THE TRAUMA OF ETHNOPOLITICAL WARFARE

The characteristics of civil wars where neighbor fights neighbor, and even relatives may be on different sides, have special long-lasting pernicious psychosocial effects. The most central issue is the loss of trust brought about through betrayal by the very people one knows and depends on in the immediate family and social network. However, people are also betrayed by their leaders, who are using and sacrificing them in political power struggles. The collective awareness of this contributes significantly to undermine the trust and belief in democratic processes.

In the former Yugoslavia there was a "powerful reservoir of traumatic memory" from World War II (Denich, 1994, p. 367) of the atrocities committed, which at that time also were fueled by ethnic ideology. This reservoir, which had existed for generations, enabled nationalist leaders to mobilize ethnic tensions and to harness these for political power agendas. Under these circumstances, it is especially important that trauma is understood not as a medical or psychiatric condition (Agger & Jensen, 1996), but as a reaction to an unimaginable betrayal of universal human ethics as expressed in the Universal Declaration of Human Rights and the Convention on the Rights of the Child. In the context of ethnopolitical conflicts, humanitarian interventions, therefore, need to have a high level of awareness of the psychological and social implications of this type of conflict, so as to avoid contributing to the sense of betrayal and lack of trust.

PSYCHOSOCIAL PROJECTS

The professional field involved in psychosocial projects cuts across the areas of mental health, human rights, social work, and education. "The term, 'psychosocial' attempts to express the recognition that there is always a close, ongoing circular interaction between an individual's psychological state and his or her social environment" (Bergh & Jareg, 1998, p. 13). The aims of psychosocial assistance under war conditions have been defined as "to promote human rights and mental health by strategies that support already existing protective social and psychological factors and diminish the stress or factors at different levels of intervention" (Agger, Vuk, & Mimica, 1995, p. 15).

In the former Yugoslavia, psychosocial work addressed several levels of intervention: (a) community development interventions such as establishing schooling and day care for refugee children; (b) network-strengthening interventions such as organizing knitting groups, language courses, or other types of occupational and educational activities; (c) mutual support-building interventions such as facilitating women's self-help groups and youth groups; (d) counseling interventions such as providing individual, family, or group consultation with a social worker around present problems and dilemmas; and (e) intensive psychotherapy interventions such as individual, family, or group therapy by psychologists and psychiatrists in which traumatic experiences were explored in more depth.

In recognition of the fact that most people exposed to traumatic experiences are living in countries where there are few or no mental health professionals (which is not the case in the former Yugoslavia), it is important to emphasize that there are many roads to recover from trauma and that there are no "right" or "wrong" levels of intervention, but there are certain overall aims that need to be followed: (a) the reestablishment of trust, (b) the reestablishment of self-esteem, (c) the opportunity to express feelings associated with traumatic experiences, (d) the reestablishment of attachment and networks, and (e) the regeneration of hope and belief in the future (Jareg, 1995). It is possible to address these aims at all levels of intervention, and the impact will be greatest when projects are addressing several levels simultaneously. In the development of projects, these aims can be discussed with participants in the process of developing the most appropriate interventions under the given circumstances.

WHY PSYCHOSOCIAL PROJECTS IN THE FORMER YUGOSLAVIA?

In the summer of 1991, war broke out in Slovenia and Croatia and, soon thereafter, the social and health infrastructures of former Yugoslavia were faced with thousands of refugees and internally displaced people fleeing the battlefields.[2] Although social welfare and health services were well developed at that time, they could not respond to the needs of so many desperate and distressed people who required all types of services: food, shelter, medical aid, and psychosocial assistance. The refugees consisted mainly of women, children, and elderly people, whereas the majority of the men stayed at the front lines as soldiers. The refugees were mostly accommodated with host families, but many in Croatia were also sheltered in tourist facilities along the Adriatic Coast.

The rest of the population showed a great deal of solidarity by receiving the refugees in their homes. However, the host families were also under stress—both economically and psychologically—from the emergency situation created by the war. It was obvious to the national mental health professionals that the refugees needed more support than the humanitarian aid and shelter they could receive from host families, centers for social welfare, and international aid organizations. Therefore, from as early as July 1991 in Croatia, the Mental Health Department of the Headquarters of the Medical Corps formulated a program for psychosocial assistance to refugees and began setting up a network of regional departments of mental health across Croatia (Moro & Vidovic, 1992).

---

[2] The information brought together in this section is based on a multitude of reports, papers, and other documents that I collected during the war.

A considerable number of national mental health professionals—psychologists, psychiatrists, social workers, and others—started addressing the psychosocial needs of refugees, attempting to help them in any way they could think of. However, they had both to establish new structures for the provision of such assistance and gain new knowledge about how to help traumatized people in the most appropriate way. Traditionally in former Yugoslavia, psychological and social services were provided through governmental institutions, and despite the presence of a relatively high number of mental health professionals, there were only a few who had work experience with war survivors. Those few were mostly working in specialized institutions with limited experience of mobile or large-scale emergency work. Moreover, there was only a rudimentary culture of providing community services through nongovernmental organizations (NGOs) or similar grassroots initiatives.

On the other side of the front line, in Serbia–Montenegro, national initiatives were also taken at an early stage to assist refugees arriving from Croatia. In July 1991, the Institute of Mental Health formed mobile teams of mental health professionals who visited refugee camps and started organizing one-day training seminars on "prevention and management of psychosocial consequences of war and crisis in children, adolescents and parents" (Ispanovic-Radojkovic, Bojanin, Rakic, & Lazic, 1993, p. 2). Generally, a great deal of the first national psychosocial emergency work was done on a voluntary basis, but gradually NGO structures began developing, and as international psychosocial projects started coming in, working in NGOs became a regular (and necessary) job for many national mental health professionals whose normal job opportunities were destroyed by the war.

During the first months of the war, not many international organizations included the issue of mental health and psychosocial assistance in their agenda. However, in November 1991 a joint appeal was issued by the U.N. High Commissioner for Refugees (UNHCR), the U.N. Children's Fund (UNICEF), and the WHO to raise funds for a program that should assist refugees and displaced people in the former Yugoslavia. Within this joint appeal, the WHO proposed, among other initiatives, immediate measures and interventions for mental health problems. UNICEF proposed to back up community-level initiatives and strengthen local social welfare services—specifically with respect to health and education needs of refugee women and children. This appeal was the first international initiative taken concerning the mental health of the war survivors.

During the second year of the war and concurrent with the extension of the war into Bosnia (in March 1992), international organizations gradually began establishing psychosocial programs for the war survivors. However, this effort underwent a radical change when notice of the war rapes hit the headlines of international media at the end of 1992.

THE ISSUE OF WAR RAPES

The media coverage of the war rapes was a turning point as far as psychosocial assistance is concerned. From then on—that is, from the beginning of 1993—international funding for mental health and psychosocial assistance began flowing into the region. However, already in December 1991, Croatian mental health professionals had learned about rape and torture when they interviewed refugees from Vukovar. At that time, coping with the overwhelming reality of torture and war, in general, did not allow the professionals to devote special attention to the issue of rape. Moreover, dealing with sexual abuse and rape was a rather unknown professional field in the former Yugoslavia (L. Moro, personal communication, 1996).

Shortly after the war in Bosnia broke out (in March 1994), news of the Bosnian war rapes also reached national mental health professionals. These professionals assisted Bosnian refugees in camps in Croatia, and they learned about the rapes along with the other gruesome details of torture related by the refugees (N. Sarajlic, personal communication, 1996). According to various observers, the practice of rape reached its peak during the months of May and June 1992 in connection with the intensive ethnic cleansing going on at that time in Bosnia. The international staff of the French NGO Partage offering psychosocial assistance to Bosnian refugees in camps in Croatia also learned about the rapes during the early summer of 1992, and French journalists were already writing about widespread raping at that time (C. Mazy, personal communication, 1996).

However, no large-scale international action was taken over the rapes until November–December 1992, when the rape issue suddenly hit the media headlines all over the world. The question of why this happened when it did is open to speculation. At that time, women's organizations around the world were making preparations for the U.N. World Conference on Human Rights to be held in June 1993, with the objective of placing sexual violence against women on the agenda (Richters, 1998). Probably, it was primarily these preparations combined with initiatives from the national women's movements in the former Yugoslavia, who collaborated with European and American feminist organizations, that brought the information on war rapes to the attention of a wider public, through which it also became a concern of international politicians and donors.

This development resulted in at least four investigative missions being sent to the war zone during December 1992 and January 1993, accompanied by a wave of journalists. A large number of international NGOs also began to arrive to assist rape survivors, and at one time it even seemed as if there were more NGOs trying to assist rape survivors than there were actual survivors to be found! Gradually, these NGOs reframed the objective of their projects, so that they offered assistance to war-traumatized women and children, in general, in the recognition of the multiple trauma of ethnopolitical warfare, such as loss of family members, life-threatening experiences, and torture.

In retrospect, the issue of the war rapes merits further reflection. At a conference, "Women's Discourses, War Discourses," which was held in Slovenia in December 1997, women from all the countries of the former Yugoslavia discussed how and why sexual violence became such a significant issue in the war. Among the explanations mentioned was the political manipulation with the number of victims—also called "the numbers game"—that lasted from the end of 1992 until the end of 1993. This numbers game was played by all parties in the conflict, including the international community, with estimations of numbers of rapes ranging from 10,000 to 100,000 women. It will never be known how many women (and men) were actually raped because of the various problems of collecting such data during war. However, there seemed both on the national and international level to be a political interest in constructing a "rape victim identity of ex-Yugoslav women"—an "image of a weak, voiceless woman whose body communicates her fate rather than her own ideas and words." This is an identity "which is compatible with stereotypical understandings of women" (Skjelsbaek, 1998, p. 13). It can probably be concluded that the war rape survivors were used—and abused—for a variety of political purposes which, however, does not deny the fact that children, women, and men were raped as part of the strategy of ethnic cleansing.

Whether there also was a national and international political interest in constructing a "trauma victim identity" of the ex-Yugoslav people merits further investigation and discussion. Recently, criticism has been raised against the export of models developed in Western psychiatry to war-torn areas in the developing countries (Bracken & Petty, 1998). The critique, which is based on a "culture discourse," fits into the eternal discussion among anthropologists about cultural relativism and universalism to which the anthropologist Clifford Geertz (1983) once remarked, "To see others as sharing a nature with ourselves is the merest decency!" (p. 16). The argument is also based on a very European "external–internal distinction," which understands cultures as separate, permanent "sociocultural wholes" neglecting "the shift in emphasis from bounded local culture to trans-national cultural flows" (Hastrup & Olwig, 1997, p. 2). Rather, anthropologists argue, culture should be explored "as a dynamic process of self-understanding among the people we study" (Hastrup & Olwig, 1997, p. 3). However, this is not to say that trauma projects should be exported uncritically to people who do not want them or need them.

This critique has also been directed toward the use of psychosocial projects as part of humanitarian relief during the war in the former Yugoslavia (Summerfield, 1996, 1998). As Summerfield rightly pointed out (1998,

p. 31), Bosnia is "Westernized"—as are the other Eastern European and former Soviet Union countries. It is, therefore, not relevant to use the culture argument here: Most mental health professionals from these countries would feel deeply offended if "we from the West" claimed that they were not part of "Western culture."

But we may ask—with Summerfield—if the context for psychosocial projects was right: Was there an expressed demand for this kind of service? There is a need for evaluating "how much client satisfaction has been a function of the mental health technologies deployed there, and how much of a social setting that provided for people to gather, share their problems with each other and muster collective solidarity at a time when many other facilities lay in ruins" (Summerfield, 1998, p. 32). Summerfield seemed to establish a strange contradiction between mental health assistance and social networking activities—a distinction that was not made by very many psychosocial projects—in fact, most of the activities were more "social" than "psycho," something that was an obvious need to most professionals working in the field.

In the following section, the results of an investigation in which my colleague and I (Agger & Mimica, 1996) actually attempted to address the above-mentioned questions are presented. The study was carried out in Bosnia and Croatia in 1995 during the last months of the war and involved the distribution of questionnaires to 2,291 participants and 165 national (and 2 international) staff members of psychosocial projects funded by the European Community Humanitarian Office (ECHO).

AN INVESTIGATION OF PSYCHOSOCIAL PROJECTS

Our study was carried out in the period from September 20 to December 9, 1995, that is, during the last months preceding the Dayton Peace Agreement of November 21, 1995, and two weeks thereafter. During that period, the peace process had already begun to move forward, and there was cautious optimism that the end of the war could be near. However, fighting was still going on in September 1995 and at the beginning of October 1995, particularly in Western Bosnia. NATO strikes were conducted against the Bosnian Serbs on October 4. On October 12 a cease-fire agreement was reached, which generally held throughout the rest of our data collection period. Thus, our study was carried out in a historical context that was slowly changing from war to peace, although not many dared believe that peace would really come. The objectives of the investigation were to assess the impact of nine psychosocial projects according to three previously defined criteria: (a) the impact of the projects on the emotional well-being of the participants; (b) the contribution of the projects to the integration of refugees and displaced people into their host communities; and (c) the contribution of the projects to development of the social infrastructure, that is, their long-term impact on social services provision in the communities.

We decided to carry out a large-scale quantitative study because this would give us a picture of important characteristics of the client and staff population, a picture that at that time was not at all clear in the midst of war and chaos. The main challenge was to develop an appropriate measuring technique that could provide us with information about beneficiaries and staff from quite different psychosocial projects that were aimed at particular, but also similar, goals. Effects of psychological treatment have always been difficult to assess, especially because psychological status is a dynamic category that is influenced by many factors among which treatment is only one. Our solution to this challenge was to use a method of self-reporting, choosing to trust that the participants are the best experts on their psychological condition. However, we also wanted to go a step beyond the technique of self-reporting, and therefore decided also to collect information from the staff working in the projects, by asking the staff to reflect on the issues of interventions and outcomes and provide us with their feedback.

Evidently, not all project activities have the same impact on different groups of participants. Because the psychosocial projects we studied offered a variety of activities, we also saw this study as a way to get an impression of which activities should be provided to various groups of participants based on their different needs. Therefore, we asked participants about which activities they themselves found most useful and compared their answers to the staff's answers to the same question.

To assess the impact of social factors within the host community and the way they influenced the reception, integration, and psychosocial healing (and/or obstacles to it) of refugees and displaced people, we studied psychosocial projects operating in seven highly differentiated regions with respect to safety, accommodation facilities, resources available for refugees, and so on. The sustainability and possible long-term effects, as well as the sociopolitical effects of the projects were also assessed, although only indirectly, through attitudes of the staff working in the projects. At the time of our study there was a consensus among the international NGOs regarding the main attitude (spirit) that should be promoted through the psychosocial projects. In most project proposals it was stated that the project attempted to promote peace and justice, human rights, ethnic tolerance, and other important universal values. NGOs also aimed at having a long-term impact on the social services provision system.

However, under war conditions this proved to be a sensitive question, and evidence of these goals in the concrete work of the NGOs were not always easy to find. It was our hypothesis that if these goals were transparent in the project activities, they would primarily be obvious to the staff working in the project. The staff would be aware of strategies built into the project and actions undertaken to achieve these goals. Therefore, we added a number of questions distributed to the staff about their assessment of the wider sociopolitical impact of their projects.

Material

To be able to compare the views of participants and the staff working in the projects, two almost similar questionnaires were developed. The questions were defined on the basis of a pilot study of 200 participants in Bosnia and Croatia in January–February 1995. Questionnaires developed by UNICEF (Mesquita, 1994) and Norwegian People's Aid (Dahl & Schei, 1995) were also a valuable source of inspiration.

The analyzed projects were implemented by nine European NGOs reaching an estimated 25,000 participants, which means that our sample (2,291 participants and 167 staff members) represented about 10% of the selected NGOs participants and the return rate for the 2,500 questionnaires distributed was about 90%. This was an astonishingly high rate, and it might be attributed partly to the fact that we (the investigators) were seen as representing the donor. Of course, this should also be taken into account in the interpretation of the answers: There might be a tendency to "please" the donor by overemphasizing positive results. However, we truly felt that both the participants and the staff were highly motivated and therefore also wanted to be cooperative.

The NGOs selected were included in the study because they provided organized psychological and social support at different levels of intervention. For both ethical and professional reasons, we did not attempt to make comparisons between NGOs: Our main focus was on participants regardless of the project in which they participated. The client questionnaire contained questions regarding sociodemographic data, traumatic experiences and coping strategies, emotional response to the war and exile experience, and evaluation of the benefit of the various activities provided by the project. As the staff was also living under war conditions, the staff questionnaire contained the same questions as the client questionnaire; however, for the staff we added a part where we asked them to reflect on the possible sociopolitical effect of their project.

We distributed the questionnaires by assembling staff members of each NGO and having them complete a questionnaire in order to become acquainted with its format. The purpose of the study was explained and questions were answered. The staff was asked to distribute the questionnaires as randomly as possible, that is, to all participants attending the project during the following few days. It was underlined that it was entirely voluntary for participants to complete the questionnaires and that the anonymity of the participants should be protected as far as possible. However, because some participants were illiterate (almost 10%), assistance was needed for them to complete the questionnaires, a fact that naturally hindered full anonymity.

Results

The results (here, numbers have been rounded and the findings simplified; see Agger & Mimica, 1996, for complete details) indicated that the participants were most often exposed to life-threatening events (85%), loss of home and property (85%), hunger and thirst (60%), torture or extremely bad treatment (30%), and illness (30%). During a war, stressful events are continuous, and in this war they happened in a context of ethnic violence in which neighbors and even family members turned against each other. This probably explains why almost half of the participants had experienced betrayal by neighbors and acquaintances and 20% by family and friends. Exposure to other stressful events was experienced on a smaller scale, varying from rape (2%) to severe physical harm and injury (10%).

Of the responding participants, 80% reported that participation in the project was of great or considerable help to them. The project also seemed to reduce all initial symptoms: About 90% reported that they were less lonely, that they had achieved more inner peace, and that they were in a better mood. Viewed as a crisis intervention, the projects seemed to have attained their goals: to keep people going even under extremely difficult circumstances.

The majority of the participants (70%) reported being less angry and bitter. Although this is a relatively high rate, changes in level of aggression were reported significantly less frequently than changes reported for other feelings (anxiety, depression, and a sense of isolation). It seemed to be more difficult to work with aggressive feelings in the context offered by the psychosocial projects. This is of course related to the social and political context in which the projects were operating. Anger and bitterness are also those feelings that ignite revenge and contribute to the continuation of war and are serious obstacles to reconciliation and coexistence. However, aggressive feelings also involve energy that could become a positive force.

The staff evaluation of positive changes in the participants corresponded quite closely the participants' own evaluation of their positive changes. However, there was a tendency for the staff to believe that the participants had become less angry and bitter than the participants themselves reported. Staff members commented on other changes they noticed in the participants: "they look better," "they are more open," "feelings of security, self-esteem and confidence in others have increased," "they have returned to the community as a social category," "they think and talk about the future;" 90% of the staff and 80% of the participants attributed the positive changes to the project.

It appeared from the answers of the staff that individual treatment goals were the primary concern of the staff members. Improvement of the mental health status of participants (in a traditional way) was rated highest by the staff, and somewhat less significance was given to the sociopolitical effects of the project. The participants, however, seemed to place more emphasis on the "healing space" provided by the project: the warm and empathic atmosphere, the opportunity to form new social networks, and the feeling of safety and contact created by the group work. Maybe a greater emphasis on the sociopolitical aspects of psychosocial projects would have given the participants a better opportunity to deal with their aggressive energy in a constructive way. This would have made projects truly psychosocial: addressing the needs of both the war-torn society and of its people.

In psychosocial projects much attention has been given to identifying strategies of how to help and support people under war conditions to integrate their stressful experiences. However, what this actually means has been neither clearly defined nor properly contemplated. One of the reasons for this is probably that the general stream of thinking among national as well as international professionals during the war was very influenced by the somewhat narrow posttraumatic stress disorder concept. Therefore, the treatment goal was often defined as helping people to be free of symptoms, thereby contributing to an individualization of the treatment procedure: Traumatized people needed mostly to relive their traumatic experiences in order to resolve their conflicts and integrate them into their lives.

However, our study illustrated that war trauma is much more than exposure to a single stressful event. It is a long and enduring state of severe stress and uncertainty about the future. In this process, people may change considerably. Feelings of antagonism, nationalism, and hostility replace feelings of altruism and tolerance. Consequently, we might ask if the true war trauma symptoms should not have been identified as nationalism, lack of tolerance for differences, and withdrawal into ethnic groups. This also leads to a major unanswered question: What should treatment goals be for psychosocial projects in future situations like this?

REFERENCES

Agger, I., & Jensen, S. B. (1996). *Trauma and healing under state terrorism.* London: Zed Books.

Agger, I., & Mimica, J. (1996). *Psychosocial assistance to victims of war in Bosnia-Herzegovina and Croatia: An evaluation.* Brussels: ECHO.

Agger, I., Vuk, S., & Mimica, J. (1995). *Theory and practice of psychosocial projects under war conditions in Bosnia–Herzegovina and Croatia.* Brussels: ECHO.

Bergh, M., & Jareg, P. (Eds.). (1998). *Health and psychosocial aspects of complex emergencies: The Norwegian experience.* Oslo: Diakonhjemmets Internasjonale Senter.

Boutros-Ghali, B. (1992). *An agenda for peace.* New York: United Nations.

Bracken, P. J., & Petty, C. (Eds.). (1998). *Rethinking the trauma of war.* London: Free Association Books.

Dahl, S., & Schei, B. (1995). *Helping women—The hidden victims of war: It does make a difference. Norwegian People's Aid's psychosocial center for displaced women and their families in Zenica, Bosnia and Herzegovina. Report and evaluation, 1993/94.* Oslo: Norwegian People's Aid.

Denich, B. (1994). Dismembering Yugoslavia: Nationalist ideologies and the symbolic revival of genocide. *American Ethnologist, 21,* 367–390.

Geertz, C. (1983). *Local knowledge: Further essays in interpretative anthropology.* New York: Basic Books.

Hastrup, K., & Olwig, K. F. (1997). Introduction. In K.F. Olwig & K. Hastrup (Eds.), *Siting culture: The shifting anthropological object* (pp. 1–14). London: Routledge.

Ispanovic-Radojkovic, V., Bojanin, N., Rakic, V., & Lazic, D. (1993, June). *Children and young people: Victims of war in former Yugoslavia (1991–1993).* Paper presented at the European Consultation on Care and Rehabilitation of Victims of Rape, Torture and Other Severe Trauma of War in the Republics of Ex-Yugoslavia, Utrecht, The Netherlands.

Jareg, E. (1995, May). *Main guiding principles for the development of psychosocial interventions for children affected by war.* Paper presented at the ISCA Workshop, Stockholm, Sweden.

Mesquita, B. (1994, August). *Outline and background of an assessment schedule: Psychosocial program for women in Bosnia–Herzegovina.* Report presented to UNICEF, Zagreb, Croatia.

Moro, L., & Vidovic, V. (1992). Organizations for assistance to displaced persons. In E. Klain (Ed.), *Psychology and psychiatry of a war* (pp. 182–184). Zagreb, Yugoslavia: University of Zagreb, Faculty of Medicine.

Richters, A. (1998). Sexual violence in wartime: Psychosocial cultural wounds and healing processes. The example of the former Yugoslavia. In P. J. Bracken & C. Petty (Eds.), *Rethinking the trauma of war* (pp. 112–127). London: Free Association Books.

Save the Children Alliance. (1996). *Psychosocial approaches to children in armed conflict.* (Working Paper No. 1). Washington, DC: Author.

Schultz, K. (1994). *Build peace from the ground up: About people and the UN in a war zone in Croatia.* Lund, Sweden: Trans-national Foundation for Peace and Future Research.

Skjelsbaek, I. (1998). *Sexual violence in the conflicts in ex-Yugoslavia.* Oslo: Ministry of Foreign Affairs.

Sperber, U. (1998). *Humanitarian assistance and humanitarian skills and knowledge in Denmark*. Copenhagen: Center for Development Research.

Stepputat, F. (1994). *Efter nødhjælpen: Fra katastrofe til udvikling?* (After the emergency relief: From disaster to development?). Copenhagen: Center for Development Research.

Summerfield, D. (1996). The impact of war and atrocity on civilian populations: Basic principles for NGOs' interventions and a critique of psychosocial trauma projects. *Relief and Rehabilitation Network*, Paper 14.

Summerfield, D. (1998). The social experience of war and some issues for the humanitarian field. In P. J. Bracken & C. Petty (Eds.), *Rethinking the trauma of war* (pp. 9–37). London: Free Association Books.

World Health Organization & Médecins sans Frontières. (1995, February). *Proceedings of the First Workshop on the Role in Health Issues of International Organizations in Conflict Areas of the Countries of Former Yugoslavia*. Geneva, Switzerland: Author.

20

SOCIAL PSYCHOLOGY AND INTERGROUP CONFLICT

MILES HEWSTONE AND ED CAIRNS

Writer and satirist Jonathan Swift was at his most cynical when he described humanity as "the most pernicious race of odious vermin that nature ever suffered to crawl upon the surface of the earth." Yet, viewed in terms of the sheer number of conflicts dotted over the map of the world or the barbarity of some of the acts carried out by one human being against another (whether in Bosnia, Northern Ireland, Rwanda, or a host of other countries), it is easy to understand Swift's jaundiced view.[1] These conflicts may be based on race, on religious differences (e.g., Northern Ireland, most of former Yugoslavia), on language (e.g., Belgium), or on various combinations of these. The diversity of phenomena subsumed under the term *intergroup conflict* is also potentially vast, including prejudice, discrimination, injustice, perpetuation of inequality, oppression, ethnic cleansing, and genocide. This chapter focuses primarily on prejudice and discrimination (i.e., negative attitudes and behaviors with respect to an out-group as compared to an in-group) and is divided into two main parts, each of which is a relatively brief and selective review of a large literature. The first part lays out some of the main social–psychological bases of intergroup conflict, and the second part presents some of the most promising social–psychological interventions to reduce intergroup conflict.

We gratefully acknowledge grants from the Central Community Relations Unit (Northern Ireland) and the Templeton Foundation during the time at which this chapter was written, and we thank Katy Greenland and Mark Rubin for their comments on an earlier version of this chapter.
[1] The interested reader can consult the "conflict data service" of the Initiative on Conflict Resolution And Ethnicity (INCORE) at www.incore.ulst.ac.uk/cds/.

SOCIAL–PSYCHOLOGICAL BASES OF INTERGROUP CONFLICT AND GROUP PERSPECTIVES

"The problem of Northern Ireland is a heady brew of history, geography, religion and nationality, of rival rights and allegiances, of competition for power and territory, of deep bitterness." This analysis of "The Troubles" in Northern Ireland by journalist David McKittrick (1998) could surely be given as accurately for almost any intergroup conflict. That is why conflict attracts and requires the research attention of, among others, anthropologists, historians, sociologists, economists, and political scientists, as well as social psychologists. But there are also distinct social–psychological bases of intergroup conflict, which primarily concern what is special about our behavior as members of social groups. Although some social psychologists have attempted to account for intergroup conflict in terms of some intra-individual factor (e.g., personality or frustration leading to aggression; see Billig, 1976), a far more convincing account can be provided by concentrating on the distinct nature of intergroup phenomena.

Ethnocentrism

The roots of these perspectives can be traced back to Sumner's (1906; see also Brewer, 1979) sociological writings on the basic state of conflict between the "we group" (or in-group) and "other groups" (or out-groups). In general, Sumner (1906) called intergroup biases *ethnocentrism*, defined as the "view of things in which one's own group is the center of everything, and all others are scaled or rated with reference to it" (p. 13). This general tendency can be seen in preferences for in-group characteristics, products, customs, languages, speech styles, and so on. Sumner saw such biases as resulting from intergroup competition and functioning to preserve in-group solidarity and justify the exploitation of out-groups. However, whereas Sumner saw ethnocentrism as universal, social–psychological research has examined what conditions lead to an increase or decrease in ethnocentrism.

Realistic Group Conflict Theory

This approach to intergroup relations (Brewer, 1979; LeVine & Campbell, 1972; Sherif, 1966) assumes that group conflicts are rational in the sense that groups have incompatible goals and compete for scarce resources. Thus the source of conflict is "realistic." Sherif and colleagues carried out a number of famous field studies of boys at summer camps, who were split up into different groups and engaged in various competitive behaviors (e.g., Sherif, 1966; Sherif, Harvey, White, Hood, & Sherif, 1961). They concluded that competition causes intergroup conflict and that there needed to be some positive and functional interdependence between groups before conflict between them would abate (i.e., they must be made to cooperate). Sherif and his colleagues created these conditions in the form of superordinate goals: goals that neither group could attain on its own and which superseded other goals each group might have had. Sherif also reported that a single superordinate goal was not sufficient to reduce intergroup conflict; a series of cumulative superordinate goals was required.

Notwithstanding the pioneering influence of Sherif's work and, indeed, the extensive, cross-cultural psychological evidence that competition promotes aggression (Bonta, 1997), Sherif's studies did not show that conflict of interest was a necessary requirement for the emergence of intergroup hostility. As Billig (1976) noted, anecdotal evidence from the early study by Sherif et al. (1961) actually indicates that the negative reactions to an out-group emerged at a stage prior to the planned introduction of competition. Thus mere knowledge of the other group's presence was sufficient to trigger the first instances of intergroup discrimination. This realization of the potency of social categorization led to Tajfel's later work on social identity.

Social Identity Theory

According to social identity theory (Abrams & Hogg, 1990; Tajfel, 1978; Tajfel & Turner, 1979), individuals define themselves to a large extent in terms of their social group memberships and tend to seek a positive social identity. This *social identity* consists of those aspects of an individual's self-image that derive from the social categories to which the individual perceives himself or herself to belong and to the value and emotional significance ascribed to that membership. Thus it is a self-definition in terms of group membership. A positive social identity is achieved by comparing one's own group with other groups to establish a positively valued psychological distinctiveness for the in-group vis à vis the out-group.[2]

Emphasizing that motivational as well as cognitive factors underlie intergroup differentiation, social identity theory holds that positive comparisons (intergroup differences that favor the in-group) provide a satisfactory social identity, whereas negative comparisons (differences that favor the out-group) convey an unsatisfactory identity. Social identity differs from earlier group perspectives in two key respects. First, in contrast to Sumner's claim that ethnocentrism is rampant, social identity theory predicts that members of social groups will differentiate primarily on dimensions that provide them with a favorable view of their own group (i.e., dimensions on

---

[2] Social identity theory argues that social categorization arouses self-evaluative social comparison processes whereby individuals strive to obtain a positive self-esteem, but the evidence for this "self-esteem hypothesis" is unconvincing (Rubin & Hewstone, 1998).

which the in-group is superior to the out-group). Moreover, intergroup discrimination is often driven by "in-group favoritism" rather than "out-group derogation" (Brewer, 1979). Second, in contrast to Sherif's claim that competitive goals cause conflict, social identity theory argues that social categorization per se can cause intergroup discrimination.

Tajfel and colleagues demonstrated the power of social categorization in their "minimal groups paradigm" (Tajfel, Billig, Bundy, & Flament, 1971). In the paradigm, participants are classified as members of two discrete groups ostensibly on the basis of trivial criteria (e.g., preference for one of two abstract painters, over- or underestimation of dots, and even allocation to group X or Y according to the toss of a coin). In fact, allocation to a group is always random. Participants then have to distribute rewards between pairs of other participants (not themselves) using specially designed booklets that assess the strength of various response strategies. The authors of the original research considered the groups to be "minimal" for the following reasons: (a) Categorization into in-groups or out-groups was based on trivial criteria, (b) there was no explicit conflict of interests, (c) nor had there been previous hostility, (d) participants did not engage in face-to-face social interaction, and (e) there was no rational link between economic self-interest and the strategy of favoring one's own group.

The most striking finding to emerge from these studies was that participants, although they made some effort to be fair in their allocations, showed a persistent tendency to give higher rewards to another (unknown) in-group member than to another (unknown) out-group member (Bourhis, Sachdev, & Gagnon, 1994; Brewer, 1979; Turner, 1981). Participants were particularly keen to ensure that their fellow in-group member received a higher reward than the out-group member, rather than to maximize rewards gained for the in-group or to maximize joint gain (i.e., for both groups). According to social identity theory, the only way for participants in these studies to obtain a positive social identity is by identifying with the groups into which they are categorized and then ensuring that their group comes off best in the only available comparison between the groups (i.e., giving more rewards to the in-group than to the out-group).

Before continuing, we might pause here and ask whether these groups do, in fact, represent "minimal" groups or, as Tajfel (1978, p. 42) himself suggested, whether in the context of an artificial and bare laboratory study they constitute "maximal" groups. They remind one of Jonathan Swift's satire on political or religious animosity in Gulliver's Travels—the implacable division between those who open an egg at the large end or at the small end ("Big-Endians" vs. "Little-Endians"). Out of quite small beginnings can sometimes grow large conflicts, and it would be difficult to overestimate the importance of social categorization and its link via social comparison to social identity and the need for psychological distinctiveness. This claim is supported by the many different applications of social identity to intergroup relations outside the laboratory (Tajfel, 1982) and its position as the dominant explanatory framework for the study of intergroup relations in social psychology (Brewer & Brown, 1998).

Outside the laboratory, social identity has had to confront the fact that groups in conflict often differ in status and that changing status relations and their perceived legitimacy are crucial determining characteristics of intergroup relations (Turner & Brown, 1978; Van Knippenberg & Ellemers, 1990). Thus when lower-status or minority groups perceive the dominant group's position as illegitimate and unstable, they may use a variety of strategies to obtain a positive identity. They may search for a positive identity by redefining characteristics of their own group that had previously been seen as negative, or they may find new dimensions for making comparisons between the groups or a new comparison group. Only later may the out-group be directly confronted, as when comparisons are made directly on dimensions such as power and status and when the lower-status group demands equality. This in turn may threaten the identity of the dominant group, leading to a backlash. All these strategies are discussed in detail by Tajfel (1978) and illustrated in the context of the conflict in Northern Ireland by Cairns (1982).

In particular, social identity theory helps us to understand the behavior of those whose identity is perceived to be threatened and whose behavior might otherwise seem quite irrational or pointless. Consider an example from Northern Ireland—the insistence of members of the Orange Order (Protestant Unionists) that they be allowed to march down Garvaghy Road, located in the center of a Catholic area of Drumcree.[3] In the same article quoted earlier, McKittrick (1998) explained that "In recent years, the parades have taken on a character of Protestant consolation, expressing not jubilation in Unionist ascendancy but a sense that at least one parade can be got through." Thus getting the parade through has become an end in itself. A Jesuit priest quoted in the same article added that "Protestants have been under pressure since 1968, and they have lost power and status to a far greater extent than many Catholics realize. As a result, they're afraid of their whole *identity* [emphasis added] being abolished completely." From the perspective of social identity theory, the insistence of the Protestant community on marching down one particular street (for just 7 minutes) can be understood in terms of their feeling that their identity is threatened and that such opportunities must be taken to stand up to the Catholic community and to show that Protestant identity is still important and valued.

---

[3] Although there are many such marches, which punctuate the summer in Northern Ireland on an annual basis, the Drumcree march is a particular trouble spot and is also particularly salient, because it took place in 1998 just a few days after the conference on which this volume is based.

IS THERE SOMETHING SPECIAL ABOUT
INTERGROUP BEHAVIOR?

At this point the reader might well be asking himself or herself this question. Tajfel's (1978) answer was a clear "yes," which he illustrated by comparing interpersonal and intergroup forms of behavior. He proposed a hypothetical continuum, with end points of "pure" interpersonal and intergroup behavior, respectively. Interpersonal behavior concerns relations that are completely determined by the interpersonal characteristics of those involved (e.g., two friends). Intergroup behavior concerns relations that are defined totally in terms of individuals' memberships in social groups or categories (e.g., a member of one group killing an innocent, unknown member on the other side of a conflict simply because he or she was a member of the out-group).

Tajfel suggested that intergroup behavior could be distinguished by three criteria. First, at least two clearly identifiable social categories should be present in the situation (e.g., a Hutu and a Tutsi, a Catholic and a Protestant, a Serb and a Croat). Second, there should be little variability of behavior or attitude within each group. Intergroup behavior tends to be uniform (i.e., "we" agree about "them"), whereas interpersonal behavior shows a range of individual differences. Third, a member of one group should show little variability in his or her perception or treatment of members of the other group (i.e., "they" are "all alike"). In Tajfel's (1978) words, out-group members are treated as "undifferentiated items in a unified social category" (p. 45).

There is evidence that people's behavior is indeed qualitatively different in-group settings (Brown & Turner, 1981). For example, when group membership is salient (e.g., during conflict), the individual tends to become "depersonalized" in the group. This is not a loss of identity ("de-individuation") but a shift from personal to social identity. A concern with the in-group takes over from a concern with the self, in-group favoritism replaces self-favoritism, the self is stereotyped as an in-group member, and the in-group is viewed as coherent and homogeneous (Turner, Hogg, Oakes, Reicher, & Wetherell, 1987). There is also now extensive evidence that groups are more competitive and aggressive than individuals (e.g., Schopler & Insko, 1992). In a similar vein, Brewer (1997) has proposed an "in-group–out-group schema," consisting of three principles likely to operate in any social situation in which a particular in-group–out-group categorization is made salient. The *intergroup accentuation principle* refers to assimilation within category boundaries and contrast between categories; all members of the in-group are seen as more similar to the self than members of the out-group. The *in-group favoritism principle* refers to the selective generalization of positive affect (trust, liking) to fellow in-group, but not to out-group, members. The *social competition principle* refers to the fact that intergroup social comparison is typically perceived in terms of competition, rather than comparison, with the out-group.

Of equal importance to the empirical evidence are the theoretical implications that follow from the distinction between interpersonal and intergroup behavior (Brown & Turner, 1981). First, theories that attempt to explain intergroup phenomena by reference to interpersonal relations are unlikely to be very predictive. Second, if the individual is depersonalized in the group, then what affects the group as a whole has implications for the individual. Intergroup behavior is likely to be influenced by intergroup relations of status, power, and so on, not by interpersonal relations. Third, some variables that have one effect on interpersonal relations may have a different effect on intergroup relations. For example, similarity may have attractive properties at an interpersonal level, but it may threaten group distinctiveness and lead to intergroup discrimination (Brown, 1984). For all these reasons, Tajfel (1979) came to conclude that intergroup behavior requires a different level of analysis from intragroup or interpersonal behavior.

TYPES OF INTERGROUP CONFLICT

Although we argue strongly that social psychology has a contribution to make to the study of conflict, we do not wish to exaggerate its importance. At the end of their seminal paper on social identity theory, Tajfel and Turner (1979) distinguished between a number of types of conflict that helps to highlight where social psychology's contribution should be greatest.

Objective Versus Subjective Conflict

When we talk about conflict, we normally have in mind what Tajfel and Turner have called "objective" conflicts over power, wealth, or territory. These objective conflicts obviously have their determinants outside the realm of psychology and require an analysis in terms of social, economic, political, and historical structures. Objective conflicts can be distinguished from psychological, symbolic or "subjective" conflicts, such as attempts to establish positively valued distinctiveness. Although distinct, objective and subjective conflicts are often interwoven, and subjective conflict can exist long after objective disparities disappear (according to Deutsch, 1973, the notion of destructive conflicts that are likely to continue after initiating causes have become irrelevant). Political scientist John Whyte (1990) has written about the conflict in Northern Ireland: "It seems to go beyond what is required by a rational defence of the divergent interests which undoubtedly exist [between Catholics and Protestants]" (p. 94). And for the very reason that the problems involved are more symbolic or psychological, they may be more difficult to deal with (Cairns & Darby, 1988).

Explicit Versus Implicit Conflict

A further distinction can be made between explicit and implicit conflicts. Explicit conflict is legitimized and institutionalized by rules or norms (e.g., the competition between groups in Sherif's studies or the World Cup competition for international football teams). Tajfel and Turner (1979) proposed that the behavior toward the out-group in this kind of conflict can, in turn, be classified into two categories. *Instrumental behavior* refers to actions aimed at causing the in-group to win the competition (such behavior can be explained in terms of the motive to win). *Noninstrumental behavior* is more interesting, psychologically, because it is gratuitous discrimination against out-groups and has no sense outside the context of intergroup relations. A prime example is the ascription of negative stereotypes to members of out-groups and, indeed, to the group as a whole. Generally a set of traits is attributed to all (or most) members of the category, and individuals belonging to the category are assumed to be similar to each other and different from the in-group on this set of traits. Treating the out-group in this way makes them more predictable, can be used to justify discriminatory behavior, and can help group members to differentiate the in-group positively from the out-group (Linville, 1998; Oakes, Haslam, & Turner, 1994; Tajfel, 1981).

Finally, implicit conflict refers to conflict that exists in the absence of explicit institutionalization (e.g., experimental participants' preference for relative gain at the expense of the out-group in the minimal groups paradigm, even when this means a decrease in objective reward and where there is no explicit conflict of interests). Tajfel and Turner (1979) referred to the many cases in "real life" where "differentiations of all kinds are made between groups by their members although, on the face of it, there are no reasons for these differentiations to occur" (p. 47). A tragic example is provided by the Hutu and Tutsi in Rwanda (Keane, 1995; Prunier, 1995).

Contrary to widespread beliefs, the Hutu and Tutsi are not ethnic or tribal groups. They have the same language, religion, and culture, and there has been a history of extensive intermarriage and even people exchanging identities. In fact, they are essentially the same people, but differences between them were emphasized by colonialists, leading to exaggeration of quite small differences in physical attributes such as height and skin color. As Prunier has reported in this volume (chapter 8), this social differentiation concluded with a deliberate genocide, the causes of which were complex but included a psychological component. As Prunier put it, "Genocide has a lot to do with how people perceive each other" (see also Staub, 1989; Staub, chapter 18, this volume).

Thus social psychological aspects of conflict are most evident in the case of implicit conflict and are also illustrated by noninstrumental behaviors associated with explicit conflicts. But they can also be important where objective and subjective conflicts have become inseparable and where a contemporary subjective conflict has outlived a more ancient objective one. This overview of social–psychological bases of intergroup conflict illustrates that there are many ways in which social psychology can illuminate the study of conflict, and many points at which a conflict can become psychological. We believe the social identity approach has the most to offer this area theoretically and that many apparently pointless conflicts become more understandable when viewed as, at least in part, attempts to establish, maintain, or defend cherished social identities. Finally, we have also argued that intergroup behavior is distinct from interpersonal behavior and that specific types of conflict can be identified in which social–psychological considerations are crucial.

SOCIAL–PSYCHOLOGICAL INTERVENTIONS TO REDUCE INTERGROUP CONFLICT

In this second part of the chapter, we give an overview of two main types of intervention aimed at reducing intergroup conflict (Hewstone, 1996). The first is based on bringing about more positive and cooperative contact between members of previously hostile groups, and the second attempts to change the structure of social categorizations. Both interventions may be aimed at changing various aspects of intergroup perception and behavior, but we will focus on three main types of change identified by Brewer and Miller (1988). The first is a change in attitudes toward the social structure as a whole, making the view of an out-group less negative or preferably more positive. The second is an increase in the perceived variability of the out-group, whereby the perceiver comes to view the out-group in a less simple, more differentiated way. The third kind of change involves a decrease in category use ("de-categorization"), whereby the perceiver comes to see the old categorization as less, or no longer, useful for identifying and classifying individuals.

Contact Between Members of Different Groups

There is now extensive evidence that contact between members of different groups, under appropriate conditions, can improve intergroup relations (Allport, 1954/1979; also see Pettigrew, 1998, for a recent review).

Favorable conditions include cooperative contact between equal-status members of the two groups, in a situation that allows individuals to get to know each other on more than a superficial basis, and with the support of relevant social groups and authorities (Cook, 1978). But there remain serious limitations to the so-called contact hypothesis (Hewstone & Brown, 1986).

One of the most serious limitations is that participants in cooperative contact programs, even if they do come to view one or a small number of individuals from the other group more positively, do not necessarily generalize their positive attitudes and perceptions. They may not generalize beyond the specific situation in which the positive contact took place, and they may not generalize from specific contact partners to the group as a whole (Hewstone & Brown, 1986). Recent work on intergroup contact is aimed at overcoming precisely this limitation.

Another serious practical limitation is that optimal contact is hard to bring about on a large scale, especially for adult participants (for young people it is somewhat easier when incorporated into formal education). Wright, Aron, McLaughlin-Volpe, and Ropp (1997) have proposed an "extended contact effect" to overcome this limitation, in which knowledge that a fellow in-group member has a close relationship with an out-group member is used as a catalyst to promote more positive intergroup attitudes. This extended contact is second-hand, rather than involving the participants in direct intergroup contact themselves, and so it could potentially bring about widespread reductions in prejudice without everyone having to have out-group friendships themselves. This second-hand contact may also overcome the problem that contact with an out-group is associated with "intergroup anxiety" (Stephan & Stephan, 1985). This anxiety may be caused by low- or poor-quality contact, negative expectations or stereotypes about the out-group, or a history of intergroup conflict. Importantly, intergroup anxiety is associated with poor recall of the contact experience, increased avoidance, and increased out-group stereotyping (Wilder, 1993).

If there are theoretical and practical limitations to intergroup contact, why the insistence on its implementation? The answer to this question has two parts, the first dealing with why contact has to be engineered if it is to take place at all, and the second justifying why we should bother to bring about contact. Why do we have to engineer contact? Unless proactive attempts are made to bring about contact, many people avoid intergroup contact, an effect likely to be exacerbated in the context of conflict where any dealing with the "other side" may be proscribed and violations severely sanctioned (e.g., in Northern Ireland people in mixed, Catholic–Protestant relationships have been frequently targeted and, in several cases, brutally murdered). In addition, society itself may be so segregated that unless we intervene there is almost no opportunity for contact.

This is the case in Northern Ireland, where there is extensive educational (Gallagher, 1995) and residential segregation (Poole & Doherty, 1996). The implications are illustrated by a problem we encountered in a recent survey on contact and prejudice in Northern Ireland, using a representative sample of the population. As part of the pilot work testing some of our questions, we received feedback from the survey organization that "interviewers found that in some of the 100 percent Protestant/Catholic areas where they were interviewing, the people had absolutely no contact with people of a different religion."

Why bother to bring about contact at all? Contact between groups can sometimes be the cause of hostility, especially when it leads to intergroup comparisons concerning inequalities of land, wealth, and so on. But in principle we believe that some contact, especially where it can be made positive and cooperative, is desirable. The absence of contact is likely to reduce the likelihood of future contact, strengthen the assumption that the two groups have different (even irreconcilable) beliefs, maintain intergroup anxiety, and reinforce the boundary between groups (Hewstone, 1996). It is worth noting that even one positive encounter with a member of the other group, although it is unlikely to change the stereotype of an out-group in general, can sometimes bring about change in perceived group variability, revealing that "they" are not "all alike" (Hamburger, 1994). Bishop Desmond Tutu told the story of his astonishment when an unknown White priest (Father Trevor Huddleston) raised his hat to Tutu's mother, a simple cook. "For the first time," Tutu said, he "realized that all whites were not the same" (cited in *The Guardian*, 1998).

Interpersonal Versus Intergroup Contact

As we have noted, a major limitation of research on contact is the failure to generalize from positive interpersonal encounters to views of the out-group as a whole. People seem to find it very easy to "explain away" (Pettigrew, 1979) the behavior of one or a few people who disconfirm their stereotype and assign these exceptions to a "subtype" that is not typical of the group as a whole (Hewstone, 1994), unless the out-group member is perceived as typical and a dispositional attribution can be made for the counterstereotypic behavior (Wilder, Simon, & Faith, 1996). Hewstone and Brown (1986) therefore argued that unless contact can be characterized as intergroup (i.e., between individuals as group representatives), it is unlikely to generalize to the group as a whole.

As specialists in this area, we are often asked "How do you explain what happened in Yugoslavia?" This European state was home to various ethnic groups who lived together (12% of all marriages in Yugoslavia and

40% in Sarajevo were mixed; Botev & Wagner, 1993), and yet it was catapulted into civil war and genocide. It became clear that close friendships with members of different ethnic groups offered no special immunity against outrageous acts committed in pursuit of the policy of ethnic cleansing. The closest friend of Dusko Tadic, member of the Serb minority in the Bosnian town of Kozarac, was Muslim policeman Emir Karabasic (his friend even served as a pall-bearer at Tadic's father's funeral). Tadic was later accused on 34 counts at the international war crimes tribunal at The Hague, one of which was beating to death four of his former neighbors, including Emir, in the Omarska detention camp. Although this case is particularly tragic, it may be quite representative in the sense that 50% of respondents to one survey in the region reported betrayal by neighbors belonging to the dominant or majority group (Botev & Wagner, 1993).

In another more positive example Ahmed, a Bosnian, related how his life was saved when Serbian forces intercepted a group of Muslims trying to escape from Srebrenica to the haven of Tuzla:

> My father was just ahead of me. In front of the tank, he turned to the left with the other men. Without thinking, I continued walking straight ahead with the women and children. After a few yards a hand reached out and grabbed my right shoulder. It was a Serb soldier, a neighbor of mine from Srebrenica. He shoved a blanket in my arms and motioned for me to put it on my head. He literally saved my life (cited in Stover & Peress, 1998).

Yet even in this latter case the close interethnic friendship was not enough to prevent the Serb joining up to a force intent on cleansing the area of Muslims.

It is obviously asking an enormous amount of any kind of contact that it should "inoculate" the recipient against the host of forces urging it in the direction of ethnic conflict (e.g., group pressures such as conformity, calls to national identity, and threats to one's family). We believe, however, that intergroup contact is more likely to provide a bulwark against these forces than is interpersonal contact. Thus we have argued that group affiliations should still be clear in contact situations and that when members of one group meet members of the other group, they should both be seen as, at least to some extent, typical of their groups (Hewstone & Brown, 1986). Only under these circumstances should cooperative contact lead to more positive ratings of the out-group as a whole, for which there is now extensive evidence (e.g., Brown, Vivian, & Hewstone, 1999; Van Oudenhoven, Groenewoud, & Hewstone, 1996; Wilder, 1984). Despite this evidence, there are some potential dangers associated with intergroup contact. Where intergroup conflict is extreme, contact may promote anxiety (Islam & Hewstone, 1993), and it may be better to begin with positive interpersonal contact, and later make group memberships salient.

Changing Social Categorizations

The interventions reviewed in this section start from the premise that since social categorization is the cause of discrimination, an improvement in intergroup relations must be brought about by reducing the salience of existing social categories (Brewer & Miller, 1984). These interventions try to achieve this, however, by very different means. The first, de-categorization, seeks to eliminate categorization; the second and third, re-categorization and crossed categorization, seek to alter which categorizations are used (Wilder, 1986).

Decategorization

Brewer and Miller's (1984, 1988) "personalization" model suggests that contact between members of different groups should be differentiated (allowing for distinctions to be made among out-group members) and personalized (allowing for perceptions of the uniqueness of out-group members). The goal then is a more interpersonally oriented and "non-category-based" form of responding that allows members to "attend to information that replaces category identity as the most useful basis for classifying each other" (Brewer & Miller, 1984, p. 288). For example, an employer who had previously been selecting only members of his or her own ethnic group might learn that this information is not very useful in predicting whether someone will be a good employee and that a much better basis for such a decision would be to look beyond the category to the individual applicants' educational qualifications.

Brewer and Miller and their colleagues have investigated their model in a series of experimental studies (Bettencourt, Brewer, Rogers-Croak, & Miller, 1992; Miller, Brewer, & Edwards, 1985). The studies confirmed the hypothesized effects of personalized contact. Participants who adopted an interpersonal focus displayed significantly less in-group favoritism than did either those who focused on the task or those in a control condition. Participants also differentiated among out-group members more in the interpersonal conditions, and there was a strong correlation between perceived similarity of out-group members (to each other) and the degree of intergroup bias shown.

Personalization aims to, and can, achieve de-categorization: Individuation of out-group members results in the category being seen as less "useful" and, thus, being used less often. This intervention may also succeed in changing perceived group variability, encouraging a more complex and differentiated perception of the out-group (Hamburger, 1994), which may ultimately reduce the likelihood of applying a stereotype to individual members in the future (Brewer & Brown, 1998; Ryan, Judd, & Park, 1996). However, the very conditions that promote personalization impede generalization of attitudes from individual members of the out-group to the out-group as a whole (Scarberry, Ratcliff, Lord, Lanicek, & Desforges, 1997). The beneficial effects of personalized contact may also be restricted to majority groups, with members of minority groups showing more bias under these conditions than when focusing on the task (Bettencourt, Charlton, & Kernahan, 1997).

Recategorization

Both re-categorization and crossed categorization are interventions inspired theoretically by social identity theory (Tajfel, 1978) and, more recently, by self-categorization theory (e.g., Turner et al., 1987). These theories emphasize that we all typically belong to several social categories and therefore may have a series of social identifications, one of which is salient at any given time. Self-categorization theory develops the earlier social identity perspective by arguing that self can be conceived on a number of levels of inclusiveness (e.g., me as an individual, me as a group member, or me as a human being). The level at which the self is defined determines how one relates to others, including members of the same group.

Gaertner, Dovidio, Anastasio, Bachman, and Rust (1993) argued that intergroup bias can be reduced by factors that transform members' perceptions of group boundaries from "us" and "them" to a more inclusive "we." They acknowledged that several factors influence intergroup bias and conflict, but their "common in-group identity" model regards the cognitive representations of the situation as the critical mediating variable (Dovidio, Gaertner, Isen, & Lowrance, 1995; Dovidio, Gaertner, Isen, Rust, & Guerra, 1988; Dovidio, Gaertner, & Validzic, 1998; Gaertner et al., 1999). Although a representation of the situation as one involving two groups is thought to maintain or enhance intergroup biases, de-categorized (i.e., separate individuals) or re-categorized (i.e., common in-group identity) representations are expected to reduce tension, albeit in different ways. De-categorization reduces bias through a process that moves initial in-group members away from the self and toward out-group members; thus former in-group members are seen less positively and as more evaluatively similar to out-group members. Re-categorization, in contrast, should reduce bias by increasing the attractiveness of former out-group members, once they are included within the superordinate group structure. The common in-group identity model resolves in-group versus out-group conflict by changing group boundaries and creating a superordinate identity.

There is extensive support for the common in-group identity model from sophisticated laboratory experiments. Bias was lower with a one-group than a two-group representation, and attraction to former out-group members was increased (Gaertner, Mann, Murrell, & Dovidio, 1989). Intergroup cooperation reduced bias via its effect on cognitive representations of social categorization (Gaertner, Mann, Dovidio, Murrell, & Pomare, 1990). It is also quite easy to find real-life illustrations consistent with the common in-group identity model, such as the national cohesion of nine different ethnic groups (half Muslim, half Christian) in Eritrea, fighting a "people's war" against Ethiopia. But common in-group identity may only be short-lived, or it may not be realistic in the face of powerful ethnic and racial categorizations (e.g., the break-up of former Yugoslavia into Serbs, Croats, Bosnians, etc.). A more successful strategy may involve a superordinate identity and distinctive subgroup identities. This would overcome a limitation of both the de-categorization and re-categorization perspectives—which they seek to deemphasize cherished identities. Yet, because membership of ethnic and other kinds of groups often provides a source of desired social identity (Tajfel, 1978), it would be impractical as well as undesirable for all parties concerned to ignore distinctive memberships.

As Brewer (1997) concluded, "De-categorization and re-categorization—as appealing as these concepts are—are inherently limited in their applicability when we move from the laboratory to real-life situations in which social groups are very large and the context is highly politicized" (p. 203). One solution to this problem, as was noted in passing, is to use a combination of different strategies. It has been suggested, for example (Hewstone, 1996), that where intergroup relations are characterized by high anxiety, initial contact should be interpersonal, only later making group memberships salient and addressing intergroup differences. Pettigrew (1998) suggested that at the initial stage, contact should involve interpersonal (de-categorized) relations to promote early positive interactions. In the slightly longer term, group differences should be highlighted to promote categorization and therefore generalization. Finally, re-categorization becomes possible over the course of extended contact.

Crossed Categorization

Most realistic intergroup contexts involve several categorizations, some of which coincide and some of which cut across each other. Thus "others" may be out-group on one dimension (e.g., Black- people vs. White- people in the United States) but in-group on another (e.g., Southerners vs. Northerners; Reed, 1982). Where others can be classified as out-group members on multiple dimensions, Brewer and Campbell (1976) labeled the situation as one involving "converging boundaries," where discrimination is likely to be increased. Many instances of intergroup conflict in the real world involve just such multiple converging social categorizations. For example, in Belfast, Northern Ireland, Catholics and Protestants tend to live in different places (e.g., Shankhill Road vs. Ardoyne), espouse different politics (Nationalist-Republican vs. Unionist-Loyalist), and even support different football teams (e.g., Cliftonville vs. Linfield).

The idea that crossed categorization might be used as an intervention comes from early anthropological work showing lower levels of conflict in societies with cross-cutting structures than in those with pyramidal–segmentary structures (see Crisp & Hewstone, 1999, for a review). Social psychologists later analyzed how crossed categorization should affect the categorization process itself (Vescio, Hewstone, Crisp, & Rubin, 1999). According to Doise's (1978) "category differentiation model," single or simple categorization leads to two cognitive processes: an accentuation of both the differences between categories (an "interclass effect") and similarities within categories (an "intraclass effect"). In contrast, the crossing of two categorizations leads to "convergence" between the categories (weakening the interclass effect) and "divergence" within each category (weakening the intraclass effect). Thus, for example, if we imagine a case in which one dimension (A/B) is crossed with another (X/Y), the accentuation of perceived similarities within one category (e.g., A) will be counteracted by a simultaneous accentuation of perceived differences, because category A contains two different subgroups according to another (e.g., X/Y → AX and AY) categorization (Vanbeselaere, 1991). As a result of these processes, intergroup discrimination based on the A/B categorization should, theoretically, be reduced or even eliminated.

The results of experimental work did not, however, typically show that crossed categorization could eliminate discrimination—or even reduce it below the level of discrimination aimed at single out-groups. Most studies do, however, show greatest bias against the double out-group, which is reduced when the target is a member of the in-group on one dimension and the out-group on the other (Migdal, Hewstone, & Mullen, 1998). This result suggests that crossed categorization can still be effective as an intervention, by helping to reduce bias against existing double (or multiple) out-groups. It should do this, in part, by making perceivers aware that the out-group consists of different subgroups (thus it may achieve differentiation). It should also reduce the importance of any one category, force the perceiver to classify other individuals in terms of multiple dimensions, and point to at least some similarities between groups (Vanbeselaere, 1991).

Like the other interventions reviewed, there remain limitations to the use of crossed categorization. Because one categorization is normally dominant in cases of conflict, even crossing multiple alternative categories may not weaken discrimination (Brewer, Ho, Lee, & Miller, 1987; Hewstone, Islam, & Judd, 1993). Crossing categories may also not help when categories are correlated (Eurich-Fulcher & Schofield, 1995), as is the case in many real conflicts (e.g., in Nigeria, the Ibo are predominantly Christian and the Hausa predominantly Muslim). There is also a need for further basic research exploring when and how various models of crossed categorization might operate (Crisp & Hewstone, 2000; Miller, Urban, & Vanman, 1998) and what type of change is brought about by this intervention. Nonetheless, crossed categorization does provide an important intervention for reducing bias against out-groups characterized by converging boundaries.

CHANGING SOCIAL STRUCTURES

Our emphasis in this part of the chapter, and our bailiwick as social psychologists, is on social–psychological interventions. Nonetheless, we acknowledge that "conflict resolution must go beyond changes in perceptions, attitudes, and qualities to the creation of enduring structures that institutionalize equality, autonomy, and respect among different groups" (Fisher, 1994, p. 61). These structures include federalization and consociational arrangements for what McGarry and O'Leary (1993) called "the macro-political regulation of ethnic conflict" (see also O'Leary, chapter 3, this volume). For example, electoral systems can be designed to fragment the support of a majority ethnic group, induce a majority ethnic group to behave moderately toward another ethnic group, or encourage multi-ethnic coalitions. We wish to emphasize, however, that whatever political structures are advocated, this decision should be guided by what we know about social categorization and its impact on conflict. At present some scholars advocate structural arrangements that cross-cut ethnic boundaries, whereas others argue that they should follow ethnic boundaries (Horowitz, 1985).

We also acknowledge that resolution of social conflict involves more than changing negative stereotypes and improving intergroup attitudes. The admirable work of Bishop Tutu's "Truth and Reconciliation Commission" in South Africa reminds us that the residue of conflict goes much deeper than prejudice and discrimination. Bishop Tutu concluded his foreword to the 3,500 pages of his final report by proposing, "Having looked the past in the eye, having asked for forgiveness, and having made amends, let us shut the door on the past—not in order to forget it but in order not to allow it to imprison us" (cited in *The Daily Telegraph*, 1998). Only very recently, encouraged by a research initiative of the Templeton Foundation, have scholars in this area considered the importance of the concept of forgiveness in intergroup conflict. Yet, in principle, interventions that succeed in reducing prejudice and discrimination could still leave participants unable to forgive, and certainly to forget, earlier atrocities. We therefore propose that social psychologists should take a wider view of outcome measures that should be addressed by their conflict interventions and a correspondingly broader perspective on the types of intervention that they should be evaluating. An interesting recent example is a study of collective guilt with respect to one's own treatment of another group and how this may affect emotions experienced and behavioral reactions (Doosje, Branscombe, Spears, & Manstead, 1998).

This overview of social–psychological interventions to reduce intergroup conflict shows that different interventions can achieve different kinds of change. We have argued that an absence of contact between groups will polarize images and reinforce group boundaries; moreover, intergroup contact under appropriate conditions can bring about generalized change in outgroup attitudes. Changing the structure of social categorizations is also important, and de-categorization, re-categorization, and crossed categorization can reduce or change the salience of existing categorization in a complementary fashion. Indeed, the interventions most likely to succeed will integrate these perspectives. Changing the social structure may also, ultimately, be necessary, but it should be guided by what we know about the functioning of social categorization.

We hope to have shown in this chapter some of the main contributions of a social–psychological approach to conflict and how this approach is different from the contributions made by specialists from other disciplines. We have demonstrated the potency of social categorization and argued that the social identity approach helps us to understand why social categorization can so easily lead to intergroup conflict. Although there is certainly more to most social conflicts than mere psychology, we have argued that most intergroup conflicts have an identifiable social–psychological component. This psychological component can exist alongside and exacerbate objective conflict, and attacking this component of conflict is important in and of itself. We have also reviewed what we see as the most important group-based social–psychological interventions aimed at reducing intergroup conflict. These include intergroup contact under appropriate conditions and attempts to reduce the salience of existing social categorizations. These interventions are not intended as a panacea for conflict, but rather as a set of ideas that can be used to achieve specific types of improved intergroup relations. These interventions, like our social–psychological perspective, are not meant to replace alternative interventions, but to be used as part of a necessary multidisciplinary approach to intergroup conflict.

REFERENCES

Abrams, D., & Hogg, M. A. (Eds.). (1990). *Social identity theory: Constructive and critical advances.* Hemel Hempstead, England: Harvester Wheatsheaf.

Allport, G. W. (Ed.). (1979). *The nature of prejudice.* Cambridge, MA: Addison-Wesley. (Original work published 1954)

Bettencourt, B. A., Brewer, M. B., Rogers-Croak, M., & Miller, N. (1992). Cooperation and the reduction of intergroup bias: The role of reward structure and social orientation. *Journal of Experimental Social Psychology, 28,* 301–319.

Bettencourt, B. A., Charlton, K., & Kernahan, C. (1997). Numerical representation of groups in co-operative settings: Social orientation effects on ingroup bias. *Journal of Experimental Social Psychology, 33,* 630–659.

Billig, M. (1976). *Social psychology and intergroup relations.* London: Academic Press.

Bonta, B. D. (1997). Cooperation and competition in peaceful societies. *Psychological Bulletin, 121,* 299–320.

Botev, N., & Wagner, R. A. (1993). Seeing past the barricades: Ethnic intermarriage in Yugoslavia during the last three decades. *Anthropology of East Europe Review, 11*(1-2), 29–38.

Bourhis, R. Y., Sachdev, I., & Gagnon, A. (1994). Intergroup research with the Tajfel matrices: Methodological notes. In M. P. Zanna & J. M. Olson (Eds.), *The psychology of prejudice: The Ontario Symposium* (Vol. 7, pp. 209–232). Hillsdale, NJ: Erlbaum.

Brewer, M. B. (1979). The role of ethnocentrism in intergroup conflict. In W. G. Austin & S. Worchel (Eds.), *The social psychology of intergroup relations* (pp. 71–84). Monterey, CA: Brooks/Cole.

Brewer, M. B. (1997). The social psychology of intergroup relations: Can research inform practice? *Journal of Social Issues, 53,* 197–211.

Brewer, M. B., & Brown, R. J. (1998). Intergroup relations. In D. T. Gilbert, S. T. Fiske, & G. Lindzey (Eds.), *The handbook of social psychology* (4th ed., pp. 554–594). New York: McGraw-Hill.

Brewer, M. B., & Campbell, D. T. (1976). *Ethnocentrism and intergroup attitudes: East African evidence.* New York: Halstead Press.

Brewer, M. B., Ho, H. K., Lee, J. Y., & Miller, N. (1987). Social identity and social distance among Hong Kong schoolchildren. *Personality and Social Psychology Bulletin, 13,* 156–165.

Brewer, M. B., & Miller, N. (1984). Beyond the contact hypothesis: Theoretical perspectives on desegregation. In N. Miller & M. B. Brewer (Eds.), *Groups in contact: The psychology of desegregation* (pp. 281–302). Orlando, FL: Academic Press.

Brewer, M. B., & Miller, N. (1988). Contact and cooperation: When do they work? In P. Katz & D. Taylor (Eds.), *Eliminating racism: Means and controversies* (pp. 315–326). New York: Plenum Press.

Brown, R. (1984). The role of similarity in intergroup relations. In H. Tajfel (Ed.), *The social dimension: European developments in social psychology* (Vol. 2, pp. 603–623). Cambridge, England: Cambridge University Press.

Brown, R., & Turner, J. C. (1981). Interpersonal and intergroup behavior. In J. C. Turner & H. Giles (Eds.), *Intergroup behaviour* (pp. 33–65). Oxford, England: Basil Blackwell.

Brown, R. J., Vivian, J., & Hewstone, M. (1999). Changing attitudes through intergroup contact: The effects of group membership salience. *European Journal of Social Psychology, 29*, 741–764.

Cairns, E. (1982). Intergroup conflict in Northern Ireland. In H. Tajfel (Ed.), *Social identity and intergroup relations* (pp. 277–298). Cambridge, England: Cambridge University Press.

Cairns, E., & Darby, J. (1988). The conflict in Northern Ireland. *American Psychologist, 53*, 754–760.

Cook, S. W. (1978). Interpersonal and attitudinal outcomes in cooperating interracial groups. *Journal of Research and Development in Education, 12*, 97–113.

Crisp, R. J., & Hewstone, M. (1999). Testing patterns of crossed categorization: Contextual antecedents and underlying processes. *Group Processes and Intergroup Relations, 2*, 307–333.

Crisp, R. J., & Hewstone, M. (2000). Multiple categorization and social identity. In D. Capozza & R. Brown (Eds.), *Social identity theory: Trends in theory and research* (pp. 149–166). Thousand Oaks, CA: Sage.

The Daily Telegraph. (1998, October 30).

Deutsch, M. (1973). *The resolution of conflict: Constructive and destructive processes.* New Haven, CT: Yale University Press.

Doise, W. (1978). *Groups and individuals: Explanations in social psychology.* Cambridge, England: Cambridge University Press.

Doosje, B., Branscombe, N. R., Spears, R., & Manstead, A. S. R. (1998). Guilty by association: When one's group has a negative history. *Journal of Personality and Social Psychology, 75*, 872–886.

Dovidio, J. F., Gaertner, S. L., Isen, A. M., & Lowrance, R. (1995). Group representations and intergroup bias: Positive affect, similarity, and group size. *Personality and Social Psychology Bulletin, 21*, 856–865.

Dovidio, J. F., Gaertner, S. L., Isen, A. M., Rust, M., & Guerra, P. (1988). Positive affect, cognition, and the reduction of intergroup bias. In C. Sedikides, J. Schopler & C. A. Insko (Eds.), *Intergroup cognition and intergroup behavior* (pp. 337–366). Mahwah, NJ: Erlbaum.

Dovidio, J. F., Gaertner, S. L., & Validzic, A. (1998). Intergroup bias: Status, differentiation, and a common ingroup identity. *Journal of Personality and Social Psychology, 75*, 109–120.

Eurich-Fulcher, R., & Schofield, J. W. (1995). Correlated versus uncorrelated social categorizations: The effect on intergroup bias. *Personality and Social Psychology Bulletin, 21*, 149–159.

Fisher, R. J. (1994). Generic principles for resolving intergroup conflict. *Journal of Social Issues, 50,* 47–66.

Gaertner, S. L., Dovidio, J. F., Anastasio, P. A., Bachman, B. A., & Rust, M. C. (1993). The common group identity model: Recategorization and the reduction of intergroup bias. In W. Stroebe & M. Hewstone (Eds.), *European review of social psychology* (Vol. 4, pp. 1–26). Chichester, England: Wiley.

Gaertner, S. L., Dovidio, J. F., Rust, M. C., Nier, J. A., Banker, B. S., Ward, C. M., Mottola, G. R., & Houlette, M. (1999). Reducing intergroup bias: Elements of intergroup cooperation. *Journal of Personality and Social Psychology, 76,* 388–402.

Gaertner, S. L., Mann, J. A., Dovidio, J. F., Murrell, A. J., & Pomare, M. (1990). How does cooperation reduce intergroup bias? *Journal of Personality and Social Psychology, 59,* 692–704.

Gaertner, S. L., Mann, J. A., Murrell, A. J., & Dovidio, J. F. (1989). Reducing intergroup bias: The benefits of recategorization. *Journal of Personality and Social Psychology, 57,* 239–249.

Gallagher, A. M. (1995). *Education in a divided society: A review of research and policy.* Coleraine, Northern Ireland: University of Ulster, Centre for the Study of Conflict.

The Guardian. (1998, April 21).

Hamburger, Y. (1994). The contact hypothesis reconsidered: Effects of the atypical out-group member on the out-group stereotype. *Basic and Applied Social Psychology, 15,* 339–358.

Hewstone, M. (1994). Revision and change of stereotypic beliefs: In search of the elusive subtyping model. In W. Stroebe & M. Hewstone (Eds.), *European review of social psychology* (Vol. 5, pp. 69–109). Chichester, England: Wiley.

Hewstone, M. (1996). Contact and categorization: Social psychological interventions to change intergroup relations. In C. N. Macrae, C. Stangor, & M. Hewstone (Eds.), *Stereotypes and stereotyping* (pp. 323–368). New York: Guilford Press.

Hewstone, M., & Brown, R. J. (1986). Contact is not enough: An intergroup perspective on the "contact hypothesis." In M. Hewstone & R. J. Brown (Eds.), *Contact and conflict in intergroup encounters* (pp. 1–44). Oxford, England: Basil Blackwell.

Hewstone, M., Islam, M. R., & Judd, C. M. (1993). Models of crossed categorization and intergroup relations. *Journal of Personality and Social Psychology, 64,* 779–793.

Horowitz, D. (1985). *Ethnic groups in conflict.* Berkeley: University of California Press.

Islam, M. R., & Hewstone, M. (1993). Dimensions of contact as predictors of intergroup anxiety, perceived out-group variability, and out-group attitude: An integrative model. *Personality and Social Psychology Bulletin, 19,* 700–710.

Keane, F. (1995). *Season of blood: A Rwandan journey.* London: Penguin Books.

LeVine, R. A., & Campbell, D. T. (1972). *Ethnocentrism: Theories of conflict, ethnic attitudes and group behavior.* New York: Wiley.

Linville, P. W. (1998). The heterogeneity of homogeneity. In J. Cooper & J. Darley (Eds.), *Attribution processes and social interaction: The legacy of Edward E. Jones* (pp. 423–462). Washington, DC: American Psychological Association.

McGarry, J., & O'Leary, B. (1993). Introduction: The macro-political regulation of ethnic conflict. In J. McGarry & B. O'Leary (Eds.), *The politics of ethnic conflict regulation: Case studies of protracted ethnic conflicts* (pp. 1–40). New York: Routledge.

McKittrick, D. (1998, July 3). *The Independent.*

Migdal, M., Hewstone, M., & Mullen, B. (1998). The effects of crossed categorization on intergroup evaluations: A meta-analysis. *British Journal of Social Psychology, 69,* 1203–1215.

Miller, N., Brewer, M. B., & Edwards, K. (1985). Cooperative interaction in desegregated settings: A laboratory analogue. *Journal of Social Issues, 41,* 63–81.

Miller, N., Urban, L. M., & Vanman, E. J. (1998). A theoretical analysis of crossed social categorization effects. In C. Sedikides, J. Schopler, & C. A. Insko (Eds.), *Intergroup cognition and intergroup behavior* (pp. 393–422). Mahwah, NJ: Erlbaum.

Oakes, P. J., Haslam, A., & Turner, J. C. (1994). *Stereotyping and social reality.* Oxford, England: Basil Blackwell.

Pettigrew, T. F. (1979). The ultimate attribution error: Extending Allport's cognitive analysis of prejudice. *Personality and Social Psychology Bulletin, 5,* 461–476.

Pettigrew, T. F. (1998). Intergroup contact theory. *Annual Review of Psychology, 49,* 65–85.

Poole, M. A., & Doherty, P. (1996). *Ethnic residential segregation in Northern Ireland.* Coleraine, Northern Ireland: University of Ulster, Center for the Study of Conflict.

Prunier, G. (1995). *The Rwanda crisis (1959–1994): History of a genocide.* London: Hurst.

Reed, J. S. (1982). *One south: An ethnic approach to regional culture.* Baton Rouge: Louisiana State University Press.

Rubin, M., & Hewstone, M. (1998). Social identity theory's self-esteem hypothesis: A review and some suggestions for clarification. *Personality and Social Psychology Review, 2,* 40–62.

Ryan, C. S., Judd, C. M., & Park, B. (1996). Effects of racial stereotypes on judgments of individuals: The moderating role of perceived group variability. *Journal of Experimental Social Psychology, 32,* 71–103.

Scarberry, N. C., Ratcliff, C. D., Lord, C. G., Lanicek, D. L., & Desforges, D. M. (1997). Effects of individuating information on the generalization part of Allport's contact hypothesis. *Personality and Social Psychology Bulletin, 23,* 1291–1299.

Schopler, J., & Insko, C. A. (1992). The discontinuity effect in interpersonal and intergroup relations: Generality and mediation. In W. Stroebe & M. Hewstone

(Eds.), *European review of social psychology* (Vol. 3, pp. 121–152). Chichester, England: Wiley.

Sherif, M. (1966). *Group conflict and cooperation.* London: Routledge & Kegan Paul.

Sherif, M., Harvey, O. J., White, B. J., Hood, W. R., & Sherif, C. W. (1961). *The Robbers Cave experiment: Group conflict and cooperation.* Norman: Oklahoma University Press.

Staub, E. (1989). *The roots of evil: The origins of genocide and other group violence.* New York: Cambridge University Press.

Stephan, W. G., & Stephan, C. W. (1985). Intergroup anxiety. *Journal of Social Issues, 41,* 157–175.

Stover, E., & Peress, G. (1998). *The graves.* Zurich, Switzerland: Scalo Verlag.

Sumner, W. G. (1906). *Folkways.* Boston, MA: Ginn.

Tajfel, H. (Ed.). (1978). *Differentiation between social groups.* London: Academic Press.

Tajfel, H. (1979). Individuals and groups in social psychology. *British Journal of Social Psychology, 18,* 183–190.

Tajfel, H. (1981). Social stereotypes and social groups. In J. C. Turner & H. Giles (Eds.), *Intergroup behaviour* (pp. 144–167). Oxford, England: Basil Blackwell.

Tajfel, H. (Ed.). (1982). *Social identity and intergroup relations.* Cambridge, England: Cambridge University Press.

Tajfel, H., Billig, M., Bundy, R. P., & Flament, C. (1971). Social categorization and intergroup behavior. *European Journal of Social Psychology, 1,* 149–177.

Tajfel, H., & Turner, J. C. (1979). An integrative theory of intergroup conflict. In W. G. Austin & S. Worchel (Eds.), *The social psychology of intergroup relations* (pp. 33–47). Monterey, CA: Brooks/Cole.

Turner, J. C. (1981). The experimental social psychology of intergroup behavior. In J. C. Turner & H. Giles (Eds.), *Intergroup behaviour* (pp. 1–32). Oxford, England: Basil Blackwell.

Turner, J. C., & Brown, R. (1978). Social status, cognitive alternatives and intergroup relations. In H. Tajfel (Ed.), *Differentiation between social groups: Studies in the social psychology of intergroup relations* (pp. 201–234). London: Academic Press.

Turner, J. C., Hogg, M. A., Oakes, P. J., Reicher, S. D., & Wetherell, M. S. (1987). *Rediscovering the social group: A self-categorization theory.* Oxford, England: Basil Blackwell.

Vanbeselaere, N. (1991). The different effects of simple and crossed categorizations: A result of the category differentiation process or of differential category salience? In W. Stroebe & M. Hewstone (Eds.), *European review of social psychology* (Vol. 2, pp. 247–278). Chichester, England: Wiley.

Van Knippenberg, A., & Ellemers, N. (1990). Social identity and intergroup differentiation processes. In W. Stroebe & M. Hewstone (Eds.), *European review of social psychology* (Vol. 1, pp. 137–170). Chichester, England: Wiley.

Van Oudenhoven, J. P., Groenewoud, J. T., & Hewstone, M. (1996). Cooperation, ethnic salience and generalization of interethnic attitudes. *European Journal of Social Psychology, 26,* 649–661.

Vescio, T. K., Hewstone, M., Crisp, R. J., & Rubin, J. M. (1999). Perceiving and responding to multiply categorizable individuals: Cognitive processes and affective intergroup bias. In D. Abrams & M. A. Hogg (Eds.), *Social identity and social cognition* (pp. 111–140). Cambridge, MA: Basil Blackwell.

Whyte, J. (1990). *Interpreting Northern Ireland.* New York: Oxford University Press.

Wilder, D. A. (1984). Intergroup contact: The typical member and the exception to the rule. *Journal of Experimental Social Psychology, 20,* 177–194.

Wilder, D. A. (1986). Social categorization: Implications for creation and reduction of intergroup bias. In L. Berkowitz (Ed.), *Advances in experimental social psychology* (pp. 293–355). New York: Academic Press.

Wilder, D. A. (1993). The role of anxiety in facilitating stereotypic judgments of out-group behavior. In D. M. Mackie & D. L. Hamilton (Eds.), *Affect, cognition and stereotyping.* (pp. 87–109). San Diego, CA: Academic Press.

Wilder, D. A., Simon, A. F., & Faith, M. (1996). Enhancing the impact of counter-stereotypic information: Dispositional attributions for deviance. *Journal of Personality and Social Psychology, 71,* 276–287.

Wright, S., Aron, A., McLaughlin-Volpe, T., & Ropp, S. A. (1997). The extended contact effect: Knowledge of cross-group friendships and prejudice. *Journal of Personality and Social Psychology, 73,* 73–90.

21

THE PSYCHOLOGY OF GROUP IDENTIFICATION AND THE POWER OF ETHNIC NATIONALISM

CLARK MCCAULEY

The psychological foundation of ethnic nationalism and ethnic conflict is *group identification*—an emotional attachment to a group. Politically, the power of an ethnic or national group is precisely the degree to which individuals will sacrifice their narrow self-interests—even their lives—to the group interest. The birth of modern nationalism is often located at Valmy, in 1792, when French troops shouting "Vive la Nation" stood up under superior Prussian fire. There is something essentially social about this kind of identification: The individual feels part of a group of people who are willing to sacrifice for the group. Emotional attachment to a group that no one else recognizes or cares about may be possible, but it is irrelevant to politics. Thus a nation is more than a group of people who recognize themselves as a nation; the group must recognize mutual feeling for their nation (Bar-Tal, 1990). The challenge for psychology is to understand the nature of this group feeling, its origins and manipulations. In this chapter, I represent some of the psychological research that may at least begin to respond to this challenge.

THE PSYCHOLOGY OF IDENTIFICATION

A Definition

Most generally, *identification* means feeling the well-being—the positive and negative outcomes of others—as our own. This is not the same as *empathy*, which is feeling what others are feeling (as anyone knows who has ever shivered for the fate of a screen character blissfully unaware of lurking danger). It is not the same as *sympathy*, which is feeling sorry for others; identification includes the glory of others' successes as well as the misery of others' troubles. Identification includes negative or reverse identification; some people care about football only to root against the Dallas Cowboys. It is not the same as Kelman's (1958) treatment of identification as persuasion based on admiring and wanting to be like others, a kind of halfway-house between internalized opinion and mere compliance. Group identification includes caring about groups that one is not a member of, including victim groups that one does not want to be a part of.

Contrary to Freudian accounts of the dissolution of ego boundaries, identification does not mean losing consciousness of the difference between self and other (McCauley, 1998b). Identification with fictional characters, for instance, does not mean losing awareness of the difference between fantasy and reality; if it did, we would run from the theater to call out the army or the police to deal with on-screen aliens or bad guys. Rather, identification means expanding the boundaries of what we care about, from narrow self-interest—"what's in it for me and mine, right now" (Kinder, 1998, p. 801)—to an interest invested in others.

Objects of Identification

Thus understood, identification is a major phenomenon, with many and varied expressions. It is commonplace to recognize that we feel the outcomes of those close to us—family, friends, co-workers, teammates—and this primary group identification is usually explained in terms of interdependence amounting to enlightened self-interest. That is, our individual outcomes are unavoidably dependent on what happens to these groups. This kind of caring is the focus of theorizing by economists and sociobiologists, who want to understand human behavior in terms of maximizing individual or genetic self-interest.

But we often care about what happens to individuals, groups, and even objects whose well-being is only subjectively, avoidably, or weakly linked to our own. Individual objects of identification include mass media personalities, both real (princesses, presidents) and imaginary (characters from print or screen). Group objects of identification include sports teams made up of individuals we would not want as neighbors or guests (professional football players), as well as secondary or common-interest groups so large that the great majority of members are personally unknown to us (ethnic or national groups, coreligionists, union members).

For most common-interest groups, it is difficult to show that the individual can expect to be better off for any investment in or sacrifice for the group. The time and effort of voting in national and local elections is not negligible, but the chance of affecting the outcome of the election is. Similarly, the investment required to attend a neighborhood meeting, a faculty meeting, or a labor union meeting is not typically repaid by the individual's impact on the meeting. The costs of going out on strike are immediate and significant, but the individual's impact on the success of the strike is not obvious. This is the free-rider problem; economists and sociobiologists have identified the problem but have not found it easy to explain how collective action could be rational for the individual member of a common-interest group (Schroeder, Sibicky, & Irwin, 1995).

Even more mysterious is the fact that we often come to care about groups that we do not belong to, even when we do not know personally even one member of the group. We sympathize with the plight of single mothers, people with AIDS, political refugees, and disaster victims, and we contribute to helping these victim groups. One can mount an argument of enlightened self-interest ("it could happen to me," "refugees unaided may flood into my country"), but the argument requires very enlightened people unenlightened about the free-rider problem. It is worth noting that, once beyond immediate self-interest, the rational expectations model fast becomes tautological: If people sacrifice for something, it must be because it is in their self-interest.

Even possessions can become objects of identification. We rejoice and suffer with our pets. We feel good when our household goods are safe, clean, and well ordered but feel bad if they are damaged, stolen, dirty, or disarrayed. The cost of burglary is more than the loss of goods; it is thinking about bad people touching and turning over our things, violating the space we call home. Of course our possessions have quotidian utilities, but human attachment to familiar possessions goes beyond their replacement cost (Belk, 1992).

Group Identification in Context

The varied expressions of identification reveal human beings as ready and even eager to pour themselves into people and things outside themselves. Against economic and evolutionary models of humans as selfish competitors—what's in it for me and mine, right now—the everyday expressions of identification raise a more generous view of self-interest. This generosity does not mean losing awareness of narrow self-interest; rather, as at Valmy, it means caring enough about others to compromise narrow self-interest for interest in other's outcomes (Smith, 1993).

Caring about the outcomes of groups we are not part of is the most mysterious form of group identification. Obviously related to this mystery is the psychology of sympathy and empathy, although the relevance is strained by the fact that research on sympathy and empathy usually examines caring about individuals rather than caring about groups. I am not representing this literature here (but see Batson, 1998). Rather I am focusing in the remainder of this chapter on psychological research that is more explicitly focused on groups, especially research that may help illuminate the power of ethnic and national groups. I begin with a quick look at some effects of group identification, then move on to examine research relevant to understanding the origins and mobilization of group identification.

EFFECTS OF GROUP IDENTIFICATION

Self-Esteem Effects

Group identification is implicated in self-esteem: We like to be part of successful and high-status groups because membership improves our social status and self-esteem. We pay more for a Cadillac than for a Chevrolet at least partly to join and to be seen joining the group of successful people who can afford a Cadillac. Similarly we attend high-status schools, select high-status occupations, and join high-status clubs at least partly to participate in the self-esteem benefits of these groups. The more exclusive the group, the more we identify with it (Brewer & Brown, 1998, p. 564).

Less obviously, being part of a low-status, disadvantaged, or stigmatized group may also help support self-esteem. Black and Chicano children have self-esteem equal to or higher than that of White children, and self-esteem is not lower for groups with disabilities, disfigurements, or obesity than for those without disadvantage (Crocker & Major, 1989). One possibility is that identification with a lower-status group permits increased self-esteem by attributing individual problems to group victimization rather than to personal failings. Thus, within a disadvantaged group, self-esteem may be positively related to degree of group identification. This prediction, to my knowledge, has not been tested.

We also like to be associated with successful groups that we are not part of and, in some cases at least, the association can affect our self-esteem. Cialdini et al. (1976) found, for instance, that students are more likely to say "we" in reference to the university football team on Mondays after the team has won its Sunday game. Students whose self-esteem has been experimentally reduced are more likely than unmanipulated students to show this effect. Hirt, Zillmann, Erickson, and Kennedy (1992) have reported that university students show higher self-esteem and higher self-expectations after watching their basketball team win than after watching it lose.

Thus our self-esteem is affected by the groups we are part of and even by the outcomes of groups we identify with but are not part of. With or without membership, caring about the right groups is an important marker of status and values. Why some group identifications may be more powerful than others in engaging self-esteem will be considered in a discussion of "terror management theory."

In-group Bias Effects

Study of "minimal groups" has shown that even the most arbitrary categorization of people can produce significant bias in favor the in-group (Tajfel & Turner, 1986). The experimenter divides individuals into two groups on the basis of their preference for art by Klee versus art by Kandinsky or even on the basis of a public coin flip. Following this division, and without ever interacting with one another, the individuals are asked to allocate rewards to, or judge the products of, members of the two groups. The consistent result is that individuals allocate more reward (e.g., money) to members of their own group and judge as better the products (e.g., essays) of members of their own group.

A notable aspect of this result is that it does not extend to allocation of negative outcomes; participants asked to allocate punishments (costs) in the minimal group paradigm do not favor the in-group (Mummendey et al., 1992). This limitation underlines the fact that in-group favoritism and out-group hostility are not necessarily linked. It is often assumed that increasing identification with the in-group implies a reciprocal decrease in identification with the out-group—reduced concern for what happens to the out-group or even negative identification that rejoices in out-group losses. The null result for minimal groups' allocation of costs is consistent with other evidence (Brewer & Brown, 1998, p. 559) indicating that in-group and out-group identification can vary independently.

Physiological Effects

Particularly with social constructivist theories of ethnic and national identification, there may be a tendency to think of group identification as something illusory, almost hallucinatory. Some indication of the substantial and material nature of group identification comes from recent research indicating the physiological impact of caring about group outcomes. The background for this research was a series of studies of testosterone levels of individuals who are involved in competition (Bernhardt, 1997). These studies showed that testosterone level (assayed from saliva) is both a predictor of behavior and a consequence of behavior.

Trial lawyers, for instance, have higher levels of testosterone than other lawyers. Tennis and chess players show an increase in testosterone before and during competition; after competition, winners show increases, but losers show decreases in testosterone. Thus it has been clear for some time that competition has effects on testosterone levels of competitors.

Recent research by Bernhardt, Dabbs, Fielden, and Lutter (1998) has taken this relationship a step further. It turns out that onlookers to competition show the same pattern of testosterone changes as the competitors.

Graduate students went into sports bars in Atlanta during the 1994 championship match of the World Cup soccer tournament. The game was on television, and the students obtained samples of saliva from fans of the two finalists, Brazil and Italy, both before and after the game. Brazil won the match, and Brazilian fans showed testosterone increases averaging around 20%; Italian fans showed testosterone decreases averaging around 20%. Group identification is evidently not all in the mind or only in the mind—not, at least, in the sense that opposes mind and body. The research cited in this section suggests that a new subdiscipline of psychology—the neurobiology of group identification—is waiting to be born.

Effects on Public Opinion in the United States

The great lesson of research on political opinions is that these opinions are not generally understandable in terms of individual self-interest. Kinder (1998, p. 801) cited studies showing that "The unemployed do not line up behind policies designed to alleviate economic distress;" "The medically indigent are no more likely to favor government health insurance than are the fully insured;" "Parents of children enrolled in public schools are generally no more supportive of government aid to education than are other citizens;" "Americans who are subject to the draft are not especially opposed to military intervention or to the escalation of conflicts already under way;" "Women employed outsides the home to not differ from homemakers in their support for policies intended to benefit women at work;" and "On such diverse matters as racial busing for the purpose of school desegregation, anti-drinking ordinances, mandatory college examinations, housing policy, bilingual education, compliance with laws, satisfaction with the resolution of legal disputes, gun control, and more, self-interest turns out to be quite unimportant."

Of course self-interest can sometimes be important in determining political opinions, but Kinder (1998) suggested that self-interest matters only when the relevant costs and benefits are substantial, imminent, and well publicized. These conditions were satisfied in the California battle over capping property taxes, Proposition 13, in which homeowners with the most to save in taxes were most favorable and public employees paid with these taxes were most negative. Kinder also noted that self-interest can be related to the importance attached to a political issue, even when self-interest does not predict position on the issue. On balance, however, Kinder agreed with Citrin and Green (1990) that "the evidence is devastating for the claim that self-interest, defined narrowly as the pursuit of immediate material benefits, is the central motive underlying American public opinion" (p. 16).

In contrast, perceived group interests are a much more reliable and powerful predictor of political opinions. Kinder cited studies showing that "Support among whites for affirmative action or school desegregation reflects sympathy for the plight of blacks," "Opposition to social welfare programs derives from hostility toward the poor," "Support for a tough-minded foreign policy reflects fear of communists," "Acquiescence in political repression depends on whose phones are to be tapped," and "Opposition to benefits for recent immigrants reflects suspicions that they are lazy or dangerous or somehow un-American." Support for the importance of perceived group outcomes comes also from interview studies, in which Americans and Europeans asked to evaluate political parties or candidates will most often refer to the positive and negative outcomes of groups they care about (Kinder, 1998, p. 803).

The group-centric nature of political reactions is also supported by research showing that political activism is motivated more by perception of group disadvantage than by perception of personal disadvantage. Runciman (1966) introduced this distinction into relative deprivation theory in arguing that it is "fraternal" rather than "egotistical" deprivation that leads to anger and political protest. Kinder (1998) cited research consistent with this argument: "Thus participation of black college students in the civil rights movement in the American South in the 1960s was predicted better by their anger over society's treatment of black Americans in general than by any discontent they felt about their own lives;" "Thus white working-class participants in the Boston anti-busing movement were motivated especially by their resentments about the gains of blacks and professionals, and less by their own personal trouble" (p. 837). Kinder concluded that the political power of deprivation lies in the perception of collective rather than personal deprivation.

The picture that emerges from studies of political opinions is that citizens understand and react to the political world in terms of group interests, including the interests of groups they are not part of. Individuals identify positively with some groups and react favorably to leaders and policies perceived to help these groups. Negative identification is also evident: Individuals see some groups as bad or undeserving and react negatively to leaders and policies associated with helping these groups. Political opinion and political action are better understood as effects of group identification than as effects of individual self-interest.

MOBILIZING GROUP IDENTIFICATION

Given the political and even commercial importance of group identification, its origins and elicitors should be of great interest. Unfortunately, this topic is understudied in psychology, especially in regard to mobilizing national and ethnic identification. Each individual is a member of many different groups, both face-to-face groups and common-interest groups; each individual is capable of identifying with many groups that he or she is not a member of. How does one group identification get control of the individual's behavior, against the interests and welfare of other groups? To return to the example of Valmy, how did identification with "la Nation" rise to dominate self-preservation and the interests of family and village as French soldiers risked their lives?

Social Groups as Categories

Group identification must begin with groups as percepts, that is, with division of people into categories and with beliefs about these categories. How these categories are acquired and how they are represented are major issues in cognitive and social psychology. The classical view was that categories are defined by necessary and sufficient conditions. Although logical categories such as "even number" can be thus defined—divisible by two without remainder—most people have nothing like a classical definition of "dog" or "vegetable." Cognitive psychologists have suggested instead that natural categories are derived from perceptions of similarity, although opinions differ as to whether similarity is represented in relation to category "prototype," in relation to previously encountered "exemplars," or in relation to abstract "feature lists" (Smith & Medin, 1981). Beyond similarity, Keil (1989) has argued the special importance of theories of ontogeny in categorizing living things: An animal is a dog no matter what it looks like if its parent was a dog.

Hirschfeld (1996) has taken Keil's focus on ontogeny a big step further with research indicating that racial categories depend upon a biologically based cognitive module that prepares human children and even adults to interpret the world of human differences in terms of essences. This human-kind-creating mechanism interacts with culture to produce essentialized categories such as gender and race. Hirschfeld argued that a similar but independent module prepares us to interpret the non-human animal world in terms of essences such as species.

An essentialized category combines immutability (essence expressed in physical characteristics or tendencies that cannot be changed in an individual's lifetime), discrimination (not all characteristics differ by essence), and heritability (essence-related characteristics determined from family background and fixed at birth). Racial and gender categories are near-universal outcomes of the human-kind-creating module, and kinship categories are likewise commonly essentialized. Occupational categories are essentialized by some cultures and, according to Hirschfeld, by many American three-year-olds. The content of racial categories is culturally variable. Irish and Italians have sometimes been essentialized in the

United States, Jews have often been essentialized by Christians, and Germans and Jews have essentialized their own groups in their "laws of return."

Hirschfeld's work implies a promising program of research for understanding ethnic group identification. The extent to which ethnic or national differences are essentialized, before or after group conflict, needs investigation, as does the question of whether essentializing a group may facilitate positive or negative identification with that group. Hirschfeld (1996, p. 61) noted that class has at least as much potential as race for explaining group conflict, but it may just be less easy to "think." Prunier (chapter 8, this volume) suggested that Hutu and Tutsi in Rwanda are better considered classes or status groups than tribes, but it also seems that these groups were essentialized or racialized before genocide was possible.

Stereotypes

The first empirical study of perceptions of ethnic and national groups was conducted in 1933 by Katz and Braly, who found few surprises: Germans were seen as efficient, Irish as pugnacious, Italians as artistic, and so forth. Katz and Braly and their successors followed Lippmann (1922) in seeing these perceptions as *stereotypes*—pictures of the social world that are inaccurate or at least exaggerated, as well as irrationally resistant to change in the face of picture-contradicting instances. Many continue in this early view of stereotypes even as modern social psychologists have agreed that the picture metaphor is inadequate. Stereotypes are not held as all-or-none pictures of group characteristic: No one reports that 100% of the members of an ethnic or national group have a stereotyped characteristic. Rather, stereotypes are probabilistic perceptions of group differences, that is, beliefs that certain characteristics are more likely in one group than another (McCauley, Stitt, & Segal, 1980).

Thus understood, stereotypes are not obviously incorrect and, statistically, should not change in reaction to small nonrandom samples of individuals who do not fit the modal characteristics expected for their group. Relatively few studies have assessed stereotype accuracy, but these do not indicate any general tendency to exaggerate real group differences (McCauley, 1995). No accuracy study has examined mutual stereotyping of groups in violent conflict, so it remains possible that under these conditions stereotypes are indeed exaggerated. The degree to which ethnic group differences are essentialized (by Hirschfeld's definition) has also been little studied, although he has reported that middle-class U.S. citizens tend to see economic and social factors as more important than race in explaining differences between Black and White people in the United States.

Stereotypes may be more the effect than the cause of group conflict. In the United States, for instance, stereotypes of Japanese and Germans took a turn for the worse in and around World War II but returned to something like 1930s stereotypes by the 1950s. In general it is probably not useful to try to understand relations between groups on the basis of group differences in personality traits. If personality differences were crucial, the United States and the United Kingdom would not twice in 50 years have been at war with Germany. Stereotypes of cultural differences in values, especially political values, might be more useful for understanding intergroup relations, but this direction of research has not attracted much attention (but see Struch & Schwartz, 1989).

Patriotism and Nationalism

Social psychologists have not given much attention to patriotism or nationalism in recent years, despite the worldwide salience of these forms of group identification. A noteworthy exception is the work of Feshbach, who has developed a scale measuring individual differences in patriotism and, separately, a scale measuring individual differences in nationalism (Kesterman & Feshbach, 1989). Patriotism is feeling love of country, which Feshbach sees as good; nationalism is feeling that one's nation is superior to others, which Feshbach sees as bad. Unfortunately for this distinction, Feshbach (1991) has found the two scales highly correlated in at least some groups. The greater difficulty, however, is that study of individual differences may not tell us much about how to mobilize patriotic and nationalistic feelings. Mobilizing these feelings does not mean that individual differences disappear or even that the distribution of feelings becomes less variable; rather it means moving the whole distribution of feelings toward increasing patriotism and nationalism. Feshbach has not had much to say about how this mobilization occurs.

Action Frames and Moral Indignation

Similarly, political scientists have been interested in individual differences in political participation and political mobilization but have had less to say about how whole groups are moved to political action. Kinder (1998) pointed to the "action frames" (Gamson, 1992) analysis of social movements as potentially useful for understanding political mobilization. There are three components to an action frame: (1) A successful frame must express moral indignation at some harm or injustice, (2) must convey confidence that action can make a difference in righting the wrong, and (3) must define a "we" who can help and a "they" who are responsible for the injustice. Gamson said that the first of these is crucial; recognizing injustice usually implies something about who is responsible and about the possibility and obligation of collective action to right the wrong recognized.

The social construction of moral violation is underdeveloped in psychology, especially in regard to group violations. It seems likely, however, that this construction may proceed incrementally or in stages. Sprinzak (1991) has described the development of terrorist groups such as the United States Weatherman group as follows: First the goal is reform (e.g., the United States has gone wrong waging war in Vietnam); then, when reform efforts fail, the system is seen as corrupt and illegitimate (the U.S. government is no longer in the hands of the people, violence against government justified); and, finally, everyone supporting the government may become a target (everyone who is not with us is against us). Sprinzak's second stage is similar to what Kinder (1998, p. 832) has called *political disaffection*. Kinder reviewed studies indicating that participants in high-risk political activism such as demonstrations, sit-ins, and riots are motivated by disaffection with the system, a kind of negative identification with government in which political leaders and the legal system are seen as exploitative and illegitimate.

Group Extremity Shift

Potentially related to the social construction of moral violation is the phenomenon of group polarization or "group extremity-shift." Group discussion tends to move attitudes and judgments of group members toward greater extremity in the direction favored by most individuals before discussion. (The shift is typically measured on a bipolar opinion scale with a neutral midpoint.) This shift has two mechanisms, which usually operate together (Brown, 1989). The first mechanism is relevant arguments. The bias in initial individual opinions is reflected in discussion, such that most of the arguments that come out in discussion support the initially favored direction of opinion. Group members are then persuaded in the direction of the new arguments they hear in discussion.

The second mechanism of group extremity shift is social comparison. Those initially more extreme in the group-favored direction are more admired and, in the competition for status within the group, no one wants to be below average in devotion to the group-favored opinion. This motivation is a push toward increased extremity for individuals initially less extreme than the group average opinion. Of course the link between extremity and admiration must, in the world outside of laboratory experiments, have some limits. The boundary between being unusually devoted to group values and being just unusual—or crazy—needs more attention than it has received.

It seems likely that these two mechanisms of group extremity shift are at work in both public and private discussions related to the moral status of ethnic and national groups. If identification with a group, either positive or negative, can be taken as a kind of attitude, then the mechanisms of group extremity shift may contribute to mobilizing group identification—once most individuals already feel for or against the group in question.

Group Dynamics Theory

One possibility for understanding the origins of group identification is to extend group dynamics theory, developed in research on face-to-face groups, to secondary groups. Group dynamics theory distinguishes between two kinds of attraction to a group (Levine & Moreland, 1998, pp. 427–428, 434). The social reality value of a group is its ability to validate opinions with the certainty of group consensus (see the later section on terror management theory). The instrumental value of a group is based on more mundane rewards: common goals, congeniality of group members, high individual status within the group, and high group status among other groups. These distinctions can be important: The rush to consensus that is called *group think* is more likely when cohesion based on congeniality is high, whereas critical examination of decision alternatives is actually encouraged when cohesion is based on the promise of accomplishing common goals (McCauley, 1998a).

It seems possible that parsing the sources of group identification may be similarly useful. Common fate, especially common threat, is a particularly powerful source of group cohesion, and it may equally be a powerful source of identification with ethnic and national groups. Extending group dynamics theory to identification with political groups suggests, for instance, that something very powerful is set in motion when a government begins to allocate rewards and costs to citizens according to ethnic group membership.

Furthermore, it seems likely that the mobilization of group identification is located in face-to-face group dynamics. The social reality value of a group, its power to define right and wrong for its members, increases to the extent that group members are cut off from participation in other groups. This is what happens in the intense religious groups often called cults and what happens in development of and recruitment to underground terrorist groups (McCauley & Segal, 1987). Similarly, Tarrow (1994) has suggested that preexisting social connections are "what makes possible the transformation of episodic collective action into social movements" (p. 22).

My suggestion here is that mobilization of ethnic nationalism or patriotism cannot be understood only at the level of individual beliefs or emotions; mobilization must occur at the level of small group norms if it is to have significant impact on individual willingness to sacrifice for the group. As small-group cohesion has been found to be crucial for combat performance (Stouffer et al., 1949), so I am suggesting that small-group cohesion is crucial for understanding how groups are mobilized for political action.

The Psychology of Commitment

Another way of thinking about mobilizing group identification is to recognize that even the smallest behavior for or against a group becomes, not just a predictor, but a cause of later and larger behaviors. The power of commitment is evident in many forms (Cialdini, 1993), not least in the obedience paradigm made famous by Milgram (1974). The surprise in Milgram's paradigm is that most normal individuals will escalate giving shocks to a supposed participant in a learning experiment—all the way to 450 volts labeled "XXX" and "Danger—Strong Shock"—if an experimenter asks them to. Equally surprising is a less-known variation of Milgram's paradigm, in which the experimenter is called away and a supposed fellow participant comes up with the idea of raising the shock one level for each mistake. In this variation, 20% of participants go all the way to the maximum 450 volts.

The authority of the experimenter cannot explain the 20%; rather it seems to be the progressive commitment of the participant that is important. There is no reason not to give the first shock; 15 volts is nothing. If 15 volts is nothing, why not 30 volts? If 30 volts is OK, why not 45? And so on. The slow escalation in shock levels is a slippery slope on which the best reason to give the next level is that the participant has already given the last level; if there is something wrong with the next level, there must have been something already wrong with the last level. Escalating commitment thus occurs in order to make sense of and to justify previous behavior (Teger, 1980); in particular, dissonance theory (see Brewer & Brown, 1998, pp. 578–579) would hold that escalation occurs in order to avoid the inconsistency between positive self-image and behavior that is stupid or sleazy. This is the psychology by which small donors to a cause become big donors, and by which idealistic protestors become terrorists (McCauley & Segal, 1987). Self-justification is a potential mechanism of escalating action in relation to positive or negative group identification. The only difficulty is in getting the first small action for or against a group; the psychology of commitment can take it from there.

Terror Management Theory

In the past 10 years, social psychologists have advanced a theory that promises a kind of master key for understanding social behavior (Pyszczynski, Greenberg, & Solomon, 1997). Terror management theory begins from the idea that humans are the only animals that know they are to die. Fear of death is potentially a paralyzing terror that can interfere with individual adaptation, with social relations and organization and, ultimately, with reproductive success. The answer to this fear is culture: all the ways in which humans are different from other animals, from the most everyday and thoughtless rituals to the most profound interpretations of the meaning of life and the individual's value in relation to this meaning. Existential terror is managed by allegiance to a cultural worldview that includes both objective standards of value and individual self-esteem that comes from meeting cultural standards.

Research has provided support for two hypotheses drawn from this theory. One is that higher self-esteem (natural variation or experimentally manipulated) should be associated with decreased anxiety about death and reduced reaction to reminders of mortality. The second hypothesis is that manipulating the salience of mortality (usually by asking experimental participants to write about what it will be like to die) will increase allegiance to the value standards of the cultural worldview.

Consistent with the second hypothesis, Americans (in the United States) made to think about their own death show increased allegiance to cultural standards: higher evaluation of Americans, those who praise America, those who exemplify American values (individual risking life to save another); lower evaluation of non-Americans, those who criticize America, those who violate cultural values (prostitute). In addition, McGregor et al. (1998) showed that mortality salience increases aggression against those who threaten the cultural worldview.

There is a crucial limitation to the effects of increasing mortality salience: These effects are obtained only when some delay and distraction occurs between thinking about death and the evaluation measure. Pyszczynski et al. (1997) suggested that the cultural anxiety buffer is engaged only when mortality is on the fringes of consciousness—primed and accessible but not in working memory. The buffer works to keep mortality out of consciousness; it has already failed when mortality concerns are the focus of conscious attention.

For purposes of understanding mobilization of ethnic national groups, the important aspect of terror management theory is that it is a theory of the power of group identification. Hope of immortality is necessarily vested in groups: So far as I know, no one has ever believed that he or she alone will live on when all other humans die. But not all groups offer the same potential for terror management. Many are willing to die for their nation, but few are ready to die for their tennis club. Why not?

Terror management theory suggests that the power of a group is the extent to which it answers the human problem of mortality. Membership in a tennis club does not offer any kind of immortality. A neighborhood, a team, a union, an economic class, even an industrial state—these offer little claim on immortality. A race, a nation, a religion, a culture—these do offer participation in a group seen to have an indefinitely long past and an unlimited future.

Terror management theory can help to explain some common observations about ethnopolitical conflict. Religion is the part of culture that offers the most explicit answer to the meaning of life in the face of mortality, and it should be no surprise that religion figures prominently in ethnic and national conflict. The contested importance of history for ethnic and national groups also makes sense in this perspective: A long group history (perhaps essentialized as Hirschfeld indicates) is a predictor or promise of an eternal future. Finally, the special intensity of double-minority conflicts is understandable because both sides of the conflict feel their culture is threatened with extinction. In Sri Lanka, for instance, the Tamil are a minority on the island while the Sinhala are a minority in relation to the Tamils of Southern India. Similarly Catholics are a minority in Northern Ireland, but Protestants are a minority in the Irish isle.

DEMOBILIZING GROUP IDENTIFICATION: THE CONTACT HYPOTHESIS

There is a large literature in social psychology associated with questions about how best to reduce intergroup hostility, discrimination, and negative stereotyping. Most of this work is some variant or development of the contact hypothesis made popular by Allport (1954/1979). I will focus on this hypothesis as the obvious candidate for psychological understanding of how group identification—both positive and negative identification—can be dissolved.

The contact hypothesis predicts that, under the right conditions, members of two groups will react positively to one another as individuals and thereby reduce intergroup prejudice and the stereotypes—understood as exaggerated and mistaken beliefs about group differences—that are occasion and support for prejudice and discrimination. The list of conditions necessary for contact to have positive effects has become quite lengthy (Stephan, 1985, offers 13 conditions), but 4 core conditions have been acknowledged since Allport (1954/1979): Contact should provide equal status for the two groups, cooperation for common goals, support by authority figures, and opportunities to interact with out-group members as individuals.

In the years since Allport (1954/1979) enunciated it, the contact hypothesis has undergone one major development: an interpretation of the necessary conditions for successful contact in terms of perceived similarity and liking. Equal status, personal contact, cooperation for shared goals, and institutional support for contact are usually understood to be important because these are the conditions in which members of interacting groups are likely to perceive important similarities and shared values. Increased perception of similarity will in turn lead to more liking. Thus the contact hypothesis has been rationalized in terms of increased perception of similarity as cause and increased liking as effect, and this similarity-liking interpretation has been generally accepted by those doing research on the contact hypothesis (Amir, 1976; Cook, 1978; Pettigrew, 1986).

Note that this interpretation makes cognitive change—increased perception of similarity—causally prior to affective change in reduced prejudice. The reverse direction of causality—affective change leading cognitive change—is conceivable (Allport, 1954/1979, p. 204; Pettigrew, 1986, p. 181) and has been recently emphasized by Pettigrew (1998). Pettigrew suggested that intergroup contact can have positive effects if sympathy or liking for individual out-group members is generalized to the whole out-group. This affect-first mechanism led Pettigrew to focus on the special importance of intergroup friendships and to interpret the core conditions of successful contact as facilitating development of intergroup friendships.

In addition to the similarity-liking and friendship-liking mechanisms, Pettigrew (1998) suggested two other mechanisms by which contact can have positive effects: behavior change (more positive attitudes following induction of more positive behavior toward the out-group, via consistency pressures) and in-group reappraisal (intergroup contact relativizing and reducing attachment to in-group norms). Pettigrew's suggestions are interesting directions for future research, particularly in suggesting the complex interplay of the four mechanisms, but here I will focus on the practical implication of the four conditions that Pettigrew agrees are necessary for contact to have positive effects.

Consistent with the similarity-liking interpretation, contact hypothesis researchers do not expect to see intergroup stereotyping and prejudice decline unless interacting members of the two groups are on the average very similar on every valued characteristic. The general failure of interracial contact to lead to improved intergroup relations in integrated schools (Stephan & Rosenfield, 1978) is usually explained by reference to the unequal status and school ability of Black and White students in U.S. schools (Cook, 1985; Slavin, 1983). Cooperative learning experiments—which have shown some success in improving Black–White interaction in integrated schools—typically use an equal-opportunity grading system that is based on improvement, rather than achievement level, in order to make the contributions of Black and White children more equal (Slavin, 1983).

These examples from the contact literature have in common a concern that group differences must be avoided if intergroup contact is to have positive effects. This condition was satisfied for the best-known example of the success of the contact hypothesis, Sherif et al.'s "Robbers Cave" experiment (Sherif, Harvey, White, Hood, & Sherif, 1961). Sherif et al. used arranged competition between two groups of boys to foment intergroup hostility and negative stereotyping then arranged equal status contact in cooperative striving for superordinate goals to reduce the hostility and stereotyping that had been created. Often lost sight of in interpretations of this result is the fact that the experimenter carefully matched the two groups to make them as similar as possible before competition began. From this experiment, the only safe conclusion is that the contact hypothesis works when two groups do not, in fact, differ on any valued characteristic. The same limited conclusion is warranted for more recent studies of intergroup contact in laboratory models that begin with groups made equivalent by random assignment (e.g., Miller, Brewer, & Edwards, 1985).

My discussion of the contact hypothesis can be briefly summarized. The contact hypothesis today is usually understood as a theory of error reduction. Prejudice and discrimination are based on mistaken perceptions of group differences—stereotypes, by the old definition—and contact under the right conditions leads to decreased stereotyping—decreased error—as out-group members are seen as more similar than anticipated. To the extent that groups have and perceive real differences, contact will not reduce group antipathy and may even increase it (Amir, 1976; Hewstone & Brown, 1986). Even in the absence of antipathy, intergroup contact under naturalistic conditions is likely to lead to contrast effects and enhanced identification with the in-group (Kosmitzki, 1996). In a world rife with real differences between groups, the contact hypothesis may have little practical significance.

Group identification is part of a larger phenomenon in which, contrary to the assumptions of economists and sociobiologists, humans find it easy to care about people and things in a way that goes far beyond narrow self-interest. This chapter has represented some of the psychological research that may help illuminate group identification, especially identification with ethnic and national groups. I have been optimistic about the potential of some of this research, notably research on essentialized categories and on terror management theory, and more pessimistic about other directions, such as the work on the contact hypothesis. My strongest conclusion, however, is that the psychology of group identification is more a collection of possibilities and starting points than a work in progress; few psychologists have yet taken seriously the power of ethnic and national groups.

REFERENCES

Allport, G. W. (1979). *The nature of prejudice* (2nd ed.). Reading, MA: Addison-Wesley. (Original work published 1954)

Amir, Y. (1976). The role of intergroup contact in change of prejudice and ethnic relations. In P. A. Katz (Ed.), *Towards the elimination of racism* (pp. 245–308). New York: Pergamon Press.

Bar-Tal, D. (1990). *Group beliefs: A conception for analyzing group structure, processes, and behavior.* New York: Springer.

Batson, C. D. (1998). Altruism and prosocial behavior. In D. T. Gilbert, S. T. Fiske, & G. Lindzey (Eds.), *Handbook of social psychology* (Vol. 2, pp. 282–316). New York: McGraw-Hill.

Belk, R. W. (1992). Human behavior and environment. *Advances in Theory and Research, 12,* 37–62.

Bernhardt, P. C. (1997). Influences of serotonin and testosterone in aggression and dominance: Convergence with social psychology. *Current Directions in Psychological Science, 6*(2), 44–48.

Bernhardt, P. C., Dabbs, J. M., Fielden, J. A., & Lutter, C. D. (1998). Testosterone changes during vicarious experiences of winning and losing among fans at sporting events. *Physiology and Behavior, 65,* 59–62.

Brewer, M. B., & Brown, R. J. (1998). Inter-group relations. In D. T. Gilbert, S. T. Fiske, & G. Lindzey (Eds.), *Handbook of social psychology* (Vol. 2, pp. 554–594). New York: McGraw-Hill.

Brown, R. (1989). Group polarization. In *Social psychology* (2nd ed., pp. 200–248). New York: Free Press.

Cialdini, R. B. (1993). *Influence: Science and practice* (3rd ed.). New York: Harper Collins.

Cialdini, R. B., Borden, R. J., Thorne, A., Walker, M. R., Freeman, S., & Sloan, L. R. (1976). Basking in reflected glory: Three (football) field studies. *Journal of Personality and Social Psychology, 34,* 366–374.

Citrin, J., & Green, D. (1990). The self-interest motive in American public opinion. *Research in Micropolitics, 3,* 1–27.

Cook, S. W. (1978). Interpersonal and attitudinal outcomes in cooperating interracial groups. *Journal of Research and Development in Education, 12,* 97–113.

Cook, S. W. (1985). Experimenting on social issues: The case of school desegregation. *American Psychologist, 40,* 452–460.

Crocker, J., & Major, B. (1989). Social stigma and self-esteem: The self-protective properties of stigma. *Psychological Review, 96,* 608–630.

Feshbach, S. (1991). Attachment processes in adult political ideology: Patriotism and nationalism. In J. L. Gedwirtz & W. M. Kurtines (Eds.), *Intersections with attachment* (pp. 207–226). Hillsdale, NJ: Erlbaum.

Gamson, W. (1992). *Talking politics.* Cambridge, England: Cambridge University Press.

Hewstone, M., & Brown, R. (1986). Contact is not enough: An inter-group perspective on the contact hypothesis. In M. Hewstone & R. Brown (Eds.), *Contact and conflict in intergroup encounters* (pp. 1–44). Oxford, England: Basil Blackwell.

Hirschfeld, L. A. (1996). *Race in the making: Cognition, culture, and the child's construction of human kinds.* Cambridge, MA: MIT Press.

Hirt, E., Zillmann, D., Erickson, G., & Kennedy, C. (1992). Costs and benefits of allegiance: Changes in fans' self-ascribed competencies after team victory versus defeat. *Journal of Personality and Social Psychology, 63,* 724–738.

Katz, D., & Braly, K. W. (1933). Racial stereotypes of one hundred college students. *Journal of Abnormal and Social Psychology, 28,* 280–290.

Keil, F. (1989). *Concepts, kinds, and cognitive development.* Cambridge, MA: MIT Press.

Kelman, H. C. (1958). Compliance, identification, and internalization: Three processes of attitude change. *Journal of Conflict Resolution, 2,* 51–60.

Kesterman, R., & Feshbach, S. (1989). Toward a measure of patriotic and nationalistic attitudes. *Political Psychology, 10,* 257–274.

Kinder, D. R. (1998). Opinion and action in the realm of politics. In D. T. Gilbert, S. T. Fiske, & G. Lindzey (Eds.), *Handbook of social psychology* (Vol. 2, pp. 778–867). New York: McGraw-Hill.

Kosmitzki, C. (1996). The reaffimation of cultural identity in cross-cultural encounters. *Personality and Social Psychology Bulletin, 22,* 238–248.

Levine, J. M., & Moreland, R. L. (1998). Small groups. In D. T. Gilbert, S. T. Fiske, & G. Lindzey (Eds.), *Handbook of social psychology* (Vol. 2, pp. 415–469). New York: McGraw-Hill.

Lippmann, W. (1922). *Public opinion.* New York: Harcourt, Brace.

McCauley, C. (1995). Are stereotypes exaggerated? In Y. T. Lee, L. Jussim, & C. McCauley (Eds.), *Stereotype accuracy: Toward an appreciation of group differences* (pp. 215–243). Washington, DC: American Psychological Association.

McCauley, C. (1998a). Group dynamics in Janis's theory of groupthink: Backward and forward. *Organizational Behavior and Human Decision Processes, 73,* 142–162.

McCauley, C. (1998b). When screen violence is not attractive. In J. Goldstein (Ed.), *Why we watch: The attractions of violent entertainment* (pp. 144–162). New York: Oxford University Press.

McCauley, C., & Segal, M. (1987). The social psychology of terrorist groups. In C. Hendrick (Ed.), *Review of personality and social psychology* (Vol. 9) (pp. 231–256). Thousand Oaks, CA: Sage.

McCauley, C., Stitt, C., & Segal, M. (1980). Stereotyping: From prejudice to prediction. *Psychological Bulletin, 87,* 195–208.

McGregor, H. A., Lieberman, J. D., Greenberg, J., Solomon, S., Arndt, J., Simon, L., & Pyszczynski, T. (1998). Terror management and aggression: Evidence that mortality salience motivates aggression against worldview-threatening others. *Journal of Personality and Social Psychology, 74*(3), 590–605.

Milgram, S. (1974). *Obedience to authority.* New York: Harper & Row.

Miller, N., Brewer, M. B., & Edwards, K. (1985). Cooperative interaction in desegregated settings: A laboratory analog. *Journal of Social Issues, 41,* 63–79.

Mummendey, A., Simon, B., Carsten, D., Grunert, M., Haeger, G., Kessler, S., Lettgen, S., & Schaferhoff, S. (1992). Categorization is not enough: Intergroup discrimination in negative outcome allocation. *Journal of Experimental Social Psychology, 28,* 125–144.

Pettigrew, T. F. (1986). The contact hypothesis revisited. In M. Hewstone & R. Brown (Eds.), *Contact and conflict in intergroup encounters* (pp. 169–195). Oxford, England: Basil Blackwell.

Pettigrew, T. F. (1998). Intergroup contact theory. *Annual Review of Psychology, 49*, 65–85.

Pyszczynski, T., Greenberg, J., & Solomon, S. (1997). Why do we need what we need? A terror management perspective on the roots of human social motivation. *Psychological Inquiry, 8*, 1–20.

Runciman, W. G. (1966). *Relative deprivation and social justice: A study of attitudes to social inequality in twentieth century England*. London: Routledge & Kegan Paul.

Schroeder, D. A., Sibicky, M. E., &. Irwin, M. E. (1995). A framework for understanding decisions in social dilemmas. In D. A. Schroeder (Ed.), *Social dilemmas: Perspectives on individuals and groups* (pp. 183–199). Westport, CT: Praeger.

Sherif, M., Harvey, O. J., White, B. J., Hood, W. R., & Sherif, C. (1961). *The Robbers Cave experiment: Intergroup conflict and cooperation*. Norman: Oklahoma Book Exchange.

Slavin, R. E. (1983). *Co-operative learning*. New York: Longman.

Smith, E. E., & Medin, D. L. (1981). *Categories and concepts*. Cambridge, MA: Harvard University Press.

Smith, E. R. (1993). Social identity and social emotions: Toward new conceptualizations of prejudice. In D. M. Mackie & D. L. Hamilton (Eds.), *Affect, cognition and stereotyping: Interactive processes in group perception* (pp. 297–315). New York: Academic Press.

Sprinzak, E. (1991). The process of delegitimation: Towards a linkage theory of political terrorism. In C. McCauley (Ed.), *Terrorism research and public policy* (pp. 50–68). London: Cass.

Stephan, W. G. (1985). Intergroup relations. In G. Lindzey & E. Aronson (Eds.), *Handbook of social psychology* (Vol. 2, 3rd ed., pp. 599–658). New York: Random House.

Stephan, W. G., & Rosenfield, D. (1978). Effects of desegregation on racial attitudes. *Journal of Personality and Social Psychology, 36*, 795–804.

Stouffer, S. A., Suchman, E. A., DeVinney, L. C., Star, S. A., & Williams, R. M., Jr. (1949). *The American soldier: 2. Combat and its aftermath*. Princeton, NJ: Princeton University Press.

Struch, N., & Schwartz, S. H. (1989). Intergroup aggression: Its predictors and distinctness from in-group bias. *Journal of Personality and Social Psychology, 56*, 364–373.

Tajfel, H., & Turner, J. C. (1986). The social identity theory of intergroup behavior. In S. Worchel & W.G. Austin (Eds.), *Psychology of intergroup relations* (pp. 7–24). Chicago: Nelson.

Tarrow, S. (1994). *Power in movement: Social movements, collective action, and politics*. Cambridge, England: Cambridge University Press.

Teger, A. (1980). *Too much invested to quit*. Elmsford, NY: Pergamon Press.

AUTHOR INDEX

Numbers in italics refer to listings in the reference sections.

SUBJECT INDEX

Clogg, Richard, 159
Cognitive dissonance, 137
Colombia, 182, 198
Combinatorial freedom, 27
Commitment, 355
Committee of Union and Progress
(CUP), 74–76, 78
Communism, 9
Communist Party of Kampuchea (CPK),
87–90
Comte, Auguste, 74
Conflict regulation, national/ethnic,
42–45
Congo, 31, 112, 114
Congress of Berlin, 154
Connor, Walker, 40
Consociationalism, 225–226
Constructionist view of ethnic violence,
120–121
Contact hypothesis, 357–359
Contamination, fear of, 28
Cooperative interdependence, 208–209,
211–212
Corporate identities, 28–29
Cosic, Dobrica, 129
CPK. *See* Communist Party of
Kampuchea
Croatia, 120, 138–141, 144–146, 308
Croats, 11, 12, 13, 126, 129–135, 138–
147
Crossed categorization, 333–335
Cuba, 200
Cultural factors, 292–293, 297–298
CUP. *See* Committee of Union and
Progress
Cyprus, 52

Dalan, Bedrettin, 171
Darby, John, 205
Dashnaksuthiun, 74
Dayton Peace Agreement, 312
De Klerk, F. W., 237, 238, 241, 243, 299
Democide, 289
Democratic Kampuchea, 83–90
Demographic reconstruction, 100
Draskovic, Vuk, 132, 134
Drljaca, Simo, 124

Ecuador, 188, 190, 194–195
Ego identities, 30

Eichmann, Adolf, 61
Elites, 6, 34, 40
Emotions, 35
END/MEND taxonomy, 43–44
Enlightenment, 36, 65
Ethnic cleansing, 119–120
Ethnic identity, 4
Ethnicity, 27
Ethnic persecution, 51
Ethnic war, 51
Ethnocentrism, 320
Ethnocontinuism, 38
Ethnopolitical conflict
and corporate identities, 28–29
and ego identities, 30
and familiarity with enemy, 5
and individual identity, 29–30
levels of, 6–20
resolution of, 20–24
and role of psychology, 24–26
and state elites, 6
without wars, 17–20
Ethnopolitical warfare
low-level, 15–17
major, 11–15
European Union, 209–210
Excess mortality, measurement of, 96–103
residual approach to, 99–103
sample approach to, 96–99
Explicit conflict, 326–327

Falklands, 188, 192–193
Fear, 121
Fein, Helen, 142
Followers, 293–294
Forgiveness, 24
France, 17, 115, 116
French Communist Party, 86
Frontier settings, 30, 32–33

Gates of Ivory (Margaret Drabble), 94,
99, 106
Geertz, Clifford, 311
Gellner, Ernest, 40
Genocidal conflicts, 6, 8–11
Genocide, 94, 289
Germany, 15. *See also* Nazi Germany
and Hereros, 52
and Tanzania, 261–262

Glenny, Misha, 133, 137
Gligorov, Kiro, 153
The Godfather (Mario Puzo), 29
Goldhagen, Daniel, 55, 57, 58, 60–62
Grau, Miguel, 193
Great Britain, 205–207, 212, 262–264.
    See also Northern Ireland
Greece, 155
Group dynamics theory, 354
Group extremity shift, 353–354
Group identification, 343–359
    and "action frames," 352–353
    and commitment, 355
    and contact hypothesis, 357–359
    essentialized categories in, 350–351
    in group dynamics theory, 354
    and group extremity shift, 353–354
    in-group bias effects of, 347
    and patriotism and nationalism, 352
    physiological effects of, 347–348
    as psychological foundation of eth-
        nic nationalism, 343
    and psychology of identification,
        343–346
    and public opinion in United States,
        347–348
    self-esteem effects of, 346
    stereotypes in, 351–352
    in terror management theory, 355–
        357
Group violence, 289–301
    culture changes and avoidance of,
        297–298
    future potential for, 301
    halting and preventing, 296–297
    instigating conditions not leading to,
        298–301
    origins of, 290–295
Guatemala, 14, 195, 200, 295

Hani, Chris, 242, 243
HDZ, 122, 134, 135, 138–140, 144
Heidegger, Martin, 65
Hereros, 52
Hess, Rudolf, 64
Hirschfeld, L. A., 350–351
Hitler, Adolf, 5, 9, 10, 17, 55–59, 62–65,
    67
Hobsbawm, Eric, 40

Holocaust, 8, 54–67
    and anti-Semitism, 60–62
    behavioristic theories of, 57–58
    demonic theories of, 55–56
    and modern/postmodern philoso-
        phies, 62–66
    sociopolitical theories of, 56–57
    socio-psychological theories of,
        58–59
Horowitz, Donald, 40–41
Hunchak Party, 73
Hun Sen, 83
Hutus, 4, 9, 23, 109–116, 294, 326

Identification, psychology of, 343–346
Identities
    corporate, 28–29
    ego, 30
    individual, 29–30
Ieng Sary, 86
IFP. *See* Inkatha Freedom Party
Implicit conflict, 326–327
Individual identities, 29–30
Individuals, role of, 23
In-group bias, 347
In-group favoritism principle, 324–325
Inkatha Freedom Party (IFP), 238, 240,
    242, 244
Insecurity, 121
Instrumental behavior, 326
Instrumentalist view of ethnic violence,
    120
Intergroup accentuation principle, 324
Intergroup conflict, 319–336
    changing social categorizations and
        reduction of, 331–335
    changing social structures and reduc-
        tion of, 335–336
    contact between members of groups
        and reduction of, 327–331
    ethnocentric perspective on, 320
    explicit vs. implicit conflict, 326–327
    objective vs. subjective conflict,
        325–327
    in realistic group conflict theory,
        320–321
    in social identity theory, 321–323
    social—psychological interventions
        for reduction of, 327–335
    types of, 325–327

Intergroup conflict, *continued*
    and unique aspects of intergroup be-
        havior, 324–325
Intifada, 216
IRA. *See* Irish Republican Army
Iraq, 295
Ireland, Northern. *See* Northern Ireland
Irish Republican Army (IRA), 206–207,
    210, 211
Israel, 16–17, 19, 215–232, 300–301
    Arab discontent in, 218–224
    citizenship status of Arabs in, 215–
        216
    consociationalism in, 225
    Declaration of Independence of,
        216–217
    future of Jewish—Arab relations in,
        229–232
    limited nature of "Arab problem" in,
        217, 224–226
    pluralism in, 224
    relative deprivation of Arabs in, 225
    system control over Arab citizens in,
        225–229
Italy, 348
Izetbegovic, Alija, 153

Jews, 17, 55–62. *See also* Holocaust;
    Israel
Jim Crow system, 276–277
JNA, 120–122, 145, 147
Johnson, R. W., 238–239
Judah, Tim, 142

Kach movement, 217
Kahane, Meir, 217
Kandt, Richard, 110
Kaplan, H., 55, 64–65
Karadjic, Radovan, 123
Karume, Abeid, 270
Keane, Fergal, 242
Kedourie, Elie, 41
Kelman, Herbert, 300–301
Kemal, Mustafa, 165
Kemal, Yasar, 171
Ke Puak, 89
Khieu Samphan, 5, 83
Khmer Rouge, 4–5, 8, 10, 83, 84, 86–90,
    94–98, 100, 101, 104–107

Kiernan, Ben, 97
Kim Il Sung, 10
Kinder, D. R., 348–349
King, Martin Luther, Jr., 21
KLA (Kosovo Liberation Army), 34
Kljujic, Ilija, 134
Kosovo, 11, 13, 17, 34–35, 130–131, 153
Kosovo Liberation Army (KLA), 34
Ku Klux Klan, 276
Kurds (in Turkey), 13–14, 163–176
    and cynicism in Turkish public opin-
        ion, 166–168
    historical background of, 164, 165,
        173–174
    and identity politics, 170–173
    limitations on nationalist move-
        ments among, 168–169
    migration of, 169–172
    in Ottoman Empire, 73–75
    and PKK, 165, 167–168, 173–175
    poverty among, 166
    and Turkey's "Eastern Policy," 163–
        164
    in Turkish propaganda, 164–165
    in western Turkey, 169–170
Kuwait, 295

Latin America, 14–15, 179–200
    border disputes in, 183–184
    causes of war in, 179–196
    class structures in, 195–196
    foreign intervention/influence in,
        184
    limited military capacity in, 196–
        199
    military thinking in, 185–189
    preconditions for conflict in, 184–
        185
    public nationalism in, 189–195
Laitin, David, 41
Le Bon, Gustave, 74
Lewin, Kurt, 54
List, Friedrich, 77
Lloyd George, David, 159
Lon Nol, 89, 90
Low-level ethnopolitical war, 15–17

Maas, Peter, 126
Macedonia, 153, 155

Major ethnopolitical warfare, 11–15. *see also* Genocidal conflicts
Malvinas, 188, 192–193
Mandel, Ernest, 41
Mandela, Nelson, 21, 23–24, 237, 241–243, 245, 299
Mandela, Winnie, 299
Mangope, Lucas, 244
Mao Tse-tung, 10, 29
Márquez, Gabriel García, 255
Martic, Milan, 143, 145
Mass killing, 289
Mass media, 128, 136–139
Mayans, 14
MBO, 145
Mein Kampf (Adolf Hitler), 56
Mexico, 19, 182
Migozzi, Jacques, 101
Militias, 141–144
Milosevic, Slobodan, 34–35, 120, 123, 125, 130–132, 135, 136, 141, 159
Minh, Ho Chi, 85
Mitchell, George J., 208, 300
Mkapa, Benjamin, 259
Mtikila, Christopher, 272
Museveni, Yoweri, 113
Muslims
    in Bosnia, 11, 17, 122–126, 134, 145
    in Cambodia, 87–89
    in Ottoman Empire, 72, 75
    in Tanzania, 271–272
Mussolini, Benito, 111
Myrdal, Gunnar, 281

Naletalic, Tuta, 143
Nationalism, 37–45
    basis of appeal of, 39–40
    beliefs about, 38–39
    and group identification, 352
    in Latin America, 189–195
    and regulation of ethnonational differences, 42–45
    sources of extremist, 40–41
    strength of, 41–42
    in Yugoslavia, 126–139
National Party (South Africa), 237, 241, 243
Nationophiles, 39
Nationophobes, 39–40

NATO, 11, 13, 34, 188, 299, 312
Nazi Germany, 5, 9, 11, 17, 33–34. *See also* Holocaust
Non-antagonistic identities, 29
Noninstrumental behavior, 326
Northern Ireland, 15–16, 20–21, 31–32, 205–214, 299–300, 320, 323, 325–326
    decommissioning of paramilitary weapons in, 210
    and emerging European context, 209–210
    execution of functional interdependence in, 211–213
    historical background of conflict in, 205–207
    "Mitchell Principles," 208–209
    social grammar of interpersonal interaction in, 207–208
    zero-sum thinking in, 205–206, 211
North Korea, 8
Nyerere, Julius, 264, 268, 270

Objective conflict, 325–327
Öcalan, Abdullah, 168, 170, 172
Omarska camp, 124
Oslo Accords, 216
Oslobodjenje, 132, 134, 145
Ottoman Empire, 9, 13, 17, 71–79, 152, 154–156, 173
Özal, Turgut, 172

Palestine Liberation Organization, 216
Palestinians, 19, 215–216. *See also* Israel
Paraguay, 192
Paramilitaries, 142–143
Pasdermadjian, Garo, 76
Pasha, Boghos Nubar, 77
Pasha, Djemal, 76
Pasha, Enver, 76
Pasha, Talat, 76
Patriotism, 352
Peer pressure, 141–142
Persecution, ethnic, 51
Peru, 188, 190, 193–195, 198
PKK, 163, 165, 167, 168, 173–175
Polarization, 127–128
Political disaffection, 353
Political identity, 5

ABOUT THE EDITORS

Daniel Chirot, PhD, is Professor of International Studies and Sociology at the University of Washington in Seattle, where he is the founder and codirector of the Center for the Study of Ethnic Conflict and Conflict Resolution. He is the author of books about global social change, political sociology, and Eastern Europe. His recent books are *How Societies Change* (1994), *Modern Tyrants: The Power and Prevalence of Evil in Our Age* (1994), and *Essential Outsiders: Chinese and Jews In the Modern Transformation of Southeast Asia and Central Europe* (edited with Anthony Reid, 1997).

Martin E. P. Seligman, PhD, works with positive psychology, learned helplessness, depression, ethnopolitical conflict, and optimism. He is Fox Leadership Professor of Psychology at the University of Pennsylvania in Philadelphia. Among his books are *Learned Optimism: How to Change Your Mind and Your Life* (1998), *What You Can Change and What You Can't* (1994), *The Optimistic Child* (with Karen Reivich, Lisa Jaycox, and Jane Gillham, 1995), and *Helplessness: On Depression, Development, and Death* (1992). He has received both the American Psychological Society's William James Award (for basic science) and the Cattell Award (for the application of science). Dr. Seligman's research has been supported by the National Institute of Mental Health, the National Science Foundation, the Guggenheim Foundation, and the MacArthur Foundation. In 1997 he was elected president of the American Psychological Association (APA).